To Letitia,

THE WALLS OF LUCCA

You are a blessing!

Steve Physioc

Steve Physioc

ISBN 13: 9780692177808

ITALY

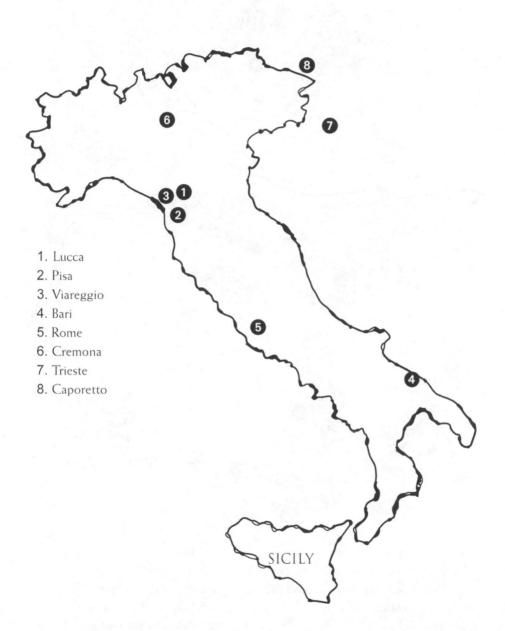

1. Lucca
2. Pisa
3. Viareggio
4. Bari
5. Rome
6. Cremona
7. Trieste
8. Caporetto

SICILY

The walled city of
LUCCA

1. Martellino Vineyard
2. Blessings Convent
3. Piazza dell' Anfiteatro / *Isabella's Market*
4. San Frediano
5. San Michele
6. Piazza Napoleone

7. Guinigi Tower
8. Botanical Gardens
9. Balvardo San Frediano
10. Balvardo San Croce
11. Balvardo San Donato
12. Balvardo Santa Maria

PROLOGUE

LUCCA, ITALY, 1914

T he Blessings Convent sisters' voices rose in unison as they neared the second *hallelujah* of "The Sacrifice of our Savior." Joy lit twelve-year-old Isabella's face as she sped up her "lightning litany" to race the sisters to the finish line with "prayforoursinnersnowatthehourofdeathamen."

The orphan girl had fought the strict discipline of the Blessings sisters at first: up each morning at five thirty; in the church navata, on her knees with rosary in hand, at six, asking God for forgiveness. When she realized she would lose this battle she reluctantly gave in, but on her own terms. While she was required to say one Lord's Prayer, five Hail Marys, and two Acts of Contrition every morning, little Isabella made a game of it. She would see how quickly she could spin off the Hail Marys and Acts of Contrition in a thrilling competition with the sisters' final stanza. Upon achieving victory, she would pump a glorious fist to the heavens to accentuate her personal finale brilliante. Then it was on to her true church, her garden.

The garden was where Isabella bloomed. This was where she prayed—never within the confines of the church walls, but always outside, embraced by the loving arms of nature. It was where Isabella felt closest to God, and the vegetables blossomed from her touch. The tomatoes seemed brighter; the kale appeared a darker green; the olives tasted more robust; the entire garden prospered in her presence. The nuns even let her wander off in the woods well beyond Lucca's walls, because she would come back with the most amazing wild mushrooms: big porcini mushrooms that she would mix into the pasta, and prized black truffles with a rich flavor that made Isabella a favorite of the Blessings Convent.

So the sisters left Isabella alone, watching her sing to each seed as she dropped it into the soil, giving the dirt a little love tap before moving on to her next plant. She clipped certain leaves from her olive trees and kissed each leaf before dropping it into her compost bin. The nuns would only shake their heads at the little girl who struggled with fundamental scripture but had little trouble blessing every living thing she passed by.

"Everything needs to be encouraged," Isabella said. "All of God's creations, whether human, animal, or plant."

Sister Anna looked out the window of the Blessings Convent in Lucca to watch the girl digging her hands into the soil of the church garden. The nun smiled as she recalled the day seven years earlier, when Isabella Roselli had arrived at their convent. She had been a waiflike child wearing a dirty white cotton dress with purple flowers all over it, her hair a mess of dark brown curls falling about her face. But what Sister Anna remembered most was the look of Isabella's brilliant, inquisitive green eyes, which showed a depth of knowledge that belied her twelve years of age. Isabella stood before the Mother Superior without a smile, her grimy hands clinging to two burlap bags: one filled with her clothes, the other stuffed with seeds. There were all kinds of seeds: apple, peach, and apricot seeds, lettuce, pea, green bean, tomato, and spinach seeds, all stuffed into the bag. It was in that moment that Anna had whispered, "Bella," meaning "beautiful," and that was the name Anna called Isabella for the rest of her life.

CR SO

Sister Anna had read the letter from Isabella's aunt, the one who could "no longer take care of the little gypsy." Isabella's parents had died the previous year from the influenza that had swept through northern Italy. Her father had had some basic schooling and could read and write. He had given this gift to his daughter, but like their family before them, he and his wife had chosen to work the wheat and potato fields of rural Italy. Isabella's family heritage was born out of a pagan philosophy, a belief that God's blessings came from the earth, water, soil, wind, and the sun, and that the meaning of life could be found in the miracle of healing.

CR SO

Anna remembered Isabella's first day: eyes studying, hands touching the walls, the art, the statues of saints, stained-glass windows—not in a disrespectful, rough manner, but simply out of curiosity, as if seeking to learn something from everything she touched. When Anna opened the door to the convent's sanctuary, the little girl's eyes went wide. The modest holy room was anything but impressive: four wooden pews; votive candles underneath a stained-glass window of Saint Scholastica, the patron saint of convents; a small statue of the Virgin Mary; and a small oak altar with the crucifix of a dying Jesus above. That was all.

"Have you been inside a church or holy room before?" Anna asked.

Isabella shook her head no, and then dipped her fingers into the holy water by the door and brought it to her lips.

"Do you know what that is, Bella?"

The little girl's green eyes flashed from the bowl to the statue, to the altar and crucifix, and then back up at Anna.

"I don't know what anything is for."

CHAPTER 1

PUGLIA, ITALY, JULY 1914

"That's it, boys—no more talk about war," Bernardino Carollo said to his sons as he stood up from the dinner table. The old wooden chair creaked from the weight of a man whose body had been sculpted from years of working the farms of southern Italy. As he thought about the growing tension in Europe that seemed to be on everyone's mind lately, he picked at a splinter that stuck out from the table, a reminder of all that he still needed to do. His wife had asked him the previous week to sand the exposed sliver, but his long days in the field left him with little energy to work in the house. And now there was this incessant talk of war—arguments about unresolved territorial disputes that had politicians pointing fingers at each other, drumming up nationalistic pride in almost every country.

"But it's coming, Papa!" his oldest son, Benny, exclaimed. "The assassination of Archduke Franz Ferdinand in Sarajevo last month has all of Europe on edge. That's why Montrel wasn't at church today. He joined the army."

The news didn't surprise Bernardino, since Montrel was a high-spirited boy from a neighboring farm in central Puglia who was prone to making rash decisions. He was much like Bernardino's own sons: raised in a small house owned by the landowner whose farm they worked. Bernardino wanted no part of any war. It was grape season, and he needed his sons here in the vineyard, training the vines on the trellises and removing any extraneous leaves to allow the sun to brighten their berries. Despite a struggling economy, his family had produced a wonderful Primitivo grape the previous season, and Bernardino wanted his landowner again praising his creation.

"If you give me your blessing"—Benny raised his voice to get his father's attention—"I promise to send every lira home to help you and Mama."

Benny's younger brother, Franco, looked up from the dishes he was washing. "You can make more money in the big cities than you can in the army."

"But there aren't any jobs left in Italy," Benny grumbled. "That's why our workers are running off to America. As soon as we join the fight, the only sure pay will be in the army."

"Italy won't go to war," Franco said as he flipped the washrag onto the sink and walked over. "Our new Prime Minister said we'll remain neutral."

"Salandra's a coward!"

"Enough!" their father snapped, still unsure of how to respond. His guide had always been one he would never question: the almighty Catholic Church.

The Carollo family followed a strict Catholic tradition. Work the fields, build houses, raise your family, tithe to the church, and trust

God's plan. Bernardino had been taught that man had been born into sin, and since his Lord Jesus had died for his sins, only the blood of Jesus could cleanse him from being thrown into the fires of hell. There was no place for "pick and choose" in the truths proposed by the infallible Catholic Church, for they were bound in heaven by God Himself. Bernardino believed that if a baptized person deliberately denied or questioned a dogma of the church, he or she was guilty of heresy and automatically became subject to the punishment of excommunication. Unfortunately, Bernardino had not thought about what happened when those baptized young people, like his sons, became teens and began to question everything.

Bernardino and Maria Carollo had two sons. The eldest, Benny, at twenty, was just like his father: strong, loyal, and dependable, and those similarities solidified a special bond. There were times when Maria heard footsteps on the porch, thinking it was her husband, only to turn and see Benny; even their gaits were similar. The youngest son, Franco, at eighteen, favored his mother. He was the child who questioned everything, from nature to religion, to the politics of Rome. The vineyards were his playground; he took to them naturally, understanding each grape's strengths and weaknesses.

The two sons could not have been more different—Benny would plow through a chore with the same dogged determination as his father, while Franco would take his time, studying the soil or weather patterns. There was many a day Maria would find her youngest son alone in the vineyard, eyes to the east, checking the clashing currents of the Adriatic and Ionian Seas to predict when they would bring cool breezes and summer rains perfect for the crop. It was that slow, deliberate, contemplative nature that aggravated his father.

Bernardino closed his eyes for a moment and asked God for guidance. Nothing came.

"I think," he finally said, "we should let our pope decide what Italy should do."

"I'm not going to let Pius decide my future," Franco groaned.

Benny shoved his younger brother. "You should want to defend your country!"

Despite their differences, Franco adored his brother, admiring both his discipline and his determination to serve others. Whether it was to serve his family, serve his country, or serve his Lord didn't matter—there was a fundamental call inside Benny to serve. But this simmering anger inside Europe was none of Italy's business, thought Franco. No country had attacked them. He had to take a stand and shoved his brother back.

Bernardino stepped between his sons just as Benny's fist shot forward, the blow mistakenly clipping his father's jaw. Both boys stepped back in shock, but it was the younger son Bernardino grabbed by the collar. "This is not your argument!"

"When will I ever be included?" Franco fired back.

Bernardino released his son, but his hand was still trembling. "You have to trust—this is all in God's hands."

"Whose God are you talking about?" Franco said without thinking. "The God of the Socialists or the God of the Nationalists?"

Bernardino slapped his son across the face. Franco was stunned. His father had never hit him before. For a long time no one spoke. Bernardino looked down at his hands, scarred from years working the fields and sore from the day's work of clearing weeds near the grapevines. He picked at a broken nail that hung from his thumb, angry with himself for striking his son and frustrated by his inability to answer his son's questions. Bernardino had sacrificed everything for his family; he had worked extra shifts to allow his sons to go to school, and this was his payback? A disrespectful child? Bernardino glanced up at his son and was struck by what he saw. He saw his wife's eyes, filled with the same disappointment he had found when Maria had lost a baby in childbirth ten years earlier.

"Please, Franco," Bernardino finally said, his voice barely audible. "Just listen to me."

CR   SO

The light of dawn streaked past the cotton drapes in the Carollos' kitchen and into Bernardino and Maria's bedroom. A rooster on the front porch crowed, and Bernardino stirred and rolled onto his side, their old spring bed creaking under his weight. Maria had been up for an hour, setting the table for breakfast and preparing for the week ahead. Sunday was gone, her favorite day, the only day of rest required by her Lord and allowed by her husband. Church was Maria's time to catch up: with friends, with children, and with visitors who had come to their village with news from afar.

As Bernardino stretched in bed, Maria caught herself gazing out the window, thinking of yesterday and the walk home from church with her family.

Maria could feel her younger son distancing himself from them. His questions of a life beyond the olives and grapes, beyond the farm, had become more frequent. He was drawn to anyone new at church who had stories of Rome, of somewhere else, of anywhere else. When the priest from Tuscany spoke at church one Sunday, Franco had lingered behind, listening to his tales of the great Apennine range and "soil so perfect, the wine practically made itself."

On this Monday morning, Maria looked outside and saw that the morning dew had soaked everything. It was hanging from the olive branches, heavy on the lupines by the gate, and as her eyes drew closer to the porch, she saw the wet tracks of a boy's boots on the wood. Franco was sitting in his father's chair, his pillowcase stuffed by his side. He was staring out at the farm as if he was holding on to this one final memory of home. Maria went out and sat next to her son.

"You don't have to go," she said.

"The farm is struggling, Mama." Franco paused for a long moment. "I wrote Papa a letter. I'll send you half of everything I make."

"Your father loves you."

"I know," he said, and then he glanced inside the house, where his father lay sleeping. "But if I go—Benny will stay."

A tiny shock ran through Maria. She had always known that their youngest child protected their oldest. He was the brother who tightened the wires on the trellises after Benny had rushed to finish. The younger had taught the older how to read and rescued him from fights on the back streets of Bari. Maria stared at Franco, so still, so poised, and the sudden knowledge of what she already knew tore at her heart. She reached for her son's hand and said, "'A man's heart deviseth his way—'"

Franco stood up and finished his mother's favorite passage from Proverbs 16:9. "'But the Lord directeth his steps.'"

She smiled. "Choose peace in every step you take."

CHAPTER 2

LUCCA, JULY 1914

I sabella grabbed tomatoes from her table at the market in Lucca and dropped them into Paolo Reggiani's bushel basket. Paolo was one of the city's bright young chefs, and he never missed an opportunity to buy produce from the most popular stand in the Piazza dell'Anfiteatro.

Isabella's table was always busy. Local trattorias came early to buy her fruits, vegetables, truffles, and fragrant olive oil. With the economy struggling and labor strikes frequent throughout Italy, the convent welcomed the extra money from Isabella's sales.

Now, at the age of twenty, Isabella was growing into a beautiful young woman. Her dark brown curls fell about her shoulders, and her bright green eyes sparkled with an inner fire, giving young men another reason to drop by Lucca's market.

"Bella, beautiful!" cried out Paolo. "You come dine with me! I'll make you the best *torta di riso* in all of Tuscany."

"With the recipe and ingredients you got from me!" she yelled back. "Create something on your own, Paolo, and I'll share a table with you."

"I'll start today! I'm off to my kitchen to prepare a meal that will make you hunger for me."

With that, Paolo tossed a tomato into the air, caught it in his basket, and was soon lost in the crowd.

"Oh, you're a lot of noise, Bella Roselli," teased her longtime friend Sister Anna. "You'll never go out with Paolo, so don't lead him on."

"I like Paolo. I'm just encouraging him to be a little more creative with his menu."

"So you'll go out with him?"

Isabella tried to stifle a grin. "Maybe."

"Tell that to Father Josefa at confession tonight."

"The only thing I'll be confessing is you stealing my *panzanella*."

"Guilty as charged! Now remember, young lady, we have Mass in less than an hour, and you're required to attend."

"I'll be there in time for communion—because I made the sacramental wine and it goes perfectly with my daily bread."

"Blasphemy, girl! You'll burn in hell for even thinking that."

"Then I'll bring a pot of water and boil up some spaghetti, because even your devil I don't believe in would be a sucker for my tomato-truffle sauce."

Anna snorted a laugh and carried their leftover produce to their horse cart. "You're lucky I'm a sucker for your truffle sauce, or I'd be going straight to Mother Superior to have you transferred to a convent in Australia."

"You'd never survive on Sister Emmilia's lumpy porridge."

Anna slid the produce onto the cart and looked up to the sky. "Oh, Lord, why can't she accept just one of your Catholic instructions?"

"Ha!" Isabella gave a crinkle-eyed grin. "Do you really believe God created the world and then turned it over to the Vatican to run?"

"You're impossible!"

"It's true. All He asked us to do was to love Him and love one another."

"And as penance He gave me you as a student."

"Maybe I'm also your teacher." Isabella winked as she helped Anna up onto the wagon and grabbed the reins. "Now off we go— Saint Freddy will throw us to the Protestants if we're late."

CHAPTER 3

ROME, JULY 1914

Franco walked the first ten miles alone. There could be no turning back now, or the Carollo farm would become his prison, smothering any chance for him to discover who he was meant to be. He didn't want to live in his father's world anymore, sacrificing his dreams for family, church, and landowner and then finally dying. As his strides took him farther and farther from home, his confidence grew, and he was now ready to question every value he had ever held.

CR   SO

A broad smile spread across Franco's face as he stepped off the miller's wagon in the capital city. He had hitched rides from Bari to Naples and north to Rome, where he was dropped off at the city's west edge. A quick look at his map told him the Spanish Steps were just a short walk away. He had read about the monumental stairway in school, but had never been to the square that drew both tourists and young political activists.

When he arrived he found a crowd covering the steps, listening to a passionate speaker. He craned his neck above the masses to get a better look, and stared full into the face of absolute power.

"The Triple Alliance has failed us!" the man screamed, and the crowd roared. He was fierce-looking, square jawed, with a piercing gaze, standing majestically at the top of the steps, legs spread wide, one hand on a hip, the other waving as if he were leading an orchestra.

"We will never align with Germany and Austria-Hungary!" He shook his fist to the crowd. "Countries that threaten to steal the lands of the Triple Entente will force England, France, and Russia to defend what's theirs! And whom do you think the greedy Nationalists will send to fight for their almighty profit?"

"The poor!" the crowd howled.

Franco turned to the man next to him. "Who is he?"

The man gave a surprised look, as if Franco should already know.

"That's Benito Mussolini. He's one of us. A Socialist who wants Italy to stay out of Europe's fight!"

Franco moved closer, to hear over the shouting.

"Down with war!" Mussolini screamed. "Down with arms, and up with humanity!"

"Yes!" The crowd thundered as Franco was swept up by the magnetism of the moment. Mussolini's energy seemed to flow into each person's mind. Looks of religious zeal flashed across the faces in the crowd.

"We have a movement going on, my friends!" Mussolini shouted. "I will not let you down!"

Franco knew he should leave and begin his search for work, but an uneasy seduction—part confusion, part fascination—made him stay.

Franco slept under a bridge his first night in Rome and in a church near the Spanish Steps his second night. On day three he found work with the railroad, building and repairing track that hugged the west coast, south of Rome. His coworkers were a mixed bag of restless men searching for any job: peasant farmers from the south, former miners from Sicily struggling with tuberculosis, and others, like him, moving to the city for adventure.

Word of Europe's declaration of war came in early August, and with the news came grumblings of what Italy would do.

"It was inevitable," Franco's coworker said as he hammered at the anchor spike to fasten another rail to the wooden tie. "Austria wanted revenge for the Serbs' assassination of the archduke and his wife."

Franco remained silent as he handed another spike to the man, who tapped three times on the head and then, with a powerful blast, drove the nail to the base. "So Austria declared war on Serbia, giving Germany the excuse they needed to join the fight, which brought in France, then Belgium, then Britain, and now Russia."

Franco handed his coworker another spike and finally joined the conversation. "Aren't we the ally to Germany and Austria?"

"It's hard to say anymore," the man answered. "Our prime minister said that when Germany and Austria declared war without being attacked, it broke our agreement to the Triple Alliance."

"Then Salandra should read Mussolini!" another worker shouted from down the line. "Benito writes for *Avanti!*, and he wants Italy to stay neutral!"

The mere mention of the name Mussolini brought a proud smile from Franco.

"I heard him speak the day I arrived in Rome!" he said excitedly, hoping the connection would draw respect from his coworkers. "He was incredible! People cheered his every word!"

His coworker nodded approvingly.

"Why"—Franco hesitated, a bit confused—"why would the Nationalists want war?"

"Greed," the man grumbled as he grabbed another anchor spike and pounded it into the tie. "Coal, iron, and oil are what every country needs to build and protect its empire." He then spit a stream of tobacco juice into the weeds and looked up at Franco. "Italy wants those resources too."

CR   ꙅ

Summer turned to fall and then winter, yet despite the weather's cooling, the political winds only stirred the embers of an angry, undecided country. Italy was in economic turmoil, losing many of its working poor to North and South America, to France, and to countries beyond. With war looming in Europe and Italian military production expanding, Franco found a better job at a munitions factory north of Rome. His days at work were filled with conversations that supported the war, while his nights in the city's bars challenged that thinking. It was as if his mind were also Italy's, being pushed and pulled, twisted and manipulated by powers both inside and outside his country. The intense debates excited the young farmer from Puglia, whose drought-stricken mind was suddenly flooded by a thunderstorm of new ideas.

CR   ꙅ

The setting sun's rays cast an ominous shadow across Franco as he walked to a political rally near Rome's historical center. The shadow was from the giant statue of Victor Emmanuel II, the king who, after centuries of struggle, finally united Italy in 1861. Now, some five decades later, Italy was again searching for a man to bring the country together.

As he crossed the street and made his way down Vicolo Doria, Franco heard cheers coming from inside the trattoria that was hosting the rally.

"Do you want to be spectators in this great drama," Franco heard a man cry out, "or do you want to be fighters?"

The voice was familiar, powerful, charismatic. Franco pushed his way through the crowd, to get a closer look. It was the same man he had seen on top of the Spanish Steps only months earlier.

"As I said in Parma last month," Benito Mussolini bellowed to those surrounding him, "if the Socialists think I am unworthy of fighting the Socialist cause—then expel me!"

"No!" his supporters shouted.

"What divides me from you now is not a small dispute," Mussolini continued, "but a great question over which the whole of Socialism is divided."

Franco looked about the room at men mesmerized by Mussolini's very words, as if receiving answers to questions they had long been craving.

"Reality cannot be done away with and cannot be ignored, and the reality is that millions and millions of men are standing opposite one another on the blood-drenched battlefields of Europe. The neutrals, who shout themselves hoarse crying 'Down with war!' do not realize the grotesque cowardice contained in that cry today. It is irony of the most atrocious kind to shout 'Down with war!' while men are fighting and dying in the trenches!"

Hisses came from the crowd as more and more men outside the bar came in to hear Mussolini's words.

"The Socialists must realize a nation has the right and duty to defend itself! When do you want to defend yourselves? When the enemy is on your chest?"

Franco was stunned. No country was invading Italy. This was the man who in August had talked only of peace. "Down with arms and up with humanity," had been his battle cry. What had changed? Franco searched the room to find anyone who shared his same concerns, but all he found were tunneled eyes in riveted concentration, soaking in Benito's every word.

"Tell me, is it human, civilized, socialistic, to stop quietly at the window while blood is flowing in torrents, and say, 'I am not going to move, it doesn't matter to me a bit'?"

"No!" came the cries.

"Intervention will shorten the period of terrible carnage." Mussolini shook his fist powerfully. "Let us take up again the Italian traditions! It is necessary to act, to move, to fight—and if necessary— to die! Neutrals have never dominated events. They have always gone under. It is blood which moves the wheels of history!"

Franco felt as if he were a little boy, back in Puglia, discovering his father's imperfection for the first time. He had thought Mussolini a fighter for the common man, the disenfranchised, the poor, yet this rant went against all he had believed the man to be. Disgust rose up in Franco's belly as he stared up at the speaker, who was gesticulating wildly to drive home a point. Mussolini was clearly a leader others would follow; his words challenged the core of a man's very being, words which spoke of patriotism over neutrality, courage over cowardice. But Franco could also hear the soft voice of his mother the day he left home—"Choose peace with every step you take"—and he suddenly blurted out, "You're a fraud!"

The crowd hushed as all eyes turned to Franco—all eyes including Mussolini's, whose gaze was penetrating, as if he were an all-knowing king looking down on one of his lowly subjects. He paused dramatically, to make sure his accuser felt the rising discomfort in the room, and then slowly crossed his arms over his chest. "It's not polite to interrupt someone when he is speaking," he said with a look of disgust, and then he glanced over at the man by his side. "Get him out of here."

All of a sudden, hands were on Franco, pushing and shoving him toward the door. A fist struck his jaw, another his ribs. He covered his face as he was thrown outside onto the brick street. The angry men returned to the bar, save one, who reached out a hand to help Franco up.

"You have more courage than I," the man smiled. "Nothing angers a man more than when you question his patriotism."

"I wasn't questioning his patriotism," Franco said. "I just wanted to know why he abandoned what he believed in."

The man laughed out loud. "Mussolini isn't interested in ideology. He's after political favors."

Franco gave a puzzled look.

"I'm Giacomo Matteotti," the man said, "a Socialist who has angered many by speaking about Italy staying out of Europe's war."

"I thought that's what Mussolini believed."

"He did. Until the political climate changed."

"I don't understand."

Matteotti laughed again and then put his arm around Franco.

"Let me buy you a drink." He pointed down the street. "Perhaps at a *taverna* that welcomes a man who interrupts the hyperbole of an egomaniac."

CR SO

They shared a bottle of red at a bar near the Santa Maria sopra Minerva Basilica, with Franco fascinated by his new friend. He couldn't remember a time he'd been more interested in listening to another man talk. Giacomo Matteotti had an eloquent yet effortless way of making the most complicated problem easy to understand. He had a total command of the Italian language and a cleanness in his thinking that had diners at nearby tables leaning in to hear what he had to say.

"Mussolini is very clever at reading the political landscape," Matteotti said as he poured Franco another glass. "He was a successful editor of the Socialist newspaper *Avanti!* because he pronounced himself 'a champion for the workers of the world.' But when the Nationalists won six seats in the Chamber of Deputies in last year's election, his commentary began to change."

"He saw a greater opportunity with the Nationalists?" Franco asked.

Matteotti nodded. "He now criticizes the liberal government because he believes the social change he wants will be facilitated more quickly by war than by peace."

"And the Socialists followed him?"

"Not all," Matteotti sighed, "but enough to weaken the party. Mussolini was asked to leave both the party and *Avanti!* Interestingly, he was immediately hired to write for a more conservative paper, *Il Popolo di Italia.*" Matteotti took a sip of wine and raised an eyebrow. "The rumors are, it's being financed by Italian industrialists and French and British interests trying to influence Italy to join the Entente powers."

"What about the Triple Alliance?"

Matteotti's eyes scanned the street as he said in a voice only Franco could hear, "Don't you find it interesting that our diplomats have been seen in England and France recently?"

Franco gave a bewildered look.

"Our politicians might be having a little talk with those two countries about joining forces."

"Why?"

"Think natural resources, Franco."

"You mean the coal and iron ore that are in Austrian colonies?"

"Don't you think negotiations with England would bring us closer to that goal?"

Franco nodded and then looked out at the Church of Santa Maria sopra Minerva. There was a young family sitting on the steps—a father teaching his little boy how to catch a ball while the mother sliced apples for a toddler. He wondered how their lives would change if Italy went to war, how one or two or three men, always men, could affect the lives of millions with one myopic decision. He thought of his own brother, inspired by honor and patriotism, ready to join the army because he loved his country, and a feeling of selfishness came over Franco. There was a part of him that was angry with the government yet another part that felt disloyal. Most of his friends were signing up because they loved their country. They were proud of Italy's history; they loved both her strengths and weaknesses and loved her resiliency too. To Franco, Italy was mythology, romance, pasta, wine, and olive groves; it was a country both charming and complicated. But Italy was his.

He turned back to Matteotti. "What is it you do, signor?"

Giacomo was silent for a moment, looking down at his almost-empty glass. Then he tossed back the last of his wine and winked. "I'm a politician."

CR   SO

The prospect of war settled on Rome like a fog across the Tiber River. One knew the water was there, but was afraid of taking a step forward, for fear of falling in. As each day passed, it seemed as if the Italian government was asking young men to take that first step.

Franco shook his head sadly as he passed a propaganda poster on his walk to work. The artwork displayed a patriotic Italian mother holding a child while pushing a soldier into the flames of war. At the bottom of the poster were the words "Cacciali Via!" ("Drive Them Away!"), as if Italy were already being attacked.

"How soon will we declare war?" Franco whispered, wishing there were something stronger he could offer that would take away his dread.

The threat of war brought Franco more work: six days, sometimes seventy hours a week at the munitions factory. He wrote to his family often, telling them of work and of Rome, of meeting Mussolini and Matteotti, and sent half of his paychecks home. But the only reply came from his mother, whose love was full, but there was a mysterious caution in her words.

"Dear Franco, " her letter started. "I pray your days in Rome are filled with peace. The cold rains of February arrived in Puglia, delaying your father's preparation for the coming season. He worries that our landowner will release us, even though he's the most respected vineyard manager in the region. The talk at Sunday service was about the war and when Italy will be invited into Europe's hell. More and more of our neighbors' sons have already signed on, and your brother plans to join them. Benny's patriotic devotion frightens me; we argue often because we need him here."

The writing ended there—no final thought, no "Love, Mother." It was as if the letter were unfinished. Franco stared at the words, trying to decide what to do. Was this life his, or did it belong to his family, or even to Italy? For a long time, Franco sat on the edge of his bed, studying the letter until finally he put it on his nightstand and went to work.

ભ   શ્ર

The news came in the spring of 1915 to the sounds of sirens and whistles throughout the factory. A worker to Franco's left banged his wrenches together to shouts of "Long live the king! Long live Italy!" A manager raced out of his office, holding up the newspaper *Il Corriere della Serra*, which proclaimed, "Our national salvation lies at the front! Italy has drawn its sword and spoken in a Roman manner from Campidoglio." Shouts of Italian pride were heard throughout the factory until a violent screeching of metal smashing against metal could be heard from the other room.

"Stop him! No! Stop him!" Muffled cries and punches could be heard through the wall as the workers from Franco's line scrambled to see what was causing the commotion.

The door opened and two security men dragged a beaten, bloody worker outside.

"What happened?" Franco asked.

As one security man shoved the anarchist into the back of a truck, the other turned back to answer, "When the boss announced that Italy had declared war, this traitor started throwing barrels and shell casings into the machine that makes our guns."

CR   SO

Franco walked the streets of Rome that night, thinking about the trouble at work and the future of his divided country. Yes, some citizens were outraged that Italy had turned its back on former allies, Germany and Austria, to join forces with Britain, France, and Russia, but most of Franco's coworkers were naive as to why Italy was going to war. This war was a strategic power grab, thought Franco. The support of the Italian army would be used for territorial gain. Italy's leaders probably speculated that only a few Italian soldiers would have to die for a political victory.

Franco opened the door to his apartment and found a letter on the floor. It was from his mother. His shoulders dropped when he read the first line. The government had sent conscription papers to their home, ordering both Benny and Franco to report to the nearest army base. His mother went on to say that their landowner had appealed to officials in Bari that one of their sons was needed to help work his farm. It was agreed that one son could stay, but the other must report. Franco stared at his mother's final words: "Benny said he would await your return before signing up." He crumpled the letter in his fist and tossed it to the floor.

He went back out into the night and wandered the ancient city, finally climbing the Palatine Hill, the centermost of the seven hills of Rome. A light mist began to fall, and he huddled inside the thick walls that overlooked the Circus Maximus. The time alone took his thoughts to the history of where he was, the very beginnings of Roman mythology, and images of Romulus and Remus made him think of his own brother. Memories of silly competitions in the vineyard or schoolyard brought a smile, but the recollection of their final argument about the war gnawed at him. With a loud exhalation, Franco reached into his jacket pocket, took out a pencil and piece of paper, and wrote a note to his boss at the munitions factory explaining why he was going home.

CR   SO

Franco opened the gate to the old wooden fence that framed his family's front yard, and walked up the stone path. He paused for a moment to breathe in the scent of the lupines, and the olives ripening on the trees behind the house. A familiar joy filled his heart as the vineyard brought back so many memories of working this land, from bud-break to flowering to *veraison* to harvest. As he stepped up onto the weathered gray porch, he saw his mother turn and her eyes go wide.

"Franco!" She burst through the front door to hug her son. "Bernardino! He's home!"

His father was standing in the shadows of the doorway, hands on his hips. "Is this the son who leaves only a note when saying goodbye?"

Franco walked inside, unsure of how his father would greet him. Bernardino put a hand on his son's shoulder and gave it a squeeze. "My prodigal son is stronger."

It was then that Franco smiled. "Now that Italy has joined the fight, there's been plenty of work—"

"No talk about war," his father said, and he patted Franco on the back. "Tell us about Rome. Has our pope invited you to dinner?"

Franco laughed until he heard another familiar voice coming from outside.

"The world traveler returns so his brother can have his own adventure!"

"Benny!" shouted Franco as his brother stepped through the door with a defiant grin. "How's the best grower in all of Puglia?"

"You never could lie, so don't start now!" Benny grabbed Franco's hand and pulled him. "You're the son with the gift in the fields! I'm just Papa's muscle—"

☘ Ș

That evening was filled with laughter, old stories, and new stories of Franco's adventures in Rome and the impending grape harvest. The Carollo family was together again, its members stuffing themselves at Maria's table with a meal that Franco had missed. When they were finished, Benny pushed himself away from the table and moved the discussion to the inevitable talk of war.

"More of our friends have signed up, brother. Dino, Matteo, Mario—all have left to serve."

Franco took his time to gather his thoughts. The look on his brother's face was one that was familiar to all who knew him; it was a stubborn look that would be difficult to change.

"What do we have against Austria?" Franco finally asked. "Last year we were their allies, part of the Triple Alliance. Now we're told they're our enemy. Why? Because some politicians told us they're now our enemy?"

Benny got up from the table, grabbed a newspaper from his room, and tossed it in front of his brother. The headlines screamed of the Italian soldiers' "love of unit and defense of country." Franco stared at the journalist's quote that asked every mother to "send her sons, brothers, and grandsons to the army… For each soldier," the writer went on, "loves his unit with absolute devotion."

Franco shook his head, which only seemed to stir his brother's anger.

"This is about protecting our country, Franco."

"Or protecting some politician's plan to make money on this war." Franco slid the paper back across the table. "But they're not the ones who will die on the battlefield, Benny. It will be Dino or Matteo—or you."

"What liberal garbage are they feeding you in Rome?"

"The politicians want to keep us afraid. They tell us that someone is out to get us so we'll build their defenses and protect them from trouble that isn't even real."

Benny rolled his eyes. "You think too much, Franco. It's action Italy needs."

The discussion pained Franco. The war had arrived. His brother would go. He glanced at his father and saw the surrender on Bernardino's face.

"It's good to have you home, little brother, but this time next week I'll be gone to fight." Benny gave Franco a playful shove. "You can read about our great victories over Austria in your liberal newspapers."

CB   BD

Franco stayed through the week, catching up with family and friends, helping his father and brother in the field, and hauling produce to be sold at the market, always at a great profit to the landowner whose farm they worked.

As the days passed, Franco knew the time with his brother was dwindling. Anytime the discussion crept toward politics or the war, Benny's jaws would tighten, and he would cross his arms defiantly across his chest. On the final day, Maria prepared a lunch of olive oil sourdough, cheese, and fresh pears, but they ate in silence until the meal was finished. Benny stared at his empty plate for a long moment and then looked up at his father. "I'll be leaving tonight, Papa."

His father said nothing, and his silence made Benny uncomfortable. "I talked to Matteo and Mario at church today, and they're going to join up as well."

Bernardino exhaled loudly to steady himself, but his voice trembled as he reached across the table and held his first child's hand. "You're a man now, Benny—old enough to make your own decisions. You've always been loyal to family and country." Their father then turned and gave Franco a disappointed look. "I thank God for giving me a son who had the courage to look his father in the eye and tell him why he was leaving home."

Franco cringed, his father's cold words driving straight to his soul. Bernardino forced a smile for his oldest son, but his moist eyes were filled with sadness.

"Your mother and I shall say our goodbyes at this table, Benny." He then turned back to Franco. "I want you to take your brother to the train station. I want YOU to be there when he says goodbye."

CR   BO

The Bari rail yard was already filled with families saying their goodbyes to fathers, sons, and grandsons who were going off to war. Many were from peasant families Franco and Benny knew; young men they had worked with in the fields under the hot sun—planting, growing, and harvesting. These were the only skills most of them knew, yet now they were stepping onto a train not knowing where the army would send them or the battles they would fight.

Franco watched his brother help young soldiers lift their bags into the railcars as they waved goodbye to their families. It was just like Benny, thought Franco. He was so much like their father: strong in character, fundamental in thought, but always willing to help others.

"Let me give you a hand," Franco said as he grabbed a bag and swung it up to a recruit in the railcar.

Benny stared at Franco for a moment before shaking his head. "You know, I was angry at you for running off to Rome. It wasn't the same after you left. All our friends stopped coming around."

Franco gave his brother a bewildered look.

"You never did see it, did you?" Benny asked.

Franco remained quiet.

"All my friends were your friends, Franco. Dino, Matteo, and Mario were your friends, not mine. I'm just glad you included me."

The words surprised Franco. He had no memory of any loneliness being part of his brother's past, but there it was, a kind of thick melancholy that hung like a heavy mist in the air. Benny was indeed a young man who relied on his parents for counsel, and their father's words were like gospel to him, never to be questioned. And now the thought of his older brother being alone on some battlefield frightened Franco.

"I know what you're thinking," Benny said with a look of false confidence. "But I'm ready to serve God and my country. As the Good Book says in Romans 13:4, 'For I am God's servant for your good. But if you do wrong, be afraid, for he does not bear the sword in vain. For he is a servant of God, an avenger who carries out God's wrath on the wrong doer.'" Benny paused as if searching for his next words. "There are countries that want to harm to our Italy, Franco—I have to help."

Franco watched his brother continue to help other soldiers onto the railcars, lifting their packs up to them, and suddenly a wave of guilt rushed over him. He wondered who the real heroes were in this conflict. Were they men like Giacomo Matteotti, who fought against social injustice, or were they men like Benny, who wanted only to defend their country, discover their purpose, and be part of a greater cause?

"How do you know what God wants?" Franco asked, and a slow smile spread across Benny's face.

"I can't answer for you. I can only follow what I believe God wants me to do."

"And you believe God wants you to be a part of this war?"

"I believe God wants me to be of service."

Franco kept his eyes on his brother, but his mind was struggling with the entire day—with his father's disappointment and now his brother's admission. He tried to summon an answer to his own emotions, but could not.

With that, Benny climbed aboard the railcar and reached out his hand. Franco looked up into his brother's trusting eyes, grabbed his hand, and allowed Benny to pull him on board the train.

CR   BO

They were miles down the track, Franco staring out at the Puglia landscape as Benny jabbered away about his younger brother's decision.

"I don't think I'll ever be able to figure you out! You have no money, no extra clothes, and once again, you left without saying goodbye to Papa. Oh, there will be hell to pay when Mama reads him your first letter." Benny laughed out loud. "And you know who he'll blame? Me!"

Franco sat on the floor, motionless.

"Why did you get on the train?" Benny asked.

"You took my hand."

"To say goodbye."

Franco suddenly felt very tired and shook his head slowly. "I just felt I—I need to be with you."

"Ha!" Benny laughed again. "As if a pacifist like you could ever help me."

Franco lay back on the wooden floor, looked up at the night sky, and tried to block out his brother's chatter as he listened to the click-clack of the train that was taking them north to the army camp near the Austrian border.

CHAPTER 4

LUCCA, SEPTEMBER 1915

The sisters of the Blessings Convent had just finished their third hymn when Isabella slipped into the back pew. She had been preparing the evening meal and had raced through the hallway, wiping her hands on her skirt before finding a seat just as Father Josefa began his sermon. San Frediano was filled with Lucca's citizens, who had gathered for a special midweek service to pray for their soldiers. Lucca had already lost several men in the first two battles of Isonzo, and the reports coming back were troubling. There were rumors that fatalities were far greater than the papers were reporting.

Isabella turned when she heard the back door to the church open. A small group had also arrived late. Two adults, stylishly dressed, walked to the front and took their seats in the first pew.

The rest of the party, looking tired and worn, sat several rows behind them. Isabella could see by their hands when they brought them up in prayer that they were laborers. Their broken nails and swollen fingers with small cuts were obvious signs that these people were winemakers. Hands that dug in the dirt, pulled vines, picked and moved grapes, and hauled oak barrels were constantly sore. She watched the mother lick her fingers and smooth the hair on her son's head. When the woman turned away from her family, there was a look of desperation in her eyes.

Isabella had known that look before; it was a reminder of her of own past. To her, it was always a memory of colors: the suffocating blackness of the day, eight years before, when the nurse had pulled the sheet over her parents' faces. The ensuing months had gone by in shades of gray, the dark gray of the grieving faces and unwelcoming homes she was moved to in the weeks after her parents passed, the pale gray of rejection by relatives she never knew. Words became her only bright colors. She remembered the words of her mother and father as they lay dying, filled with the worry of what would happen to their only child. Her father had handed her the basket of seeds and pulled her close. "Isabella, these can be seeds of doubt and fear—or seeds of opportunity. Be careful where you plant them."

"I'm afraid, Papa."

She remembered his final words. "Take the hand of God, child. He created you like Himself. It is you who rule your destiny."

That moment had been her conviction. It was as if she knew this world was not her true home, as if somewhere in her mind she recognized a voice that was calling out to her. It was a voice of strength and trust, of patience and peace, untouched by fear and doubt. It was a certainty that had carried her from the dark colors to the bright ones over the eight years since the death of her parents.

Now the woman's desperate look pulled at Isabella's heart, and as she looked down at her hands, she knew how she could help. The bright red peel of a tomato that had stuck to the back of her hand was her tap on the shoulder.

She snuck out the back of San Frediano, a frown from Anna following her every step, and ran the two blocks to her friend's restaurant.

"Paolo, I need your cutting board!"

"I knew you couldn't stay away from me, Bella!" Paolo grinned, "but I'm in the middle of—"

"Get me tomatoes and garlic!" She pushed past him, sweeping what he'd been preparing off his cutting board.

Paolo did as he was told but held the vegetables just beyond her reach. "What's in it for me?"

"I'll go out with you," she said impatiently, "if you'll just shut up and get out of the way."

He laughed and handed her the tomatoes and garlic. She sliced them up, mixed them together with a little salt, pepper, and dried salt cod, tossed the mixture in a wooden bowl, and hurried back to church just as the service ended.

Sister Anna was the first to greet her. "Mother Superior asked why you missed communion again."

"Get me five place settings," Isabella said as she searched for the family.

"I pray you have a good explanation!"

"Please, Anna." Isabella swept the newspapers and church bulletins off the side of the table and set her bowl down. She saw the family leaving the front of the church and ran over to greet them.

"Excuse me, signora! I'm Isabella Roselli. I cook for San Frediano and was wondering if you and your family would like to try my *baccala*."

An out-of-breath Sister Anna arrived with the place settings and sarcastically added, "I beg you to at least try it. The poor girl is desperate for a compliment."

Isabella playfully elbowed Anna in the side.

"Yes, thank you," the mother said with a weary smile. "I'm Angelina Venero. We work the Martellino farm." She then turned to introduce her children, whose eyes and noses were focused on Bella's creation. "This is my son, Bartolo. He's eleven."

Isabella bowed as if he were royalty.

Angelina nodded to a pretty girl with sparkling blue eyes and tight, thick curly hair. "Rosa is eight and helps in the field." She then introduced her twin girls. "Elena and Elisa may only be six, but they wash and dry the dishes and take care of the chickens."

Angelina's smile then faded to a look of deep sadness. "My husband was the Martellino winemaker until he was conscripted into the army—he died on the battlefield." She paused and inhaled a deep breath. "The grape harvest was difficult without him, and I'm afraid this year's wine will be bitter."

"The wine will be bitter because her husband should have stayed through the harvest," another voice said.

Isabella spun around in shock and stared at the person who had spoken. Before her stood a fashionably dressed woman in a charcoal-gray Edwardian silhouette, with lace that rose up to a high neckline, accentuating her slim figure. Her outfit was something you'd wear to a party, thought Isabella, but not to church.

"His volunteering to support Italy's cause was indeed a noble gesture," the woman continued, "but it cost us a good winemaker and perhaps this year's vintage."

Isabella's eyes met the woman's straight on, as if studying her very soul.

The woman cleared her throat and offered a gloved hand. "I am Susanna Martellino."

Isabella shook it, but she turned back to Angelina. "I'm very sorry for your loss."

Angelina only nodded, her eyes low.

"I can't begin to imagine what your family has gone through," Isabella said as she began to spoon the *baccala* onto plates. "If there's anything we at the Blessings Convent can do, please don't hesitate to ask."

The vineyard owner's wife fixed Isabella with an inquisitive, interested stare. "You're the girl from the market I read about in the newspaper, aren't you?"

Isabella did not answer. Instead, she handed a plate to one of the children. Her silence bothered Susanna.

"Young lady—did you hear me? I understand your crostini were well received at San Michele in Forno's bazaar."

Still no response from Isabella.

"Our meeting today could be of good fortune for you. My husband and I have been looking for someone with your skills to work at our villa."

Isabella turned to face her. "I'm not for sale, signora—and I prefer to work for someone who truly understands the suffering of another."

Susanna flinched back, feeling the words as if they were a slap to her face. She took a moment to calm her rising anger. "You—should know I give graciously to your convent."

Isabella shrugged. "Good for you."

"You, disrespectful little girl!" Susanna snapped. "I demand an apology."

"Then I shall apologize," Isabella said with an exaggerated sigh. "I shall apologize for not appreciating your insensitivity, and I shall pray that you become a more considerate Christian."

"How dare you!" Susanna's fists clenched at her sides. "I—I will be taking this up with your Mother Superior!"

"Then do that, signora." Isabella said with a crinkle-eyed grin, "But I should warn you—she is also a fan of my *baccala*."

"There you are!" a gentleman called out as he hurried down the front steps of the church. He smiled at Isabella. "I was hoping the two of you could meet. I'm Giovanni Martellino. I met you at the bazaar." He turned to his wife. "This is the young lady I was telling you about, darling—she served the most delicious crostini I've ever—"

"I'm sure they were fine"—Susanna cut him off and grabbed his hand—"but we must leave immediately. I'm already late for several errands in town."

Giovanni gave a confused look to both women and only nodded.

Susanna inhaled strongly through her nose and stared at Angelina. "Please return to our estate as soon as you're finished eating this—charity offering."

CHAPTER 5

THE ISONZO VALLEY, SEPTEMBER 1915

Franco and Benny stared at the bodies of their dead countrymen lined in rows by the trenches near the Isonzo front. They watched a chaplain move from corpse to corpse, making the sign of the cross over each body of an Italian boy no older than twenty. Franco stood frozen, his eyes riveted to the death surrounding him, until a medic pointed to a wounded soldier who lay on a pushcart.

"That one's still alive. Bring him to my tent."

Franco did as he was told, but the smell inside the tent almost made him retch. The medic noticed.

"First day?"

Franco only nodded.

"Our army wasn't ready to carry on a campaign this big," the medic continued.

"How many?" were the only words Franco could come up with.

"More than I can count."

Franco's hand went to his mouth as he watched the medic slice open a patient's thigh, infected blood and pus oozing from the black-and-green skin onto the dirt floor.

"The damn generals brag that we're such great fighters, but they don't see what I see." The medic wiped a surgical knife with a dirty rag and pointed to a cot where a sheet had been pulled up over a soldier's head. "The dead come to me—they're just boys, ill prepared to fight, most right off the farm." He raised his eyes to look at Franco. "Farmer?"

Franco nodded.

"Ever shot a rifle?"

"No."

The medic shook his head. "Good luck."

‘‘ ’’

Franco jammed his spade into the frozen ground and came up with nothing but ice and rocks. He and Benny had spent the last month digging trenches and bunkers in the Isonzo valley, a sixty-mile stretch in a mountainous region separating northern Italy from Austria. Franco turned his spade over, dumping the stones and frozen water on top of the wall of mud to build the Italian defense.

"Make sure you leave a gap wide enough to get our rifles through!" Benny yelled from inside their bunker as he poured dirty water into a coffee pot.

"I've done this before," Franco grumbled as he pushed the mud into the creases of the wall. He jammed his spade into the ground and went inside. They had built an underground sleeping hut using tree branches to support the walls, and a wire-net-and-tarp roof. With winter approaching, the mud would freeze and better support the structure, but as the sun came up, its warmth revealed the stench of the death the valley had suffered in the first two battles.

"How much longer will we have to stay in this stinkhole?" Franco asked as he sat down next to his brother.

"We'll be here until God orders us to attack," Benny said, and then he poured his brother a cup of coffee. "In the army, God is General Luigi Cadorna."

Franco shook his head. "He's not held in high regard by his own officers."

Benny remained quiet.

"Thousands of our men died because of his tactics in the first two battles," Franco said. "I'm told we didn't have enough rifles, enough shears to cut the barbed wire, or enough artillery shells."

"Maybe Cadorna doesn't want them." Benny tossed the rest of his coffee onto the fire. "They say his hero was Napoleon, who loved the full-frontal assault."

Franco took a deep breath, his face filled with dread. "But Napoleon didn't face machine guns and barbed wire."

They quieted when the flap of their shelter opened and three men from their platoon joined them for coffee. Two were privates from southern Italy, peasant farmers in their past lives; and the third was a lieutenant from Matera, known for his strict discipline. Franco despised the lieutenant, as he had a reputation for eavesdropping on conversations and reporting any discontent back to his captain.

The lieutenant eyed Franco suspiciously as he twisted the tips of his waxed mustache. "Did you polish my boots?"

Franco nodded to the corner of the room, where two shiny black boots were next to his bed.

The lieutenant snatched them up. "You left them in the dirt?"

Franco only gave an annoyed look.

"Damn you, Private! Your lack of discipline will get you killed on the front!"

"Then have Cadorna throw me in the brig," Franco said in a barely audible voice.

Before the lieutenant could respond, Benny grabbed his brother by the arm, jerked him to his feet, and pulled him outside. He led Franco down to the banks of the Isonzo.

"What the hell is wrong with you?" Benny growled as he released his brother's arm. "You can't question army leadership!"

"You did."

"I'm your brother!" Benny snapped. "I'll listen to your damn complaints and make sure no one else hears them! But you gave up your freedom to question authority when you joined."

Franco, still pale and short of breath, was beginning to recover. "I never should have followed you."

Benny's shoulders slumped forward, and the guilt of his having induced his younger brother to follow him pulled them even lower. "But you did join. And we both became subjects to the Italian army when each of us made his decision."

"Look who's on the front lines, Benny! The poor! The rich sons like that damn lieutenant show up with no experience and are made junior officers, but every private in our platoon is a peasant. Most of them can't read or write. They don't even know what we're fighting for."

Benny shook his head. He still couldn't understand why his brother had stepped onto that train. Franco was not a soldier. He wanted answers to questions that soldiers could not ask. Benny did the only thing that made sense to him. He reached into his backpack and pulled out his Bible.

"That won't stop Cadorna from sending more men to their deaths," Franco grumbled.

"No—but it gives me comfort." Benny handed his brother his Bible. "I pray that it gives you comfort too."

Franco stared at the book in his hands: its worn leather cover faded by time, pages yellowed and curled from being constantly turned, little bits of paper sticking out of the top, marking his brother's favorite passages. This was the only book Benny had ever read; the book he'd learned to read with. It was the very foundation of who Benny was. Franco slowly looked up at his brother. Benny's face was grim, his eyes searching.

"Please, forgive me," Benny finally said.

Franco's mouth fell slightly open. He was unsure of why his brother would seek his forgiveness.

"Forgive me for pulling you onto that train, little brother. I need your forgiveness before they send us out to fight."

CR   ℘

Benny's message stayed with Franco the rest of the day and into the night. When he woke in the morning, he dressed for battle and walked to a hill overlooking the Isonzo River. As he studied the ridge where the enemy was waiting, he thought of the thousands of Austrian soldiers just like him, in some cold muddy trench, holding on to fear of an unseen enemy, ready to attack, ready to defend, and why? Because that was the order they had been given. His eyes went to the Isonzo, to the water carrying leaves and twigs downstream, the river not caring at all that thousands of soldiers, both Italians and Austrians, had spilled their blood in its current. The river continued to drift by, taking those tragedies and horrors of war out to the sea. The river did not care. Through war and peace, triumph and tragedy, it did not care. Franco closed his eyes as his thoughts went back to his brother's words. "I need your forgiveness."

When he opened his eyes, he seemed to see the river in a new light this time—a vibrant life source connected to everything. The river knew its truth, never doubting its ability to give and sustain life. Franco now saw the river's brilliant brown and green colors, and how they harmonized perfectly with the surrounding oaks and pines that swept down the hill in pursuit of the river's life. A gentle peace warmed him, and he inhaled the beauty of the Isonzo valley until he felt a hand touch his shoulder.

"I've been looking all over for you!"

It was Benny. There was eagerness in his eyes that scared Franco.

"Our battalion is readying to attack!"

The brothers ran back to their bunker, gathered their gear, and joined the march to the river. For the assault to be successful, their commanding officer told them, they must capture the summit of San Michele, north of the Isonzo.

CR   SO

A bitter autumn wind swept in from the north, chilling the Italian soldiers as they waded into the river. All Franco could hear was his own shallow breathing and the icy water lapping against the legs and waists of his countrymen as they headed to the Austrian side. He turned to his right to make sure his brother was close. Benny had a fierce look about him—brow furrowed, rifle ready, eyes studying the forest. The quiet morning heightened the tension until the crack of a single rifle shot shattered the silence. Franco looked up to see birds scattering from the trees, their solitude broken as the shot echoed off the valley walls. A lone sparrow swept down toward the river. A fellow soldier fell backward into the cold water, and a dull pool of blood drifted up from his chest and was carried downriver by the current.

"Charge!" a captain roared, and the men lifted their water-soaked legs and ran to the Austrian shore. More shots rang out as the Austrian marksmen picked off the young Italian soldiers. Franco saw Dominic, a young miner from Sicily whose sarcastic wit he'd grown to enjoy, fall into the shallow bank at the shoreline. He saw Gustave take a shot to the face and drop into the frozen mud in front of him. Gustave was like Franco, a peasant farmer from Puglia; they'd shared stories of winemaking and argued which soil from their homeland was best. As Franco dove behind a log on the Austrian side, he feared for his brother. Where was Benny? He'd been off on his right when they entered the river. He frantically searched the Austrian shoreline, but with so many of his countrymen diving for cover, he couldn't tell who was alive and who was dead.

"Benny!" Franco screamed. He scrambled to his feet and raced down the bank, yelling his brother's name. A bullet ricocheted off a log in front of him, and then another zipped past into the river. Someone grabbed him by the collar and threw him down behind a log.

"Stay down, you damn fool!" It was a sergeant from his battalion, who stole a quick glance at the hills before looking into Franco's frightened eyes. "Keep your head down until we find their marksmen."

A second charge came from the Italian side, diverting the Austrian marksmen's attention to the easier targets in the water.

"Now!" shouted the sergeant, grabbing Franco by the arm and leaping forward. Italian soldiers, fed by the sergeant's courage, charged ahead into the woods, firing their rifles whenever they saw a flash of Austrian gunfire. Two of the enemy came through the brush, but the sergeant was too quick; dropping the first with a shot to the chest and then quickly slamming another bullet back into the chamber and killing the second attacker. The Austrian fell at Franco's feet, clutching at the wound to his neck, blood spilling out onto Isonzo ground. Franco froze in sudden panic, staring at death face to face for the first time. The sergeant again pulled him to the ground.

"Now's not the time to be afraid!" he growled as he pulled Franco's bayonet out of its sheath and stuck it onto the end of his rifle. "You know what this is for, soldier. Don't be afraid to use it."

CR   SO

Franco stumbled through the forest on the enemy side of the Isonzo, blindly following the sergeant through the brush and trees near the river. Despite support from their artillery, and despite outnumbering the Austrians two to one in manpower, the Italian army had gained only forty meters over the last two days. Austrian machine gunners and snipers hunkered down in the hills, waited for the shelling to cease, and then slipped out and picked off the Italians as they charged the hill. Franco had slept only three of the last forty-eight hours, for he'd gone to each campsite searching for his brother. He'd lost count of the dead he'd seen along the way. The sergeant had had him help the wounded back to a makeshift hospital near the river. Most would not live through the night. At first, Franco had been shocked at seeing the horrors of death, but now he was numb from watching so many of his countrymen die in the first two days of Isonzo's third battle.

A cold mist was falling as the sergeant leaned back against the muddy trench with a distant look on his face. He had killed five of the enemy in the Italian charge to set up defenses on the north side of the river. His actions and leadership had been courageous, if not heroic, but he didn't seem to care. He drew a cigarette from his breast pocket and covered the flame with a dirt-caked hand as he inhaled and turned to Franco. "We've been together two days, and I still don't know your name. I know your brother's name because you're shouting it all the time, but I don't know yours."

"Franco Carollo," Franco mumbled. "From Puglia."

The sergeant stuck his hand out. "Nice to meet you, Franco Carollo from Puglia. I'm Sergeant Antonio San Stefano, from Sicily."

Franco said nothing as the sergeant flicked off the first ash from his cigarette. "I can tell you don't like fighting—so why the hell did you enlist?"

Franco only shook his head.

"You haven't fired your rifle yet, have you?"

Again, Franco only shook his head.

"So, tell me if I've got this right. You're a pacifist. You're against the war. You hate Italy's politics and the men who sent us to fight."

Franco remained quiet as the sergeant studied him.

"Well, join the fucking crowd," the sergeant snorted, and then he suddenly became serious. "But let me tell you something—as soon as you stepped foot onto this battlefield, you were no longer fighting for family or politicians or even Italy. You're fighting for the soldier next to you." Sergeant San Stefano made sure Franco raised his eyes to meet his. "Right now, the man next to you is me."

Franco's voice was barely above a whisper. "Yes, sir."

The sergeant handed him his rifle and patted him on the back. "Now that we have that straightened out, let's go find your brother."

They left the trench and crawled on hands and knees to a log that three Italian soldiers were using for cover.

"Have any of you seen Private Benny Carollo?" Franco asked. The exhausted soldiers shook their heads. They checked two more foxholes with no luck. Sergeant San Stefano nodded to the forest. "Let's work the trail ahead toward our east camp." He pointed up the hill. "See that rock crag next to the stand of oaks?"

Franco nodded.

"Perfect cover for snipers. Stay low."

The sergeant led the way, crawling several meters in front, and turned in to the trees. Franco followed, but his jacket caught on a scrub oak limb, and when he went to untangle it, he heard a rifle shot followed by men's voices grunting, as if they were in a struggle. Franco ripped his jacket free, jumped to his feet, and raced through the trees. He saw his sergeant grappling with an enemy soldier. The Austrian wrenched his way on top, held Sergeant San Stefano's head down, and pulled his knife from its sheath. Franco tried but could not move. The enemy raised his knife, and for the first time since they had been together, Franco saw fear in his sergeant's face. He wanted to cry out, but no words came. Instead, with his hands shaking, he raised his rifle and somehow pulled the trigger. The rifle kicked and the bullet flew through the air, shattering the Austrian soldier's left shoulder blade and ripping his throat open. Machine gun fire followed, coming from the rock crag in the hills as the sergeant had earlier predicted. Bullets slammed into mud as Sergeant San Stefano scrambled for cover.

Someone suddenly grabbed Franco and pulled him behind a tree. It was Benny.

Franco threw his arms around his brother as Sergeant San Stefano circled around through the trees and joined them by the oak.

"You must be fuckin Benny!"

Benny nodded as he held Franco, whose face suddenly went ashen when he saw the Austrian soldier he'd just killed. The enemy lay twisted on the ground, his head turned awkwardly toward Franco, hollow eyes staring back as if desperately searching for help. Sergeant San Stefano said nothing. He turned the brothers away from death and led them back to camp.

CR   SO

The steady mist that had been falling all day finally let up as they arrived at the muddy trench that would be their home for the night. Franco's childhood friend, Matteo, was sitting alone with his head in his hands.

"Matteo!" Franco cried out, but his friend barely lifted his head and gave a look that was both pain and defeat.

Benny pulled Franco to the side. "I was with him when the fighting started. It was chaos at the front. Matteo's errant shot hit one of our own. He was with that soldier when he died."

A streak of despair went through Franco. He was suddenly angry: angry with Benny for joining the army, angry with himself for following him into this wretched war, and now angry with God.

"I prayed the last few days," he said, his voice growing in anger. "I prayed that I would find you and that the killing would stop." He looked past the river to the battlefield strewn with dead young soldiers. "How can God allow this to happen?"

"Perhaps it's as Papa says." Benny's face was grim. "We must simply trust that all of this is part of God's plan."

It was almost dark, and the sun's rays cast a soft glow across the frozen corpses: young men, perfect only hours before, whose deaths were not yet known by mothers and fathers, sisters and brothers, wives and children. Franco shivered at the realization and turned back to his brother. "There has to be another way."

Benny sought the right words to answer Franco's assertion, but nothing came.

ଔ   ଓ

The Italian cannon fire started early on October 21. Sergeant San Stefano walked up and down the second line to make sure his soldiers were ready for the assault of the hill, San Michele. As soon as the cannons stopped, the first Italian charge started up and was immediately cut down by Austrian machine gun fire; hundreds were killed on the first charge.

Franco's line was next. His heart pounded as he went through his checklist. Bayonet secure. Ammunition clips. Cartridge in chamber. Safety off. He inhaled deeply, trying to calm his fears, and he peeked above the log that served as his cover. Smoke mixed with fog blurred any chance to separate friend from foe. It would be a blind charge into a ravaged field of dead and dying. The waiting was deafening. Finally, the captain yelled, and Franco reached for his brother, but Benny was already gone, over the log and into the gloom. Franco followed, keeping Benny in his sight as the enemy responded with small-arms fire. They raced past the Italian dead and wounded that littered the hillside from the first wave. Austrian machine guns opened up, and Sergeant San Stefano yelled for his soldiers to take cover. The Carollo brothers dove into a ditch framed with barbed wire set to slow the Italian charge. Their chaplain was tending to the wounded only twenty meters away.

"Get down, Father Mario!" screamed Franco as the enemy guns ripped the ground in front of the chaplain. Benny sent a shot at the enemy's nest, which gave Sergeant San Stefano time to charge the Austrian gunners and take them out. Franco turned to find their chaplain still on one knee, caring for a soldier, oblivious to the bullets zipping past. Benny crawled underneath the barbed wire with a burst of machine gun fire following his every move.

Jumping to his feet, Franco fired two shots at the Austrian machine gun, giving his brother time to rush ahead and pull Father Mario and the injured soldier down into a ravine for cover. Franco breathed a sigh of relief.

CHAPTER 6

LUCCA, NOVEMBER 1915

Isabella could feel a frost coming. She had harvested the grapes in her small garden in early September, then removed the top layer of dirt and brought in new soil from the Serchio River for her winter crops. She planted leeks, squash, asparagus, garlic, and snap beans in October, believing that the first cold spell would bring a sweeter taste. Those who shopped Lucca's market agreed. Her plants thrived under her tender care, and consequently, the convent's vegetable sales remained strong despite a down economy in wartime.

Now, on a chilly November day in 1915, Isabella was digging, but not to plant. This time she was digging in the convent vineyard for a sturdy young grape plant that would relocate easily. She dug it up, wrapped the roots in plenty of soil, and gently placed it in a knapsack for travel.

"Don't tell me you're going to run away again?" Sister Anna asked as she stepped outside.

Isabella laughed. "A convent in Switzerland has made me a better offer."

Anna squeezed her arm. "You're going to help the Venero family, aren't you…"

Isabella said nothing as she pulled the knapsack over her shoulders.

"You have a heart for those who suffer," Anna smiled, "and God loveth a cheerful giver."

"I made today's meals," Isabella replied quickly, trying to change the subject. "If I'm not back before dinner, there are leftover crostini that should get you through tomorrow."

Anna put her arm around Isabella and walked her to the road. "I know you don't think it's possible, but somehow we'll survive without you."

Isabella hiked north to the Martellino vineyard, making a four-kilometer journey across the Serchio River and into the hills, olive groves, and vineyards of Tuscany. A broad smile creased her face as she looked back at Lucca's powerful walls built from local brick and stone, at first designed to defend, and then in the 1800's transformed into a tree-lined promenade for locals to enjoy. The promenade was a spectacle, even in late fall with the leaves gone from the chestnut trees and the sun peeking through the oaks that grew on top of the Torre dei Guinigi.

When she saw the Martellino property, Isabella understood why the family had built its vineyard on this land some four hundred years before. While the strong winds and dust did not penetrate, just enough breezes off the Ligurian Sea pushed the fog perfectly against the hills. There was a spring at the top of a hill that gushed cold, clear water down east of the vineyard, flowing down to the Serchio River. The rare rains they enjoyed in the summer months combined with the soil and made it perfect for growing grapes and olives.

The main house had been restored at the turn of the century and still boasted the old oak beams of the original, but the hand-made terracotta floors had been a gift from Giovanni's father to his mother only weeks before she died.

Isabella turned down the drive, went past the villa, and cut through the courtyard to a smaller back house where the Venero family lived. Angelina was in the field with her family when she saw Isabella.

"Look, children!" she cried out. "It's the chef from San Frediano!"

"I'm no chef!" Isabella yelled back. "I'm just Italian!"

They hugged briefly, and Angelina held her at arm's length. "I read the story about you in the newspaper. Very impressive. What brings Lucca's 'Garden Girl' to our modest farm?"

"Your compliments," laughed Isabella, and she glanced back at the grand two-story villa. "But this place is anything but modest."

Angelina forced a smile.

Isabella squeezed her arm. "I came to see if you need any help."

"You are too kind." Angelina nodded, recovering herself slightly. "I try to remember what my husband would do. We covered the wine for the secondary fermentation, but—but—"

Isabella finished her sentence. "You're not quite sure when you should separate the wine from the deposits before you move it into the final containers?"

Angelina nodded.

"I'd be happy to take a look," Isabella said, and then she changed the subject back to why she'd come. "And how are—?"

"The children have been a big help. We're now cleaning the barrels and—"

Isabella touched her arm. "I came to see how you are doing."

Angelina looked away and stared across the vineyard. "My husband did so much. I'm trying to remember half of what he did in both the vineyard and the olive orchard."

Isabella said nothing.

"Mariano loved Italy," Angelina continued. "After he was drafted, he hired two hands to help me, but they were gone by late July, tired of the Martellinos' criticism. I was told Mariano had been killed two weeks before the harvest." She looked to the villa. "The signora gave me one day to grieve."

Isabella took her hand but remained quiet.

"I met Mariano at the Cathedral of San Martino." The memory made Angelina smile. "He was very shy for such a big man, but he finally worked up the courage to ask me to marry him at a picnic on the banks of the Serchio. He was so nervous he dropped the bread in the river, and as it floated away, he said, 'I hope this doesn't mean you won't marry me.'" There were tears on Angelina's cheeks. "I—I can't lose this job—but I don't know how long the Martellinos will keep us on."

Isabella wrapped her arms around Angelina and let her cry. As she looked out at the field, she saw the Venero children watching. They had a look in their eyes—a look Isabella had once seen in her own eyes.

"Show me the wine," Isabella whispered when Angelina was ready. Angelina wiped her tears and waved for her son to join them at the barn. They walked down to the cellar, where Isabella checked the first barrel and turned to Bartolo. "Go get me three eggs, please."

As the boy ran up the stairs, Angelina gave her a quizzical look.

"I'll put the white of an egg in the cask. Egg whites are good for removing tannin particles, so the wine has a rounder and softer texture."

"How do you know this?"

"My parents were farmers, and even though they died when I was eleven, they ignited my spiritual fire and gave me a love of nature. For that, I'm very grateful."

Angelina's mouth twitched slightly; she was shaken by the ease with which Isabella spoke of death. "When did you—get over losing them?"

"They're always in my heart," Isabella said matter-of-factly. "After they died, my aunt and uncle couldn't take me in, so they asked the Blessings sisters for help."

"The nuns raised you?"

"I fought the sisters at first, but they were patient. Especially Sister Anna, who was given the task to convert me." Isabella gave a sarcastic roll of her eyes and crossed herself. "Convert me from ignorant heathen to enlightened Catholic. Anna had me memorize scripture, study the saints, sing in the choir, and polish every crucifix in the convent."

"Did it work?"

Isabella chuckled lightly. "I have a different understanding of God. Anna finally left me alone in the garden. It was in the garden where I found His peace."

"You didn't feel as if God had abandoned you?"

"When I was finally able to forgive," Isabella smiled, her green eyes bright and encouraging, "forgive my parents for dying, forgive my relatives for placing me in a convent, and forgive myself for thinking that I was unwanted and unloved—only when I let those feelings go was I able to understand God's real world."

"His world is my agony," Angelina said heavily as she stared into the barrel of fermenting wine, cloudy and mysterious, its future as unpredictable as her own. Mariano had been her rock, and now he was gone. She was alone—alone with the responsibility of raising four children while managing one of the largest farms north of Lucca. This would be her solitary prison, whose walls would be impossible to surmount.

"I don't know what to do," Angelina said. She paused for a long moment, trying to compose herself. "I've been so angry—angry with Mariano for leaving, and then for dying in this awful war. Now, I'm afraid this wine will fail and I'll lose this job. I don't know where we'll go or how we'll survive."

CR   SD

Isabella stayed with the Veneros that day, helping with the wine, cleaning their house, and cooking their dinner. They didn't have much, but she found a zucchini in the kitchen, sliced it, and grilled it until it was a tender brown. She then raised the fire to char it and sprinkled spices on top: basil, red pepper, salt, and olive oil. She sliced up some homemade country bread, brushed it with olive oil, and then grilled it too until it was a crisp golden brown. She placed the zucchini on the bread, added a little ricotta cheese to the top, and carried it to the dinner table. All ten eyes stared at Isabella's creation as if it had come from the hands of Michelangelo himself.

Their anticipation suddenly cooled when Susanna Martellino stepped into the doorway of their cottage. The setting sun silhouetted her thin frame as she walked to the kitchen table and plucked a zucchini stick off Isabella's platter.

"Well, if it isn't the cynical convent cook," she said with an icy tone, and then she took a bite of the zucchini. "I take it you've reconsidered my offer to work for us?"

"I came to see if I could help Angelina."

"Then you'll need my permission first. But if I said yes, how would you help?"

"I can't come every day, but when I can, I'll cook meals and help to bring a better flavor to your wine."

Susanna's head jerked up in momentary shock. "How dare you criticize our wine! My husband's family has owned this winery for four centuries, and we will not be told—"

"I apologize for my choice of words," Isabella interrupted, "but I sampled your wine at Lucca's festival and found it rather bland. I believe I can help."

Susanna was not used to this type of raw honesty from a commoner, but had heard of Isabella's excellence at the market. Still, she wondered what angle the young lady was trying to work. "And all this help you'll give without pay?"

"When I'm able, signora. I still have responsibilities at the convent."

Susanna's upper lip stiffened as she stared at the young girl. Isabella was a common orphan, thought Susanna. Her drab brown skirt and blouse were obvious hand-me-downs, probably given to her by some family who attended San Frediano. There was dirt under her fingernails, and her shoes had holes in them and were too big for her feet. Yet everything about her reeked of confidence.

"You act rather high and mighty for a peasant girl who should be grateful that the Blessings sisters took her in."

The comment startled Angelina but not Isabella.

"I'm very grateful," Isabella said matter-of-factly, "and as an incentive for my proposal, whatever I cook for the Veneros' I shall make for you and Signor Martellino."

Susanna bristled at the absolute gall of this girl telling her what she would and would not do.

Angelina broke the tension. "She can stay here when she visits."

Susanna took another slice of zucchini. "Let's just not forget our roles."

Isabella gave a lopsided grin. "Our roles?"

"Of course. My husband and I are the landowners. You will be treated as one of the field workers."

"I'm simply volunteering to help—"

"And I'm helping you! There's a reason God made the rich and also the poor. It says so in the Bible, but I doubt you can even read!"

Isabella ignored her and continued to serve the meal. The quiet bothered Susanna, who suddenly felt a need to defend herself. "Jesus said that blessed are the poor and blessed are they who hunger and mourn. I believe God gave me this vineyard so that I may help the poor by giving them jobs. I'm sure the Veneros' are very grateful." She then turned back to Isabella. "I expect my dinner promptly at eight thirty."

"Your dinner will be on time," Isabella answered. "But just to clarify, I can read, and I believe that in the beatitudes you refer to, Jesus said, 'blessed are they who hunger and thirst for righteousness.'"

"I know that!"

"I'm sure you did, signora. But I don't think it's about jobs or vineyards or even going to church, but that you must be hungry to serve to achieve these." Isabella then smiled at the Veneros'. "I believe the children are hungry, so I shall serve them now."

Susanna gave Isabella a look of absolute contempt. "Eight-thirty dinner!" Then she stormed out of the house.

CR BD

The Venero family ate every last bit of Isabella's dinner that night. When they finished, Isabella took from her knapsack a small package that had a leaf sticking out of the top. She undid the twine and opened the paper.

"This is a young Barbera plant from our convent vineyard. It may look a little frail, but it's actually very tough and can withstand many climates."

Angelina's daughter Rosa raised her hand. "I know where we can plant it."

"We can mix soil from the creek bottom," Isabella pointed to their chicken coop, "with the droppings from your chickens."

They looked at her in surprise.

"The droppings have a nutrient which stimulates the plant's growth."

Bartolo raced off to the chicken coop as Isabella followed Rosa and the rest of the family out to the end of the vineyard. She dug a hole, placed the Barbera plant inside, and surrounded it with the soil Bartolo had mixed.

"Let's place our hands on this plant," Isabella said, "and bless it with love every time we are near."

"Why does it need love?" Rosa asked.

"Because everything is energy. Animals, plants, thoughts, and ideas are all energy. There's a communal flow when we bless something together. When we combine our positive thoughts, amazing things happen."

They walked back to the Veneros' cottage, where Isabella said good night and headed to the villa to make the Martellinos' dinner. She washed her hands and face in the well outside, dried them on her skirt, and knocked on the back door. A middle-aged woman with a dour expression greeted her.

"You must be Isabella. I'm Josephine. I run the house. You have thirty minutes to make dinner. The Martellinos are never late."

Isabella walked through an entryway that opened up into the most beautiful kitchen she had ever seen. There were marble floors with huge wood beams that supported a ceiling at least five meters high. From the ceiling hung pots, pans, spoons, and ladles. There was a big, open brick oven that would be perfect for bread and pies. Next to that was a stone grill, waist high, with a brass chimney above that led the smoke out to the top of the roof. Isabella had never seen anything like it and stood staring.

"Well?" Josephine asked impatiently. "What are you waiting for? You now have twenty-eight minutes to prepare dinner. Whatever you need can be found in the pantry next to the stove."

Isabella grabbed a fistful of wood chips, tossed them onto the grill to make the fire hotter, and hustled to the pantry. With little time, she made the same meal she had prepared for the Veneros. Josephine led Isabella into an elegant dining room with a long oak table. Giovanni got up from his chair and clapped his hands.

"I'm delighted you've agreed to work for us!" he said excitedly. "Susanna said you had a wonderful talk."

Isabella only smiled as she placed a plate before Susanna and then served Giovanni.

"Lucca's chefs tell me her fruits and vegetables are the best of any market," Susanna added with a bored tone. "Unfortunately, I have not shared in their experience."

Isabella looked at Susanna in the light this time and saw a striking woman with sharp eyes, long dark hair, and a beautiful olive complexion. While Susanna smiled coolly, she did not raise her eyes to meet Isabella's. There was a calculated coldness to her every movement. She took a bite and paused as if in thought. "This—is missing something. Salt. Isabella, bring me salt."

The shaker was within her reach, but Isabella moved it closer. Susanna added the salt and brought the grilled zucchini and toast to her mouth, "Yes, that's all it needed."

Isabella said under her breath, "And some people like sardines with their gelato." Josephine, standing in the corner, heard the comment and stifled a laugh.

"What's that?" Susanna frowned.

"Nothing, signora. I'm glad you like it."

CHAPTER 7

THE ISONZO VALLEY, JANUARY 1916

F ranco pounded the butt of his rifle into the icy stream and dipped a metal pail into the muddy water. While the Italian infantry was freezing on the Isonzo front, Cadorna's senior officers were resting comfortably miles back. Recently word had leaked down to Franco's battalion that seven hundred Italian Alpine troops had frozen to death because the Italian leadership had not come to their aid. Yet any dissent was met with punishment.

Franco blew into his cold, chapped hands to warm them before lifting the water pail to bring back to his squad. Winter had been particularly brutal. The icy winds off the Alps had filled the makeshift hospital with soldiers dying from disease and others suffering from frostbite. Benny had wisely stolen blankets from an Austrian farmhouse in December that were now saving his comrades. As Franco pulled back the tent flap and lowered the pail to the dirt floor, his brother sat up on his cot.

"Does Cadorna even care about us?" Benny asked as he dipped his cup into the muddy water. "What's his plan when this iceberg finally thaws? Charge up another damn hill?"

"Watch what you say," Father Mario whispered. "Cadorna has spies everywhere. He gave one soldier a three-year jail sentence for writing a letter to his parents criticizing his leadership."

Benny gave a disgusted look. "Jail would be better than this."

The chaplain raised his cup as if offering a sarcastic toast. "I recall the words of the elitist Francesco Crispi: that we peasants should 'respectfully accept the benefits that trickle down to us from the bourgeoisie and be glad to be given a place at the banquet of life.'"

"Quite a banquet we have," Franco said as he touched his cup to Father Mario's. "Muddy water and moldy bread sent respectfully by the bourgeoisie. How unfortunate that their own sons were unable to join us on the front lines."

ᘒ   ᘓ

Winter turned to spring, another battle on the Isonzo was lost, summer came, and still little ground was taken by the Italian army until finally, on August 4, Sergeant San Stefano was given orders to send his men forward. As the sun crept over Mount San Michele, Father Mario went from soldier to soldier, offering encouraging words and making sure packs were tightened before their unit's assault on the town of Gorizia. There was a new fear among the soldiers on that day. In Cadorna's most recent setback near Trentino, the Austrians had introduced their first gas attack, and over four thousand Italians had been killed, wounded, or gassed in a matter of days. That terror now stretched tightly through the Italian trenches.

"Steady!" yelled Sergeant San Stefano to the soldiers at the edge of their muddy defense. "Steady!"

The cannons roared as an artillery barrage, which was designed to be a diversionary tactic to draw the Austrian army units around Gorizia to the south, began. Franco covered his ears to muffle the noise of the cannons pounding the Austrian hills. There was a moment of quiet followed by a cry from the sergeant. "Charge!"

The earlier fear that had gripped Franco now became a heightened awareness as he climbed out of his trench and ran tight against his brother. Despite his hatred of the war and disdain for the Italian leadership, he felt as if all the men he ran with were his brothers, and their voices gave him the courage and strength to continue his charge.

The Austrian defense let the Italians advance the first forty meters. Then their machine guns ripped through the first wave, cutting the Italians apart. Franco dove into a trench, bullets tearing up the ground around him. He crawled to the bottom and through a mash of mud, blood, and urine over to a dead body at the edge of the ravine. He peeked over the corpse and saw the enemy machine gun nest. It was a lone gunner with his partner, loading the strip of bullets into the gun and firing at Franco's countrymen. Franco slid his rifle across the dead man's belly, aimed, and fired, hitting the gunner in the face. The dead gunner's partner gasped in shock and then reached for the gun. Franco leaped from his trench and charged the enemy nest. The Austrian swept the machine gun around, but he was too late. Franco's bayonet tore through the man's neck, the man's body jerking up as blood burst from his throat. Franco tried to pull the bayonet free, but his rifle stuck in the enemy's neck. The man's eyes locked on

Franco in a desperate plea as blood continued to pour from his throat and mouth. Franco shoved his rifle aside in sudden panic and let go a primal scream that was part rage and part fear. He fell flat on his back and stared up at the sky, listening to the sounds of bullets and screams and cannon fire and moans and the man next to him dying. He wondered if he would be the next to die. He did not care anymore.

CR SO

It was a mournful day for the city of Lucca in early October of 1917. The news from the Italian front that three more locals had been killed hit the Venero family especially hard. Bartolo had been coached in football by Tony Verelli, one of the soldiers who had been killed on the Isonzo.

The memorial was held at San Michele in Foro, where a painting of Saints Helena, Jerome, Sebastian, and Roch appeared to be looking down and comforting the mothers and fathers of those children whose lives had been cut short in the Isonzo valley. Isabella wiped her tears when Signora Verelli went to light a candle for the soul of her son. Friends and family members held her while little children stared awkwardly, not understanding the depth of the moment. Mothers knelt in pews, silently thanking God that it wasn't them at the altar.

When the service ended, Isabella headed for the door. She needed to get outside, to breathe the cool night air and let go of the sorrow that filled the church. She felt a tap on her shoulder. It was Susanna Martellino.

CR SO

Susanna was the kind of person who believed that love was dangerous, and the memorial only reinforced that conviction. The father she had loved had left when she was ten, and the mother she had wanted to love had not reciprocated. When the henpecking became too much to bear, her father took off, and his abandonment made Susanna's mother even more determined to have her daughters marry well. She taught Susanna and her sister that life was a struggle. It was about competition, suffering, and loss, and the only two alternatives were being poor and being rich. She drove both girls hard, and Susanna tried desperately to please her. But it was Susanna's only sibling, Margherita, who would marry rich. It had happened so easily for Margherita—going to that fancy school in Rome and finding and marrying the rich banker. When Susanna met Giovanni, she misjudged his fortune and didn't discover until after they were married that the vineyard was in debt.

On this evening, though, her trouble wasn't about money. It was personal, and she needed help. She felt she needed someone like Isabella. There was something about the girl that she wanted. Whether it was her self-assurance or fearlessness or faith, Susanna wasn't sure. But it was something that she was looking for that night.

They walked in silence up the great ramparts as the moon sent a soft glow across the chestnut trees that lined the brick path. Susanna stopped at the edge of the Piazza Napoleone and turned to face Isabella. "I've wanted to talk with you for some time."

Isabella said nothing.

"I—uh—wanted to thank you for helping the Venero family and our vineyard the last year. Your—influence will help us produce a good wine this season."

Isabella cocked her head to the side. "But that's not why you asked me to walk with you, is it?"

Susanna felt a twist in her gut. How was this peasant girl always able to take control of the conversation and put her on the defensive? She decided to change her strategy. "My husband wants a child very badly. I miscarried two years ago. Giovanni was very angry. He blamed me for his loss. He says I'm too weak, and now— I'm pregnant again. Please, I want your help. Having you with me will give me confidence. I want you as my midwife."

Isabella gave no answer. She walked to the edge of the walls and stared out toward the Serchio River. The news surprised her. She had expected a conversation about the memorial, how to help those in Lucca suffering the loss of loved ones. Instead, it was about Susanna, always Susanna. This woman indeed was in the midst of some emotional pain, but Isabella felt that Susanna created problems to appease her own guilt. And guilt was an emotion foreign to Isabella. For months she had been warmly welcomed into the Venero family—eating, laughing, and working the fields with them, yet the only time she was invited inside the Martellino villa was to cook and serve the Martellinos' dinner. She had never even seen Susanna speak to Angelina. The walls between the two families appeared greater than the walls they walked on that night. Yet now the lady of the villa was practically begging her to accept a job. Susanna's honesty about her fears of being pregnant and her revelation of her husband's anger had caught Isabella off guard. She wanted to help, but her intuition said no.

"I can't give you confidence," Isabella said. "I've already overstayed my time, and I'm needed back at the convent. You have Josephine, who is completely capable—"

"Josephine is capable of nothing!" Susanna snapped. "She was there when I miscarried the first time! I want you and will pay for your help!"

Isabella let out a long breath. She should have expected the response. Susanna was a woman who was used to getting what she wanted and would use Isabella's friendship with Angelina as leverage. Still, this request was foolish.

"I grew up in a convent," Isabella said. "That should tell you all you need to know about the experience I've had with babies."

Susanna cleared her throat. "I want you."

Isabella shook her head. "Josephine and Angelina have delivered babies before. If you would like, I'll help out in your final weeks, but for now, I must return to the Blessings."

Susanna's eyes were cold and expressionless. "I shall talk with your Mother Superior."

Isabella held her gaze. "I believe I told you before, signora—I'm not for sale. I will not be your midwife."

She then started back toward San Michele, followed by a fuming Susanna. When they went down the steps to the church, Giovanni was waiting in the shadows.

"Where have you been?"

His words surprised them, and Isabella saw Susanna's discomfort, so she answered for her. "It was such a beautiful evening, signor, that we went for a walk."

Susanna grabbed Isabella's arm. "Please stay."

"I'm sorry, signora. I'm needed at the convent." Isabella then smiled at Giovanni. "My heartfelt congratulations to both of you."

As soon as she saw Susanna go pale, Isabella realized her mistake. Giovanni looked at his wife. "Congratulations?"

Susanna's eyes dropped. "I'm sorry, Giovanni. I—I was afraid to tell you."

"Tell me what?"

"I am—with child."

Giovanni's surprise was immediate, but Isabella also saw a look of joy in his eyes before she said goodbye and headed to the convent.

CR   SO

DeAngelo Giuliano Martellino was born on March 1, 1917.

Isabella was there, helping Josephine with the delivery. Susanna, weakened by the labor, had fainted after watching Josephine cut the umbilical cord. They washed the child in olive oil, and Isabella covered him with a blanket she had knitted at the convent. A soft tap on the door was followed by Giovanni peeking inside.

"You have a son," Isabella smiled.

There were tears on Giovanni's cheeks as he gently touched his newborn's head, and Susanna's eyes flickered open, dim and cheerless as if indicting her husband for the pain she was in. But just as quickly she fell asleep again, and Isabella placed DeAngelo in the arms of his father.

CR   SO

Isabella placed her hands on her hips as she studied what was available in the kitchen pantry. She wanted to make a meal that would help Susanna recover from childbirth. She found potatoes, kale, spinach, and other dark green vegetables, sliced them up, added seasonings, and tossed them into a pot of boiling water.

"Sister Anna told me of your many gifts," Josephine said as she inhaled the aroma. "A gift with food—and a gift with people."

Isabella smiled her silent thanks and then thought back to the evening with Susanna on Lucca's wall. "The signora told me of a previous miscarriage. Why was Giovanni angry with her after that loss?"

Josephine raised an eyebrow. "Is that what she told you?"

Isabella nodded.

"Giovanni was devastated when she lost the baby—but Susanna never cried. It was as if she never accepted the baby's death." Josephine paused. "Do you know they named the boy after Giovanni's father?"

Isabella shook her head.

"His father was a tyrant. When his wife and older son died from an illness, he blamed Giovanni."

"Why?"

"Because Giovanni survived—and his older brother was his father's favorite. DeAngelo Martellino was a mean drunk and rode Giovanni hard. That's why I have a soft spot for him. He's still trying to prove himself to a dead man."

Isabella was taken aback. "I've never heard him mention his father before."

"He never does. I thought he hated him. Now he names his first child after him."

As Isabella stirred the soup, a slow smile began to spread across her face. "Perhaps it's Giovanni's way to forgive his father. The name DeAngelo means 'from an angel.'"

CHAPTER 8

THE ISONZO, OCTOBER 1917

B enny Carollo leaned back against the trench he and his brother
had recently dug and wiped the sweat from his brow.

"I know the generals don't want our advice, but it seems as if
they've positioned our artillery too close to us."

Franco nodded. "Sergeant San Stefano said they've positioned
the first THREE lines too close together."

"What happens if the enemy breaks through?"

Franco looked back at the proximity of the cannons. "We'll have
no support, and they'll be able to march straight through."

Benny shook his head. "I'm tired of following the same stupid
mistakes, brother."

"And Cadorna keeps promising reinforcements." Franco's voice
was sharp with agitation. "So, where the hell are they? We need
help."

"We take a hill and then lose it, take another hill and lose it
again. Thousands of our soldiers sacrificed—for what?" Benny
tossed his shovel aside in disgust. "All our friends from Puglia farms

are gone. Matteo on the Isonzo, Josefa taken by Austrian mortars at Trentino, Dante gassed at San Martino."

The brothers turned when they saw Father Mario come out of a bunker after giving last rites to another soldier.

Franco breathed heavily for a moment, trying to calm his rising anger, but he could not. "How many is that, Father?" he growled. "One thousand? Two thousand? Where's your God in this?"

The question stunned Father Mario, who had been with the Carollos the last two years. While they had been through the horrors of the Isonzo together, he had prayed they had not lost their faith. "God is everywhere in this, Franco."

"Then He's weeping on His heavenly throne."

The chaplain's face softened. "He weeps so that we'll change our hearts and turn to him."

Franco grabbed his pack, pulled out the Bible his brother had given him two years before, and threw it on the ground. "I've read your damn Holy Book and found only a God who plays favorites!"

Father Mario's face tightened, but he said nothing.

"Your God drowned thousands to save Noah's family because the world was so evil!" Franco continued to rant. "Your God had Samuel order King Saul to crush Amalek! He told them to destroy everything! Kill both man and woman, infant and suckling."

Father Mario raised his hand, but Franco cut him off.

"Your God saved Moses's people at the Red Sea, but killed the Egyptians! Who were the Egyptians but men just like us—fathers, brothers, sons, following orders from some power-hungry leader."

Outrage gripped Franco's face as he pointed to the morgue. "Is your 'God of love' in there, Father? Is He with us?" His voice was strained. "Is your God on our side—or with the enemy?"

Father Mario took a deep breath and looked down at the dried blood on his hands, the blood of the soldier to whom he had just given last rites. He took time before answering to reach down and pick up the Bible.

"A person can use biblical stories to defend his fears, Franco—or he can use them to understand the depths of love and forgiveness. I won't begin to explain the biblical verses you mentioned because I don't know what the authors were feeling or what they'd been through when they wrote of those experiences." He paused for a long moment. "But I can tell you that I think it's dangerous when we literalize the stories of the Bible to defend our actions."

"You didn't answer my question," Franco said in a low voice. "Both our soldiers and the enemy are praying for God's help."

"God does not choose sides, Franco. But I do believe it takes great faith to choose His side."

"And what side is that?"

"The side of love and forgiveness."

"That's your answer for everything!" Franco shot back. "And yet I haven't seen any love and forgiveness on the front. I've only seen death and suffering!"

Mario grabbed Franco's arm. "WE created the horrors of this war, Franco. God is waiting for US to change our minds, rise above this battleground, and return to Him."

Franco turned away from his priest and stared out at the Isonzo River, the river that had seen so much death and suffering, and now carried the blood of Italian, Austrian, and German soldiers to the sea. The God he had grown up with had abandoned him. He had never felt so alone.

03   80

Two weeks passed, and the anxiety of the coming battle continued to build. Finally, on a cold afternoon in late October of 1917, Sergeant San Stefano came to Franco's bunker.

"I need you to go to the command center. General Cavaciocchi has again asked for reinforcements before we advance. He's sent several requests and has been told they're on the way, but there's no sign of them." He handed Franco the general's requisition. "Get this to whoever's in charge. We need them to listen."

The sergeant then drew his bayonet from its sheath. "The rest of you, check your ammunition and fix your bayonets. I have no idea when this battle will begin."

Franco moved quickly to his brother's side. "Stay with Father Mario. He's our good luck charm. I'll be back before we attack."

☙ ❧

It was near sunset when Franco arrived at the Italian army's command and communications center, and his confidence immediately dropped. The place was absolute chaos. The leadership was bickering about where to set up defenses, how the enemy would attack, what bridges should be blown up, and if the Italian army had the right equipment to thwart a gas attack.

Franco ran to a captain coming out of the command tent. He came to attention, saluted, and handed the officer General Cavaciocchi's request. The captain read it and took a deep breath. "I don't have an answer for you right now."

"Sir, the enemy is advancing. Our line desperately needs help."

The captain didn't speak for a long time, his gaze fixed on the requisition, and then he finally nodded. "I'll take this to my superior. Please wait here for our answer."

Franco saluted, waited for the captain to leave, and then sat down on the ground, opened his backpack, took a bite out of some bread and cheese, and waited. It was now seven in the evening. He would wait another five hours for the answer that would never come.

At midnight Franco shook his head to keep from nodding off. He'd gone in several times to get an answer to General Cavaciocchi's request but had been sent away each time by the captain, who ordered him to stay patient. At 12:01 Franco's head bobbed forward just before he heard an explosion in the distance. He heard another and another booming to the north. He jumped up, grabbed his rifle, and raced back down the hill.

CR   &O

Intense fog and the Italian army's mass confusion slowed Franco's return to his battalion. When he reached his brother's bunker, everyone was gone.

He ran from trench to trench, searching for any soldier who could connect him with his division and his brother. He came across soldiers retreating with the Second Army.

"What happened?" Franco called out.

"We couldn't stop them!" the soldier yelled back. "The Germans broke through!"

Franco ran into the fog, begging the God he'd earlier rejected to help him find his brother. Without a map, he stayed close to the river to center his bearings and keep from getting lost. Another cannon-and-mortar barrage came hammering down, but he wasn't sure if it was friendly or enemy fire.

As the sun rose, the fog started to burn off, and Franco could see figures silhouetted in the mist headed his way. He ducked into a bomb crater and fixed his bayonet before peering over the rim of the mud. He saw hundreds of Italian soldiers without their weapons running his way. Several ran past, but he grabbed one by the arm. "Why are we retreating?"

"It's over!" the soldier cried out. "The Germans have taken Mount Jeza. We're getting out before they gas us."

"What of the Forty-Third?" Franco demanded.

The man pulled his arm free. "Caporetto!" was all he said.

Franco continued on before machine gun fire forced him to dive into a ravine near the river. He crawled on his hands and knees to a small bridge across a creek entering the Isonzo, which gave him cover to slide from bomb crater to bomb crater while enemy fire sprayed haphazardly around him. The artillery barrage picked up again, only this time it was directed at Caporetto. He looked over his shoulder and saw more soldiers approaching, but they weren't Italian. Austro-German troops had used roads paralleling the Isonzo valley, putting the Italian army in a pincer-like grip. Franco knew he would be surrounded if he didn't move, so he turned away from the river, used the trees for cover, and pushed on to find Benny.

It took Franco six hours to make it to Caporetto, and when he arrived, the scene shocked him. Hundreds of Italian soldiers were retreating down the heights along the Isonzo valley, ditching their weapons and racing across the bridge. At the same time, captains were waving them back because army engineers were planting explosives to blow up the bridge in an attempt to slow the enemy's advance. Soldiers were throwing wagons and carts off the bridge in their effort to retreat. Franco pushed his way past the chaos, past his countrymen as they carried and dragged their wounded over the bridge.

"The Forty-Third," he pleaded, "where are they?"

Exhausted soldiers did not answer.

Franco moved on, and as he passed the remains of a bombarded stone farmhouse, he saw in the distance an army chaplain kneeling over an Italian soldier by a single oak tree. What followed was a moment Franco would relive in his nightmares for years to come. He would recall images of a heavy mist falling on the frozen, muddy battlefield, a ground littered with the dead, whose hollow eyes stared up at him as if begging for help—help that never came. In those dreams Franco was always running in slow motion—either running to save his brother or running away from something, he never was quite sure. But in every dream, he never reached his destination. He remembered yelling out their names and remembered the smiles that creased their faces when they recognized him, the smiles that quickly changed to looks of terror when the familiar whistle of the artillery shell came screaming toward them. It took one-tenth of a second for the two hundred pounds of dynamite to tear apart the ground and knock Franco off his feet. Time seemed to stop as he wiped the dirt and ash from his eyes and picked himself up. When the smoke cleared, he saw that the oak tree was gone. He dropped to his knees. Father Mario was dead, cut in half by the explosion. Benny's left arm and leg were gone, and he was shaking as the blood rose from his chest to his throat. He reached for Franco and coughed, "Where's— Father—Mario?"

Franco choked back his sobs. "He's gone! They're all gone!"

Benny said seven more words before he died in his brother's arms. "Go home, Franco. Go home—and forgive."

CHAPTER 9

LUCCA, OCTOBER 1917

As the months passed, Isabella found herself spending more and more time at the villa. The Mother Superior had been understanding because the Martellinos had suddenly become an important benefactor to the convent. At first, Isabella thought Susanna had manipulated the Mother Superior to get her to work, but now it didn't matter; she felt a special closeness to the boy. It was as if their connection was beyond coincidental. Despite DeAngelo being a newborn, every moment together felt comfortable: theirs was a love that was at times silence, at times laughter, and at times tears, but DeAngelo always seemed at home in Isabella's arms.

೮౩ ౩౦

"There must be something wrong with him," Susanna complained one day as she handed her crying baby to Isabella. "I nursed him and rocked him for almost an hour, but he just keeps screaming."

Isabella took DeAngelo outside to the fresh air, gently laid him on his back on the courtyard table and lifted his knees to his belly. The baby let out a loud fart, and Isabella winked back at Susanna. "Just a little gassy." She then picked up a now calm DeAngelo and began to dance with him slowly, singing a song her mother had sung to her when she was young.

"Go to sleep, go to sleepy, in the arms of your mother. Go to sleep, lovely child, go to sleepy, child so lovely, go to sleep, go to sleepy, in the arms of your mother."

Susanna watched from the door, lips pressed tight together, relieved but resentful, waiting impatiently for her son to doze off. As soon as he did, she hurried over and snatched him from Isabella's arms.

"Thank you," she said with a false smile. "But please choose another song next time. You're not his mother."

CꙨ 🙰

Giovanni stared out at the vineyards that lined his drive home from Pistoia. His gaze was abstracted as he thought about yet another failed wine sale. It seemed as if there was no end in sight with the war in Europe stifling the economy and hurting vineyards and olive orchards throughout Tuscany. Maybe, he thought, it was time to get away for a spell. Let Angelina and the two men he had recently hired run the farm, and he would take Susanna on a holiday. They rarely had time alone, and it seemed that every time he returned from work, his wife was either gone seeing friends in Lucca or at political rallies. She had taken a sudden interest in the Nationalist effort in Italy and was constantly giving her opinions about the war. Giovanni had read that the Nationalists were having an important rally and fundraiser in Rome, and thought they would be something that would interest his wife. Susanna was indeed excited and immediately sent word to the convent that its cook was needed to care for DeAngelo.

CZ SO

"Be careful, darling!" Susanna said as she watched Giovanni pack their car. "That gown was designed by Mariano Fortuny. I don't want to have to press it again when we get to Rome." She walked around the car, inspecting his every move. "Please don't push my jewelry box up against my scarves; they wrinkle so easily." When he finished packing to her satisfaction, she clapped her hands and walked over to Isabella, who was holding DeAngelo.

She's finally going to say goodbye to her son, thought Isabella.

Instead, Susanna only spun around and pointed to the back of her neck. "Would you be a dear and redo my necklace? The chain on my pearls is catching on my hair." Isabella did as she was asked. Then Susanna turned back to face her, smiled sweetly, and not wanting to smudge her lipstick, simply kissed the air that separated her lips from DeAngelo's forehead.

CZ SO

The Martellinos spent the first part of their holiday enjoying Rome; touring the Vatican and Saint Peter's Basilica. On the fifth day, Giovanni surprised his wife with tickets to a Nationalist rally, to hear Italy's new prime minister, Paolo Boselli, speak. Giovanni knew Susanna was a fan of the seventy-eight-year old politician who promised to bring national unity by empowering the military and controlling angry workers inside Italy.

But the message that evening only confused Giovanni. There was much talk of Austria's eastern enemy, Russia, falling into a revolution and the United States joining the war, which would dramatically change the international political climate. After listening to Boselli's call for mass conscription into the army, Giovanni thought it unfair. He knew most of Italy's peasants were like his dead winemaker, Mariano. They couldn't read or write and probably didn't understand why they were fighting. Meanwhile, the landowners' sons were not being asked to fight. The result, of course, was an angry working class.

෩ ෨

"Did you hear what that gentleman said about the southern landowner who was attacked by his own workers?" Susanna said after the rally.

"Are you talking about that Obizzi blowhard?" Giovanni replied. "He's anything but a gentleman."

"He's a brilliant speaker! And his story about those ungrateful peasants attacking the very landowner who gave their families gainful employment for centuries has me worried." As they headed up the steps to the post-rally party, she grabbed Giovanni's elbow to emphasize her point. "He told me that could happen to us if you're not tougher on our help."

"The Veneros aren't going to cause any problems." Giovanni opened the door to the politician's mansion. "Angelina is grateful to have a job that feeds her family."

Susanna's face flamed as she followed guests into a grand ballroom filled cheese and bruschetta and wine and brandy. "But we know very little about those new workers you hired," she

78

complained. They're former soldiers with no experience in a vineyard."

Tired of Susanna's questioning his business decisions, Giovanni grabbed a goblet of brandy and raised it over his head.

"To Italy!" he cried out, and the room roared back, "To Italy!"

"To Italy winning the war," Alfredo Obizzi said as he walked over and touched his glass to Susanna's. The young politician was about her age, twenty-five, of medium height, but he appeared much taller because of the way he carried himself—chest out, with a noble cleft chin and dark, penetrating eyes. He gave Susanna a roguish wink. "At least this war is controlling that damn peasant union, Fedeterra."

Susanna's eyelashes fluttered up at him as if asking him to continue.

"The longer the war goes on," Obizzi explained, "the greater chance we have of controlling the peasants."

She turned her prettiest smile on the Nationalist politician. "Did you serve?"

"I would have loved to have joined our gallant men at the front." He gave a dramatic sigh. "But unfortunately, I had responsibilities at my father's bank and then was hurt in an equestrian accident." He pointed down at his foot. "Damn horse stepped on me."

"Oh my!"

Obizzi had already had too much to drink, and spilled his wine as he continued to lecture. "Now these poor soldiers will be coming home, looking for jobs, and when they can't find them, what do you think they'll do?"

She shook her head innocently.

"They'll follow the damn Socialists, which will only bring trouble."

Giovanni heard the comment and thought it insensitive. "Excuse me, signor, but you're talking about the young men who have fought for our country. We must at least listen to them."

"We'll listen, but they must be controlled." Obizzi paused and gave a contemptuous glare. "I'm sure you heard what happened in Turin?"

Giovanni stayed silent.

"A riot over bread. Fifty people were killed."

"The Socialists want too much!" Susanna added. "They must pay for the trouble they're bringing our country."

The conversation ended abruptly when the door to the room burst open. It was another politician, face white, breathing heavily.

"We've taken a terrible defeat at Caporetto!" he yelled out. "The enemy has broken through! They're saying Venice could be next!"

Giovanni gasped as he imagined the enemy storming across Italy, and suddenly his fears went to his eight-month-old son. He grabbed their coats and headed for the door. "Come, Susanna. We've got to make sure DeAngelo's safe!"

CR   SO

While the Martellinos were in Rome, Isabella and DeAngelo were inseparable. She would lay a bedroll on the floor next to his crib so she could comfort him at night, and would carry him in a knapsack while working the farm during the day. She cut two holes in the knapsack to put DeAngelo's legs through and wore the bag on her chest, so the baby could enjoy being outside.

"It's a good day to begin that garden you've been after us about," Angelina said as she helped Isabella pull DeAngelo out of the knapsack. The baby began fussing, and Isabella reached into her pocket, pulled out a grape, peeled it, crushed it in her hand, and popped it into the baby's mouth. She placed the happy child on the ground and let him crawl in the dirt next to her.

"Now is indeed a perfect time to plant winter vegetables like kale and carrots and broccoli." Isabella grabbed a hoe to prepare the soil. DeAngelo picked up a stick and mimicked her, scratching the ground with his twig.

"That boy is your shadow," laughed Angelina. "Dig a hole for a broccoli seed, and I'll bet he copies you." Isabella did, and the boy matched her every move. She dug a hole and he dug a hole. She placed a seed in a hole and he placed a seed in a hole. She covered the hole with dirt and he covered the hole with dirt. By the twentieth plant, the two of them were filthy. DeAngelo had dirt everywhere: in his hair, under his nails, between his teeth. When the sun began to set over the western hills, Isabella knew it was time for the child's dinner, so she picked him up and carried him like a loaf of bread back to the Veneros house. She let him crawl on the floor while she made his meal: spinach and warm milk ground together to make a creamy texture, easy for the baby to eat.

Angelina's oldest child, Bartolo, made a silly face that got DeAngelo giggling. As Isabella sat on the floor to feed DeAngelo, the child was laughing so hard that his hand hit the spoon, flipping the creamed spinach directly into Isabella's face. After a mock look of shock, the room exploded in laughter, and Isabella dipped her finger in the spinach and placed it on DeAngelo's tiny nose. The baby shrieked with delight, grabbed a handful of his dinner, and heaved it at Isabella, splattering her face and hair. She countered with her own handful of spinach on top his head that dripped down the sides of his face. Bartolo took a fistful of flour and threw it, covering both of them in white. Isabella embraced DeAngelo and they rolled on the floor, laughing out loud, until they heard a scream from the doorway.

"What in God's name are you doing with my child!"

It was Susanna, back from Rome and staring at the mess in front of her. Giovanni was behind her with a broad grin, amused at the sight of his happy child with flour and dirt and spinach all over him.

"I've been looking all over for my son!" Susanna hissed. "I leave for one week and you have him looking as if he lives in a pigsty!" She stormed over and pulled DeAngelo from Isabella's arms. The baby, surprised by the sudden anger, reached out for Isabella and started to cry, which only angered Susanna further.

"You've turned my child against me! Get out! Go back to your damn convent!"

CHAPTER 10

CAPORETTO, NOVEMBER 1917

On a drizzly, desolate evening, Franco buried his brother and his chaplain by an oak tree near Caporetto. Italian soldiers in retreat urged him to join them, but he silently ignored their calls and continued to dig the graves. He did not leave a cross to mark the graves, having abandoned his faith on the battlefields of the Isonzo. Instead, he marked their final resting place with two large stones he carried from the river. He stood, wiped the tears from his eyes, and headed south. As he crossed what was left of the bridge from Caporetto, the snow began to fall, but Franco trudged on, numb to the cold and the inner pain that plagued his every step. When the snow stopped, he looked back and saw that everything was ablaze. Dreczenca was burning, and the reflection of the flames lit up the sides of Mount Nero. He turned off the road and plodded on toward the Julian Alps.

Franco was done with fighting. He was dead emotionally. The horrors that he'd seen had taken much from his soul. He moved on, almost invisible to the soldiers he passed along the way, powerless to recognize his own exhaustion and hunger. He walked for three days without sleep, finally stopping at a farmhouse at the southern base of Mount Matajur. The family fed him and gave him clothes and a place to sleep, refusing his offer of money. The next day he ascended the Julian Alps and headed southwest through a pass, following a road the Italians had built in 1915 to bring supplies to the Isonzo front. He caught a ride with an empty supply truck returning to Udine. The man spoke of soldiers he had met along the way, the looks of despair and defeat he had seen. When he asked Franco if he'd been in battle, his response was silence.

On a chilly evening in early November, they drove into Udine, where Franco was dropped off near the church of Santa Maria della Purita. Franco joined other refugees and slept on the church steps. The next two days were spent begging for work. Nothing came. At night he sat against the church wall and pulled a wool blanket around himself, shivering from the cold and the battle memories that haunted him. As he looked up at the crucifix on the side of the church, he wondered how God could allow His only son to be crucified. He could not forgive a God who would allow this world to suffer so much. Darkness came. Franco slept fitfully, with nightmares of his comrades' pained looks of death from the fields of Caporetto.

He left Udine and continued southwest, stopping at a dairy farm to ask for work. The farmer said he couldn't pay, but offered food and shelter in exchange for work. Franco accepted and stayed with the family through the new year; his gloom stayed with him. The ache, shame, and grief would not go away. He had not written to his parents since the death of Benny because every time he sat down to write, his guilt pushed the pen away from the paper. Who was he now? He questioned every one of his motives. Do all men need war, he wondered? Was there some primitive, unconscious desire to kill, cruelly, brutally, as he had seen on the battlefields of the Isonzo? Or was there the hope and forgiveness that Father Mario preached?

That night, Franco wrote a letter to his parents. He started with the 'I'm sorrys' that filled his heart. He was sorry he had boarded the train with Benny; sorry he had not been able to save his brother; sorry for the rage and fury within his heart; sorry for the anguish and tears he knew this letter would bring. He was sorry he could not return home until he had relinquished the demons of war. Franco signed the letter through his own tears, and mailed it the next day. He left the farm in mid-January, unsure of where his journey would take him.

Hiking through the rolling hills of Triviso and then on to Bologna, Franco found odd jobs along the way. He helped paint a house outside Bologna, and made enough money to buy a ticket on the Porettana Railway to Pistoia. As the train meandered through the Apennine Mountains, he picked up a newspaper and read reports of the war. The heaviness returned to him, along with a new feeling of guilt—the guilt of a man who had left his countrymen on the battlefield. Yes, he was a deserter, but thousands of Italian soldiers had gone home after Caporetto. He read about the Italian army's making a fierce stand to hold off the Austrians at the Piave River. He read also that the war had cost Italy the lives of more than half a million young men, and that now the government was declaring a *ragazzi del 99*, a call to arms of all males age eighteen and older. The Nationalist writers were trying to revive Italy's fighting spirit by reminding their readers that as dark a moment as

Caporetto was in the nation's history, "no people [had] obtained greatness without having passed the test of suffering." Franco tossed the paper aside, thinking it was so easy for the man with the pen sitting in a warm home to send someone else to fight his battles.

The Porettana rail took Franco through the heartland of central Italy and finally into Tuscany. He left the train in Pistoia and headed west, moving through the most breathtaking farmlands he had ever seen. He recalled a day in church, years ago, when a stranger had told him of land where the "soil was so perfect, the grapes practically grew themselves." As he walked along the Pescia River valley, the beauty grew with each step, and he stopped to inhale the fragrances that surrounded him. He could breathe again. The knot in his chest was beginning to unwind. The terror he had felt on the battlefield was being released to the beauty of Tuscany.

Franco looked out from the hills, across the endless acres of vineyards. He knelt down and felt the soil that had nurtured the grapes that produced Italy's most famous wines. Spring had come early that year, with warm, soft rains that allowed the wildflowers to bloom early. There were red and yellow poppies glistening on the hills as far as the eyes could see. To the right was a dirt road lined with cypress trees leading west. He covered his eyes and squinted at the horizon, feeling that something beyond was drawing him to these lands.

Franco moved on, stopping at three different vineyards. He was reluctant to reveal his past, so the conversations ended quickly, with the landowners rejecting his requests for work. As he continued toward the next vineyard, Franco thought of a conversation he had had with Father Mario before Caporetto. The army chaplain had told him men were raised to believe that miracles were amazing, rare occurrences that only a few special people were given. The priest said it was that limited thinking that held miracles back, and that all we needed was the willingness to change our minds. Franco needed that miracle right now.

He stopped at the next drive and looked up at the sign that read, "Martellino Vineyard." Walking down the path, he decided that whomever he met, he would be completely open about his past and see where it led. When he came to the main property, he saw a man striding from the workers' house on his way to the villa, throwing his arms into the air as if he was upset about something. The man saw Franco approach and yelled, "No handouts!"

Franco continued forward, came to attention, and offered a handshake. Giovanni did not accept it.

Instead, Franco saluted him. "I'm Private Franco Carollo. I spent two and a half years with our Second and Third Armies in the Isonzo valley."

"I don't have time to talk," Giovanni said with a flip of his hand. "Two workers left me in the middle of the night."

Franco remained confident. "I've worked vineyards with my family in Puglia, mainly growing the dry red Rosso Barletta and Sangiovese. I have experience in all areas, both with grapes and with olives. I'm a hard worker looking for a job."

Giovanni slowly raised his eyes to meet Franco's. He wondered how badly this young man wanted to work.

"Two of my field workers ran off last night after I advanced them a week's wages. If you're that interested, give me one week—no— make that two weeks without pay, so I can see for myself the employee I'll be getting."

Franco extended his hand again. "I'll work three weeks for free, and you'll not be disappointed."

This time Giovanni took the young man's hand and shook it.

"Go to the workers' house and ask for Angelina. She'll show you where you can stay and give you your responsibilities."

For the first time in months, Franco smiled.

ଓ   ଙ

The rare sound of silence seemed to calm Giovanni as he entered the villa that night. He had grown accustomed to DeAngelo's persistent crying ever since his wife had sent Isabella back to the convent. In an effort to replace her, Susanna had tried three different nannies in the last five months. She had fired the first two for not meeting her demands, and the third had recently quit. To make matters worse, when Susanna spent the day in Lucca, she would drop her child off at the convent and return later to find DeAngelo in a splendid mood, only to have to endure his sobs the entire drive home.

As Giovanni fixed himself a drink and sat down in his favorite chair, he heard a car door slam and his wife's angry footsteps across the stone kitchen floor; he waited for her to burst into his study.

"That's the last time I leave our son with Isabella!" Susanna yelled as she kicked the door open. DeAngelo was in her arms; there were tears on his cheeks and his thumb was in his mouth. "I left DeAngelo for only two hours! When I returned, she had taken his shoes off and had him walking for the first time! In her filthy garden!"

"I'm so very sorry," Giovanni said, faking an effort to share her disappointment.

"I wanted to see him take his first steps!" she snapped. "I know she taught him to spite me!"

"So, tell me darling." He tried to hide his grin. "What did she say when you confronted her about our little boy not waiting for you?"

Susanna let out an exasperated exhalation. "She made some sarcastic remark about DeAngelo giving a sermon this Sunday on Luke 13:12. I tell you, Giovanni, she mocks me!"

"And what does"—as he bit his lip, "Luke 13:12 say, Susanna?"

She turned up her nose. "How should I know?"

Then she was gone, storming out of the room and upstairs to put DeAngelo in his crib. Giovanni went over to the family Bible and turned to Luke 13:12. A broad grin spread across his face as he read, "When Jesus saw her, he called her over and said, 'Woman, you are set free from your ailment.'"

CƆ ＆Ɔ

It was true. Isabella missed DeAngelo. The child was a delight to be around and enjoyed every part of the outdoors, from playing in the garden to walking along Lucca's walls to watching leaves floating down the Serchio River. The Blessings nuns loved him as well and would argue over who would hold the baby when Isabella was in the kitchen. But with wounded Italian soldiers now returning from the war and the convent volunteering to help in the hospital, Isabella didn't have as much time to spend with the Martellinos' son. She was too busy in the kitchen, preparing extra meals for the patients. On this day she prepared a dish that was healthy and easy to digest—slicing up cucumbers, tomatoes, onions, mint, parsley, and garlic with bulgur wheat, then mixing it with boiling water to make tabbouleh. Sister Anna walked into the kitchen and inhaled the smell from the wooden bowl that held Isabella's creation. "Oh my. Isn't that lovely—green and more green. Shall I serve it with Chianti or a nice Barolo?"

Isabella tossed an onion at her friend. "I'm just thinking of their health, Anna. What have they had on the Isonzo but bread and potatoes? They need greens to get iron back into their bodies."

Anna grinned as she pinched her nose. "And the bulgur wheat should help release it from their bodies."

Every day before entering the hospital, the Blessings nuns said a prayer of love and acceptance. The prayer helped prepare the sisters for the horrors of war that were inside. Broken, battered bodies and hollow eyes that stared at the ceiling greeted them. Isabella grimaced when she saw a doctor stick a large anti-tetanus needle into a soldier's chest. The smell of chloroform was everywhere, as doctors used it to induce sleep in their patients, before removing limbs from their ravaged bodies. Isabella offered broth and her tabbouleh to the soldiers. There were no complaints. The sisters wondered what had happened to these young men who had once been so excited about becoming soldiers, and now returned crippled, both physically and mentally. Much of the suffering Isabella could handle, but the burn unit was another matter. There were only five soldiers in this unit in Lucca, but all had sustained 4th degree burns over half of their bodies. And regardless of how the sisters tried to comfort the young boys, the pain was unbearable and constant. Every night they left in tears, with Sister Anna asking the question they were all thinking: "Where will these young men go? What will become of them?"

 C? S?

An exhausted Isabella returned to the convent that night to find Susanna waiting for her.

"Where have you been?" Susanna asked, obviously annoyed. "I told you I had tickets to the opera. Lucca's own Giacomo Puccini will be singing in the performance of *La Bohème*."

Isabella swept her hair away from her tired eyes. "I told you I couldn't tonight."

"But DeAngelo loves you," Susanna said with a planned look of sadness. "I can't leave him with anyone else."

At that moment the baby boy reached out for Isabella, and of course, Isabella took him and sat down on a chair in the kitchen as Susanna hurried out. Isabella leaned back with DeAngelo in her arms and closed her eyes.

CHAPTER 11

LUCCA, 1918

T he cool quiet of the vineyard before sunrise invigorated Franco. He was back doing what he loved. He had grown up working with grapes and olives in the fields of Puglia, and the serenity of the farm comforted him. As he lay in bed waiting for morning light, he finally lost patience, tossed his blanket aside, lit a kerosene lamp, and went out to the field. The morning fog was deep in the valley, as if lifting the Martellino property up toward the dark sky. Franco inhaled a deep breath and smiled, then walked out to the first row of plants and touched the leaves, checking for pests and disease. He dropped to a knee and grabbed a handful of dirt, wanting to see how the workers had fertilized and irrigated the plants. He noticed that someone had redirected part of the creek into a small channel that led across the vineyard. The vines were planted on a slight decline on the hill that would carry a determined amount of water across the field. If it rained, the arm from the creek could easily be dammed off. Franco nodded approvingly, thinking someone had done good work. Had it been Angelina and her family, or the two men who had quit in the middle of the night?

The sun's rays started to creep across the eastern hills, offering a soft glow to the vines. The plants had already gone through the bud-break of early spring and the flowering of May. Franco held the small fruit in his hand. This was a critical time of the season, one that would determine the potential crop yield. He felt the size of the berries, knowing that if the skin-to-pulp ratio differed, it could be a sign of disease and a bad crop. This cluster felt just fine.

Hearing footsteps, Franco turned to find Angelina.

"You're up early," she said cheerfully and handed him a plate of bread and apricots. "My children will join you as soon as they've had breakfast."

He thanked her and then pointed to the creek. "Good idea with the irrigation system. Was that your design?"

Angelina smiled, thinking of Isabella. "No, it was a friend of mine in town who has a gift when it comes to nature."

Franco nodded. "How many work the vineyard and olive grove?"

"It's just my family and you right now."

He paused for a moment as his eyes scanned the expanse of the property. "It would seem to me that more help would be needed for a farm this size."

"We're allowed to hire boys from neighboring farms during the planting and harvest, but Signor Martellino would like to eliminate that expense in the future." She paused until he looked back up at her. "The Martellinos need a vineyard manager. My husband had that responsibility until he was killed on the Isonzo three years ago."

Franco stiffened and looked away. "I'm sorry."

"This land has been in the Martellino family for centuries," she continued, "but I get the feeling they're not as rich as they seem."

He remained quiet.

"We need this year's crop to be a success, Franco, for the Martellino family—and for my family."

☙ ❧

Franco was true to his word, working fourteen-hour days without pay for three weeks. Giovanni came every day to check on him, and despite being impressed with his work, he challenged Franco with questions.

"We should be seeing color from the berry now, yet it's still green and firm."

"It's still mid-July," Franco answered. "We'll see color soon, and then we'll get a better understanding of the potential of the juice."

Giovanni pointed across the field. "Why don't those plants by the creek have berries yet?"

"Angelina said those are the newer plants, so this won't be their season."

Giovanni became serious. "This is an important year, Franco. If I'm to keep you on, the wine must be a success."

Franco only nodded.

As Giovanni started toward the house, he stopped suddenly and turned back to Franco. "Your three weeks of proving yourself are over. I'll start paying you this week."

☙ ❧

News of the war came to Franco through Giovanni's visits to the vineyard. The Martellino landowner had heard through Josephine that Franco had fought in several battles of the Isonzo, and he asked him about what he had experienced. Franco disclosed how long he'd served, but said nothing else.

"Our troops were victorious at the Battle of Piave River," Giovanni said, hoping for a reply.

Franco only nodded as he continued to cut away at a cluster of leaves that was blocking sunlight from the berries.

"We held off the Austrian assault, and that, combined with a rebellion inside Austria, could mean we're close to victory."

Still nothing from Franco.

"You—should be very proud, being part of Italy's glory."

Franco put down his shears and stood up. "Did they report how many died?"

Giovanni shook his head innocently.

"I didn't think so," Franco said with a blank look. "I didn't find any glory in watching my friends die."

Giovanni tried to be respectful. "But they died for their country, and that will not be forgotten."

Franco inhaled strongly through his nose. "They'll be forgotten until the next time our nation goes to war. And then their names and memories will be recalled by the politicians and generals who will benefit most from the next conflict."

"That's a rather unpatriotic statement, Franco," said Giovanni. His voice was low, kind but with a hint of warning. "It would benefit you to keep those feelings to yourself."

Franco stared across the vineyard, beyond the farm, beyond Lucca, as if searching for words to explain what he'd experienced in battle. Instead, he stayed silent, perhaps silent for too long, as the only sounds he heard were of his landowner's boots walking back to the villa.

CHAPTER 12

LUCCA, AUGUST 1918

It was an unseasonably cool night in late August 1918. Franco spent the afternoon sharpening tools, cleaning trays, and readying for a harvest that could come any day. From sunset to midnight he worked on the wine barrels until his body could take no more. Sleep came quickly, but within two hours the first raindrop fell, then another and another. A rare August storm had blown into Tuscany, and a downpour followed. A flash of lightning followed by a loud crack of thunder woke Angelina. She heard the rain and ran to the door. Another bolt of lightning lit up the sky, and in the split second of illumination, she saw the disaster.

"Bartolo!" she screamed out as she ran to her children's room. "Get Franco! The vineyard is flooding!"

She woke even her youngest children, as every member of the Venero family would be needed to keep this year's crop from being ruined. If the rain soaked the fruit and diluted the grapes, it would begin to spread rot through the vineyard and destroy even the finest harvest.

"Signor Franco!" Bartolo cried out as he pounded on the door of Franco's bunkhouse. "Wake up! A storm is flooding the vineyard!"

Franco bolted from bed and ran barefoot to the field. When he reached the first vine, the water was already over the top of his feet. He knew this could be a disaster. He had forgotten to dam the arm of the creek that brought water to the field. Bartolo followed him to the overflow, and the two of them used rocks and boards to try to dam the creek. Angelina came with her three daughters to help and then grabbed her son.

"Bartolo, listen to me!" she yelled through the pounding rain. "Go and saddle a horse! Get Isabella! Tell her what's happened!"

As the boy took off for the barn, Angelina and her girls ran to help Franco.

"Do whatever you can to divert the creek away from the vines!" Franco screamed. "I'll find out why the water isn't draining from the field!"

Franco pushed through the water, but by the time he made it to the end of the vineyard, the water was midway up his calf. He searched the road and found the obstacle. The water was flowing down through the vineyard into a ditch, but branches and leaves and debris had collected at a drainage tunnel, blocking the flow that went underneath. If Franco could clear it, the channel would lead the water out to the Serchio River.

He ripped the smaller branches out, but each time he pulled one out and tossed it across the road, another branch floated down to take its place. He continued to pull the debris out from both ends of the tunnel for what seemed like hours until he came to a branch too large to dislodge. The suction of the tunnel pulling against his strength was too much. Exhausted, he collapsed in the muddy road.

The morning sun was rising in the east, offering enough light for Franco to view the vineyard. There was water from the first vine to the last. It was a disaster. Franco knew his fate. He was a failure. He had failed his brother and Father Mario at Caporetto, and now he had failed again.

"Get up! Get up!" Angelina ran over and grabbed Franco by the arm. "We have to at least try!"

He struggled to his feet, and together they grabbed the branch and pulled. It didn't budge. They pulled again. Nothing. The heavy blanket of failure swept over him again as the rain pounded down. Just as Franco reached one final, desperate time for the tree limb, a high-pitched yell made him stop. It was young Rosa, splashing through the flooded field, out of breath.

"Mama! She's here!"

They turned to see two trucks coming down the drive, loaded with people dressed head to toe in black, each holding a push broom. A dark-haired woman leaped down from the truck and began shouting instructions. The black-robed figures followed her.

"Praise God!" Angelina laughed through her tears. "It's Bella and the sisters from the convent!"

Bartolo rode up on his horse and tossed a rope to Franco. "Bella said to tie this to the branches and let my horse pull them out!"

Franco jumped into the water and wrapped the rope around the biggest tree limb. Then he tied the other end to the horn of Bartolo's saddle. When he gave the horse a pop on the backside, the horse jerked forward and the limb came out of the drain. He tied the rope to two more limbs, and when the horse pulled them out, the drain rushed free. Now bone weary, Franco struggled to his feet and looked up to see the dark-haired girl leading the nuns toward the edge of the vineyard. The sisters tied their robes above their knees and walked into the flooded vineyard as the girl shouted over the roar of the storm, "Start here and push the water to the ditch. Try to keep it from soaking the grapes!"

Franco could not believe what he was seeing. There must have been twenty nuns wading in the water. They had push brooms and were shoving the water into the ditch and beyond through the tunnel toward the Serchio River.

Angelina gave Isabella a quick hug. "Where did you get so many to help?"

Isabella wiped the water from her face. "Anna went to San Michele, Sister Marie went with your son to San Martino, and everyone wanted to join in the fun!" Then she winked at their transportation. "The trucks we—borrowed. Now let's go! We must work quickly or the harvest will be lost!"

She then turned and pointed at Franco. "You there! Go to the trucks, get the sheets we brought from the convent, and spread them on the floor of the barn. Take the Venero children with you to pick the grapes and dry them with the sheets."

A startled Franco couldn't believe what he was hearing coming out of the mouth of this bossy young woman.

"Signorina!" he said with a look of defeat. "The grapes are ruined."

Isabella pulled a grape off the closest vine and popped it into her mouth.

"Tastes good to me. Now get them to the barn."

He nodded dumbly and went with the Venero children, grabbing a cluster of grapes along the way. He looked at Bartolo. "I want you and Rosa to lay out the sheets and dry the grapes. I'll get the trays and bring in some more."

The nuns made quick work of the field. With the creek now dammed off from above, the sisters pushed enough water into the ditch to free the water that had soaked the field. Isabella then released several sisters to help carry grapes inside the barn.

"Lay the grapes on top of the sheets," Franco instructed, and then he opened another sheet and covered the wet berries. "Gently rub the sheets across the top to remove any excess water."

As he picked up three trays and ran outside, he felt a hand grab his upper arm.

"What in God's name have you done!" Giovanni Martellino roared. "You fool! You've cost me everything!"

Franco no longer cared about his fate. He had endured enough on this difficult morning and handed his landowner a tray.

"You can fire me later, but right now you can help us save the grapes!"

Franco pushed past him and ran out to the field.

03   80

The work at the Martellino vineyard that August morning was inspiring. Sister Anna had the nuns singing hymns in the field as they pulled the clusters from the vines. As they carried the grapes to the barn, their joyful voices sang out in prayer.

"For Thee the stream of beauty flows. For Thee the gale of summer blows. And in deep glen and wood-walk free, voices of joy still breathe for Thee!"

Their harmony carried through the vineyard and to the neighboring farms. The nuns of Lucca's churches had swept the water off the field and had the grapes off the vines and in the barn before noon that very day.

Franco, Angelina, and Isabella began the busy work of separating and de-stemming the most desirable grapes. They dropped them into huge oak bins and had the sisters hold up their robes, stomp on the grapes, and turn them into a mushy liquid. Then they poured the mushed fluid into earthen jars and took them to an area in the basement below the barn, to prevent an early fermentation. Franco knew this time before fermentation was important and would maximize the flavor from the grape skins. It was eight in the evening when the last earthen jar was carried down to the basement.

"Your children were incredible," Franco said to Angelina as he gave her a hug and then nodded up the stairs. "Now go cook them a fine meal and tell the signor he can take it out of my pay so they can eat meat."

She laughed and gave him a playful shove and then headed up the stairs.

The room was silent save for the sound of the barn door closing. Franco stayed in the cool cellar, checking the bins and still feeling miserable. He walked between the earthenware, muttering in a barely audible voice. "I'm such an idiot. If I don't get this right, I'm done. Why didn't I see the storm coming? It's all my fault if this crop is ruined."

Franco's complaints were suddenly interrupted by the sound of sarcasm.

"Well, that's a wonderful attitude."

He spun around but saw no one. "Who said that?"

The voice had come from behind the earthenware, near the stairs.

"If you're talking to yourself, you should lower your voice, but if you're trying to be heard, then I've got to tell you—all your worrying is a waste of good time."

Franco walked toward the stairs and saw the dark-haired girl with the soft green eyes sitting on the floor.

"Sorry to interrupt your inspiring conversation, but I'm a little tired after being awakened at three in the morning." She reached up with her hand. "I'm Isabella. I work at the Blessings Convent and am a friend of the Veneros."

Franco took her hand and pulled her up. "I'm Franco, the fool who forgot to dam the creek, which led to the flood and probably ruined the grapes."

She broke into a quick grin. "Well, aren't you a bundle of optimism?"

He looked at her through narrowed eyes for a moment, debating what to say next. He'd failed his family, his brother, his countrymen, and now his landowner; there wasn't a hell of a lot to be optimistic about.

"I'm responsible for this year's wine," he said with a serious tone, "and my stupidity could get me fired."

"Signor Martellino won't fire you." Isabella laughed as if she knew something he didn't. "You saved him today. The grapes are ready. Just give thanks to God that you rescued them in time."

He looked down. "I don't believe in God."

"Yes, you do—you're just constipated."

His eyes widened with surprise and embarrassment.

"That's right. You're constipated. You're like the drain by the road. You have all this anger and negativity clogging you up. You just have to clear the drain and let it flow."

She stuck her finger into one of the earthenware jars that was filled with the mushed grape fluid and held it in front of Franco's nose. He didn't know what to do.

"Taste it," she insisted, and a red-faced Franco licked it off her finger.

"The wine will be fine," she continued. "Let me ask you: What grapes do you know that have been sung to and blessed by nuns?"

He only shrugged his shoulders.

"Prayer works, Franco. Instead of talking about what went wrong today, why don't you take a look at what went right? You and the Veneros dammed the creek, Bartolo got help to come, and together we drained the field and dried, de-stemmed, and crushed the grapes. It was a very good day."

Franco was taken aback by the confidence that flowed so easily from this young lady. He opened his mouth to reply, but then reconsidered, thinking it might lead to a subject he wanted to avoid—his faith.

All of a sudden she grabbed his hand and pulled him upstairs. "I'll show you why you shouldn't be afraid of losing your job." She went over to a basket of leftover grapes, plucked out the best one, and opened the barn to find Giovanni talking with Sister Anna.

"Congratulations, Signor Martellino!" Isabella cried out. "Despite the weather, this is a great harvest! Try one of your delights!"

Giovanni eyed the grape, placed it in his mouth, bit into it, tasted the burst of flavor, and smiled.

"This is very good."

He then turned to Franco. "And you, my winemaker, are very lucky."

As Giovanni walked to the villa, Franco looked at Isabella with a puzzled expression. "How did you know he'd like it?"

"Two reasons: number one, the grapes were ready, and number two"—she gave him a wink—"while you may think I'm a silly girl, Signor Giovanni thinks I'm pretty smart."

CHAPTER 13

LUCCA, 1918

F ranco slept well that night. His job had been saved for another day, and the Venero family, for whom he felt some responsibility, would continue working at the Martellino vineyard. Despite a difficult start that August morning, Franco's first harvest as vineyard manager had ended well. As he laid his head back on his pillow, he thought of the green-eyed girl with the fearless attitude who had helped him that day, and with a grin on his face he closed his eyes and fell fast asleep.

The following morning, Franco joined the Veneros at their breakfast table for the first time. His face lit up when Angelina's daughter Elena brought him a bowl of grapes they'd picked the previous day. He picked up a grape and held it up to the sun to admire the potential inside.

"It's been a long time since I've felt this good."

Angelina only smiled as she handed him a plate of eggs and bread.

"How did she do it, Angelina?"

"How did who do what?"

"You know who. How did she get all those nuns to help us?"

"Isabella can be very persuasive. She has a gift for making people look at things differently."

Franco raised an eyebrow. "By yelling at us?"

"No. By helping us believe we're stronger than we think we are."

Franco scratched his head. He wasn't a big talker, but for some reason, Isabella's actions brought his words to the surface.

"Does she always talk to Signor Martellino that way?"

"She speaks her mind."

"That sharp tongue could find her looking for a new job."

"Bella doesn't work for the Martellinos."

He leaned back in his chair, looking curiously at Angelina. "She seemed to know this property inside and out. Why, it's unfair not to pay her!"

"She comes to help me, Franco."

He looked down, mildly embarrassed. "That's very kind—but why did I only meet her yesterday? I've been here for months."

Angelina cocked her head to the side and grinned. "Because you're always in the orchard or vineyard. If you came in before dark you might have a few more friends besides the olives and grapes."

Franco stared at a grape before dropping it into his mouth. "Does she come often?"

"Not as often as she used to. For some reason, the lady of the house doesn't like Bella. I think Susanna is the only one who can say no to her big brown eyes."

Franco looked up quickly. "I thought they were green?"

Angelina bit her lip to keep from smiling. "Yes, I believe you're right. They are green."

He stared out at the vineyard. "We did save the harvest—but I still don't know if the wine will be as good as it could have been."

"And how many times, Franco, do we get exactly what we want?"

"I just want to prove to Signor Martellino that this vineyard can produce both a great Sangiovese and Trebbiano grape."

"Then believe you will."

"But one more day of sunshine would have made it so much better."

"If you expect the world to give you perfection, Franco Carollo, you'll wind up unhappy. Just give the world the best you can."

Then Angelina took him by the arm. "So how about you and I do a bit of giving this morning? Let's get to the barn and add a little yeast to the glorious wine that Bella says will be better than you expect."

CR   SO

September of 1918 was the first time in almost four years that Franco was able to enjoy the smell of crushed grapes turning into wine. After cleaning the field and checking each plant for water rot, he went down into the cellar to add yeast and sugar to the slurry as the primary fermentation began. He plucked out a few stems that floated to the top, but left some in to add to the tannins and flavor. Angelina helped him cover the vats with the sheets left from the convent so oxygen could enter, but the fruit flies could not. Now it was time to leave the wine alone and allow the flavor to come out.

There was no rest for Franco, who rose early each morning to repair the dam at the creek, check the plants for mildew, and clear the excess debris from the ditch that led to the stone tunnel underneath the road. He returned to the isolation of the fields believing hard work would keep his thoughts from the war. The evenings were not as kind, as the nightmares of Caporetto returned—dark dreams that always ended with his failure to save his brother and Father Mario. He would awaken in a cold sweat and stare up at the ceiling. His only peace came from work—relentless, obsessive work.

CR   SO

From her kitchen window, Angelina watched Franco going from plant to plant only to return again. This was a man whose job was already finished, yet he continued to labor. Angelina understood the burden Franco was carrying; she had felt it in the letters she had received from her own husband in his first weeks on the Isonzo. And Franco was a man who had seen much more than her Mariano had. Behind his silence were memories of darker things than she could even imagine. Franco had seen his brother die and arrogant generals survive. Angelina knew his seclusion would not heal his nightmares, so she tossed aside her dish towel and walked out to the field.

"Franco, I need your help at the market."

He stayed with his work. "Not today, Angie."

"Yes. Right now. Since you've been here, you've never left the farm. I want to show you our beautiful city."

He stood up and started for the barn. "I need to check the wine."

She followed him. "You need to leave the wine alone. The barrels need a break from you."

He continued on until she grabbed him by the elbow. "I'll peck at you all day if you don't come to town with me!"

He made a face at her; the thought of Angie following his every step, from cellar to vine, made him shake his head.

She gave him a playful shove and said, "Now, get washed up and change your clothes. You need to look nice for Lucca."

The entire Venero family took Franco to town that morning in a wagon pulled by two big draft horses. As they crossed the Serchio River and rode through a tunnel of oak trees that lined the road to Lucca, the view took Franco's breath away. There was a vast green lawn that stretched from the main road to the huge walls that surrounded the city. The walls must be twelve meters high, thought Franco. They were of red brick with vines crawling up the sides, and as he looked left and right, the walls seemed to go on forever. There were chestnut trees beginning to take on their rich fall color atop the walls, and as they passed through the northern medieval gateway of Porta dei Borghi, Franco began to smile. "The walls don't seem so fearsome once you're inside."

"I'll take you for a walk on them some time," Angelina said. "It's a pleasant four-kilometer stroll around the city."

He saw children playing on top of the wall, an older gentleman teaching his grandchild to ride a bicycle, and a family having a picnic on a bench overlooking the city. "They look wide enough for us to drive our wagon."

"They're big enough for two wagons. There are tunnels inside, so back in the day, troops could move through to attack the enemy or retreat from danger. The builders also developed a network of moats and ditches so they could flood the low area near the walls to slow down an enemy attack."

Franco pointed to a tall tower that had trees on top. "What's that building?"

"Guinigi Tower. It's over five hundred years old."

He snorted slightly. "Looks like they came from money."

"And from pride. The Guinigis insisted that they have the tallest building in town. It's almost forty-five meters, and there are seven oak trees growing on top."

Franco's smile grew as Angelina swept the wagon to the right and followed a road past the Basilica of Saint Frediano with its striking thirteenth-century colorful mosaic on top of the church. They turned left down a narrow street and through an archway into the Piazza del Mercato. Inside were buildings of various shades of terracotta, ochre, and tan that ringed the plaza, forming a beautiful frame for the brilliant colors inside. The market burst with a delightful mixture of reds, purples, and yellows from the flower, vegetable, and fruit carts on display. Franco smiled inside as he remembered his mother telling him that broccoli always looked greener if next to the bright red tomatoes, and here they were, side by side at Lucca's market. There were apples and apricots and large stacks of sweet onions, eggplants, and string beans piled high. Local buyers inspected beef, ham, and fish that they would sell in their trattorias that week. The sounds of violins filled the air, as musicians hoped passersby would toss coins into their hats.

"Come, try a few samples!" a vendor cried out. "Our oil is the best in all of Tuscany!"

Another pointed at Bartolo. "Ciao, little boy! Tell your mama to buy you a little Italian butter rum!"

"This reminds me of home!" Franco exclaimed. "We have a fine market in Alberobello. Not as big as this, but the apricots and olives and meats and—"

Before he could finish, he felt a pop on the back of his head, then another on his neck. He turned to find a giggling Isabella throwing grapes at him from behind a fruit-and-vegetable stand.

"Well, if it isn't the Martellinos' rainmaker!" she yelled out as she fired another that bounced off his shoulder. "Are they going to call your wine Miraculous Rosso, or perhaps Blessed Sisters Sangiovese?"

Isabella's teasing had the Venero family roaring in laughter and Franco turning red as he wondered who this girl was who taunted him at every chance.

Before Franco could pull the wagon to the side, the Venero children were already off, playfully dodging Isabella's throws as she now pelted them with grapes. She grabbed all four children and hugged them to her as Angelina pulled Franco to the table that was filled with buyers.

"Popular table," he said as they squeezed through the crowd.

"Every weekend," Angelina grinned.

"Signor Franco!" he heard someone call out. He spun around to find Sister Anna waving at him, her hand filled with paper money. "Pray tell us you have good news about our wine!"

Franco yelled back over the crowd, "If you're buying, it has a chance!"

"I'm simply in charge of the convent sales!" Anna winked and stuffed the money into a wooden box. "But I believe that our good Lord invented the grape, so we could all be happy!"

He sat down next to Anna but his eyes stayed with Isabella, who was introducing the Venero children to her friends in the market.

"How long has Bella lived at your convent?" he asked.

"Eight years. She came to us in 1909 at the age of twelve, having never stepped foot in a church or heard the story of Jesus."

"Never heard Jesus's story?" He sat back, startled. "How is that possible in Italy?"

She laughed. "I thought it was impossible, too, but Bella has her own ideas about faith."

Franco raised one brow.

"When I first told her about Jesus, she became very excited and said, 'I know who you're talking about! I just didn't know He had a name before today!'"

At this, Franco raised both eyebrows.

Anna nodded. "I asked Bella what her parents called Him, and she said, 'One Who Knows the Truth.'"

A heaviness fell over Franco, and his next words seemed an effort. "Then who does she believe God is?"

Anna raised her eyes and looked directly at him. "The One Who IS the Truth"

Franco sat silently for a spell, watching Bella work the market as if she were some conductor leading an orchestra, helping one chef select the right bell pepper to go with prosciutto while pointing out a tomato to another man who scanned her table.

"I remember when Bella was only fourteen," Anna continued, "our Holy Mother asked her to prepare a birthday meal for the new mayor."

Franco managed a smile. "That's pressure."

"Even more so when you consider that because of her upbringing, Bella didn't believe in eating another of God's creations."

"Sounds like a good heart but a lousy menu."

Anna laughed. "You should have heard those arguments, Franco. Little Bella would open a Bible and read us the first chapter of Genesis. 'God said, I give you every plant yielding seed that is upon the face of all the earth, and every tree with seed in its fruit; you shall have them for food.'" Anna's eyes brightened at the memory.

"Then she would hand me back our Holy Book, give me one of her crinkle-eyed grins, and say, 'I can't find anything in here about God eating meat!'"

He chuckled lightly. "She makes a pretty good argument."

"Bella insisted that God is a vegetarian and that if He walked through our convent door she would fix him her *panzanella*—and that He'd probably ask for seconds."

Franco watched Isabella move about the market, pick up an apricot, smell it, and say something kind to the vendor. She grabbed a melon from another vendor, held it up to Rosa's ear, and thumped it with a finger as she explained why one was better than the other. Then she made her way back over to her table, closely followed by the Venero children.

"Bella!" Anna called out. "I was telling Franco about the birthday meal you fixed for the mayor!"

"The first one?" Isabella yelled back, "or the time I burned the chocolate biscotti?"

"The first one. The time you put all of the sisters to work."

Isabella placed her hands together in mock prayer. "It was a day of collective love."

"It was exhausting," Anna groaned. "It took us two days to clean up her mess in the kitchen. Bella had Sister Teresa boiling the spaghetti noodles, Sister Emmilia crushing and boiling the Roma tomatoes into a paste, and Sister Mona slaving away at the oregano, basil, and olives."

Isabella raised an impish brow. "That's what a good leader does."

"She came into the kitchen with her arms filled with garlic cloves, black truffles, and parsley, then prepped seasonings of red pepper flakes and ground black pepper."

Bella laughed, remembering. "Then I found some dry red wine—"

"She poured half the bottle in!"

"And then a little more," Bella giggled.

Tears of amusement were beginning to run down Anna's cheeks at the memory. "And then Sister Mona hid in the pantry and drank the rest!"

Franco was enjoying the back-and-forth banter between two friends. It reminded him of home, before he had left for Rome, before the war, before Caporetto. He wondered how this world could be so happy for people like Anna and Bella when the pain of living gnawed at him. His world was one of death, sorrow, and disappointment.

A hearty slap on the back from Anna brought him back to the now. "You should have seen her, Franco! Bella climbed up on a chair, lowered her nose to the pot, and declared, "A wonderful event is almost ready!"

Franco shook his head to rid himself of any lingering dark thoughts and summoned a polite smile. "Was it a success?"

Anna put her hand on her heart in feigned reverence. "Bella prepared a meal that was pure artwork, as if she were a maestro, slicing and dicing and seasoning to perfection. And she was only fourteen! The mayor has since requested she prepare at least one meal every single year."

Isabella rolled her eyes at Anna's exaggeration, picked an apricot off her table, and handed it to Franco. He took a bite. It was indeed delicious.

"What's your secret?"

She shrugged again, as if the question were silly. "I just love what I do and believe that when you have a passion for something, the result will be good."

Franco gave a look of doubt.

"You don't believe in positive thoughts, farm boy?"

"I'm a realist," he answered defensively. "Life is not that easy."

"I never said it was easy. I said it works better if you think positively."

Franco didn't reply for a moment. Then he raised his eyes to the north, where his wine was maturing in the cellar underneath the Martellino barn. He knew how uncertain the future could be.

"I believe in hard work," he finally said.

"And I believe in smiling while you work." She grabbed some dirt that was at the bottom of a box of kale and held it up. "We look at the land and hope the soil is fertile, but our minds and hearts are like fertile soil as well. This kale needs good soil, and we need good thoughts. Good thoughts create good actions."

Anna handed a kale leaf to Franco. It was a deep, dark green. He inhaled the aroma as Anna leaned in and whispered, "Get ready for Isaiah 30:23."

"I heard that!" Isabella laughed. "But Isaiah 30:23 makes perfect sense. 'He will give rain for the seed with which you sow the ground.'"

Franco gave a puzzled look.

"We think the dirt, the sun, and water are the only elements needed when we plant a seed. But everything in nature, including human beings, needs love to reach its true potential. I simply plant the seeds of divine ideas in my garden, and the fruits and vegetables flourish."

He let out a long sigh. "Until there's a drought or a flood."

"There will always be challenges in life, Franco." Her eyes fixed on his with a penetrating stare. "But does that mean we should stop living or stop loving? Those are the times we need more than ever to relax into silence and open our awareness to divine ideas that will create incredible possibilities." She held up a bright purple grape. "Look, Franco—the possibility of the perfect Sangiovese."

She then hooked her arm through his and pulled him away from her table. "Come, there's something I want to show you." She led him through the market and down a street to the Basilica of San Frediano. They went to the side of the church and down the cellar stairs past old, dusty furniture and pictures. They came to a back room that was filled with wooden barrels.

"These oak barrels have been here the last two years," Isabella said. "The church used them only once, until a benefactor gave them new barrels. I noticed that the ones you use at the vineyard are not of the best quality and consequently the Martellino wine stinks of wood."

Franco was a bit stunned at her candor, but then looked inside one barrel. "This is quality French oak."

"And the cooper who charred the inside obviously loved his work."

She rolled the barrel toward the cellar door. "They're simply taking up space in the church basement. Saint Freddy's groundskeeper is a friend of mine, and he told me they're yours if you want them."

"You already assumed I'd want them?"

She narrowed her eyes and gave him a long, level look. "You're not the only one I want to see succeed, Franco. The Veneros need this wine to be successful or they won't have a job."

"I—I didn't mean it that way."

Isabella leaned against the barrel and crossed her arms over her chest as if impatiently waiting for Franco to make a decision. Her body language irritated him. Why the hell was he letting this church cook tell him how he should do his job?

"No offense, Isabella, but you only make sacramental wine at the convent—"

She slapped her hand on the side of the barrel. "Don't make this about me! The red you have is ready to barrel. Do you want these oak barrels or not?"

He glared at her but his embarrassment was evident, his face red, the tips of his ears burning. "Of course I want them," he stuttered, "but, how am I going to get them to the vineyard?"

"Didn't I just tell you that divine ideas create incredible possibilities?"

"And your divine idea is?"

"Do you remember the trucks I borrowed to bring the nuns to your flooded field?"

He nodded.

Isabella gave him a crinkle-eyed grin. "I believe they'll be available again tonight."

☙ ❧

Franco, Isabella, and the Venero family put those trucks to good use and delivered the barrels in front of the Martellino barn by nine o'clock that night. Inside the villa, Susanna watched Franco and Bartolo carrying the barrels to the barn and immediately went to tell her husband.

The villa door banged open, and Giovanni's voice rang across the courtyard. "Would someone please tell me what's going on at my vineyard without my knowledge?"

Franco lowered a barrel to the ground. "I'm sorry, signor—I—we—were given these French oak barrels."

116

"Why was I not told of this first?"

"I just found out today and didn't want to bother you this late."

"I'm here now, Franco!"

Isabella came up from the cellar just as Franco was trying to explain.

"Bella said the groundskeeper at Saint Frediano had these casks and offered them to us. We thought they might draw a nice flavor—"

Giovanni stopped him. "This is Martellino wine. I'll make the decisions on how our wine should taste."

Franco dropped his eyes to the ground. "Yes, signor."

Giovanni walked around the barrel, giving the impression he was studying its design and potential. "What's the price for the barrels?"

"There was no charge."

"Don't be a fool, Franco. There's always a price. What does the church want?"

"No price, signor. The groundskeeper said we—"

"Put the barrels in the barn." Giovanni again cut him off. "I'll make my decision in the morning." He then turned and went back to his villa.

Isabella stood still by the door of the barn for a long moment, eyes fixed on Franco. The courtyard was quiet as she slowly walked over to him. "Are you the winemaker for this vineyard or a servant boy?"

Franco flushed hotly, shocked at her question. "This is his vineyard."

"And YOU are his winemaker. He deserves to know your opinion. Do you believe you are less than Giovanni?"

Franco didn't know how to answer. He had been raised in southern Italy, where the landowner was never questioned.

"Well?" she asked again. "Do you believe you are less than Giovanni?"

Franco stood as if paralyzed, desperately wondering how to answer. Finally, he said, "He's the landowner, and I'm his worker."

Bella crossed her arms and eyed him. "Tell that to the Veneros when they're fired because their winemaker, who knows more about growing grapes than the vineyard owner, didn't have the courage to give his opinion."

Franco's mouth fell open. "I—I didn't hear you give your opinion!"

"I'm not his winemaker."

"Who are you?" he said, his anger growing. "You're kind to everyone in Lucca—except me!"

"Finally, some emotion from you!"

"Emotion?" He fired the belt he had been using to haul the barrels to the ground. "Is that what you want?"

"Giovanni needs to know what you think, Franco. And the Veneros also need to know what you think, instead of watching you do everything by yourself."

He started to walk away. "I don't have to listen to this."

She followed him. "Why are you honest with me yet won't speak your mind to Giovanni?"

"Leave me alone."

"Is it because I'm poor and he's rich?"

Franco spun around and glared at her. "You don't know me!"

Isabella's entire body softened. "No, I don't. I don't know anything about you, or your past. But we're dealing with the here and now—and right now this vineyard needs a winemaker."

Franco was shaking in anger as he grabbed the last barrel, hoisted it to his shoulder, and pushed past her into the barn.

CR   ᘓ

It was a restless night. He lay in bed, angry with Isabella and angry with himself. She was right. He was afraid of losing his job. He was afraid of having his opinion criticized. He was afraid of the sadness that would not go away. He believed the guilt of what had happened on the battlefield was something he deserved. It was life's payback for all he'd done wrong.

As he stared up at the ceiling, he thought back to something Isabella had said in Lucca, something about divine ideas creating incredible possibilities. Did that belief work only for people like Bella? All of a sudden, his brother's final words at Caporetto came to him. "Go home and forgive."

Franco knew what he had to do. He went to the barn, cleaned and prepared the new oak barrels for the wine, and then waited for the lights to come on inside the villa.

A second-floor lamp suddenly lit, followed by one inside the kitchen. Franco inhaled a deep breath and knocked on the door.

Josephine opened it.

"I need to speak with the signor," he said.

Twenty minutes later Giovanni opened the door.

Franco didn't wait for his boss to acknowledge him.

"Signor Martellino, I've thought a lot about what you said last night, and while I respect your wishes, I must let you know how I feel about your vineyard. Come with me."

As they walked out to the vineyard, Franco grabbed a spade from the side of the barn and carried it to the middle of the field. He dug down about a foot and a half and pulled up the soil. "Look at this, signor. You have good soil on top, full of broken slate, rich in minerals that will give good flavors to the grapes. Despite my mistake in not reading the weather correctly, the slope of your land is good for drainage, and these hills hold just enough moisture before the sun burns off the fog. It all means we will produce an excellent Sangiovese grape."

Franco put the spade in the ground and pointed to the barn.

"Now let me tell you about the barrels. The French oak will produce a better wine. The cooper who charred the oak did a splendid job. There's a light toast on both the head and body of seven of the barrels that will give us a lighter red wine, and a medium toast on five more that will give us a more full-bodied wine. We'll still have some left that we can put in our old barrels to see how it matches up. I believe your Sangiovese grapes will benefit from the minerals in the ground and the oak and smoke from these barrels. I believe—no—I know, the result will be an outstanding red—as good as any in Tuscany."

Giovanni stroked his chin, impressed with what his winemaker had to say, but before he could respond, Franco added, "I'll finish this season, and then I'd like to take a week off to visit my parents in Puglia. They haven't seen me since I left for the war."

Giovanni looked up slowly. "How do I know you'll return?"

"I gave you my word when I arrived and worked three weeks for free. I'm nothing if I go back on my word." Franco spoke briskly to dispel the doubt in his landowner's eyes. "I'll return because I'm your winemaker, and because I want to be the first to taste the beginnings of your Martellino red."

A slow smile started across Giovanni's face. "Then you shall work, Franco. There will be no days off for you before you leave. There will be no hiring boys from the local farms to help. The Venero children will be your only help. We'll try your idea with the new barrels, but if it doesn't work out to my satisfaction, your services will no longer be needed."

"That, Signor Martellino," Franco said as he grabbed the spade and started back toward the barn, "will not be a problem."

CR   SO

Two days later the fermentation was complete, and the wines were ready to be poured into the barrels for aging. The Veneros were up early that Saturday morning, with Bartolo off to the convent to ask Isabella for help. He passed Susanna on the road and waved, but the Martellino matriarch's mind seemed elsewhere as she stared across the wheel of her car and drove past him.

CR   SO

Susanna had her regrets. There were things she wanted to do with her life, and mothering was only getting in the way of those ambitions. She sensed a change in Italy and wanted desperately to be part of that change. The war would soon be over, and with it, Socialism would be out as well. In its place would emerge a stronger, more disciplined government. The politicians she was to meet today would be part of that future, and she wanted to join them in helping to build Italy's new empire.

Susanna gripped the wheel tightly, trying to force out the guilt that grew the farther she drove from her villa. At the core of her guilt was Isabella. The convent girl was again back at the vineyard, her return an agreement Susanna had made with her husband in exchange for time with those who would build the new Italy. Still, the heaviness in her heart would not go away. Why did mothering come so naturally to Isabella? Why did DeAngelo prefer that gypsy to his own mother? She had tried to keep the boy away from Isabella as often as she could by putting him in the care of Josephine. But every time she turned her back, Josephine would innocently leave the back door open, letting DeAngelo wander outside to join Isabella and the Veneros in the field. Susanna was sure it was happening now, and the thought made her grip the wheel even tighter.

CB BO

"Little D.!" Isabella shouted when she and Sister Anna walked down the Martellino drive and saw DeAngelo playing in the courtyard. The little boy came running into her arms. "How's my favorite little winemaker?" She picked him up and carried him into the barn. It was time to start pouring the wine into the barrels for aging.

At the sight of Isabella, Franco flushed hotly and offered only a slight nod before turning back to work.

Isabella followed him, holding DeAngelo on her hip. "Little D., would you like to see how Uncle Franco blends different grapes from your vineyard to make a fine Martellino red?"

DeAngelo giggled, but Franco remained quiet. Isabella made a puppet with her hand, as if it were talking to DeAngelo. "Is Uncle Franco still mad at me for speaking my mind the other night? Look how his jaws clench like a Roman gladiator's as he tries to hide his smile."

DeAngelo was now giggling so hard that Franco had to bite his lip to keep from smiling. Finally, he gave up and offered a reluctant smile, giving Isabella exactly what she wanted.

"We did it, DeAngelo! We made the big *brutto* from Puglia smile!"

Franco dipped his fingers into a bucket of water and flicked spray at Isabella and DeAngelo. The little boy squealed as Isabella yelled, "Help me, Little D! I can't swim! I can't swim!"

Franco laughed and took the boy from Isabella's arms.

"Would you like to help us barrel the wine, Little D.?"

The little boy nodded enthusiastically as Franco took him down to the wine cellar, where Bartolo was siphoning off the first jar into one of the French oak barrels.

As Franco walked around the cellar, explaining to DeAngelo about the quality of the wood and how the toasted oak would bring out a smoky flavor, Giovanni entered the barn and moved to the cellar stairs. He stood quietly at the top, listening to his winemaker explain to his son about the art of turning grapes into red wine. A proud smile spread across Giovanni's face and grew as he walked down the cellar steps and called out, "Is that my son, the winemaker?"

An apprehensive Franco turned, only to see the delight in his landowner's face. "DeAngelo is helping me decide what wine should go in what barrel."

"And what has my little winemaker decided?"

Franco brushed some breakfast crumbs off the baby's face. "I think he's partial to the light toast."

Giovanni laughed. "My son will be the finest vintner in all the land!"

Franco handed DeAngelo to his father. "Would you like to help him siphon the wine into the barrels, signor?"

"If my son wants my help, I'd be delighted."

Father and son walked to the end of the cellar to join Bartolo, who had just started another barrel. Isabella walked up behind Franco and poked him in the ribs.

"You made Giovanni smile."

"No, I didn't. His son did."

Isabella nodded at Giovanni, whose joy was evident as he carried DeAngelo from barrel to barrel. "I think both of you did."

He watched them for a bit. "It's easy to be happy when you're with children."

"I don't think life is meant to be difficult, Franco. When we're free and playful, everything seems to work out so much better."

"But I doubt we'd get very much accomplished."

"Look around you!" Isabella said with a raised eyebrow. "Everyone is working—and everyone is happy." She again poked Franco in the ribs. "Even you. Even the relentless workhorse from Puglia made somebody smile. It feels good, doesn't it?"

She slid past him and was gone up the stairs.

Franco watched her leave with both bewilderment and enchantment. Who was this girl from the convent? He found himself furious with her one minute and charmed the next. He looked over to Sister Anna, who was just finishing a barrel of red.

"I've never met anyone like Bella," he said. "She seems to be this little bird that flits from branch to branch without a care in the world."

"You think she doesn't care?" Anna asked. "I've never met anyone who cares so much."

"But she's so darn sure of herself. It's as if she has life all figured out and everything works out easily for her."

"What do you know of Bella's past, Franco?"

"Well—nothing, really."

Anna inserted the bung on the side of the barrel to seal it and nodded toward the stairs. "Then go ask her."

Franco walked to the Veneros' cottage, where Isabella was preparing lunch. He stood in the doorway for a moment, staring at the young woman in front of him. It was the first time he had noticed her unaffected beauty, and he admired her slim frame as she washed the lettuce and cilantro. She wore a white cotton blouse that was tucked into a green skirt the color of her eyes. As Isabella leaned forward, a breeze swept through the kitchen window and billowed the top of her blouse open, allowing Franco a glimpse of her breasts. He found himself staring and caught his breath.

Isabella looked up and smiled. "I hope you're hungry, because what I'm making will refresh you."

"Uh—yeah," stammered Franco, suddenly unable to speak.

She cocked her head to the side. "Is anything wrong?"

"No—uh—no," he bumbled, asking himself the same question. What the hell was wrong with him?

Isabella dried her hands on her skirt and waved for Franco to join her at the wooden chopping block. "Here, you cut up the parsley. I'll do the cilantro and chives."

He almost tripped as he walked through the doorway.

She chuckled. "Are you all right?"

He took a deep breath as he tried to straighten out his thoughts and then suddenly blurted out, "Where do you come from?"

Her brows drew together as if she was confused. "Is that a question or a statement?"

"Uh—question?"

"Are you asking where I was born or about my life journey?"

"Life journey—yes."

Isabella reached into the small stone oven and pulled out the tray of sliced almonds she had been toasting. She lifted one off the tray and placed it between Franco's lips. "Pretty good, don't you think?"

He felt dizzy. "Yes, delicious."

She smiled. "I love a man so generous with his words." Then she started her tale of where she'd come from to the path that had brought her to the Martellino vineyard. She ended with, "It seems as if everything in my life, good or bad, has led me to where I'm supposed to be right now."

Franco studied her face as if he were trying to read her. "You believe something divine gave you the difficulties in your life?"

"I believe you get what you get, Franco. My father encouraged me to question everything; even the very existence of God. He said it was in the seeking that I would find my answers, and that I could not fail if I sought to reach the truth."

"You're not angry that God didn't save your parents?"

"God didn't take my parents," she said with a serious tone. "Influenza did. Some of my past I may not have wanted—but every experience has been a great lesson."

Franco thought back to the war and the memories that still haunted him.

"Some of our past is hard to let go of."

She didn't speak for a long time, but her eyes stayed on his, soft and understanding. "I'm sorry for what you've been through."

He had to pause to compose himself. Then, for the first time since he had left the battlefield, he shared with someone his time in the Isonzo valley: he spoke of a mismanaged war and of the defeated looks of Italian soldiers in full retreat, but he could not bring himself to tell her the details of the deaths of his brother and chaplain.

They were quiet for a spell. Franco stood erect, fists clenched, staring out across the barren vineyard. He struggled to breathe, but the guilt held firm until a leaf broke free from a grapevine branch and fell to the ground. It was the same leaf that weeks earlier had changed from green to yellow and was now golden red, and as the wind picked up, he watched other leaves pulled from their source fall gently to the ground. Isabella saw what he saw and placed her hand on top of his. She said nothing, but her touch stirred something inside him.

"Tell me about Sister Anna," he said.

"My greatest teacher," Isabella smiled. "Anna helped me understand that simply caring for others is how healing occurs. She said it was not her responsibility to take my suffering away but only to be a loving presence in my life. I remember one time I was very angry about having to live at the convent, and Anna left me alone in a room with my chair facing directly at a quote she had hanging on the wall. It was from a Frenchman named Voltaire. The quote read: 'The longer we dwell on our misfortunes, the greater is their power to harm us.'"

She took the parsley that Franco had chopped and tossed it into a large wooden bowl with the lettuce, cilantro, chives, and almonds. He looked at her hands, at how easily they moved around the kitchen table. When she took a knife in her right hand and a lemon in her left, it was as if this movement had taken place a million times before. Without looking she sliced the lemon into quarters, squeezed the juice around the salad with one hand while adding vinaigrette dressing with the other, and then slowly licked the mixture off her fingers. For the second time, Franco noticed her natural beauty, how the sun had browned her olive skin, making her green eyes more pronounced and the curls that framed her face in the color of dark chocolate.

"It's time," Isabella said as she handed him the wooden spoon and fork.

The word *time* brought him back to his previous thoughts, and as he followed Isabella outside to the dining table he asked, "Do you think I've been dwelling on my past?"

"I think you've been through a lot," she said as she placed the bowl in the middle of the table. "I think you should be a little easier on yourself."

"I should have been there for my brother."

"Then be there for him now."

He stared at her, his mouth slightly open.

She reached across the table and took his hand. "What do you think your brother would want for you right now—this very moment?"

Franco took in a deep breath, exhaled slowly, and looked across the vineyard at the leaves that continued to fall to the ground. "I think—" he finally said. "I think he would want me to be happy."

CHAPTER 14

LUCCA, OCTOBER 1918

To Franco, the Martellino vineyard had become his calm, the eye of the hurricane that was still storming across Europe. But the peace he had found on the fields north of Lucca was shaken when he arrived at the train station. Boxcars were filled with broken soldiers on their way home. The war was almost over. News of the Allied capture of the Hindenburg Line was the talk of every citizen, but you could not see any joy in the faces of the weary Italian veterans. As Franco walked past a soldier reading a newspaper, he glanced at the headline that told of Germany's Third Supreme Command admitting that they were beaten and handing over power to Max von Baden and the Reichstag. The end was near.

Franco found a seat in the railcar next to a wounded corporal. The young man had lost his right leg below the knee, and the right side of his face was scarred.

Mortar fire, thought Franco as he nodded to the young man.

"Where are you headed?" he asked.

"Toranto," the soldier muttered. "You?"

"Alberobello station, then to my parents, near Bari."

"Good country. I was a farmer before this." The corporal pointed to his amputated leg. "They say it's almost over."

"I hope so," was all Franco could think of saying, but the soldier wanted to talk.

"If it's almost over, why does our new prime minister, Vittorio Orlando, want General Diaz to launch one more attack?"

Franco took a deep breath to steady his growing outrage. "Politics," he grumbled.

"Of course," the corporal sighed. "With help from the British and French armies in this final assault, Italy will finally be able to claim the lands we wanted before the war."

"More will die because we need military victories to strengthen our political position in Europe when this war ends."

The corporal looked up. "You fought?"

Franco nodded, and the corporal reached out his hand. "Then you know what I saw."

Franco shook his hand but said nothing more.

ଔ ഔ

It was late in the afternoon when Franco stepped off the train in Alberobello. He remembered being with his brother at that very station almost three years before. Benny had been the reason he'd boarded that train. Now he was dead. Franco thought he might recognize an old friend in town but saw none.

As he walked up the path to his parents' farm, he felt sad about the place. The front yard was overgrown, and paint was peeling off the house that now seemed old and tired. He looked to the backyard and saw his mother in the garden. She stood up and held her hand over her eyes to cover the glare from the sun.

"Franco?"

He nodded.

"Franco!" she screamed as she ran to his open arms. "My baby boy!"

"I'm sorry, Mama. I'm so sorry," was all he could say.

When his father came from the barn and saw the two of them, he dropped the pails he was carrying. For a moment he wore the expression Franco had expected: of a man with an iron reserve who rarely showed emotion. Then his father's face began to curl into a cautious smile, and he came to hug his son.

CR SO

The Carollos had a fine dinner that night. They talked of happy times, of friends from church, of successful seasons. But although Franco's father was pleasant, he was distant. It wasn't until the meal was finished that Franco spoke of his brother.

I need to tell you about Benny."

His father shrank back, but Franco pushed on. "He was a good soldier, Papa. Everyone liked him." Franco tried for words, but everything he thought dissolved into the guilt he was feeling. "I—I tried to protect him. But my orders were to take a message to the communications center."

"Stop," his father said, but Maria squeezed Franco's hand to signal him to continue.

"When I got back—my battalion was gone. I tried to find him, Papa—I tried to find him."

Bernardino stared past his son, "Why did you go?"

131

"I wanted—I wanted to—protect Benny."

"No!" His father slammed his fist on the table. "Why did you leave the first time? None of this would have happened if you had not left for Rome! Because you had your adventure, Benny wanted his own, and now my son is dead!"

The statement caught Franco by surprise, and the guilt he had pushed away in recent weeks came roaring back.

Maria put her hand on her husband's arm to calm him, but he shoved it away.

"Your job was here! With your family!"

Franco tried to answer, but the only thing he found was misery.

"Do you know what our priest said when he heard of Benny's death?" his father snapped. "He said it was God's will! God's will? Damn His will! Is it God's will to make the landowner rich and me poor? Is it God's will to let our landowner's son live while my son dies?"

Franco sat frozen to his chair while his father stormed out of the house.

Maria watched him go and then turned to her son. "When we received your letter, part of your father died. He's been angry ever since."

Franco couldn't respond. Instead, he brought his fists to his forehead, trying to force the guilt out of his mind.

Maria put her hand on his. "He loves you, Franco. But he needed to say those words. I think he believes if he says them he will suffer less."

"What about you, Mama? What about your suffering?"

She paused for a long time and then took a deep breath to keep from crying. "Benny's death changed me as well. But I no longer believe his death was God's will."

"Why?"

"Because I believe man made God 'almighty'. Man gave God the power to remedy any wrong or to prevent any disaster. But wrongs and disasters still happen. I've come to believe that's simply part of life."

Franco stared into his hands. "Then what use does man have for God?"

"We long for God's miracles," she said. "And then we blame Him when He doesn't part a sea or move a mountain or prevent a war— or a son dies. But I now believe a miracle is something very different. A miracle can be the simple change of my heart."

Franco was silent for a spell before two thoughts entered his mind. The first was something Isabella had told him. "Some of my past I may not have wanted, but every experience has been a great lesson." The second was the memory of his brother's final words: "Go home and forgive." It was time, thought Franco, and as swiftly as a leaf being carried down a waterfall, he let go and forgave his father's bitterness and judgment—but he could not yet forgive himself for what he had failed to do at Caporetto.

The Carollo family did not speak of Benny or of that first night again. Franco quietly worked next to his father in the vineyard and olive grove. They helped their landowner with his wheat field and even joined Maria at church on Wednesday night. Father and son did not talk of the future until the day before Franco was due to return to Lucca.

"I must leave tomorrow," Franco said as he cut off a dead branch from an old olive tree. "Signor Martellino trusted me to be gone only a week, and there's still much to be done."

"Tell me about this Giovanni Martellino," his father asked. "Is he a good man to work for?"

"His pride gets in his way sometimes, Papa. He wants to be right, wants control, but then I saw a wonderful moment with Giovanni and his son before I left. It reminded me of you when Benny and I were little, and you would get so excited talking to us about pruning and pressing and aging."

They laughed, and Bernardino began to open up. "Do you remember the time you and Benny got inside an old barrel and rolled it down the hill? When you tried to walk, it looked as if you'd had too much wine."

"And the first time you let us take the olives for pressing by ourselves. We ran our horse too quickly and left half the load on the side of the road."

Bernardino sighed as he looked across his field. It had been a difficult year with so many field workers gone to fight Europe's war. "Are the soil and weather good in the north?"

"They're perfect for both grapes and olives, and there's plenty of water." Franco thought back to the night of the flood. "I didn't tell you how I almost ruined the crop. I forgot to block a dam before a big rainfall, and it flooded the field."

"Signor Martellino didn't fire you?"

"This crazy girl, Isabella," Franco grinned, "brought a truckload of nuns out to drain the field and saved both the grapes and my job."

His father could tell by the way Franco's face lit up when he said Isabella's name that she was someone special. "So, tell me about this—Sister Isabella?"

"Oh, Bella's no nun!" Franco laughed. "Every sister at the Blessings Convent loves her, but can't believe she still lives with them."

"So, she's more than a friend?"

"No, Papa. I hardly know her."

"Then get to know her."

"I'm sure she has plenty of suitors."

"Then be one of them."

"I don't know."

"Are you afraid of being hurt, son?"

The question made Franco pause, and for a moment he wondered if he was holding back. He took a breath and tried to straighten out his thoughts.

"I've never met a girl like her. She makes me feel stupid one moment and special the next. She's honest to a fault."

"Sounds like your mother," Bernardino laughed as he put his arm around his son. "But let me tell you something very important. Fear can be deceiving. There was a time I was afraid of your mama's confidence. Thought I wasn't good enough for her."

The statement surprised Franco. He had always thought his father a rock, rigid in his beliefs, like an oak in the middle of any storm.

Bernardino let out a long exhale and picked up the dead olive branch. "I don't know how I would have gotten through your brother's death without your mother."

It was the first time his father had mentioned Benny's death since Franco's first night home. They were quiet for a spell until Bernardino said, "I don't want you to leave before I tell you something. I'm sorry for what I said the other night."

"And I'm sorry I left years ago without telling you."

"No, son. You did nothing wrong. A father raises his boys, and they're his legacy. I thought I had lost both of my sons on the

Isonzo: one to the war, and one to his memories of the war. Your mother is right. I must learn to forgive. I hope you can do the same."

ʘ ʆ

They had a wonderful dinner that night and shared a bottle of the vineyard's best red. Bernardino and Maria took their son to the Alberobello train station the next day, November 3, 1918, and as they walked to his railcar, Franco had a question for both of them. "I would like to show you Lucca. If I send you rail tickets, will you come?"

Bernardino thought about the difficult expense for Franco, but the look in his son's eyes changed his mind. "Only if you take us for a walk on the great walls that you've been bragging about."

"I would love that, Papa."

His mother's eyes were wet as she hugged her son goodbye.

Franco stepped up on the train and heard his father roar from the sidewalk, "Tell Sister Isabella that Bernardino and Maria Carollo look forward to meeting her!"

As the train headed north, Franco looked back, sporting a broad smile.

Sitting alone in a passenger car, Franco was amused by his thoughts. He had come so far in the last few months, from the battlefields of Caporetto and the depths of depression to the leap of faith he had taken by accepting the job at the Martellino vineyard. Was it as Isabella had told him, that everything in a person's life, good or bad, leads him to where he's supposed to be? Maybe, he thought, he was supposed to meet Isabella. He had to admit, he was charmed by her smile and passion for life; and now, as he looked out the window at the pines that seemed to be rushing by, he couldn't get her off his mind.

As the train pulled into the Florence station, he heard shouts and laughter coming from the platform. He stuck his head out the window and saw men and women hugging and children waving Italian flags.

"What's going on?" the man across from him asked.

"It's some kind of celebration," Franco answered.

When the train stopped, people jumped aboard, crying out, "It's over! The war's over! Our boys took Cadore, and the Austrians and Germans have surrendered!"

Throughout the train, people were embracing. An old man grabbed Franco and shouted, "Praise God! My son is coming home!"

The rest of the ride was a party. Wine bottles that had been handed through the railcar windows in Florence were now open, and people were getting drunk on the joy of the war ending. Yes indeed, this was a great day, Franco thought. Peace with his mother and father, the end of the war, and now Franco himself on his way to Lucca to find that incredible spirit, Isabella.

CHAPTER 15

LUCCA, NOVEMBER 1918

Franco grabbed his suitcase, leaped off the train, and caught a bus loaded with people celebrating the end of the war. Seizing the joy of the day, he laughed and hugged complete strangers, kissed the cheeks of a toddler, and then blew kisses to fellow passengers as he jumped off near Lucca's east gate and raced to the Blessings Convent. Flinging open the door to the church kitchen, he saw Sister Anna packing vegetables into a box.

"Hello, Sister!" he shouted with joy. "Are you going to Lucca's grand celebration?" He then looked around the kitchen and hallway for Bella. "I was hoping you and Bella might want to celebrate!"

But Anna did not smile. Instead, she moved quickly to his side and touched his arm.

"Bella's very sick, Franco. She was working the market when Signora Martellino brought DeAngelo for her to watch. The child fell ill. Bella took him home, and now both are very sick."

Franco stood frozen, grabbing the back of a chair to steady himself. "How serious is this?"

"It's the worst sickness I've ever seen. Several have died." Anna took his hand, led him to the sanctuary, opened a Bible, and pointed to Exodus 23:25. "Pray on this while I get the wagon?"

He stood with his head bowed, eyes closed for a moment, trying to will himself to read scripture. Finally, he opened his eyes and read, "And ye shall serve the Lord your God, and He shall bless thy bread and thy water, and I will take sickness away from thee."

Franco refused to go to his knees, furious with a selfish God who demanded that man worship him in exchange for simple compassion. He pounded his fist on the wooden altar, knocking over a silver chalice, and as he went to catch it, he saw his reflection in the cup. It was the look of his father, the same look of suffering he had seen earlier in the week. He sank to his knees. "Damn you, God! What do you want from me?" He looked down at his hands, still holding the silver chalice. "I beg of you, please save these two. They're only good. They're only joy. Please heal them."

He stood up and lit a candle, touched the holy water, made the sign of the cross, and left the sanctuary to join Anna and go on to the Martellino villa.

CR   SO

Franco sat in silence on the ride, listening to Anna's soft prayers of thanks, healing, and peace. His own attempt at devotion only seemed to be a form of desperate pleading, which ended in uncertainty. He stared out at the dark, cloudless night, the logical part of his brain searching for an answer, any answer. Instead, he found only more questions.

CR   SO

"Isabella is upstairs with DeAngelo," Josephine said as she opened the kitchen door, holding a cloth napkin over her face. "Everyone else is at the Veneros.'"

"Is the doctor with her?" Anna asked.

"Every doctor in Lucca is busy. The baby's fever has not broken, and his breathing now comes in gasps. I'm afraid if he doesn't improve soon—he'll die."

Franco's head dropped in despair.

"Signora Martellino has blamed it all on Bella." Josephine picked up a wooden spoon and began to stir a pot of boiling water filled with eucalyptus leaves. "Bella is also very sick. She has the same chills and fever as the baby and could be in the first stages of pneumonia. Susanna sent a courier to Rome for a vaccine, but Bella doesn't want it."

Franco's mouth fell open.

"She thinks a simple water cure and baths will be of greater help."

"More than a vaccine?"

"She believes the vaccine is poison."

"Why?"

"She says the vaccine will stimulate the sickness and that it's better to keep the child hydrated with water and a tea of raspberry and lemon juice to loosen the mucus that's hardening in his lungs."

Josephine then took an onion from Anna's basket and sliced it in half. "Bella also said onions attract bacteria and placed them next to their bed. It must work, because when I went in this morning, the onions were black. We needed more. That's why she sent Anna back to the convent."

They heard a baby's raspy moan and turned to see Isabella, with DeAngelo in her arms, struggling down the stairs. Her hair was stuck to her face in tiny ringlets of sweat; her lips were white, her breathing heavy.

Franco went to help.

"Stay away!" she coughed as she carried the baby to the pot of water and placed a towel over his head to help him breathe in the steam.

Josephine led Franco and Anna to the door. "I've been exposed. Bella wants everyone else away from the house."

As they headed to the Venero's cottage, Anna placed a rosary in Franco's hand. For the space of a moment he stared at the crucifix, still unconvinced how the worn olive wood and faded silver could or would change anything. His thoughts were suddenly broken by a woman's angry voice.

"If my son dies, I'll kill your friend!"

It was Susanna, waiting by the Venero's door, pointing an accusing finger at Sister Anna. Giovanni held her back.

Startled, Anna froze in the middle of the courtyard.

"Isabella is saving your son, signora. She didn't make him ill."

"When I left him yesterday, he was healthy! She exposed him to all those sick people at the market!"

Giovanni pushed his wife inside the Venero's home and waved for Anna and Franco to join them. Susanna stood alone in the corner, her dark eyes searching for someone to blame. Anna went to her.

"Don't come near me!"

"Please, signora, we're all afraid, but being angry will not allow miracles to happen."

"Don't you dare tell me not to be angry! He's my son!"

"Then see him well. Believe that the spirit of healing flows through him—"

In a rage, Susanna shoved Angelina's dishes to the floor and they shattered at Anna's feet. "Your prayers haven't worked! I've sent a courier to Rome for the vaccine!"

Giovanni shook his head. "I was told they're out of the vaccine."

"Then find another hospital, dammit! Just get it for me!"

☙ ❧

As Franco walked back to his room, the emotional exhaustion of the day hit him, and he thought about all that had taken place since morning: leaving his parents' home, the news that the war was over, the celebration on the train, his excitement at the prospect of seeing Isabella, and then the shock of the news that two people he adored were close to death. It was then that he realized he was still holding the rosary Anna had given him. He opened his hand and found blood on his palm. He had been clutching the rosary so tightly during Susanna's tirade that he'd cut himself on the base of the cross. A dull ache in his heart slowly started to rise up to his mind and turn into fear. He could not believe how foolish he'd been to think that the world would get better, that he might have a future with Isabella. A familiar sorrow crept over him as he lay back on his bed. Sleep did not come easily.

☙ ❧

Franco was awakened the next morning by a scream. He bounded from the bed and raced to the Venero's house. Angelina was on the floor, sobbing. Sister Anna was by her side, her habit off, perspiration dripping down her forehead and face. Her sleeves were rolled up past her elbows, and her hands held a bloody cloth.

"The sickness came so quickly," Anna said in a voice barely above a whisper. "Her breathing got worse and worse and then just stopped."

"What? Who?" stammered Franco.

"My Elena!" cried Angelina. "My sweet Elena!"

The twins, Elisa and Elena, had shown signs of illness the previous night. The children were separated in tents outside the house, with Anna tending to the twins while Angelina treated Bartolo and Rosa. Elena was gone within three hours of her first cough.

Franco sat on the floor and put his arms around Angelina. He had been here before, intimate with this sadness, and his mind traveled back to Caporetto, to images of Benny's and Father Mario's deaths. Would he ever be rid of these nightmares? He wished desperately for some way to break the pain that joined them, some act that could return him to the joy he'd felt earlier in the day. Instead, he held Angelina closer, tormented by her sobs against his chest. He wanted to cry, but no tears came.

◌ॐ   ॐ◌

Isabella remained isolated on the second floor of the villa, fighting to keep DeAngelo alive. She rejected Susanna's attempts to find a vaccine, believing the baby's only chance was to stay hydrated, to somehow not let the mucus solidify in his lungs and suffocate him. If she could move the disease through and out of his body, he had a chance. Cradling the feverish child in her arms, she soaked a towel with water and squeezed drop after drop into DeAngelo's mouth.

◌ॐ   ॐ◌

"You can't blame Isabella for getting sick, Susanna!" Giovanni growled as he grabbed his wife by the arm and pulled her to a quiet spot behind the barn. "YOU were the one who brought our son to the market! Why didn't you take him with you or simply leave him with Josephine?"

"He—he wanted her," Susanna tried to explain. "He was crying and—wanted to be with Bella."

Giovanni remembered losing his own mother and brother to an illness when he was young, and the memory infuriated him. "Why did you have to go to town? What the hell was more important than being with your son?"

Susanna felt as if she couldn't breathe as guilt gripped her.

"You could have taken him with you!" Giovanni pounded his fist against the wall of the barn. "Instead, our little boy is fighting for his life because you had to be—God knows where!"

"I sent for the doctors! I sent for the vaccine! What more do you want?"

Giovanni clenched his hands together, as if afraid that if he separated them he might strike his wife. "I want you to try—just one fucking time—to be our son's mother!" He then stormed back to the Venero's house.

Susanna collapsed to the ground and covered her face, but she made sure Giovanni was gone before crossing herself and looking to the sky. "Please, God, I'm sorry I sinned. Just don't take my son."

CR   SO

Cold weather arrived in Tuscany later that week. Bartolo was the first to recover, and he helped Franco build a little coffin for Elena as he waited for his mother to come out of their house. Angelina was still in mourning and had not come out since her daughter's death. Bartolo had been a great help both to Franco and to Anna, who had stayed to help nurse the other Venero children back to health. The boy had not said one word since his sister's passing. He would silently leave the house and grab a shovel or rake and join Franco in the field. Now, as Franco watched Bartolo take a plate of food from Anna and sit alone by an olive tree, the boy's head hung so low it rested on his chest.

Franco walked to Anna. "I'm going to town to get some more coal for the fire."

Anna gave him a puzzled look. "We have enough coal."

"We need more. I'm going to take Bartolo with me. Is there anything you need in town?"

She reached out for his hand. "If you can swing by the market, perhaps that olive oil sourdough the Veneros love."

He tried to leave, but Anna held his hand until he turned to face her.

"You're a good man, Franco Carollo. Thank you for taking the boy. He's holding so much in."

As Franco led the horse-drawn wagon to town, he sat quietly next to Bartolo. Angelina's son stared away from Franco through the oaks that lined the street.

"Thanks for helping me in the field," Franco finally said. "I needed an extra hand."

Bartolo only lowered his eyes.

"Do you know why I went home to Puglia?"

The boy shook his head.

"I had not seen my parents in almost three years. I needed to make peace with them."

Franco hesitated, but Bartolo remained silent.

"I never said goodbye when my brother and I joined the army. His name was Benny. Great brother." He smiled. "I once broke our kitchen window throwing a rock, and then he took the blame. Can you believe that? I looked up to him, but for some reason, I also felt I had to protect him. As if I had any control over that." Franco took a deep breath. "I saw my brother die at Caporetto and I've held onto that guilt ever since."

Bartolo's voice was shaking when he finally spoke: "Me too."

"Why do you feel guilty?"

Bartolo's tears started flowing. "My papa—could do anything. He would not have let Elena die. I—I was too sick to help her."

Franco pulled the cart off to the side of the road and put his arm around Bartolo. "You did nothing wrong. A sickness took your sister. The war took my brother. It's our damn guilt that tells us we could have done something, and it's our guilt that demands that we be punished." He paused and waited for the boy to face him. "You did everything you could, Bartolo. Now, your mother needs to see you smile. She needs to see you happy again."

Bartolo wiped the tears from his eyes but remained quiet. Franco squeezed his shoulder.

"You've been a big help to me, young man. Do you remember when you rode the horse to town in the middle of that thunderstorm to save my job and our grape harvest?"

A slow smile began to curl at the corners of Bartolo's mouth. "I helped you pull that branch out of the drain."

"Yes, you did. Saved my backside, you did, or both of us would be out looking for a job."

Franco cracked the backs of the horses as they headed to town. "I'm going to need more of your good work, Bart, if we're going make the Martellino wine the best in all of Tuscany!"

CHAPTER 16

LUCCA, DECEMBER 1918

One week after Elena's funeral, Franco walked outside and saw a lone figure sitting in the vineyard. He knew it was Isabella. He wanted to walk out and greet her, but something told him she wanted to be alone, so he continued on to the courtyard where Sister Anna was mending clothes.

"What's Isabella doing?" he asked.

"She's in mourning," Anna said softly. "I just told her about Elena. She and DeAngelo were so sick I decided to wait until they were strong enough before telling her of Elena's passing."

Franco watched Isabella sitting all alone, legs crossed, hands on her knees, palms up, as if offering herself up to some invisible deity. He turned back to Anna. "Why doesn't she go to church to pray?"

"Bella is not religious, Franco." Anna put down her needle and thread and looked up at him. "Yet she is the most spiritual person I've ever known."

"But she was raised in a convent."

147

"And we've had many debates about my Bible," Anna sighed. "Some parts she accepts; others she does not. Bella can quote scripture perfectly that makes sense to her."

"What makes sense to her?"

"Only love. She doesn't believe in sin, or hell, or the wrath of God."

Franco thought back to the horror he had seen in the war. He had seen man at his worst. "Her God is not one I'm familiar with."

"But it's a source that she's deeply connected to, Franco." Anna then nodded to Isabella. "This is her Elijah moment."

He gave a confused look.

"There's an Old Testament story about Elijah meeting God at Mount Horeb, and it explains the nature of a person's relationship with God. In the story, a great wind blew, but God was not in the wind. An earthquake shook the ground and fire followed, but God was not in the quake or the fire. Next came the sound of sheer silence. It was in the silence that Elijah met God. That is where Isabella is this morning. Some call it prayer, others meditation. Some need church; Bella needs nature. This is where she will leave her sorrow."

Franco avoided working in the field until Isabella was finished with her meditation. It was about noon when she came in from the vineyard and walked to the Veneros. She held Angelina for several minutes. When they separated, Isabella wiped her friend's tears and kissed both cheeks. She embraced each of the Venero children and then looked at Franco. It was the same unblinking stare he had envisioned every day while he was away in Puglia. He welcomed her open arms and lowered his head to her shoulder, letting the breeze carry her hair across his face. He felt a peace he had not experienced in years. It was as if, for a holy instant, the feeling of grief left him.

The sound of the villa door closing interrupted their peaceful moment. It was Susanna, wearing a fashionable dark gray outfit. She appeared to be in a hurry as she nodded to Isabella. "DeAngelo is still recovering from his illness, and I can't be exposed to him just yet. I have responsibilities in town and need you to stay with our boy for the night. Giovanni has gone to Florence to meet with men who are interested in buying our wine."

Isabella's mouth fell open in shock. "But I'm needed back at the convent. I—I have responsibilities also."

"I've already talked with your Mother Superior, and those duties can wait. I need you here." She hesitated a moment, knowing Isabella would be vulnerable to her next words. "And DeAngelo needs you as well." She then smiled sweetly, got into her car, and headed to Lucca.

Franco couldn't believe what he had just witnessed and turned back to Isabella, whose sad eyes continued to follow Susanna's car.

"I don't understand," he grumbled. "You're more than honest with me, and even Signor Martellino, but you just allow—"

Suddenly Isabella collapsed into Franco's arms. The weight of the last two weeks, of recovering with DeAngelo and learning of Elena's death, was all too much, and now she released it all onto Franco. He held her and searched for words, any words that might comfort her, but found none and simply let her cry. When her heavy sobs finally slowed, she raised her head and forced a smile.

"I'm sorry," was all Franco could think of saying.

"No," Isabella whimpered. "I've created this problem."

Franco knew exactly what she meant. "She takes advantage of you because she knows you'll do anything for her son."

"I do love him—and I don't want DeAngelo to grow up and be like his mother. But I can't protect him. I can't keep him from learning the lessons he's supposed to learn."

"He's learning from you too, Bella."

"And he's learning from his mother."

"What? How to be selfish?" She raised a hand to stop him, but he could not stop.

"She's a cold woman only interested in herself! I can't believe she didn't go to Elena's funeral!"

His words made Isabella stiffen, and they stood in silence for a moment.

"Susanna's afraid," she finally whispered.

"We're all afraid of something, Bella."

"Not all of us," she said, as her eyes continued to stare down the hill at the dust trail of what was left of Susanna's escape.

Franco gazed out over the Martellino land from the vineyard to the olive grove, and finally rested on their beautiful villa. "You'd think everything she could ever want is right here."

Isabella only nodded as she headed to the villa to look in on DeAngelo.

CZ   ZO

"I tell you, my friends, our great country needs a new direction, a powerful fist that will not back down to the demands of outsiders!" Alfredo Obizzi shouted as he raised a glass to salute the party at the Piazza Napoleone in Lucca. Obizzi was proud to have been asked to speak at the historic square. On this day in late 1918,

Lucca was hosting a gathering of political leaders who would address Italy's future.

"What we need is unity!" Obizzi roared. "Caporetto showed us that we must be strong! We must become one! We must take our open hand and pull our fingers together into a powerful fist! ONE voice demanding obedience from peasant to king!" Obizzi shook his glass so violently that wine splashed onto the piazza bricks.

"Yes!" shouted the political leaders.

When he finished, a mayor from a nearby village pulled Obizzi aside and whispered in his ear, "The Socialist Party is growing every day. Do you think the peasants will revolt and demand their own lands?"

Obizzi repeated a quote he had heard recently. "'Our rulers have given us life without grandeur and a war without leadership. We need a new and decisive direction.'"

Obizzi moved on, shaking hands and greeting others with slaps on the back, but his focus changed to a dim-lit corner of the piazza. He walked to the edge of the square, took the woman's hand, and kissed it.

"Ah, my beautiful Susanna, I was hoping you'd come. These governmental elitists bore me. Can you escape with me tonight?"

Susanna smiled as she took the hotel key from Obizzi's hand and moved back into the crowd.

ogni ogni

Franco knew he would be busy all the way through the new year. The wines were poured into barrels for aging, and it was time for the second racking. Franco, Angelina, and Bartolo pumped the wine from one barrel to another, and then Rosa and Elisa removed the solids from the bottom of the barrel, so it could be used again. Franco was hoping some of the light reds might be ready in six to eight months, while the full-bodied reds would probably need a year or two.

There was also the work in the vineyard, cutting back the buds on the young plants and training the vines to grow on the wires. Even though Franco was working fourteen-hour days, he still felt he was falling behind. He was spending much of his time with the grapes while Angelina and her children worked the olive grove. The end of the war had at first brought joy, but soon revealed a depressed economy throughout Italy. The lira was sliding on the international money markets, and with men returning from the war, unemployment was rising. Giovanni had sold the previous year's wine, but not at the price he had hoped. Still, Franco thought the Martellino wine and olives had great potential, but if the vineyard was truly to be successful, he would need to speak with his landowner about hiring one or two more men.

℞ ℥

New Year's Day came and went. Because of work, Franco saw little of Isabella except at Sunday Mass. She always seemed to be busy cooking or taking care of DeAngelo while Giovanni and Susanna attended the service.

Franco inhaled deeply and tried to concentrate on the Sunday sermon at San Frediano. The priest spoke about the war being some metaphor for life, but his message only stoked the coals of disappointment that still burned inside Franco. He forced his mind to think of anything else, and soon his thoughts drifted to the green-eyed girl who usually attended this service. He glanced around the church but couldn't find her, so he slipped out during communion and headed for the kitchen. DeAngelo was the first to see him and came running into his arms.

"Hey, Little D.!" Franco exclaimed. "What's cooking at the Bella trattoria this morning?"

Isabella winked as she pulled two clamshells out of a basket. "Some friends brought me a gift from the beaches near Venice. I thought I'd make a nice little *spaghetti alle vongole.*"

"Sounds delicious."

"It should be. The spicy chili pepper sauce I made has Anna coming in every five minutes for another taste."

He dipped his finger in the sauce and brought it to his mouth. "It is spicy. Like you."

She pinched his stomach. "You look tired and hungry. Why don't you come for dinner?"

"I'd love to," he laughed, "but I'm so far behind I've asked Sister Anna to petition God for an eighth day of the week!"

She gave him a sour look. "Why don't you ask Giovanni to get you some help?"

"I've wanted to, but he has a lot on his mind lately. We're selling more wine, but not at a good price. I don't know if he can afford another worker."

"Have you thought about sitting down with a pencil and paper and writing down what the profit will be with just you and the Veneros working and then writing down what the profit would be with another big, strong, good-looking man like you working that vineyard?"

Franco grinned. "I'm glad you're finally noticing."

"Don't change the subject. Giovanni understands money, so you have to talk his language. Tell him you could spend all your time with the apricots, grapes, and wine, while the man you hire could spend his time with the olives, apples, and pears."

He raised one eyebrow. "We don't have any apple or pear trees."

"I have good seed from our trees in the convent garden," she said matter-of-factly, "and you have unused land near the creek that would be perfect."

He slowly nodded his approval.

"With the war over," she continued, "Lucca's olive mill should be running twenty-four hours a day. It's a win-win situation. You'll have the help you need," she then curtsied and pushed out her lower lip in a sad expression, "and then perhaps you could find time to join poor little me for dinner."

Franco gave DeAngelo a wink. "I like the way your second mama thinks, Little D.!"

"But since you're not dining with us tonight," Isabella shrugged, "I shall walk the walls with Paolo Reggiani. He's one of Lucca's bright young chefs, and he always makes time for me."

Franco's head snapped up as he realized Bella wasn't teasing. He tried to speak, but no sound came. Another sharp poke in the ribs brought him back to reality.

"Now write down your proposal for Giovanni to hire another man," Bella said as she handed him a pencil, "and tell him that you sold some of his wine to a restaurant in Lucca."

"I sold what to where?"

"You sold four barrels of the Martellino red to Paolo's restaurant." Isabella's twinkling eyes seemed to be taunting him. "You know, the man I shall stroll with on the walls of Lucca tonight."

Isabella then sashayed her hips as she walked out of the kitchen, giving Franco yet one more opportunity to change his mind.

CR ꙮ

Three days later Franco asked Giovanni to join him between the vineyard and the olive grove. He spread a map he'd drawn of the entire property, with detailed plans on how he would change their irrigation system.

"Not only will I improve the flow of the creek to your grapes and olives," Franco said, pointing to a vacant plot of land on the rise of a hill, "but we can expand your vines up this hill."

"If we're going to expand," Giovanni disagreed, "we should plant the new vines near the creek. That's where the water is, and the soil is much better."

Franco shook his head. "The low areas have cold air pockets and high humidity; therefore, the grapes would be at greater risk of disease. Grapes don't want good soil. They like a rocky soil that encourages their roots to reach down farther into the ground for the best flavor." He paused. "But I would like your permission to plant apple and pear trees in the rich soil by the creek."

Giovanni stroked his chin as he studied the hill for a long moment. "How many more hectares do you think we can add?"

"Four for the vines and two for the apples and pears."

A broad smile began to stretch across Giovanni's face as he realized the potential to his wallet. "You may hire the other man you say we'll need to expand. But I want him to prove himself as you did—the first three weeks without pay.

Franco laughed out loud. "Nobody's that stupid! Only a fool like me would agree to three weeks without pay!"

Giovanni chuckled. "Two weeks to prove himself, then."

"One more thing, signor." Franco had waited until the very end to seal the deal with good news. "We sold four barrels of your red to Trattoria da Giulio in Lucca."

"Well done!" Giovanni clapped his hands together. "That's one of our city's finest restaurants, and four barrels is an excellent start!"

As they walked back to the barn, Giovanni put his arm around Franco.

"I too, have made a sale. Ten barrels of our red to a seafood restaurant in Viareggio. I want you to take them there tomorrow."

CR SD

Franco drove into Viareggio late the next day and found the beachside resort in a festive mood. The town was known for its carnival that was held every January and February, and with the war finally over, the city was more than ready to party. As Franco turned his truck down the main road, he found himself in the middle of a parade. There were colorful floats with people dressed up and mimicking Italian politicians, military officers, and showmen. A group of soldiers high atop a float were passing around a bottle of whiskey and singing out, "If Lenin comes, we'll have a great party and go to the bosses and cut off their heads! Hi, ho, and the union will grow!"

Franco laughed at the silliness of the scene, but also wondered what direction his country was headed.

It was almost dark when he finally turned off the parade route, a bit unsure of where he was, squinting through the dim light to read the street signs. He took a right down an alley, trying to get away from the crowd, but that proved to be a dead end. As he backed up, he drove over a bottle that had shattered across the alley, and he pulled over to check his tires. Stepping down from the truck, Franco saw that three men had followed him down the alley.

"What have we here, boys?" said the biggest man as he wiped his mouth with a filthy sleeve.

His partner, a grizzled man with a scar across his cheek, pulled up the tarp on the side of the truck and smiled at the barrels of wine. "I believe we just struck gold, Bruno."

"This wine's already been paid for." Franco stepped between Bruno and the truck. "I don't want any trouble."

The third man circled around and lifted a barrel off the back of the truck. Franco started toward the thief but was shoved up against the truck by Scarface. Then Bruno slammed a fist into Franco's gut, dropping him to his knees.

"This wine is ours now," Bruno growled as he grabbed Franco's hair with one hand and pulled a dagger out of his belt with the other. Franco reached for the knife, but suddenly Bruno collapsed to the ground, blood gushing out the side of his head. A man moved from the darkness with a wooden bat in his hand and whipped it left to right, shattering Scarface's teeth and jaw. He fell to the ground, out cold. The third man dropped the barrel of wine and sprinted out of the alley.

Franco's defender stepped out from the shadows. "When the hell are you going to learn to keep your head down?"

Franco squinted through the darkness. "Sergeant San Stefano?"

The man lifted his left arm, showing a stump where his hand used to be. "No sergeant anymore. Even the Italian army doesn't take cripples." He then helped Franco to his feet.

"I thought you were invincible," Franco said. "What the hell are you doing here?"

"I was working on the floats and saw you drive by. I followed and thought you might need help when those three gentlemen escorted you down the alley." The sergeant, now Antonio, grinned, his white teeth shining in the dark. "It's the second time I've had to save your sorry ass."

Franco laughed as he opened the door to the truck, "Get in. You can save my ass again by helping me find the restaurant that bought this wine."

As they drove to Trattoria Martino, Franco told Antonio what had happened after Caporetto: of the deaths of Benny and Father Mario, getting a job at the Martellino vineyard, and his return to Puglia to see his parents.

Antonio's face tightened as he stared out at the darkness. "I thought all of you had been killed or captured. It was total confusion on the front. No one knew where anybody was. I can't remember the date, but we were defending the river when a shell landed near me. I woke up in the field hospital with my left hand gone and shrapnel from my hip to my knee. The medics sewed me up; the captain said 'thank you very much' and sent me home. But how does a one-armed miner from Sicily find a job? I've been wandering this country the last few months with other boys like me, who came home damaged by the war and are looking for work. That's what brought me to Viareggio."

Franco gave a look of disgust. "The politicians have no problem sending us to the front, but they want nothing to do with us when we return."

"To the rich, the mere mention of Socialism means the end of their glory; but to peasants like us, it's hope for our future." Antonio paused in thought. "I like to think of myself as a Social Democrat, because the extremists scare the hell out of me. They want the same thing that happened in Russia to come to Italy."

Franco said nothing, wanting his friend to continue.

"The Reds stormed the Winter Palace in Moscow, and many were killed. Now Italy's extreme Socialists want the same thing here—revolution." Antonio stared down at what was left of his left arm. "I'm tired of following some damn politician's ego."

Franco parked the truck at the back of the restaurant, and the two of them hauled the wine into the cellar. After the owner signed off, they walked back outside before Franco suddenly stopped in the middle of the street.

"Hey Sarge!" Franco grinned. "I've got a proposal for you."

Antonio cocked a brow in interest. "I'm listening."

"I need help at the vineyard and olive grove. And you need work."

"I'm still listening."

"Now I know you don't know a thing about farming, but you know how to lead and get things done. It's not much money, and you'll have to work for free the first two weeks to prove yourself to Signor Martellino, but it's beautiful land and good people. How about climbing back in the truck and checking out Lucca?"

Antonio scratched his chin as if he were pondering the offer, "I don't know, Franco. I really should consider all my options. There's that float on Third Street I've been working on, and I have a nice little bed in a box in an alley by a trash dump off Via dei Pini." Then he laughed out loud. "Hell yes, I'll join you in Lucca! I'll work a month for free to land a job!"

Franco's smile grew as he put his arm around his old friend. "Don't tell the boss that, because he'll accept your offer. Now let me show you Lucca!"

They jumped into the truck and headed east, talking nonstop. The sergeant was quiet for a moment as he looked down at his damaged left arm. "I was pretty low before Christmas, seeing so many people celebrating with their families, and I hadn't even heard from my mama after the war. It was a neighbor who told me she passed away two months before I came home. I had nowhere to go. One night I snuck into a church in Salerno and slept under a pew. The whole place was an eerie quiet. I woke up after midnight and walked around the chapel. There was one candle lit for someone's prayer that night, and there was a note next to the candle, as if it had been left for me. It was from Isaiah 41:13. 'For I the Lord will hold thy right hand, saying unto thee, Fear not; I will help thee.' So I lit a candle and asked God, 'Tell me what to do, Lord; tell me what to say,' and a thought came to me—I still have this one good right hand that can reach out and take His. So I grabbed hold of God's hand that night and told Him I would let Him lead the way. I know it may sound crazy, Franco, but my surrendering gave me hope, a feeling I haven't had in a long time."

Franco thought about Antonio's words as he drove toward the light on the horizon that was Lucca. He still wasn't sure if he was ready to trust a God he didn't understand. The church he had grown up in had talked more about sin than love, more about fear than forgiveness. Then he had met people like Father Mario, Sister Anna, Isabella, and now Antonio, who were prompting him to think differently. He felt as if his entire belief system was being turned upside down. Were his eyes and ears deceiving him? He had been through a terrible war, seen his brother die on a battlefield, and watched a disease take a child from her mother. He was still angry about why those things had happened, and he was not ready to forgive a God who had taken them.

"What have I learned?" he whispered.

"I hope you learned to hire the right man!" Antonio grinned.

Franco sat up straight. He had forgotten there was someone sitting next to him when he uttered the question.

"I want you meet this girl in Lucca—Isabella."

"She's special?"

"I've never met anyone like her. She challenges every belief I've ever had."

"What do you mean?"

"Bella believes we're on earth to learn lessons," Franco said with a far-off look, "and that everything that happens to us, whether we consider it good or bad, is simply an opportunity to get closer to God."

Antonio smiled. "I like your girl already."

"Oh—she's not my girl," Franco quickly replied, and then he nodded to the light on the horizon. "She belongs to that beautiful city."

There was a full moon reflecting off the walls that seemed to welcome them inside as Franco drove through the Porta Santa Anna, proudly pointing out churches and towers and piazzas to his old friend. He parked along Lucca's main shopping street, the Via Fillungo, and headed to the heart of town. The foot traffic was rather heavy with locals enjoying fine meals and wine. As they passed by one of Lucca's most famous restaurants, Buca di Sant'Antonio, Franco glanced inside, and his eyes went wide. There in the middle of the restaurant was Isabella, dining with the young man she had teased him about. Paolo Reggiani. A dull pain in Franco's chest began to tighten as he watched Paolo dip his bread into olive oil and offer it to Isabella's waiting mouth. As she took the bite, she spotted Franco and waved. Franco jerked his head away and tried to act as if he hadn't seen her. He couldn't think straight. He wanted to run, but his feet moved as if stuck in cement. Isabella, though, had seen him and ran to the door.

"If it isn't the great winemaker, Franco Carollo! Come, join us!"

Antonio stopped dead in his tracks and stared. "Who is that vision of loveliness?"

"That"—Franco's shoulders slumped forward—"would be Isabella."

Antonio grabbed his jealous friend and hauled him toward the restaurant. "I'm liking this town of yours more and more, brother!"

Antonio was the first through the door and gave Isabella a hug that lifted her off the ground. "Hey, baby! I feel like I know you! Franco's been telling me all night long about his bee-yoo-tee-full EE-sa-bella!"

Franco turned red, but Antonio was on a roll. "I'm Antonio! Franco and I served together in the army! I saved his skinny ass more times than I can remember!" He held up his left stump for the two of them to see. "Franco came back with more of himself than I did, but we had a coincidental rendezvous in Viareggio, and now I'm going to work with him at the Martellino vineyard!"

"Delightful!" Isabella clapped her hands. "Perhaps you can get Franco to cut his work from one hundred hours a week to eighty so he can have a fifteen-minute dinner with me!"

Antonio reached across the table to shake the hand of an annoyed Paolo. "You, sir, must be Franco's competition! Nice firm handshake—good hair—I understand you can cook—yes—you'll be a difficult man to beat!"

Franco wanted to crawl into a hole, but Isabella grabbed his hand and pulled him down to sit next to her.

"What are you guys eating?" Antonio peeled back the napkin over Paolo's bread basket and smiled. "It's my favorite! Sourdough and olive oil!" He tore off a piece of bread and waved it in front of their faces. "You know, there's an art to dipping. The bourgeoisie like to dip very quickly to get just a hint of the taste." He barely touched the bread to the oil and tossed it into his mouth with a frown. "In Rome, they do it with a twist of the hand so the flavor spreads along the bottom of the bread. That's all in the wrist." He wiggled the bread around and offered it to Paolo, who reluctantly took it. "But I'm from Sicily! We don't dip! We dunk!" He ripped off a big piece of bread, poured more oil on the plate, and swirled the bread around, covering almost the entire piece with oil before stuffing it in his mouth. "*Mama mia*, now that's what I'm talking about! That's the way we enjoy olive oil at the San Stefano house in Sicily!"

Isabella's laughter brought tears, while Franco and Paolo were a little stiff to Antonio's humor.

"Tell me, Bella," Antonio beamed. "Did Franco tell you he's going to put me in charge of the olive grove?

"No!"

"Yes! Now, I've never farmed a day in my life, but I guarantee you by this time next year they'll be talking about Antonio San Stefano's oil in this very restaurant!" Antonio grabbed Paolo's elbow and lifted him out of his chair. "My new friend with the perfect hair, it appears we're out of bread. What do you say you and I go pull some hot stuff out of the oven?" Antonio winked at Franco as he pulled Isabella's date across the room to the kitchen.

Franco turned a sharp shade of red as he turned back to Isabella. "I'm—I'm so sorry," he stammered. "It wasn't right for us to barge in on your date."

Isabella smiled sweetly and brushed a lock of Franco's hair away from his face. "Don't ever say that, Franco. You're always welcome at my table. It's been difficult to get you away from work, so I'm thankful for such a happy moment."

Franco could still feel the touch of her fingers as they left his face.

"Antonio's a good man," he nodded, recovering himself slightly. "He saved my life in the war and may have saved it again tonight when we had trouble with some men in Viareggio."

"I like his energy. I think you made a good decision."

"Giovanni wants me to plant five more hectares—"

"No talk of work." Isabella cut him off. "That's all you do. With the schedule you keep and my being ill, you never told me about your visit home!"

Franco told her the entire story, from his father's anger to their time of forgiveness to the wonderful healing his family had experienced before he left. He told her of the train ride home, when he had learned of the war's end outside Florence, and how he had wanted nothing more than to get back to Lucca and share the joy with her.

She stared at him for a long moment, and then her mouth curled into a teasing grin. "You came to the convent to see me?"

"Yes—uh," he stuttered, once again a bit embarrassed. "Of course."

"Why?"

Franco squirmed uncomfortably, avoiding her eyes. "Well—I—I missed you."

Isabella touched his chin and raised his head to meet her gaze. "And I missed you, too."

"Comin' through! Hot bread! Watch yer nose and toes!" Antonio broke Franco and Isabella's sensitive moment by barreling through the restaurant with hot sourdough in his right hand and a white napkin over his left stump. A resentful Paolo Reggiani followed behind him with the olive oil.

Antonio made sure everyone at the surrounding tables could hear him. "So how's Paolo's competition doing over here!"

Isabella laughed as she took the hot bread from him and placed it on the table. The four of them ate and talked and laughed the rest of the evening—Franco, of course, now feeling a little more comfortable and a little less jealous about interrupting Isabella's dinner with Paolo Reggiani.

CHAPTER 17

ITALY, 1919

G iovanni was not pleased. He called Franco into his study for an explanation. "A one-armed man? With no experience in the field? That's your idea of help?"

"But—"

Giovanni quieted him with a flip of his hand. "Italy has all these able-bodied men coming home from the war, and you hire—this broken-down soldier?"

"Signor Martellino, Antonio knows how to work. I'll stake my reputation on him."

"Yes, you will. I don't think you realize the importance of this next season. We're finally making sales into towns our wine and oil have never been to in the past, and that momentum must continue."

"It will, signor."

"You've made some very interesting decisions in your time here, Franco. You almost ruined your first harvest by not reading the weather correctly, and now you hire a cripple to help you in the field."

"Sergeant San Stefano is no cripple!" Franco straightened up in anger. "Countless lives were saved in the war because of his leadership. Even with one hand, he'll do the work of three men."

Giovanni studied him coolly. "He'd better, Franco. Each of you had better do the work of three men."

☙ ❧

Franco jerked the barn door open and found Antonio sitting on a wine barrel in the corner. Franco gave him a quick, distracted glance and snatched a pair of shears off the wall.

"Well, don't you look happy?" Antonio laughed as he picked up a baling hook from the floor and walked over to Franco. "Did the boss question my suspicious physical resume?" He held the baling hook in front of Franco's face. "Does he think this one-armed Sicilian pirate is going to steal all of his precious grapes?"

"This is serious," Franco frowned. "Giovanni says this is a critical year, and he won't hesitate to fire both of us if sales go down."

Antonio held up his damaged left arm. "Then I shall work my fingers to the bone for you!" Grinning at what he thought was a fine joke, he raised the hook in his right hand. "If that doesn't work, I'll fish for dinner."

Franco did not laugh; instead, he handed the shears to Antonio. "Take these to Angelina. I'll work the vineyard today with the Venero children while Angie teaches you about olives—" He paused and then let out an exasperated exhalation. "Just listen to her, Tony—Angie hasn't had it easy. She lost her husband in the war and a child to influenza."

Antonio quickly snapped to attention and saluted. "Yes sir, Private Franco. I'm off to defend the olives!"

Franco could only shake his head as he wondered if Giovanni had been right about his decision to hire an old army friend. Antonio did nothing to calm his worries when he put the shears on his shoulder and marched out of the barn.

CR   ₧⁂

Angelina had a polite yet serious expression on her face as she walked with Antonio out to the olive grove. He was conscious of her mood and decided to drop his playful bravado and simply wait for her to speak.

"We produced twenty percent more oil last year than the previous season," Angelina finally said. "But our profits were down ten percent. This farm can't afford that again."

He nodded but said nothing.

She led him into the grove and turned to face him. "Before we begin, I want you to take a moment and look at the trees we'll be working with today."

Antonio did so out of respect, but wasn't quite sure what this woman wanted him to see. He remained quiet as Angelina touched the leaves of a tree. "I think the olive tree is the most beautiful tree in all of Italy. There are days in the spring when the blue-gray color of the wood against Tuscany's bright green land takes my breath away."

He waited a moment before commenting. "My mother told me about one back in Sicily that was over five hundred years old."

"There are many older than that throughout Tuscany." She knelt down and grabbed a handful of dirt. "This land may not be good for wheat and corn, but the olive tree has deep roots which allow it to thrive in the rocky soil."

"Sounds as if difficulty brings out the best in an olive tree."

A slight smile began to crease Angelina's face. "Yes, and that's where the olive tree is similar to our grapevines. They both seem to like the tougher ground. It's as if the richer the soil, the more prone to disease both are."

Antonio remained quiet as Angelina moved her hand to the roots. "The olive tree can withstand much—drought, disease, fire, bad soil—and still be productive for centuries if it is cared for properly."

Antonio wondered if Angelina was talking about an olive tree or herself. She stood up and continued her instruction, pointing out the proper pruning technique, what branches needed to be cut back, and at what angle. She went on about pests and disease and talked about when to harvest and when to cure; then she gracefully moved the shears in her right hand, cut back a branch at the desired angle, and handed the limb to Antonio. "Did you know olive oil has long been considered sacred?"

Antonio gave her nothing more than a slight nod that told her she was welcome to continue.

"Like anything, it needs a little work for the great taste to be realized. That's why we treat it with lye or brine or ferment it before it becomes oil. But everything on the tree is useful. A friend of mine even uses the leaves for a medicinal tea."

He rubbed his chin. "So, what you're saying is the olive is considered sacred because adversity brings out the best in it."

Angelina nodded and stared past the orchard as if her thoughts were elsewhere. "The olive has long been a symbol of wisdom, hope, and peace," she whispered.

Antonio thought it all right to lighten the mood. "I didn't know I'd be getting an agricultural and spiritual lesson today."

She laughed. "I'm sorry for carrying on, but the success of this vineyard is very important to my family."

Antonio did a quick sign of the cross. "You made me a believer, Sister Angie. So when do we spread the holy water on the grove?"

She gave him a playful shove and handed him the shears. "Franco said you are a jokester, but vowed you'll be a good worker. So, let's at least act busy. I don't want Signor Martellino questioning our work ethic."

"Work ethic?" Antonio grinned mischievously as he followed her to the first tree. "Nobody said anything about work ethic in my job interview!"

CR   SO

"These damn liberals have no backbone!" Alfredo Obizzi grumbled as he read the newspaper in his hotel room in Lucca. "The same fucking leadership that failed us in wartime is now screwing us in peacetime."

Susanna came out of the bedroom, buttoning up the neckline of her dress. "But our Prime Minister, Orlando, and his assistant, Sonnino, were pushed around by the other countries at the conference. What could they do?"

"Don't be so naïve, Susanna!" Obizzi threw down the paper. "They were simply pawns in an international chess game. That damn American president refused to let Italy work out our own territorial agreement with Yugoslavia."

Susanna was confused. "Why would they let someone who isn't from Europe be part of Europe's treaty?"

"Because America helped win the war," Obizzi hissed. "Orlando and Sonnino tried to bluff the council by walking out of the meetings in Paris."

"And they made the treaty without them?"

"Of course! Those idiots thought their bluff would work. That the world leaders would beg them to come back to the table and write the treaty for them."

"Instead—"

"Instead the other countries signed the deal and shit on us! I tell you, Orlando's government is finished!"

Susanna poured each of them a glass of wine. "We need a strong man running our country."

"A man like Mussolini!" Obizzi said, and then he picked up the paper from the floor and searched for the correct story. "Benito's the only Italian with the courage to criticize other world leaders. Listen to what he said: 'Italy's future policy must be directed toward establishing a modicum of justice between us proletarians and the fatter and more bourgeois nations of the world.'"

Susanna wasn't sure what a proletariat was, but it sounded impressive, so she nodded in approval. "Those are indeed the words of a true leader."

"We need a new and younger enthusiasm for the cause. That's why Mussolini wants to lower the voting age to eighteen. His charisma will get the young vote."

"But what of the older and richer powers in our country?"

"Don't worry—Mussolini wants a corporate chamber in the Senate, so those who know how to work will be making the important decisions. He'll also make sure we have a strong international policy, so what was signed in Versailles will never happen again."

"What about Tuscany, Alfredo? How will he support us landowners?"

"That's the one area where I disagree with Benito. He wants our farms either to be extremely productive or to be given to peasant cooperatives." He paused and laid a gentle hand on her shoulder. "With a preference, of course, that those lands go to soldiers returning from the war."

A long moment passed as he waited for Susanna to understand the ramifications of his statement. "Now, you know I like helping our soldiers, Susanna, but I'm afraid that if you give the peasants too much power, Italy could experience the same troubles that have torn apart Russia."

"What happened in Russia?"

"The workers revolted and the tsar was overthrown. A thug named Lenin has taken over and encouraged peasants to intimidate wealthy landowners and demand pieces of their property."

"Oh my!" Susanna gasped, her face going pale. "The two men my husband hired are former soldiers."

Obizzi gave a condescending glare. "Do you want an uneducated peasant to take what's yours simply because he fought in the war?"

"Of course not."

"Then make sure your husband controls his workers."

The thought angered her. "Giovanni has given them free rein to run the vineyard while he's been away selling our olives and wine. They've also planted unnecessary fruit trees that won't benefit us for years. What should I do?"

"Get rid of them," he said with a huff. "You can find any number of peasants who will work for far less than your husband is probably paying. Unless, of course, you want to share the profits of your Martellino brand with simple commoners."

She slowly nodded. "I'll take care of it."

Obizzi was silent for a moment and then made sure she caught his gaze. "Why don't you have your husband check the Trieste market?"

"Trieste? Where's Trieste?"

"It's just past our northeastern border. There's a Fascist I've been trying to connect with in that region. His name is Antonio Mosconi. Perhaps your husband could do business with him. That connection could benefit both of us—politically and financially."

"How?"

"Trieste isn't like liberal Tuscany, Susanna. Mosconi is actually trying to control the Serbian ingrates."

"There's trouble in the northeast?"

"Trouble always reveals opportunity." He stared at her intently. "Imagine controlling the entire wine trade in that region."

The thought of wealth brought a smile to her face.

"And if there's trouble in Trieste," Obizzi said as he pulled her in and kissed her full on the lips, "that may be exactly what you need to rid yourself of the workers who want to steal your land."

CR   SO

At two and half years of age, DeAngelo loved playing in the church garden, imitating Isabella as she dug in the dirt and planted her seeds. After watching the boy's enthusiasm, Isabella designed a plot next to her garden where the little boy could raise his own vegetables and fruits. It was a small five-by-ten-foot enclosure, squared off with wooden slats. The pair had gone to the Serchio River for the best soil, hauled it back, and planted tomatoes, peppers, basil, parsley, and oregano.

"Little D., your plants will be the spices that bring to life the meals we cook for the Blessings Convent," Isabella said as she sat on the ground and pulled the boy onto her lap.

Rosa joined them. "I could smell his basil all the way from the kitchen."

"Perfect for tonight's pasta."

DeAngelo giggled, "Pasta yummy."

Isabella hugged DeAngelo to her. "And your basil will bring out all the yummy flavors that we want!"

She ran her hand over the soil. "We planted the basil next to your tomato and peppers, Little D., because the basil will help the flavor of its neighbors, and who doesn't like a hint of basil in a tomato?"

DeAngelo clapped his hands in delight.

"And since flies and mosquitoes don't like basil, the plant helps your garden in another way."

As she picked off a basil leaf and held it up to the little boy's nose, Franco peeked out from the kitchen window and winked at Rosa to stay silent as he tiptoed behind Isabella and DeAngelo.

"Now parsley is a different matter," Isabella continued. "It can be very picky and needs a lot more attention."

"So what should we do?" asked Rosa, trying to hide her smile.

Isabella pulled a tray of seeds over in front of DeAngelo. "I soaked the seeds for two days in cool water and then poured boiling water over the soil plug."

"Why?" Rosa bit her lip.

"Because parsley seeds have a chemical in them that can prevent the plant from sprouting, and the hot-cold process works to get rid of the chemical. I then plant parsley in the sun next to the peppers and tomatoes, and together they bring out one another's wonderful flavors."

"I believe that if you were a plant, Bella," Rosa giggled, "you'd be basil."

Bella raised one brow. "Why would I be basil?"

"Because you bring everyone together."

Franco could keep quiet no longer, "Rosa is one perceptive young lady."

"Franco!" a surprised Isabella cried out, and then she lifted DeAngelo up to him.

Franco kissed the boy on each cheek and asked, "Which vegetable would I be, Little D.?"

Rosa whispered into the boy's ear, and DeAngelo repeated, "To-ma-to."

"Tomato?" Franco asked. "Why am I a tomato?"

Rosa tried to keep from giggling as she spoke for DeAngelo. "Because tomatoes like being around basil, and everyone knows you like being around Bella."

Franco turned red with embarrassment and then reached down to help Bella up.

"Well—I guess that makes me a tomato."

"A bright red one, too." Bella grinned.

He smiled, recovering himself slightly. "I hope you don't mind my dropping by without an invite. I had to deliver some wine to Buca di Sant'Antonio, and I thought, why not check out Little D.'s garden?"

Isabella bowed to him dramatically, "We are so honored to have the hardest-working man in all of Tuscany give us a few minutes of his precious time."

Franco lifted DeAngelo onto his shoulders and offered Bella his arm. "Do you have some precious time to go for a walk?"

"Indeed!" Isabella nodded in a royal way as she took his arm, and the four of them headed up the east-gate steps.

"Do you know the story of the walls?" she asked.

"Just the little that Angie has told me."

"Well then, count your blessings, because Sister Anna used to lecture me daily about the history of Lucca's three walls."

Franco gave her a quick glance of amusement. "Educate me, Professor Bella."

"It all started with the pre-Christian walls some two thousand years ago," she began as they walked toward the Villa Guinigi and botanical gardens. "The medieval walls were built in the thirteenth century." She spread her arms wide. "And finally, they constructed the ones we walk on today."

"How long did it take?"

"One hundred five years!" she exclaimed. "They broke ground in 1545 and finished in 1650. These Renaissance walls were designed to fight off an assault from Florence and the Medicis. But Florence never attacked, and this great project was never really put to the test."

Franco looked across the massive ramparts to the plane trees that lined their path. "People sure spend a lot of money trying to defend themselves from what they think might happen."

A peaceful smile lit Isabella's face. "Fortunately, we can be as free from fear as we want to be."

Franco gave a puzzled look until Isabella pointed at the Cathedral of San Martino. "Have you seen the Sacred Visage and the temple created by Lucca's famous sculptor, Matteo Civitali?"

He shook his head no.

"You should stop by and see the Volto Santo," Isabella said. "It's a beautiful dark-colored carving of Christ on the cross with a mystical history."

Franco pointed up to DeAngelo. "You have our undivided attention, professor."

"As legend has it, the great Nicodemus was instructed through a vision from God to carve the crucifix and leave it in a cave in the hills of Lebanon. Many years later, a deacon in Lebanon received a vision to go to this cave and load the carving onto a ship. He did that and was astonished to see the ship sail away without a crew."

Franco gave a look of doubt. "This sounds like something Sister Anna made up."

Isabella put her hand on her heart in mock reverence. "I trust everything Anna tells me."

"Go on then."

"In the year 742, a ship arrived at the port of Luni, some forty miles northwest of Lucca. When the citizens approached, the ship moved away." Bella jumped in front of her audience as if a great Shakespearean actor on stage. "But the gallant citizens of Luni would not be denied! They captured the ship, and much to their amazement, they found no crew on board!" Bella's eyes and mouth went wide in melodramatic shock. "Mystified by their discovery, they sent for the bishop of Lucca. When the bishop arrived, he was so inspired by the carving that he arranged to have it transported to the diocese in Lucca."

Franco rolled his eyes. "How convenient."

Bella thrust a finger to the sky. "That's what the citizens of Luni also said! They contended that their city should have the carving. After much debate, the bishop suggested they place the carving in a chariot, hitch bulls to it, and let the bulls decide where the carving should go." Bella spun around and acted as if she had a heavy yoke around her neck. "When the bulls set off for Lucca, the Lunise people accepted this as the will of God. The bishop transported the carving to San Frediano for the night to determine where it should go the next day."

"Don't tell me there's more?" Franco said with more than a hint of sarcasm.

"Yes! The following morning the crucifix was gone! The bishop ordered an immediate search of the city and found it in San Martino, where it remains to this day."

Franco laughed out loud. "God willed it from Freddy to Marty!"

Isabella put her hands on her hips and gave him a wry smile. "Don't take everything so literally, Franco. I love the divine nature of the story—the ability to let go and listen to the Holy Spirit. Whether the legend is true or not doesn't matter. It's about listening to your heart instead of your head."

When they approached the steps that would take them back to the convent, Franco lifted DeAngelo off his shoulders and let Rosa run ahead with the Martellinos' little boy. As they walked down the stairs, Isabella slipped her hand inside Franco's. Her touch stirred him, and he was suddenly aware of the fullness in his heart. There was a peace and familiar comfort that came to him whenever he was in her presence, and when they reached the garden he turned and met her gaze. His hand seemed to rise by itself and brush her hair from her face. She smiled knowingly, lifting her chin to meet his first kiss, and—

"Where in God's name have you been?!" It was Susanna, storming out the kitchen door of the convent.

Isabella turned in surprise. "I'm sorry. We went for a walk."

"Do you always leave without telling anyone where you're going? DeAngelo is my son! Not yours!"

"I'm sorry for not telling the sisters where we were, but quite frankly, signora, I'm not your servant whom you can—"

"Enough!" Susanna snapped, and then she turned to Franco. "And you, winemaker, are like all the others. You want your own lands but aren't willing to work for them. My husband pays you well, and now, when he's away, you neglect your responsibilities so you can flirt with this—this—orphan!"

"Signora Martellino!" Franco cried out in shock, but before he could say more, Isabella squeezed his hand and stepped in front of him. "It was my mistake, Susanna. In the future, I'll tell the sisters where I am."

"Yes, you will!" Susanna picked up her son and then snapped her fingers at Rosa. "Come with me, young lady."

Rosa winked at Isabella and whispered over her shoulder, "I think I'd better go with parsley."

Isabella bit her lip to keep from laughing.

When Susanna left, Franco didn't speak for a long time. He watched as his landowner's wife slammed the convent door and pulled DeAngelo to her car. Franco turned to face Bella. "I've asked you this before—it's something I just don't understand. Why do you let her take such advantage of you?"

"That's your perception, Franco. I see it differently."

He let out an exasperated groan. "And you believe that if you listen with compassion you can help her to be less selfish."

She cocked one brow at him. "You make a good point about listening with compassion. It's worked very well for you with Giovanni."

"What are you talking about?"

"He's changed since you and Antonio started working there. He's more understanding, both as a boss and as a father." She snapped off a leaf from the garden and handed it to him. "I think you just might be the spice he needed."

The comment made him grin, but he turned the conversation back to her. "So will you deal with Her Highness differently?"

"I'll talk with her," she nodded, "but I don't want you to get involved. I don't work for her. You do. Your defending me could cost you your job."

He let out another sigh. He knew she was right. He had seen the vindictive side of Susanna, and it was not pretty. "All right," he said, and then he started for the gate. "I'd best be on my way before Queen Susanna feeds me to the lions."

Isabella grabbed his hand and pulled him forward, giving him a quick kiss on the cheek. "Thank you, kind sir, for finding just a little bit of time in your busy day to spend with a—a poor orphan like myself."

Franco laughed and then took a step back and bowed dramatically. "The pleasure was all mine, m'lady. For this tomato always enjoys spending time with a little basil."

CHAPTER 18

AUTUMN 1919

A ntonio pulled out a bottle of Martellino oil and grinned at the label that read "Susanna's Best." It boasted an artist's rendition of a woman who had an uncanny resemblance to Giovanni's wife, scantily clad, hanging from an olive branch as she sipped from a bottle of Martellino olive oil. Giovanni had asked his winemaker to stop by a popular Lucchesi restaurant, Bosco's, with a sample. When they entered the trattoria, Franco was surprised at the large crowd for a Wednesday evening. Many of the men there were peasants like him, field workers, and men from the olive oil and textile mills. The jovial Antonio had already made friends in town, and those at the bar greeted him as if he were a long-lost brother.

"Sergeant Tony!" several shouted when they saw him enter.

Antonio swept his arms out and bowed at the waist.

"Gentlemen, gentlemen, I am your humble servant!"

Franco rolled his eyes as Antonio grabbed a plate from a nearby table and uncorked the top of the Martellino olive oil with his teeth.

Splashing the oil onto the plate, he roared, "You must try this sensational oil, my brothers! I have slaved the last two months under the iron fist of this Franco tyrant—to give you my masterpiece! This oil is better than virgin! I would call it 'Virgin Mary' if not for the church! So instead I call it 'Three Virgins I Met in Viareggio'!"

The restaurant erupted in laughter until Franco pulled Antonio aside and whispered in his ear, "This is last year's oil, and we're supposed to give it to the proprietor."

Antonio gave Franco a wink. "The guys here don't know when it was made, and believe me, if the boys like it, the owner will love it."

Antonio took off dancing from table to table, spreading his olive oil for all to enjoy, but kept the last of the bottle for the owner, Cesare Bosco, who had been watching Antonio's routine from the kitchen.

"Signor Bosco!" Antonio cried out when he saw him. "You have the perfect trattoria for my people!"

Bosco only smiled as Antonio pointed to the crowd.

"Look how all my friends delight in the divine oil I now want you to savor."

The proprietor broke off a piece of bread and dipped it into the oil. After a proper tasting, he then checked out the crowd, which had perked up since Antonio's arrival. "This is very good."

Antonio placed his hand over his heart and with great drama grabbed a napkin and acted as if he were wiping tears from his eyes. "Signor, you have made a broken-down army sergeant weep tears of joy."

He then turned to face the crowd, thrust out the stump where his left hand used to be, and shouted, "Gentlemen, the bastard who walks among you has worked my fingers to the bone so that you may deflower the Virgin's greatest olive oil!" The laughter rose as Antonio roared. "Yes! I can see it in your faces! Your happiness is my reward! *Grazie, grazie, grazie!*"

⚭

An embarrassed Franco came over to shake the hand of the trattoria owner. "Signor Bosco, I'm Franco Carollo, the winemaker and vineyard manager for Giovanni Martellino. He asked me to bring you a sample of his olive oil in the hope that we might be able to do business in the future. I'm proud of our wine and oil, and our prices are very competitive."

The owner looked around the room at the men now singing and dancing with "Sergeant Tony" and said, "If your buddy can bring his friends and personality back to my trattoria, I believe we can work together."

"Thank you," Franco said, and then he looked around the room before turning back to Cesare. "Why such a large crowd on a Wednesday night?"

The owner chose his words carefully. "Socialist Party gathering. These men are tired of the rich not sharing any of their profits, and they want to unionize. The owners tell the government that sharecropping is working, but that's simply what the rich want the politicians to believe."

Franco's mouth twitched slightly. "But aren't the landowners and industrialists also taking a risk?"

"The government doesn't bail us commoners out when we fail or return from the war damaged men. But they bailed out industrial firms like Ansaldo and Ilva."

When Franco didn't answer, Cesare asked, "On what side of the fence do you stand, Franco Carollo?"

Franco looked out at the men reveling in the trattoria. He didn't know what to say because many of them were like him; they had defended their country and now had come home only to struggle to find jobs in a down economy. Finally, Franco said, "I'm not sure what to think anymore. I just want to work."

Cesare put a hand on his shoulder. "These are tough times, my friend, but the Socialist movement is growing. We thought we had a friend in Mussolini, but he's like a chameleon, constantly changing his words to be accepted by whatever company he's in. And now he's surrounded himself with some very dangerous people—anti-Socialists who scare people into believing that unions are the beginning of Communism."

Franco continued to stare out at the crowd before turning to shake the owner's hand. "I'll give what you say some serious thought and discuss it with Antonio."

"Do that, Franco, and while you're at it, return tomorrow with five cases of Martellino oil."

Franco thanked him and started to leave, but Antonio grabbed him. "Where do you think you're going?"

"Home," he shrugged.

"No, you're not." Antonio pulled him back inside the bar. "You need to spend time with these people, Franco. They're called neighbors. People who live next to us. People who might help you enjoy life a bit more—and buy some of what we're selling."

Antonio poured him a glass of beer and took Franco from table to table, introducing him to new friends and future clients.

They left after midnight, riding the cart back to the vineyard, with Antonio singing his favorite Italian songs as loudly as he could. Franco sat quietly until he nudged his friend to settle down.

"I have something serious to ask you."

Antonio quieted.

"I looked at all those men at the trattoria tonight, and I couldn't help but think—how many horrible memories did they bring back from the front? Did we win the war? Did we lose the war? How does life just go on after what we witnessed on the Isonzo? And now, God bless them—they all gather to see if a union will get them out of the dire straits most of them are in."

Antonio chuckled as he snapped the reins to the backs of the horses. "Franco, you are one deep thinker. Do you know why the men were there tonight? Or why we go to church, or why we get together and play or cheer for our football teams? Because it might be that rare moment, that two- or three-hour stretch, when we can forget about the war, forget our troubles, and laugh, and brag, and be with our brothers!"

"Did we win the war?"

"Who cares?!" Antonio yelled out. "Enjoy these moments! You never know when they'll come again!"

Franco sighed. "You're probably right."

"Of course, I am. I mean, look around you. Look at all you have to be thankful for! You have a good job. You work for—a fairly decent boss. The Veneros are loyal and hard workers"—he paused for effect and straightened up proudly, "your roommate is the most handsome and brilliant fellow I've ever met. And now—you have Isabella."

"I don't have Bella."

"Arrgh," Antonio growled. "Everyone sees the way she looks at you! You should rejoice every day of your life that a woman like Bella would show even the slightest interest in a poor buffoon like you!" A wicked smile then began to light Antonio's face. "I'm jealous of you, Franco Carollo. That girl is like the stars in the sky, like the sun slowly setting across our vineyard, like the—"

"Quiet!" Franco laughed. "What can I do to shut you up?"

"Answer me! Do you doubt she likes you?"

"No. I just don't think I'm—good enough for her."

"Enjoy the moment, Franco! Stop thinking for just one second and enjoy the moment! It's all we have!" Antonio again tapped the reins as he turned the horses up the hill. "But as for the union meeting tonight, I think I'll bow out for a while. I feel an underbelly of anger growing in our country, and I'll not be a part of that anymore. Anyone who sings about love, I'll sing with them." He nudged Franco. "Have you heard the love song about the peasant boy and church cook?"

He stood up on the front seat of the wagon and spread his arms. "Ohhhh, Franncoo and Bella were kissing under a full Tuscan mooooooooon!!!"

Franco could only shake his head as he resigned himself to the fact that Antonio's musical teasing was going to wake all the new friends he'd just made.

ca   so

There were no happy songs or delight in Susanna's life, for those fantasies would certainly be followed by disappointment. Her life was filled with small dissatisfactions and constant comparisons. Those with money were to be envied; those without were to be chastised. Her displeasure intensified as she paced her bedroom, thinking about what was taking place in the vineyard. As she pulled back the curtain to watch Antonio chasing Angelina's girls back to the barn, all she could think of was the ledger in Giovanni's study, the bottom line that showed a third straight month of barely breaking even. Mussolini's plan to give unproductive farms to peasant cooperatives worried her, and if her family was going to suffer, then the vineyard workers should suffer as well.

The Venero girls' squealing laughter from outside only made Susanna angrier. With so much gaiety now taking place in the field, she was sure these workers were taking advantage of her husband. They didn't want Giovanni to be successful. They wanted his land. No, Susanna thought, Alfredo was right—these new workers must go. Yet she had said nothing to her husband and wasn't quite sure why. Her life had become too complicated. Before, she'd had only herself to worry about. Now there was a husband, a child, the farm's financial dilemma, and Alfredo. It was all so confusing, and with it came guilt. The guilt of not measuring up—of not being the mother, the sister, the wife, and the friend she wanted to be. That guilt kept her from seeing the joy taking place in the field.

She stormed into her husband's bedroom. "Giovanni, we must talk."

He gave a tired exhalation. "What is it, dear?"

"Have you been watching what's going on outside?"

"Yes, the work is getting done and the profits are up."

"Up from where?"

"They're up, Susanna, and much of the credit goes to Franco."

"Well, I don't like that other fellow with the one arm. He ingratiates himself with everyone, is always being foolish, and then—watch him turn on us, join a union, and take our farm."

"You can't be talking about Antonio," Giovanni said. "The man does more than his share and has fun doing it. His enthusiasm has picked up everyone on this farm."

"Don't you see, Giovanni, he's an imposter. Why, I heard in town the other day that—that he and Franco were seen at a Socialist union meeting."

She then repeated what her lover had told her the week before. "Did you know that despite our country's economic troubles, the days lost to strikes by agricultural workers leaped by four hundred percent in the last year? That is a recipe for disaster."

He cut her off. "Why do you do this, Susanna? For the past two weeks, I've been to Florence, Pisa, Prato, and Pistoia, selling our wine and oil. We've had no trouble from any of our workers, and this farm seems to finally be moving in the right direction."

"Well, I don't like them. They're going to steal what's ours."

"Nonsense. Franco is a loyal employee and a talented winemaker. Antonio is better than I thought he'd be, and I've been tough on both of them. Our sales are up, and people are talking about our Martellino red. Now please, let me rest."

Because Susanna knew her husband was vulnerable, she did not back down.

"You know I'm thankful for how hard you work for our family, but you've been away and haven't read the papers. Our economy is struggling, yet even though the workers make more, they still want to strike." She paused to make sure she had Giovanni's attention. "I told you Franco and Antonio were seen at union rallies. After all that we've worked for, they could break us. I won't allow that to happen. I—I want them gone."

A drained Giovanni fell back on his bed. "All right, Susanna. I'll talk with them tomorrow."

CR SO

The morning brought a pleasant Tuscan sunshine. The ground glistened a tannish green, and a cool November breeze swept through the olive trees. Franco surveyed the orchard and knew it was a perfect day to pick. Angelina pulled an olive from a twisted, gnarled branch. "We couldn't have asked for better weather leading up to today, Franco. This will be a good crop."

He nodded. "The goddess Athena said the flesh of an olive is as bitter as hate and as scant as true love—"

Angelina finished his sentence. "And that it takes hard work to soften the olive, to squeeze the green-golden blood for our sustenance."

"My father used to pray for days like this." Franco smiled. "And when they'd come, he said it was a reminder to be grateful."

Josephine walked up with DeAngelo. "I couldn't keep the boy in the house any longer. He was up before dawn, wanting to join you."

DeAngelo showed them his pillowcase tied to his waist. "Pick olives."

Franco swept the boy off the ground. "You shall be the first picker, Little D.! Now go find the best olive in our grove and start the harvest!"

Franco put DeAngelo down, and the little boy raced off to the grove, searching for the perfect olive. Antonio came from the barn with the sacks and nets for the harvest and put his arm around

Angelina. "Have I told you, Signora Venero, that you look absolutely ravishing in this dismal gray horse blanket you're wearing this fine morning? What did you use to make it—a wood loom?" Angelina pushed him away as he picked at the sleeve of her shirt. "I think I saw this same fabric in Signora Martellino's garbage."

This time the shove wasn't playful, and Antonio escaped into the orchard singing, "My Angeleeena—bringing fashion to the peasant women of Tuscaneeee!"

She couldn't keep from laughing. "He's such a silly fool."

"Tony may play the fool," Franco said as he handed Angelina an olive sack, "but you should see him on the road. He's the best salesman I've ever seen. He has everybody laughing."

As Angelina watched Antonio chase the children around the olive grove, her smile grew. "It feels good to laugh again."

DeAngelo ran from tree to tree, picking an olive off a branch, holding it up to the light, and then shaking his head before moving on to the next tree. Each picker was waiting by a tree for DeAngelo to complete his mission, and finally, after inspecting a green-golden orb, he lifted the olive to the sky.

"Let the harvest begin!" Antonio roared.

Rosa and Elisa shrieked with delight as they raced up the ladders to begin their picking. The jovial banter stretched from one tree to the next as the nets around the pickers' waists quickly filled with olives that bulged all the way down to their ankles.

"Company, halt!" Antonio shouted from atop an olive tree when he saw Isabella and Sisters Anna and Emmilia cutting across the field, carrying burlap sacks. "Reinforcements have arrived!"

The three women came to attention and saluted in the general direction of Antonio's voice. The old sergeant was hiding behind a branch as he continued to tease. "The Martellino Army doesn't recruit slackers. You nuns either pick a man or pick an olive."

"I'm shocked to find you here, Sergeant!" Sister Anna called out as she searched the trees for Antonio. "I thought most Sicilians went to confession AFTER they stole from the farm!"

"Tell me, Anna," Antonio yelled back. "How does our pope know when he's in a Sicilian church?"

Anna covered her mouth to hide her grin. "I don't think I want to hear the answer."

He yelled so everyone in the orchard could hear him. "When he sees nuns with machine guns hanging from their belts!"

Then she saw him, peeking from behind a branch with that huge, idiotic grin on his face. As the laughter rang through the orchard, Anna ran over and shook his ladder. "God will forgive me if you fall and break your neck!"

"Keep shaking, Sister!" Antonio roared as several olives fell from the tree. "You're helping me find the perfect olive for tonight's martini!"

ᘒ   ᘔ

It was a wonderful time on the Martellino farm that afternoon. The air was crisp and clear, and the green from the soft summer rains was two months gone, revealing now the golden fields of autumn in Tuscany. The blue-gray olive trees stood out against the tan hills, their branches pulled low with the weight of their fruit. And the olives were perfect—big, juicy Frantoio olives with their robust fruity flavor and bold aftertaste. Those who worked the orchard that day were one big happy family—laughing, singing, and picking olives late into the afternoon until they heard a cry from Antonio.

"Incoming!"

Franco turned to see Giovanni headed their way. There was a troubled look on his face. Franco stepped down from his ladder, hooked his olive net to a branch, and walked over to greet his landowner.

"I want Antonio here too," Giovanni said sharply.

Franco waved for his coworker to join them.

They stood silent until Antonio arrived, and then Giovanni asked with an irritated tone, "Do you men like working here?"

"Yes sir, very much," Franco answered, a bit confused.

"I believe I've been fair with both of you. I've honored our agreement and even let you make decisions with the crops."

"Have we done something wrong, signor?"

Giovanni's face tightened. "Where have you been going late at night, Franco?"

"We've been here—getting ready for harvest," Franco said, still puzzled. "This time of the season we always work late. The only times we've been gone were to run errands for you—or to stop by the market or church."

"Then why have I heard that both of you were seen at a Socialist meeting that's trying to start a union in Tuscany?"

Franco was stunned. "Signor Martellino, I swear I have no idea what you're talking about."

Antonio started to chuckle, which only gave rise to Giovanni's anger.

"I don't see anything funny about your being part of a union, Antonio. If you're involved, you can clear out your things right now. I'll not have anyone work here who is trying to undermine the success we've had."

Franco looked worried as Antonio continued to laugh.

"Don't blame us," Antonio grinned. "You were the one who sent us to the Socialist meeting."

Giovanni glared at him. "What are you talking about?"

"Remember when you sent us to Bosco's to have the owner sample your oil? We walked IN on a Socialist meeting. But I guarantee you, the only union Franco and I were interested in starting was the one to get Cesare and the boys to buy your oil. They loved it, by the way, and they want more."

Giovanni's mood softened as Antonio continued. "I don't know about you, Signor G., but I don't think I'd trust anyone who would want a lame-brain like me to be a part of their club. Franco, maybe—but not me."

The joke started Giovanni laughing. "I couldn't believe it when I heard it, but I had to make sure." He slapped Antonio on the back. "Please accept my apology. I shall deliver that oil to Bosco's myself."

"The oil can wait," Antonio said as he put his arm around Giovanni and turned him toward the grove. "Take a look at your little boy out there picking olives for his papa. Why don't you join us?"

At that moment DeAngelo saw his father and held up his pillowcase stuffed with olives. Giovanni laughed out loud and looked at the olive net in Franco's hand.

"May I?"

"Absolutely." Franco smiled, and together they headed to the grove to join the harvest.

From the second story of the villa, Susanna watched the entire scene unfold. She had been waiting impatiently for her husband to fire their winemakers, but now she stared in disbelief as he helped his workers pick olives. What had gone wrong? Why had Giovanni ignored her demands about having these men removed? And now, what would she tell Alfredo?

CHAPTER 19

CHRISTMAS 1919

I t was time, Franco thought. It was time his parents came to Lucca to see their son's work. His heart was full as he sat on the wooden fence outside the barn, contemplating the Martellino farm's success. He thought the wine he was blending had great potential, and now the olive harvest had been a success, with orders coming from as far away as Bologna and Modena. His landowner was pleased and had even sent railway tickets to his mother and father to visit for Christmas.

Franco inhaled the crisp December air as his eyes studied the snowcapped Alpi Apuane mountains to the north. There was something pleasant about this land. From the soft, round-flanked mountains he now enjoyed to the rolling hills lined with vines and orchards, everything about it seemed to say, "Welcome home."

He jumped off the fence when he saw Giovanni step outside. "Beautiful day, eh, signor?" he called out.

"And getting better every minute!" Giovanni said and headed his way. "One of the best markets in Pontedera placed an order for both our wine and oil."

"That's fantastic," Franco beamed.

"I'd like to celebrate!" Giovanni clapped his hands together. "What do you say we invite the entire neighborhood for dinner?"

"I'll have the children decorate the front of your house."

"That's a grand idea," Giovanni said. "Invite Bella as well. Tell her I'll pay her to pick out the food and prepare a Christmas feast."

◌◌   ◌◌

Franco had the children working on the project that very afternoon. They framed each doorway with evergreens and hung holly from the stone entrance to the driveway. Antonio built a manger in the front yard, and the Venero girls decorated it with colored paper and gilt pine cones. Bartolo filled the top shelf with fruit, candy, and small gifts for the neighbors' children as Franco posted a sign at the top of the road that read, "Welcome to the Martellino party."

"This celebration sounds expensive," Susanna grumbled as she handed her husband a piece of string to finish an evergreen wreath. "Please tell me you invited only our neighbors."

"It's the holidays. I invited everyone!" Giovanni smiled as he tied the last branch down and then hooked the wreath to the front door. "I can't remember a Christmas when I've had so much fun."

She gave a loud exhalation and reached over his shoulder to straighten the wreath. "Remember, Giovanni—Franco, Antonio, and the Veneros—are—our—workers. You pay them—to work."

"I'm not paying them anything, darling. These decorations were all Franco's idea." He nodded to the end of the driveway, where Bartolo was lifting DeAngelo up to tack colored paper onto an ornament. "Just look at the joy on your son's face. He loves this."

"I don't want DeAngelo spending so much time with the Veneros," she said through clenched teeth. "Our son is very bright, but you let him play in the dirt with our workers instead of teaching him to read and to do his figures."

"DeAngelo's not even three years old, Susanna. Let him be a little boy."

"Leadership takes discipline, Giovanni. And that begins at birth."

He turned and gave her a narrow eye. "Can't we just enjoy the day, Susanna?"

"Of course," she answered quickly. "But when our boy is old enough, I'm going to find a good school that will help him reach his full potential."

Giovanni seemed not to hear his wife as his gaze fixed on DeAngelo, who was proudly attaching a ribbon to another ornament. He smiled.

Susanna watched her husband closely and then took his hand and brought it to her lips. Her heart beat a little faster as she thought now might be a good time to bring up another subject which had long been on her mind.

"One more thing, dear. We need to discuss this vineyard's future."

Giovanni said nothing, but there was a hint of caution in his eyes as he looked at her.

"Our business may be improving," she said with a bright smile, "but I think it's time to expand. I believe now would be a good time to look into the Trieste market."

"Trieste?" he said slowly, as though thinking it over. "That's a long way from here."

"Yes, but I was reading in the newspaper about all the exciting opportunities there. The new Italian government is just now taking control of the northeast, and Trieste could be wide open for our goods."

Giovanni rubbed his chin. The idea did sound interesting. Perhaps it was time to branch out and test other markets. The chance to strike it rich was appealing.

"I'll be in Florence next week with wine buyers," he nodded. "I'll look into it."

Susanna patted his arm and gave him a quick kiss. "Thank you, sweetheart. I think this could be a very exciting time for our family."

Before she could walk away, Giovanni reached for her hand and nodded to the children, still working on their final Christmas decoration. "Let's join them, darling."

She stood still for a moment, wondering how she could respectfully decline his offer to engage in such frivolity, and then a stiff smile forced its way across her face. "Of course," she finally said. "That would be lovely."

CR &O

Franco was like a five-year-old on Christmas morning as he paced the train station outside Lucca, anxiously waiting for his parents' arrival. When they finally stepped from the train, Franco almost ran over a porter in his sprint to greet them.

"Mama! Papa! Welcome to Lucca!"

They hugged briefly, and Franco carried their luggage to the back of his wagon.

"So, this is the town you've been writing us about?" his mother said as she scanned the neighborhood.

"No, Mama!" he answered quickly. "The real Lucca is inside the walls!"

He helped his mother and father climb up on the wagon and snapped the reins to his horses.

As they left the rail station, Franco stood up on the wagon board, impatiently waiting for the walls to come into view.

"There they are!" he finally gushed, and his mother giggled as she pulled him down next to her.

"Ahead is the Porta San Pietro," he rattled on. "Our southern gate that was built almost four hundred years ago."

Maria bit her lip to keep from laughing, but she was delighted at her son's enthusiasm. They passed through the walls and headed down Via Vittorio Veneto, which only escalated Franco's pride as they approached a large square lined with plane trees.

"This is the Piazza Napoleone!" Franco beamed. "It was redone for Bonaparte's sister when she lived here in the early 1800's! Look over there! That's the Palazzo Ducale! It goes back to the 1300's, when Castruccio Castracani was lord of Lucca!" He again snapped the reins to hurry his horses. "Let me show you the Cathedral of San Martino. Isabella told me they carved the Virgin Mary's family tree on one of the outside columns. It's magnificent!"

Maria laughed out loud. "Slow down, Franco! We've just arrived. We have plenty of time for you to show us your beautiful city."

They headed out the northern gate and past the Serchio River, up into the vineyards, Franco talking nonstop, until they finally reached the lane that turned down to the Martellino villa.

"Impressive," Bernardino said.

It was the first time Franco's father had spoken since stepping off the train, and he seemed to be studying the Martellinos' two-story villa.

"Family money?" Bernardino asked as he stepped off the wagon.

"The Martellino wines go back four centuries," Franco answered.

His father's gaze went to the barn and workhouse, both recently painted.

"That's your work, isn't it?"

"Yes, sir."

Bernardino gave a proud smile. "I could tell. It has your attention to detail." He pointed to the red barn door, trimmed in white. "Not one drop of red on white."

Franco laughed. "My papa used to tell me that if a job's worth doing—"

Bernardino gave his son a playful shove: "—it's worth doing right!"

"Welcome, parents of the Prince of Puglia!" It was Antonio, busting out of the Venero cottage with an open bottle of wine in one raised hand and Angelina chasing after him with bread and cheese.

"How do you like my place?" Antonio called out. "It was a mess until your son hired me. The grapes tasted of cow dung, and the olives were as hard as Carrera marble until I signed on—"

Angelina tore off a piece bread and shoved it into his mouth. "Don't believe a word out of this Sicilian shark's mouth. He'd take credit for Jesus walking on water if he were here today."

Antonio spit out the bread and feigned a look of innocence. "You know it was a Sicilian who stole those wooden shoes so Jesus could perform his miracle."

Franco stepped forward to make the introductions, lips pursed tightly in an effort to hide his grin. "This is the sergeant I wrote about in my letters." He then nodded to Angelina. "Signora Venero is the sane one."

They all laughed and then sat down and ate, drank, and visited for a spell, until Franco's patience ran out.

"Angie and Tony—uh—I'm sorry—but would you mind if I showed my parents the property?"

Antonio's eyes went wide in mock surprise, and he grabbed Angelina's arm. "Did we just get a promotion, Angie? Did the Prince of Puglia just ask OUR permission on a most important decision? This is a subject I must give my full attention."

Franco shook his head and turned to his mother. "He thinks his job is secure because he can make people laugh."

"My job is secure because I can fake that I'm in charge!" Antonio winked at Maria. "Watch closely how I control your son." He narrowed his eyes and stared at Franco. "No! You may not take your parents to the vineyard. Instead, they must clean our wine barrels and shine Signora Martellino's many shoes."

Angelina smacked Antonio on the back of his head, their laughter carrying across the courtyard to the villa, prompting a disapproving glare from the second-floor window. Those in the courtyard did not see Susanna watching.

"Don't listen to this old windbag!" Angelina giggled as she gave Antonio a playful shove and then smiled at Bernardino. "Go see what your son has created."

Franco led his parents past the barn to show them the Martellino land. The vast Tuscan valley sprawled out before them—rolling hills, gullies, and a creek perfectly framed by rows of brown vines whose canes had been cut precisely by Franco the week before.

"Beautiful land," his father said. "How many hectares?"

"Fifty."

They walked into the vines, where his father knelt down, brushed away the dry leaves, and dug his fingers down into the roots. His smile grew. Franco could tell his parents were proud of him and all that he had accomplished as wine manager of the Martellino farm.

"Do they appreciate your work?" his mother asked.

"I think so. Signor Martellino has become more interested in what goes on in the field ever since his son, DeAngelo, was born."

"And his wife?"

"The signora has little interest in the farm, and I rarely see her. Isabella says I should be patient with her."

Maria raised an eyebrow at her son. "We keep hearing you talk about this Isabella. Is she someone special?"

Franco turned red. "We're friends, Mama—just friends. You'll get to meet her tomorrow."

CR BO

He took them down to the cool, musty cellar of the barn to show them his most recent work. "This is the most promising time since I've been here," Franco said as he pulled back the curtain to reveal the barrels. "We've sold to restaurants in Lucca and towns throughout Tuscany that we've never been able to get into before."

His father inhaled deeply through his nose, taking in the aroma of grape coming together with the oak. He noticed hints of vanilla, clove, and smoke. He smiled. "The wine will be good."

"But we still have to be able to market and sell it," Franco said. "That's where Antonio comes in. He may play the part of a fool, Papa, but he's a great salesman."

"Does your landowner agree?"

"Giovanni doesn't feel comfortable giving us that kind of control yet. But in the rare times he's had us deliver to a new market, if Antonio is with me, we always come back with a sale."

They left the barn at dusk, the sun setting low in the southwest, a soft orange glow peeking through the dark olive trees. Franco smiled proudly. "I'm glad you're here. I've wanted to share this with you for a long time."

Bernardino put his arm around his son's shoulders. "You've done an excellent job, Franco. I wish Benny were here to share—" His father caught himself, but Franco's quick smile calmed him.

"I wish he were here too, Papa."

03　80

The Martellino Christmas Eve party began with Giovanni handing the Venero children gifts of money and dark chocolate. Susanna followed behind, offering only an uncomfortable smile and a pat on the head. There was a part of her that wanted to be involved, but she struggled with the words to be included. It was as if she were a guest in her own home. Suddenly, DeAngelo grabbed his mother's hand and pulled her to the children's game of *lupo delle ore*. As she watched DeAngelo count out his steps and stumble at the edge of the carpet, a pang of jealousy bit her when he dove into Rosa's arms. And when she turned to see Angelina and Antonio talking with her husband in the corner, it only made her feel more alone.

Seeing her discomfort, Franco picked up a box of matches and walked over.

"Excuse me, signora—we would be honored if you would light the Ceppo."

Her eyes suddenly brightened. "Why yes, thank you. I'd—I'd like that. My family followed that tradition when I was a child."

"Then you know the rules." Franco handed her a match. "The person who burns the Yule log makes a toast and expresses her wishes for the new year."

Franco poured a glass of wine, handed it to Susanna, and then whistled to get everyone's attention.

"Quiet, everyone! The lady of the villa is going to light the Ceppo this year!"

Susanna felt all eyes on her as she raised her glass.

"To family—may our 1920 wines be even better than 1919's."

Everyone cheered. DeAngelo ran to his mother and hugged her. Franco held up his glass of wine to toast Susanna. "Thank you, signora. Thank you for opening up your heart and home and inviting us to be part of your Christmas."

 os so

The sun rose on Christmas morning of 1919 to a heavy frost that covered the grounds. Franco had been in the vineyard, checking to make certain the roots were well covered in leaves. He found no damage and returned to the courtyard to find DeAngelo waiting for him, all dressed and ready for church.

"What do you think Bella made me?" DeAngelo asked excitedly.

Franco tousled the little boy's hair. "I don't know, Little D. You're going to have to be patient."

"Last year she made me an apron to help in the kitchen."

"And you did a wonderful job with—"

Suddenly the villa door opened and out stepped Susanna, wearing a shimmering dark-green dress, pearl necklace, and matching earrings. DeAngelo ran to his mother and threw his arms around her legs. "Mama, what do you think Bella got me for Christmas?"

She peeled his hands away from her dress as if they were diseased.

"DeAngelo, this is Mama's best dress—please be careful."

"But Mama, what do you think she—?"

"I don't know, child—perhaps a book."

"I hope it's shears, Mama! I can help Franco with shears!"

She paused and looked down at her child. "Yes. Shears. How dignified."

Then she lifted DeAngelo into their car, and together with Giovanni they began the drive to San Frediano. The Carollos and Veneros followed by horse and wagon.

CR ❧ SO

They had just begun the Liturgy of the Word when Franco noticed Isabella's absence. Of course, he thought, she was busy preparing her traditional Christmas meal of *cennone*: spaghetti with anchovies mixed with fresh broccoli, fish, and herbs. He so wanted his parents to meet her. Isabella was the most interesting person he had ever met—thoughtful, confident, pure. He had seen how others were drawn to her as if they, too, wanted what she had.

He let out a long breath of impatience and tried to listen to Father Federigo's sermon. The man had one of those voices that would put a frightened cat to sleep. He spoke slowly, enunciating each and every word, eyes bulging as he droned on. He was saying something about Jesus being the one mediator between God and man. Now it was time to pray. Finally. Franco knelt down and clasped his hands together, absentmindedly tapping his pinky against the back of the pew. His mother reached over, put her hand on top of his, and said in a voice barely above a whisper, "I'm looking forward to seeing her too."

When the Mass ended, Franco hurried everyone to the Blessings Convent. He glanced at his image in the window, ran a hand through his hair to smooth it, and opened the door. He wanted to go in last, still a bit apprehensive because he wasn't completely sure how Isabella would receive them. He heard her before he saw her, that happy sound of joy, welcoming everyone she met while dishing her *cennone* to those in line. Then suddenly she stopped and looked his way, her face lighting like a candle.

"Mama and Papa!" she cried out, and then she ran across the room, dodging churchgoers and their children. "You must be starving after having to eat Franco's cooking!" She hugged Bernardino and Maria with an embrace that surprised both of them. "What did he serve you? Grape leaves and boiled olive pits?"

Maria laughed. "Angelina made sure we were taken care of."

"Come." Isabella put her arms around them and led them over to Sisters Anna and Emmilia. "I want you to meet my friends."

They visited for a bit until Isabella felt a tug on the back of her skirt. It was DeAngelo, standing with an expectant look on his face.

She dropped to one knee. "Merry Christmas, Little D.! May I help you?"

He shuffled his feet and gave her a hopeful look. "Present for me?"

"Was I supposed to get you a gift?" she teased.

DeAngelo stuck out his lower lip in disappointment.

"Ah, now I remember," Isabella smiled. "Why don't you show Franco's parents your garden while I find that little something I have for you?"

As DeAngelo led Bernardino and Maria over to his garden, Susanna watched Isabella pull a gift from under the table. The scene made her feel guilty, and she suddenly saw herself as a very little girl, so small she had to reach high for her father's hand. He had always been there for her; he had always remembered the holidays and birthdays her mother had forgotten—until her mother had pushed her father away. And now she was doing the same thing, only to her son.

She watched with envy as Isabella snuck up behind DeAngelo and snapped a leather belt around his waist. On it hung a wire cutter, a tiny trowel for working in the vineyard, and small shears. The look on his face was all Susanna needed to know that Isabella's gift was perfect for her son. DeAngelo spun around, searching for his parents.

Alarm shot up Susanna's spine when he spotted her and ran over.

"Mama, look! I be like Franco!"

But instead of sharing in his delight, she snapped. "I don't want you playing in the dirt!"

She immediately regretted her outburst and reached for DeAngelo, who backed away. Then, with his head bowed, he shuffled off to find his father. In that moment Susanna saw her mother, bitter and judgmental; the guilt overwhelmed her, and she withdrew back against the church wall. She knew she shouldn't go, but she needed something, anything, to change the way this dreadful day was going.

"Damn you, Alfredo," she said to herself. "I don't want to—but I need you!"

CR SO

Bernardino was smiling to himself as he followed Isabella on a tour of her small convent garden. He let her talk as she moved from plant to plant, touching the leaves as if they were long lost friends. This was a woman, he thought, who seemed to understand, and perhaps even enjoyed, the challenges that come with life.

"A garden is a perfect example to show us that happiness is a choice we must make," Isabella said. "While some may be unhappy about rain spoiling a picnic, at the same time a farmer might be thankful for the moisture to nourish his plants."

He studied her face for a moment. "My son says the plants respond to your touch."

"I just give them love," she laughed. "I know there will always be good seasons and bad."

"So a bad crop doesn't bother you?"

"Who determines what's good and what's bad? We judge too often with our eyes rather than our hearts."

She showed him one of her olive trees, a small, gnarly, seemingly lifeless growth in the back of her six-tree orchard. "Some of the sisters want me to cut down this olive tree because of the way it looks—but I'll have you know this old tree produces the best olives I've ever tasted."

Bernardino pointed to where two old branches had recently been removed.

"It looks as if the tree might be dying?"

"Those branches were sapping the tree of its energy to feed the younger branches that needed nourishment. If I hadn't cut them back, the entire tree would have suffered. It's a bit like us human beings. Sometimes we need to let go of the past to realize our potential."

Franco's father nodded. He knew why this young woman so enchanted his son, and when Isabella was called away, Bernardino hurried over to Franco and pulled him over to a quiet area. "If you don't marry that girl, you're an idiot."

"Papa!" Franco's eyes went wide in shock. "You just met her! Why—I—I don't even know if she'd have me!"

"Go get her, then."

Franco looked away, but his father's grip tightened on his upper arm. "Remember my words, son—the two most important decisions you shall make in your life are what you want to be when you grow up and who you want to spend it with."

"Papa, we're just—"

Bernardino put a finger to his son's lips. "I've seen your work at the Martellino vineyard, and you're an excellent winemaker. Now for the second decision." He leaned forward to make sure his son understood the seriousness of his words. "Don't you dare let her go. If you do, it will be the biggest mistake of your life!"

When Franco saw Isabella coming with two plates, he quickly changed the subject. "Papa, why don't you have some more of Isabella's *cennone*."

Bernardino swept the forkful of spaghetti to his mouth and closed his eyes as he savored the flavors. "Ah, Isabella, this is fantastic." He then winked at Franco. "Remember my words, son. This is a most important decision."

As Franco's face turned a darker shade of red, his mouth opened as if he were trying to find the words to quiet his father. Instead, Isabella took it as an opportunity to thrust a bit of spaghetti into his mouth.

"What important decision must Franco make?" she asked

Franco almost gagged on the *cennone* as his father laughed out loud. "He's a smart boy, Bella! He'll know what to do!"

☙ ❧

As the party continued into the afternoon, Isabella sensed anxiety in Susanna. The signora seemed distracted throughout the meal and spent much of the afternoon alone. While the children played on the steps of the walls and parents congregated beneath, Susanna backed into the shadows of a chestnut tree. The woman seemed to be in pain, and Isabella thought if she approached her in the right way, she might be able to help.

Susanna's eyes flickered back and forth as she stepped out the side gate. Isabella watched her move up the steps and decided to follow to see if they could have some time alone. She hurried up the stairs and caught a glimpse of Susanna moving along the path that led to the Piazza Napoleone. There was a purpose in her walk, some destination to be met, and just as Isabella was about to call out, Susanna suddenly stopped and turned toward a stand of plane trees. The look on her face sent a chill down Isabella's spine. Susanna's eyes were filled with longing as she stepped into the shadows, where a man took her in his arms and kissed her full on the lips. For a moment Isabella stood frozen, and then she quickly hid behind a tree. Flushed and breathing hard, she waited to calm her nerves before stepping away and hurrying back to the convent.

CR   SO

"Bella! Where have you been?" Franco's shout startled her, and she tried to hide her surprise.

"I'm sorry. I—I just stepped out for a moment."

"You look as if you've seen a ghost! Is anything wrong?"

"No—nothing."

"Little D. has been looking all over for you."

The little boy was seldom far from Franco and came running into her arms. "Bella, show Franco's mama garden!"

She took a deep breath to calm her nerves and joined Franco's parents.

"I understand you made this little garden just for DeAngelo?" Maria said.

"Yes." She swallowed hard, trying to straighten out her thoughts. "He—he planted everything."

Giovanni joined them, and you could see the pride on his face as his son pointed to his plants. "This parsley—this basil," DeAngelo beamed. "Plant by tomatoes—taste better."

Isabella looked up, only to see Susanna walking briskly down the steps, weaving her way through neighbors and friends to take her husband's hand.

DeAngelo pulled at Isabella's dress. "Bella?"

She didn't hear him.

He pulled again. "Bella, can you show Mama how make garden?"

But all of Isabella's attention was fixed on Susanna's hand in Giovanni's. Then her gaze traveled up Susanna's arm to find a smiling Susanna staring back at her.

"Bella?" The little boy asked again. "Can you?"

When she hesitated again, Susanna spoke for her. "That would be lovely, child, but Isabella's very busy at the convent, and I'm sure she wouldn't have the time."

DeAngelo looked up to his mother with sad eyes. "Please, Mama?"

Susanna glanced around the courtyard and saw that all eyes were watching her. "Why, yes, DeAngelo—" she stammered. "Of course—I'd love to."

CHAPTER 20

LUCCA, 1920

D espite Italy's economic hardships, the vineyard's wine and olive oil sales were holding well. Giovanni cut his prices from the previous year, allowing him to get into markets where he had failed in the past. He was also beginning to notice that his sales improved on the days he brought Antonio with him. His newest employee had a natural charm that seemed to make everyone around him comfortable and happy. It was as if the most prohibitive questions were allowed and everyone was at ease in his company.

Giovanni lifted the final barrel of wine onto the back of the flatbed and sat down next to Antonio to begin their drive to Pistoia.

"You were one of many returning soldiers looking for work after the war," Giovanni began this day's conversation. "How do you now see Italy's future?"

Antonio rubbed his chin as if he were giving his boss's question serious consideration. "I think the future will be better tomorrow."

Giovanni laughed. "Seriously, Tony."

"Well, I'm just an old soldier, so I relate things to the military, Signor G. In the army the generals lead and the soldiers follow. There are times a soldier may think his general has erred, but he can't protest his authority. We took an oath when we signed up."

"Franco said you followed orders very well."

"But that was the army. Being a citizen is different. Our government made laws to ensure that every Italian has a voice. If we don't like our jobs, we have the freedom to move to another one. If we want to join the Socialist Party or the Nationalist or the Republic, we're free to do so."

"And that's fair."

"But now we have this new Fascist Party, which is more like the military." Antonio gave a half smile, but his brows were drawn together in concern. "They speak; we obey. It bothers me when one speaks with such venom about the opposition."

"What do you mean?"

"The Fascists scream that they're the real Italians, the only true lovers of our country, and that everyone else is a coward who's trying to bring down our beloved Italy."

"Don't you think we need change?"

"Change, yes. But I'm not a person who sees only black and white. There are a multitude of colors—or considerations—between these two extremes, particularly after a war that tore apart our country."

Giovanni grinned. "And your plan, Senator Tony?"

"We need a peaceful solution!" Antonio banged his fist against the dashboard and laughed. "Fear always divides us, Signor G. It never brings us together. I believe the Fascists are dividers."

Giovanni was enjoying the discussion and countered, "But if Fascism is our future, we must learn to work with the new leadership."

"Will the new leadership be willing to have a sincere negotiation with the workers?"

"The unions have received a wage increase despite the nation's economic struggles, and still the workers revolt. If this violence continues, don't you think someone needs to step in and stop it?"

"But who is creating this violence?" Antonio cocked his head to the side and stared at his boss. "I've heard stories of Fascist squadrists bullying anyone who gets in their way, and beating Socialists for simply stating their opinions at rallies. Is that the way to unite our nation, or do the Fascists want the dissension so they can come in and give the impression that they're saving Italy?"

"It's a difficult time," Giovanni sighed.

"I just hope what's happening in the northeast doesn't infect the rest of Italy."

Giovanni straightened up as if taking a greater interest. "Those lands were given to us in the Treaty of Versailles."

"We did indeed win their lands in the war, but don't you think we should learn to get along with our new brothers instead of eliminating them?"

"What are you talking about?"

"There was a story in the paper last week about Italy's borders being 'afflicted by Austrian heritage.' The writer made it sound as if they had a disease."

Giovanni held his breath, concerned yet determined to make his point. "Susanna thinks there's great opportunity in the northeast."

Antonio's eyebrow rose skeptically. "Where's she getting her information?"

"I don't know, but she's taken an interest in the Fascist party and reads everything she can get about Mussolini."

"The Fascists have their own newspapers," Antonio frowned, "so they can twist information to make themselves sound as if they are saviors—or victims." He hesitated. "But when that writer said Italy must 'energetically cleanse Trieste'? Well, that's wrong."

Giovanni said nothing as he continued to drive.

"They're talking genocide, Signor G."

"That's one writer," Giovanni muttered, and he forced his mind back to the thought of finally striking it rich. "Trieste is a new market. Susanna and I believe they're hungry for Italian business, particularly wine and olive oil. This can be very lucrative for us."

Antonio drew a deep breath. "And very dangerous for anyone who sells there."

CR   &O

Antonio's charm prevailed at the Pistoia market. He made quick friends with a trattoria chef, and the result was the sale of three cases of oil and five barrels of wine. At lunch, he struck up a conversation with a gentleman who owned three restaurants in town, and when they discovered that they had served together in the Second Army during the Great War, the man bought five barrels of red and five of white. When they departed Pistoia, the Martellino truck was much lighter, and Giovanni's wallet was a bit heavier.

CR   &O

"How's my little boy!" Giovanni called out when he arrived home that evening and saw his son pulling a small wagon from the field.

DeAngelo came running, spilling half of the load of wood he'd been hauling. "Papa! I help Franco!"

Giovanni laughed as he picked up the small logs scattered behind the wagon and hugged his son. "I hope you worked up an appetite, because I'm starving!"

Susanna joined them, and Giovanni gave her a thumbs-up. "Much success, darling! We sold our entire load and made contact with a man who knows Trieste."

She gave him a quick kiss. "If we control that market, Giovanni, our wine will be the talk of Italy."

"Mama?" DeAngelo pulled at his mother's dress. "Show Papa olives."

She gave her son a pat on the head. "Not right now, sweetie."

"Please! I'll race you!" DeAngelo took off running, and Susanna waited for her son to get beyond the barn before she turned back to her husband. "I don't have time to play these silly games with DeAngelo."

"But you promised him."

"I—" she hesitated before moving on to the villa. "I've been busy with you away."

"Busy?"

"Yes. Helping with Italy's new direction."

"And what direction is that, dear?"

"Mussolini, of course."

He stopped before opening the door. "So you've been attending more Fascist Party meetings?"

"When I can." She glanced down at the ground. "But Isabella has been of little help. Why—I believe she's been avoiding me."

"I don't have to remind you, darling. We don't pay Bella, so she owes us nothing."

Her head snapped back up. "She does indeed owe us! She talked you into retaining the Veneros, and now—she's taking important time away from our winemaker."

Giovanni laughed out loud as he opened the back door and followed his wife inside. "You mean Franco has cut his hours back from eighty to seventy-five? Please, Susanna, their relationship is none of our business."

His defense of Isabella only irritated her more. "You don't see what I see."

"What do you see?"

"A girl who doesn't know her place. Isabella doesn't respect her superiors."

"My God," he muttered. "Now you sound like a Fascist. One voice. Everyone else? Get in line."

"That's what has always made our country great," she said very slowly. "From the Roman times to right now. We need strong leadership. Someone, I think—like Mussolini."

"That chameleon?" Giovanni groaned. "He changes his colors to suit whatever company he's in. Antonio believes Fascism is dividing our country instead of bringing it together."

"Now you're listening to our help?"

"Antonio fought for Italy."

"He's nothing but a Socialist sympathizer who wants what we have."

He shook his head. "You're wrong, Susanna."

"You don't read the papers?"

"I don't read—your Fascist papers."

"It's the truth!" she snapped. "The unions ask for more every week! You're spending way too much time with the workers and caving in to their deceit."

Giovanni tried to calm himself as he walked to the dinner table.

"Have you seen our sales, Susanna? They've grown since Franco and Antonio arrived. They deserve some of our profits."

"This is our vineyard. A vineyard they'll take from us if you're not strong."

"I've found none of your accusations about them to be true. They're two men who genuinely are interested in the success of this vineyard." He paused before adding, "As a matter of fact, I now look at them as part of our family."

"Family?" she said with a flip of her hand. "The workers are not our family. They're employees."

Giovanni's hand was shaking as he grabbed a bottle of Martellino red and held it in front of her face. "This is the wine that was the talk of Florence today! And Franco's the one who sweated in the fields, worked the vines, nurtured the grapes, and blended a wine the critics loved. This—wasn't—me."

"But it's our land and our grapes."

He gave a loud exhalation and poured her a glass. "I want you to try this and tell me it isn't better than the wine we produced before Franco was here."

She refused and then delivered the words she knew would cut straight to his heart. "What happened to the man who ruled this vineyard? Who didn't allow his workers to manipulate him? Oh, I'm sorry—that was your father."

Her words were like a punch to Giovanni's gut, and he jerked back so quickly he spilled some of the wine.

"Don't bring my father into this! He ran the vineyard his way, and I'll run it mine!"

"The workers respected your father."

"They didn't respect him. They feared him."

"I respected him."

"You barely knew him. And our wine never lived up to its potential."

"Because you were not strong enough."

Giovanni took another deep breath to cool his growing anger. His thoughts again went to Isabella as he recalled watching her in Lucca's market. Even in the chaos and frenetic whirlwind of buyers and sellers in the square, there was a certain peace and safety that drew others to her. He admired how calmly she listened to an impatient customer and then without even speaking seemed to soothe that person's anxiety. It was as if she listened with her heart rather than her ears.

"Why is it that everyone stops by Isabella's stand at the market?" he asked.

"I don't care."

"It's about her kindness, Susanna. That girl gives more of herself than anyone I know. And the goodwill she gives seems to return to her tenfold."

"And look how far it has gotten her. She's still penniless."

He sighed. "Are money and power all that matter to you?"

"I've tried poverty and I am unimpressed."

"Look deeper, Susanna. Something has changed on this vineyard ever since that girl stepped foot on our property. The Veneros' spirits have been lifted. Look at the joy our son has with her in the garden. His joy has changed me."

Giovanni's compliments of Isabella cut a nerve deep in Susanna, one that stabbed at her guilt and demanded defense. Instead, she simply shook her head and said in a condescending tone, "First you listen to a common peasant, Antonio, and now you listen to a three-year-old child. You're being taken for a fool, Giovanni—and the same will happen to our country if we don't get a man strong enough to lead us."

He shoved his chair against the dining room table and stormed out of the house.

Far off in the field, Giovanni saw Franco teaching DeAngelo how to clip off old leaves from the vines. A flight of sparrows seemed to dance around them in search of seeds that had fallen, and then they soared back up to the sky in perfect unison. It was as if all were one.

Giovanni stood frozen, hands gripping the iron gate while his eyes softened at the scene before him. It was then he knew what he must do. He would show Susanna how successful their vineyard could be. He would send Franco to Trieste.

ભ   છ

For seven dreary, rain-drenched days, Susanna listened to DeAngelo plead with her to take him to his garden at the Blessings Convent. When she finally gave in, they drove to town on a day when the sun came out and the spring flowers seemed to come alive that very morning. The whole valley floor and foothills were covered with yellow daffodils and purple azaleas swaying in the soft Ligurian Sea breezes. All Susanna could think about on the drive was the letter she had received the night before. It had come from her sister, inviting Susanna's family for the Easter holiday. Included was an apology for a past argument, but Susanna saw past her sister's words and knew it was a sham. Margherita was rich, and this would be another opportunity for her to flaunt her wealth. It had been years since the two had spoken, yet even in this unpleasant moment, Susanna couldn't recall what their argument had been about, only that her sister had been wrong. Susanna had thrown the letter into the fireplace that morning, hoping it would make her feel better, yet all her action brought up was guilt, and a reminder of her own shortcomings.

"Let's play in garden, Mama!" DeAngelo squealed as Susanna turned the car in to the convent drive. As soon as she stopped he was out the door, running to the church kitchen.

"DeAngelo, wait for Mama!" she called out, but her son ran on. She threw up her hands in a gesture of profound annoyance and then followed after him. When she opened the door, Isabella was already holding DeAngelo.

"Susanna!" Isabella called out from across the room. "Come meet one of my dearest friends, Father Angel!"

"It's Antonio Costa," the man laughed as he extended his hand.

Susanna shook it but offered only an uninterested smile.

"I'm no father," Costa continued, "but Bella and I have known each other for years."

Susanna was in no mood for conversation, so she remained silent.

"We met at a dinner in 1915 while I was in the seminary, and we've been friends ever since."

Another uninterested nod came from Susanna as she turned to watch Isabella make a swing with her arms and lift DeAngelo up toward the ceiling. Susanna didn't feel a need for such foolishness, but still, it made her jealous to see Isabella do it.

"After some health issues," Costa continued, "I returned to civilian life, working at a bank in Bologna. I was on my way to do business in Pisa, so I thought I'd drop by the convent and was overjoyed to find Bella."

"Yes," Susanna said in a tone that was both expressionless and cold. "Isabella apparently is everyone's friend."

Sensing the tension, Signor Costa decided it was a good time to leave. "I really must get back to work, Bella," he said with a quick smile. "Thank you for the wonderful lunch and visit." He then nodded to Susanna. "It was a pleasure meeting you, signora."

Susanna waited for him to close the door and then turned back to Isabella. "Why have you been avoiding me?"

Isabella hesitated and then took DeAngelo's hand. "Come. Your son wants to show you his garden."

Susanna opened her mouth to reply but instead just shook her head and followed them outside. When Isabella sat on the ground, DeAngelo immediately jumped into her lap. A resentful Susanna pulled a chair up to the side of the garden.

"We planted this kale last month," Isabella began. "It was a beautiful, warm, and sunny day when we planted the seeds. The next week was cold, then back to warm, then cold again; then the rains came and drenched the garden, and today we have sunshine." She hugged DeAngelo to her and touched a leaf. "Look. Your kale survived. And all the worries we may have had meant nothing to the kale, for worries are the spell we cast upon ourselves, believing trouble will find us—unless we give it our complete attention."

At first, Susanna wanted to return to her question about why Isabella had been avoiding her, but Isabella's last statement made her pause.

"There is a unity and flow to nature that I trust," Isabella continued, her eyes focused only on DeAngelo and his garden. "And when I awaken to that thought, the world is healed. For I know I can't change the world—I can only change my thoughts about the world, and then all my troubles seem to disappear."

Her words brought Susanna back to the recent letter from her sister—the invitation to come to Rome and be reminded of her own lack, to see what fate had given her sister and denied Susanna.

"Look how the leaves reach up to the sun," Isabella pointed out to DeAngelo. "Despite rain and wind and gravity, the leaves press on in quest of their source." She smiled down at the little boy. "Something will always be in our way, Little D. It's up to us to be vigilant in seeking the truth."

Susanna had finally had enough.

"What is the truth?" she groaned. "Some mystical illusion you invented so the oppressed can be happy?"

Isabella sat up straight, unsure of what Susanna was talking about. "We all deserve happiness, Susanna. But happiness is a choice. No event or person should be able to determine our happiness."

How could Isabella ever understand, thought Susanna? She'd never had anything. No house or land or money. No husband, no child or responsibility. Finally, she thought it best to explain. "Perhaps you would understand if you met my mother and my sister."

"They hurt you?"

"I was never good enough. I loved my father and he loved me, but he could take no more of my mother and left when I was a child. My mother was desperate to be rich, and suddenly we had nothing. But she continued to play the part of being wealthy. She was obsessed with having my sister marry rich—and she got what she wanted. Margherita married a banker from Rome who is related to Giacomo Matteotti."

Isabella's mouth fell open in surprise. "The Socialist leader?"

She nodded. "You should see my sister's home. It makes our villa look very poor indeed. My mother was furious when I married Giovanni, and she reminded me of her disappointment every time I saw her."

"When was the last time you saw your mother?"

"At her funeral. Five years ago."

Isabella was stunned. Susanna had never mentioned her mother before. She remained quiet, knowing Susanna was not finished.

"My sister sobbed at the funeral, while I felt nothing. I cried later that night—for myself, for the love they never gave me—but not for my mother."

Isabella didn't know what to say. As she thought of how to respond, DeAngelo leaned forward and pulled a weed that was next to the kale. That simple act sparked a different thought.

"There's more than just the wind and rain that threatens this plant, Susanna." Isabella took the weed from DeAngelo. "If I leave this weed next to the kale, it could strangle its roots. So I remove the weeds that would keep the kale from realizing its potential."

"I have no problem separating myself from others."

Isabella paused to look at Susanna, who seemed to be lost in thought. For just a moment Isabella had an impulse to do or say something that would shock her out of her self-pity. Instead, she said, "But there are times when bad things make kale better. Frost can kill some plants, but it produces a sweeter flavor with kale."

Susanna stared at the leaf for several moments until Isabella touched her hand. "Our thoughts are like seeds, Susanna. It's important which seeds we select and where we plant them. Wrong thoughts create the trouble in our lives. We compare, we judge, we condemn, and all that does is hurt us. We need to change the way we think and understand that droughts and floods will come. We must learn from those challenges to grow."

Susanna's eyes began to well up with tears as she continued to stare at the leaf. Isabella lifted DeAngelo up and placed him in Susanna's lap. "Be grateful for what you have right now. Being with friends, today's warm sunshine, and the time to spend with your little boy."

Susanna's lower lip began to tremble as she looked into DeAngelo's eyes. She saw innocence, but she also saw a boy so vulnerable. And to Susanna vulnerability was weakness. She'd been vulnerable as a child, and all it had brought her was pain and loss. Only the poor were vulnerable; only the poor were ignorant. She wanted to be away from Isabella, away from the words that seemed to attack all that protected her. Her head snapped up in near panic.

"Don't you ever tell me how to think!" she lashed out. Then she stood up defiantly, grabbed DeAngelo's hand, and left.

CHAPTER 21

TRIESTE, 1920

O n a humid July afternoon in 1920, Franco drove into Trieste, the recently annexed territory of the Kingdom of Italy. There were few citizens on the streets, and those whom Franco saw seemed anxious. He sensed the discomfort as he parked the truck in the front drive of the Hotel Balkan. The hotel manager waved him in and hurried him down a hallway to a private room where a man with dark hair and a salt-and-pepper beard was waiting.

"I wasn't sure if you'd show," the man said, "but Signor Martellino insisted you're a man to be trusted."

Franco shook the man's hand.

"I'm Vlade Kuric. I met your landowner in Florence. I'll have my men help you get the wine from the truck."

Franco thanked him but then asked, "Forgive me, signor, but there was hardly anyone on the streets when I arrived. Is anything wrong?"

Kuric picked up a newspaper and handed it to Franco. "This is the Fascist paper *Il Popolo di Trieste*. Their writers have been trying to stir up trouble."

"Why?"

"Ever since Italy was given our land in the Treaty of Versailles, the Fascists have been even harder on us Slavs."

Franco read the editorial, which claimed, "a Slavia inside Italian borders cannot be allowed to exist."

"Last month your Mussolini said Italy should 'energetically cleanse' our city." Kuric continued. "He said what they should have done from the beginning was annex Trieste and separate Italians and Slavs. That statement has given Mosconi free reign to terrorize our city."

"Antonio Mosconi?" Franco asked.

"Yes."

"That's the man Giovanni's wife suggested I see if I had any trouble."

Kuric glared at him. "Are you a Fascist?"

"No."

"Then Mosconi won't help you."

Franco's shoulders slumped forward. Why had Giovanni sent him this far from Lucca? Why was the Trieste market so important for their vineyard? His gut had told him this was a bad decision, and he had not listened. His frustration grew as Kuric showed him to his room.

଼ଷ   ଼ୠ

Franco awakened to the sounds of gunfire the next morning. He quickly dressed and hurried outside, only to find that the front and back lights of his rented truck had been smashed. The driver's side window was gone, and on the seat was a note that read, "Die, Slav. Get out, murderer."

He scanned the area for whoever might be responsible, but the streets were empty. God, how he wished he were back in Lucca. In the last few months, he had spent every available moment with Isabella and couldn't remember a happier time in his life. There were romantic picnics on the Serchio River, silly talks while walking the walls, and their last evening together atop the Giunigi Tower. The view was spectacular, of every rooftop in Lucca and all the way to the Apuan Alps. But what he remembered most was his nervous anticipation of how he would offer Isabella his first kiss. Not one of the quick, embarrassed pecks he'd awkwardly given the cheeks of teenage girls back home in Puglia, but the full-blown, lips-on-lips, amorous embrace he'd seen on unrestrained lovers on the walls of Lucca. Now it was his turn, he had thought, as he clumsily searched for her hand while respectfully continuing to stare at the great Tuscan beyond.

"Beautiful." It was all he could think of to say.

Isabella said nothing, only waited for his eyes to meet hers, and when he finally turned, he found an amused look, as if she had known what he had planned. It was she who made the first move, pulling him into the oak trees that grew on top of the Giunigi Tower. Her expression was magnetic, drawing his face to hers, and the surprise of her tongue darting into his mouth made his knees go weak. Thank God for the oak trees, he'd later tell her—if they hadn't been there for him to lean back on, he was sure he would have fallen on his ass. Yes, he was falling in love; perhaps he was there already.

Now, as he recalled his last conversation with Giovanni, he was angry with himself for not speaking his mind. He thought they were extending the Martellino market too far from Lucca, but he had remained silent. Antonio had warned him of the trouble brewing in

Trieste, but Franco had not listened, and now he was in a foreign city where most of the people did not speak his language, far from the Giunigi Tower and Isabella's sweet lips.

He crumpled the note, flung it to the floor, and then drove until his exit was blocked by a barricade. He parked in front of a cafe and found a Slav who spoke Italian.

"Why is the road blocked?" he asked.

Her eyes searched the room before she answered in a hushed voice. "Mosconi and his thug, Francesco Giunta, are rallying their forces to attack."

"Attack? But why?"

The woman led him to the window and pointed to where he'd just been. "The Narodni Dom in the Hotel Balkan is the headquarters of the Slovene movement. Mussolini wants all Slavs out of Trieste."

"But Mussolini doesn't rule Italy."

"No, but his henchmen run our town, and their squadrists have bullied anyone who isn't Fascist."

A blast suddenly erupted from outside, followed by the roar of a crowd. The Hotel Balkan was on fire. Franco ran to his truck, cold horror rippling up his spine as he saw men pouring gasoline around the hotel and beating hotel workers who tried to stop them. A squadrist chased down a man and his wife and struck them with a chain. Franco raced over and leaped in front of the couple just as the terrorist drove his chain down. The metal ripped into Franco's left arm and the side of his head, but with sudden fury, he grabbed the chain with his bloody hand, jerked the squadrist forward, and smashed his fist into the man's jaw. The man let go of the chain and stumbled away.

Franco helped the woman and her injured husband to his truck, but he knew trouble would soon follow. The terrorist who had attacked them was talking with fellow squadrists and then started his way. Franco pounded his foot on the gas pedal, blasted through the wooden barricade, and drove directly at the terrorists. They leaped out of the way at the last second.

"Where should I go?!" Franco yelled.

The woman looked up, and her eyes went wide. "You're bleeding!"

His heart was pounding as he reached up and felt blood dripping down his head and neck, soaking his shirt. He grabbed a rag, held it to the wound, and drove on.

Another blast lit the sky behind him, and he glanced back to see the Hotel Balkan, with its Slavic cultural center and community archives inside, engulfed in flames. Franco fled to the northwest, away from Trieste.

It took them almost an hour to get out of the city before the woman directed him to a small farm outside Trieste. As he pulled down a path to the rear of the cottage, an older gentleman came out to help him carry the wounded husband into the house. Franco collapsed on the floor and stared at his bloody hands. He knew he had lost a lot of blood, and his breathing now came in gasps.

"I'm Dr. Volpi," the older gentleman said. "I must care for this man first, but my wife will help you."

Franco leaned back against the wall and tried to clean his own wounds with a wet rag, but instead, he dozed off. When he opened his eyes, the doctor's wife hovered over him with a needle and surgical thread.

"I was afraid of this," she said as she drew the needle through his wound. "When Mosconi accused the Slavs of being a 'cultural menace,' we knew it was only a matter of time before he brought violence."

"I don't understand," Franco coughed. "The Fascists lost in the last election. Why would they attack—"

"Because they're angry they lost!" It was Dr. Volpi, who had come into the room. "They'll terrorize anyone who's against them. They lie to angry soldiers returning from a failed war, telling them the Socialists or the Slavs are the reason for their troubles."

Franco slumped against the wall. "Dear God, not again."

"The Fascist numbers are growing," Volpi grimaced. "I'm afraid for Italy."

As soon as his wounds were bandaged, Franco could think of nothing but getting home to Lucca. He was grateful, so grateful, for this family's help, but he wanted desperately to move on; he had to get home. He struggled to his feet, the pain in his side deepening, and stumbled to the door. The doctor's wife tried to stop him.

"Please." He pushed past her. "I have to get home—thank you for your help."

She helped him to the truck. He sat for a moment trying to calm the pain that was shooting down his neck and arm. Finally, he took a deep breath, started the engine, and headed for the rail yard where he had rented the truck. There were angry young men everywhere, looking for a fight. Franco waited in the shadows for them to pass and then steered clear of the main station, hiding behind railcars as he waited for the train to move. When it did, he slid behind an oil drum and climbed into a boxcar. Huddled in the corner was a frightened family of four.

"Help me," Franco mumbled.

The father went to Franco's side. "What happened?"

"Hotel Balkan," were the only words he could gasp.

"Mosconi," the man said in disgust. "He's why we're fleeing to Pistoia."

"But—you're Italian," Franco said in a raspy voice, his words beginning to slur. "I thought—Mosconi—was against Slavs?"

"It doesn't matter anymore. If you don't join the Fascists, you're the enemy. When they burned the hotel today, we knew we had to leave."

Franco tried to answer, but his mouth was caked and dry. He licked his lips and summoned all the strength he had left. "I work—the Martellino vineyard—not far—from Pistoia—please—help me—get home."

The wife took Franco's jacket and folded it in half. "Lie back, signor. You need to rest."

The train rolled southwest through the mountains and into Tuscany as Franco fell in and out of sleep. He awoke with a throbbing headache, and the swelling in his arm and neck was much worse. He was feverish, weak, and almost delirious when they arrived in Pistoia late the next day. The family helped Franco off the train and onto a waiting truck. Fortunately, the driver knew of the Martellino vineyard and drove him there that night.

☙ ❧

With the summer sun setting late, the Martellino workers were still in the field when the truck turned down the drive. Giovanni was the first see them and ran to help. He listened to the man explain what had happened in Trieste, and his shoulders slumped forward. "It's my fault. I should never have sent him."

The back door of the villa opened, and there stood Susanna, her eyes wide with shock, knowing it had been her idea that Franco go to Trieste. Her lover had insisted that his friends in the Fascist Party would help them sell their wine in the northeast and that this could be a great political and business opportunity for both of them. The phrase "both of them" had been what Susanna held on to, but she hadn't realized until after Franco left that her husband's business connections lay with Slavs at the Hotel Balkan.

Isabella was already at Franco's side, her hand on his forehead.

"Antonio, bring me water!" she called out, and then she turned to Angelina. "Fill a cool bath—we must get his temperature down."

She removed his bandages to check the stitches and turned to Rosa. "I need vinegar and olive oil to clean these wounds."

Antonio returned from the well and helped Franco drink as much water as he could. When he put the pitcher down, Isabella urged him to drink more. "Get the sickness through and out of your body."

"I'm so sorry," Giovanni said, fumbling with his words. "What happened?"

Franco winced in pain as he reached into his pocket and pulled out a promissory note for the wine. "When I left—the Hotel Balkan was in flames. I don't know if—if Signor Kuric is alive."

Susanna snatched the note from Franco's hand. "That means this paper is worthless!"

Franco's head dropped in defeat.

"Unacceptable!" Susanna snapped. "We must be paid for the wine we delivered!"

"Hush!" Isabella lashed out. "Franco's sick! We need to get him inside!"

Susanna jerked as though she'd been slapped. Isabella had never spoken to her like that before. How dare she! Giovanni held his wife back as Antonio and Isabella carried Franco to the villa.

Susanna glared at her husband. "I want all of them gone! Is that understood?"

Giovanni waited for them to enter the house before he lit into his wife. "What is wrong with you?! Do you have any idea what Franco's been through?"

At the moment all she could think of was the money—the money and the promise she had made to Obizzi. "But this was our investment, and this is our vineyard—"

Giovanni cut her off. "We were the ones who sent him to Trieste! We both knew how dangerous this could be! Now you want me to fire the people who bleed for this vineyard?"

"They're damn Socialists, Giovanni! Why can't you see that?!"

"You're wrong! They want the same thing we want! A great wine and olive oil and nothing more!"

"You're a fool!" She grabbed his arm. "You'll be taken as you've always been taken, and I—" She gripped his arm tighter to make sure her point hit home. "I won't be around when they do!"

Giovanni wrenched his arm free and headed inside to see if he could be of help.

Susanna looked around the courtyard, but everyone was gone. She was furious. Dammit, didn't they know that money would be needed for this vineyard to survive? She put her fist to her mouth to keep from screaming, and started for her car. She needed someone who believed in her, someone who would sympathize with what she alone was going through. As she slammed the car door, she decided to go to the one person who understood her.

CHAPTER 22

AUGUST 1920

With cool baths and cucumber water, Isabella was able to get Franco's fever under control. She covered his wounds with vinegar and olive oil to clean the area and calm the inflammation, and then she let him rest while she sought out Giovanni.

"Franco can't do anything until his body heals," she said when she saw the Martellino landowner in the kitchen. "I think it would speed the healing process if I take him to the mineral baths in the mountains."

Giovanni's expression suggested a feeling of guilt. "I'll help Antonio and Angelina in the field until you get back."

"There shouldn't be that much work." She grabbed some lemons from the top shelf of the pantry and tossed them into her knapsack. "The grapes are in the flowering stage, and the olives are still months from harvest." She looked directly into his eyes to make sure he understood her next words. "And Angie can help with DeAngelo."

"Susanna's still in bed," he muttered. "She came home late last night, still angry about our loss in Trieste."

Isabella said nothing as she finished packing healthy vegetables to both feed and heal Franco on their trip.

"Let me help you." Giovanni picked up the crate and followed her outside. "I'm sorry about what happened, Bella. I don't know where this vineyard would be if I had run Franco off when he asked for a job. He's a good winemaker—and a good friend."

Isabella only nodded as she headed to the wagon.

"Bella!" he called out and nodded to his car. "I want you to take my auto. Please."

She startled him with a hug, and together they packed the Martellinos' Lancia Theta, then went to wake Franco and help him to the car.

For the first time since he had returned from Trieste, Franco smiled and gave his landowner's hand a thankful squeeze. Closing his eyes, he leaned back into the soft leather seat and drifted off to sleep as Isabella began the drive to the Alpi Apuane mountains.

CR SO

Franco awoke to absolute beauty. There were jagged peaks that seemed to rise up from the river; boulders teetering on the edges of cliffs, appearing ready to fall at any moment; and broad, green, rolling meadows dotted with yellow, purple, and white flowers that would suddenly disappear down into a deep gorge. They crisscrossed the river several times on small stone bridges as the water snaked its way through the canyon, away from the mountains. Isabella pointed to some deer grazing in a meadow that seemed to have been placed between two boulders by the Apuan gods themselves. She turned the car down a path away from the river into dense woods, and they passed through oak, chestnut, and beechwood trees as they rose in elevation. After they passed through a dark-green archway of trees and blue-gray boulders, Isabella pulled over on the side of a dirt path and parked the car.

She helped Franco down to a cool, sandy area by a pool of water that flowed from the mouth of a cave. He rested while she unpacked the car and spread out food, herbs, and medicines on a wool blanket. Lifting up on one elbow, he swept his dark hair, wet with perspiration, away from his face and looked around. Blue jays screeched high among the pines, while a squirrel darted up a massive hornbeam that jutted out from the bronze limestone. The reflection of the cave on the pool mirrored perfectly, making it nearly impossible to tell which one was real.

"How did you find this place?" he asked.

"The sisters used to bring me here on their spiritual retreats." She nodded to where he was looking. "That cave is one of over two hundred in this mountain range. Some are small like this one, but others are like the Abisso Enrico Revel-Vetrico, which is said to be one of the deepest wells in the world. I picked this spot because of the mineral bath and the juniper trees."

She went to the woods and returned with several branches from a juniper, crushed the berries into a pulp, pressed them into oil, and then spread the oil on a bandage. She then re-dressed the bandages on Franco's arm, ear, and neck with the juniper oil, making sure the oil had direct contact with his skin.

"The vinegar and olive oil will clean the infection, and the juniper will keep the swelling down and help in the healing." Isabella finished the dressing and sat down next to him. "When I was little, my mama and papa told me of the old days when people believed juniper had magical powers to protect against evil."

Franco's mouth twisted slightly. "Why don't you grow it in Susanna's bedroom?"

She laughed. "She didn't send you to Trieste to hurt you."

"Are you sure? Because Trieste is not a place anyone should be investing in right now."

"She probably just received bad information."

He shook his head. "Why do you always give her the benefit of the doubt?"

Isabella thought back to the night on the wall, seeing Susanna in the arms of another man. She had done nothing to stop her and had said nothing since. Why did she give Susanna, as Franco called it, the benefit of the doubt? She was lost in those thoughts when the sun suddenly peeked through gray clouds, lighting the opening to a cave. For a moment she thought of Susanna being lost inside; she imagined that with each deception, with each attack, Susanna's guilt took her farther into the cave, away from the light and away from true happiness.

"I don't think Susanna likes herself," she said softly, still looking at the cave. "And when you don't like yourself, you want to bring others down too. Then your guilt is doubled."

"What about you?" Franco turned to face her. "Do you like yourself?"

She sat up straight and said proudly, "I love myself."

"You're the most confident person I've ever met," he chuckled. "Is that because you have no guilt?"

"None at all. Guilt was man's invention. Not God's."

He raised one doubtful brow. "You never feel guilty?"

"No."

"How is that possible?"

"My discipline to pray and forgive."

"So because you pray, God smiles on you?"

"God smiles on you too, Franco—and on Susanna."

"Then what separates you from the rest of us?"

"Nothing, except the belief that I am not separate from God."

Franco was smitten by how easily he could talk to Isabella—about both serious and trivial subjects. There was an ease to their conversation that always felt comfortable, an ebb and flow that seemed as natural as being in the vineyard every morning. Seeing her now, poised and relaxed, made him smile. "Interesting." He bit his lip to hide his grin. "You believe you are—God?"

"I believe I'm an expression of God's love," she said matter-of-factly.

"Like Jesus?"

"Like all of us."

"Where I come from, that's called blasphemy."

"Says who?"

Taken by surprise, he took in a deep breath. "It's—it's in the Bible…"

"Mark 3:29," she said promptly. "'But whoever blasphemes against the Holy Spirit never has forgiveness, but is guilty of eternal sin.'"

He nodded, looking pleased he remembered.

"Guilty of eternal sin?" Isabella gave a look as if she had bitten into a lemon. "No wonder there's so much anger in the world when guilt and sin are at the core of who we believe we are."

Franco paused for a long moment and then looked directly into her eyes. "Then who do you believe you are, Bella?"

"I certainly don't believe I'm a sinner."

"You don't?"

"Absolutely not. Sin is the only thought that makes the goal of God seem impossible."

"Then what do you call the evil that we see in the world?"

"Pride. Greed. Ego. But the belief in sin is the source of our guilt, which of course demands punishment and suffering, and—I find that stupid."

"You don't believe in original sin?

"That concept was introduced by a man named Irenaeus in the second century."

"Really?"

"Yes."

Franco cocked his head to the side. "So—what are we?"

"We—are—perfect. Only our guilt and our belief in sin stand in the way of our remembering God."

"So that's the problem with Susanna!" Franco laughed. "She forgot who God is!"

"No!" Isabella clapped her hands to make sure she had his attention. "Susanna has forgotten who SHE is, a perfect child of God. Instead, she has allowed guilt and fear to take her off her true path. It's the same problem with the world, Franco. Fear and ego started the war you fought in. Fear and ego are at the center of the fight we're currently having in our government—and they are also what troubles Susanna."

Franco propped himself up on his elbow. "I'm a bit confused."

Isabella grabbed more of the juniper berries and began to crush them against a stone. "Your confusion tells me you need more juniper. My father told me that juniper helps with memory loss."

"That's right," he grinned. "I forgot who I am."

"Obviously you lost your mind in Trieste, because even an idiot wouldn't travel after he'd been beaten with a chain."

"I just wanted to come home to you."

"Next time you try to do something that foolish, they'll bring you home in a box."

He wanted to laugh again, but his neck hurt, and he lay back in the grass.

"When your wounds are well enough, you can bathe in this natural mineral spring," Isabella said as she taped the final bandage to his arm. "Hopefully that will be enough to heal an old, broken-down body like yours."

Franco tried to look serious. "Oh, why do you torment me, woman, when I'm only on this earth to get rid of my guilt and fear so that I can find the true path to you."

"Don't patronize me." She stifled a laugh. "You're the moron who got in the fight with terrorists."

"I didn't want to fight." He pressed his lips together and sighed. "I was just trying to help a couple escape from an angry mob."

She smiled sweetly and gently brushed his hair away from his face. "That's what I love about you, Franco Carollo. You care about others." She lightly touched her lips to his, but as she did, her elbow grazed his injured left arm.

"Ow."

She gave a lopsided grin, "That's the first time one of my kisses has brought you pain. I guess I'll have to stop that."

He pulled her to him, his soft, wide mouth opening on hers. She bit his lower lip, giggling as she held it between her teeth, and then flowered his face with kisses, kissing his forehead, eyelids, nose, and cheeks before returning to his lips. His heart swelled with the love he felt for this woman. Then she kissed him a final time and leaped to her feet.

"Enough mischief! You must heal, and I must put our camp together and prepare dinner."

Franco watched her hurry about, spreading a canvas tarp on the ground and covering it with blankets.

"What? No tent?"

She spread her arms to the sky. "This, my love, is the dry season in the hills. You'll not want a tent to hide the stars tonight. There's only a crescent moon, so the heavens will be spectacular!"

She pulled a wooden bowl out of her bag, and Franco knew what that meant. "No more vegetables. This gladiator needs meat."

Isabella shook a wooden spoon in his face, "God gave us everything we needed to heal naturally! I shall make you a meal that will heal your bones, keep your fever down, and bring much-needed iron to your blood."

Franco lay back and groaned.

She reached into a large basket, pulled out a wild cabbage, ripped the leaves off, and tossed them into the bowl. Then she pulled out some familiar green leaves. "Kale! Good for your blood and reducing inflammation."

Next were lemons and sea salt; she sprinkled the salt and then cut up the lemons and squeezed the juice all over the kale leaves. "Sea salt! Good for the kidneys and stress. It will help you sleep tonight. Lemon is great for the liver and digestion. Why, it's even been known to cure hiccups."

Franco's smile widened as he watched her mix the ingredients as if she were in a well-orchestrated opera. She sang him songs about food, friendship, and love that her mother had taught her when she was young. Then, with her hands dripping with the lemon juice, she pulled a bottle of dark brown liquid out of the basket. "Balsamic vinegar! It fights viruses and infections."

She reached in for another bottle, and Franco saw that it was her homemade olive oil from the convent garden.

"Lucca's finest! Good for everything!" She poured in the oil, ground some pepper over the top, and winked. "I don't know what pepper is good for—I just like the taste!"

She mixed it all together, placed it off to the side, and grabbed a loaf of bread and bottle of wine from the bottom of the basket. "While the salad blends, why don't we have a little Martellino red." She pulled the neck of her blouse over her shoulder and gave him a sultry look. "It's not only good for your heart—it's the liquid of love!"

CR   SO

They dined by the side of the mineral-spring pool that night, the crescent moon rising just above the pines like a towering candle to light their meal. Isabella talked about growing up on farms in northern Italy, the influence of her parents both during their lives and afterward, and how they, along with the Blessings sisters, had helped her through dark times.

"Tell me about Sister Anna."

"Anna is my dearest friend," Isabella said with a smile that showed deep affection. "She knew my grief in a personal way. Her own mother died when she was fifteen, and because her father could not care for her, he placed her in the convent. Can you imagine the pain for both parent and child? I think that's why she understood my suffering, even encouraged my love of the natural world. Anna would search city markets for fruit and vegetable seeds for my garden. One time she went all the way to Pisa because she had heard they carried special bell pepper seeds." Bella looked up into the night sky and inhaled the scent of the clean, pure pine forest. "I love Anna. She never forced her faith on me—only honored the spiritual path that I was traveling."

Franco listened quietly, moved by the ease with which Isabella shared her past; he knew it was time for him to do the same. He began with simple memories: of his upbringing in Puglia, the tension between father and son, his time in Rome, and finally, the war. Much like the blood he had seen flow on the Isonzo River, his thoughts moved on the current of his mind to where they had to go.

"I still don't know why I got on that train," he said in a voice barely audible. "I was against Italy going to war, and yet I went." He paused for a long moment, a faraway yet intent look on his face. "I still have nightmares of a man I killed on a hill near Gorizia."

Isabella put her hand on his but stayed silent.

"We were ordered to advance—always to advance—and wave after wave of my friends was cut down." A deep sadness came to his eyes, which were darkened by flashbacks of that final day. "It was at Caporetto that my brother died. I searched for him—but I was too late."

He broke down and wept when he told her about his brother dying in his arms. She held him and let him cry. She held him until there were no tears left; then she laid him down and covered him with a blanket.

"It's time for you to rest," she whispered. "I want you to breathe deeply—try to inhale the greatest peace you've ever known—and as you exhale, say, 'I rest in God—I rest in God.'"

Franco said the words and drifted off to sleep.

He slept peacefully for a few hours until old demons crept into his dreams: he was back in Trieste, but when he saw the Fascist squadrist beating citizens with a chain, the victims were his brother and his chaplain. In the dream, Franco tried to stop the violence, but he couldn't move. It was as if his feet were frozen to the ground, and each time he tried to raise his arms to ward off the attacker's blows to Benny and Father Mario, he was too slow to help. His brother cried out to him, but Franco could do nothing. Benny and Father Mario's images slowly drifted away. Franco reached for them and cried out, "Come back—don't leave me—"

He opened his eyes to find Isabella shaking him out of his nightmare.

"It's only a dream, Franco. It isn't real." She dipped a cloth into the cold mountain water, stroked it over his sweat-covered face, and pointed to the midnight sky. It was a view he had seen a thousand times in the past—growing up on the remote farms of Puglia, and later on the Isonzo battlefields, when the smoke and ash would finally clear to reveal the evening sky. But for some reason, on this night, the vision took his breath away. It was as if he were seeing the heavens for the first time, as if the mountain gods had brushed infinite points of light across a black canvas. Millions of stars seemed to be dancing above them.

"To me—that is God," Isabella whispered. "That is my celestial reminder that all is perfect in the world." She gently placed her hand on his chest. "That same perfection is inside you, Franco. God created you in His image. His image is only love. That is the truth. The war twisted your mind. Violence, pride, greed, ego—all these confused your understanding of who you really are. You are not sin,

Franco. You are love—and once you accept your holiness, nothing can make you afraid."

A soft wind blew through the trees as Franco lay back on the blanket and stared up at the sky. With Isabella's hand still on his heart, he drifted off to a peaceful sleep.

ଔ   ଔ

He woke the next morning invigorated, but Isabella insisted that he still rest. She handed him a bowl of sliced apples and a cup of water.

"I was hoping for bacon and eggs," he grumbled.

"Apples awaken your mind and stomach," Isabella said firmly, and then she pointed at the cup. "Drink three full cups of water, take a mineral bath, and then nap before lunch."

"Yes, signora," he said with a wry grin as he bit into an apple slice.

She raised one eyebrow and gave him a stern look. "I'm not kidding."

"No, signora."

She shook her head and headed for the forest.

"Where are you going?" he called out.

"I'll be back in an hour or two. I'm going to find some wild cabbage for your lunch."

He rolled his eyes and gave a dramatic sigh. "Sounds delicious."

He didn't hear her answer.

ଔ   ଔ

He awoke from his nap to the familiar scent of soup cooking. Isabella was watching him as she stirred the pot over white-hot coals.

"Ah, the lovely smell of wild cabbage boiling," he wisecracked.

"This is what your body needs." She ladled out a bowl and walked over. "Tell me what you can taste."

He brought the spoon to his lips. "Garlic," he smiled, and then took another sip. "Kale, uh—spinach, tomatoes, uh—"

"The rest is simply salt and pepper and olive oil. But every ingredient is designed to bring goodness into your body while pushing out dis-ease."

He raised one brow. "Why did you make it sound as if *disease* is two words?"

"All living organisms are designed to work perfectly, Franco. When something is out of order, there is a lack of ease. For humans, it takes mental discipline to get back to ease. That's why you see me praying every morning and night." She winked at him. "You should try it."

He paused for a long moment, suddenly taken back to his nightmare. "Do you remember last night?" he finally asked.

She nodded.

"I was back in Caporetto. I tried—but couldn't save my brother and chaplain."

She remained quiet.

"When I woke up, you said something about my being without sin and created out of love. What did you mean?"

A warm smile suddenly lit Isabella's face. "I don't believe God makes mistakes, Franco. I don't believe He would create sin. I believe we created a belief in sin, which led to guilt, which led to punishment, which leads to anger, greed, and envy, which can only result in war."

He inhaled a deep breath. "I never should have gotten on that train."

"But you did," Isabella said softly, her green eyes filled with understanding, "and you did the best you could to save your brother and chaplain at Caporetto." She touched his hand. "I'll never know what you saw on the battlefield. But I do believe with all my heart that only forgiveness will set you free. Caporetto did happen, and that hurt you terribly—but if you allow the past to affect the present, you're allowing it to defeat you a second time. Let go of the past. God's will for you is perfect happiness."

Franco turned away and stared at the mineral springs, the seemingly never-ending flow of water off rock to the pool and down to the valley below. He closed his eyes and thought about his brother, imagining scenes of growing up with Benny: laughing at the dinner table, picking grapes in the vineyard, on the train to join the army, charging up a hill, and finally, seeing his brother die at Caporetto. He opened his eyes and picked up a stone.

"It's time to let you go, big brother," he said softly, and then he tossed the rock into the mineral pool. All of a sudden, he felt dazed with gratitude, overwhelmed by grace, and without thinking he reached for another stone. Staring at the rock for a long moment, he visualized his army chaplain, remembering his prayers before battle, and then he dropped the rock into the pool. "I wish you well, Father Mario."

A new brightness seemed to light Franco's face, as if he were seeing for the first time, and he confidently looked back at Isabella. "I've now done what my brother asked me to do," he whispered. "I've gone home—and forgiven."

She squeezed his hand. "Then see yourself healing right now."

He lay back down and closed his eyes, visualizing his body strong and healthy, untouched by man's world or by fear. Suddenly, the smiling faces of Benny and Father Mario came to him. He blessed them and saw them walk toward a distant white light, disappearing into his mind, gone from any perceived pain and suffering. A kind of joy lit Franco's mind and body as a new image came to him.

"I'm visualizing something else now," he said with his eyes still closed, trying to stifle the slow grin that spread across his face.

Isabella playfully pinched his side. "You're being silly."

"No. I'm seeing the two of us growing grapes together."

She giggled. "A fine blend, I'm sure."

"But the grapes I'm working with are much better than yours."

"But mine still taste better."

"No, they don't."

"Yes, they do."

Franco's grin turned into a wide smile. "All right. They're both very good and we mix them together and win at next year's wine tasting festival in Florence."

"That's impressive," Isabella said as she placed her hand on his heart.

"I see myself walking through the vineyard to hand you the trophy."

"I'm sure it will look lovely over the Martellino's fireplace."

He opened his eyes. He wanted to ask her. The setting was perfect: alone in the mountains, the dark green junipers contrasting with the bright blue sky, Isabella's smiling eyes staring into his. He thought of his father's advice: "Don't you dare let her go. If you do, it will be the biggest mistake of your life." He was there, at the precipice of a most important decision. A thousand words flew through his mind; he tried to catch one or two or three to string together for some kind of enchanting sentence. Instead, he just gulped and grinned stupidly back at her.

"Yes," he bumbled. "A trophy would look nice over their fireplace."

The mood inside Isabella's eyes seemed to change as she simply gave Franco a polite tap on the chest. "Thank you for sharing that lovely vision with me."

CR   SO

They spent the next day bathing in the mineral bath and hiking the trails of the eastern slopes of the Serchio River valley. Their hike took them down into a dramatic gorge with steep walls that seemed to reach into the clouds. They rested for an hour next to the Pelago Creek, a biting slice of water that had cut its way through limestone over millions of years to form the breathtaking geology of the Orrido di Botri. As Franco stared at the magnificence, a sweet calm came over him, and he soon drifted off to sleep—perhaps for seconds, perhaps for an hour, he wasn't quite sure. Isabella woke him, nodded to the sun's position in the sky, and helped him to his feet. "You're still recovering. We should head back to camp."

Franco found that the hike had indeed sapped his energy, and when they returned he relaxed in the cool mineral water while Isabella fixed their dinner. They ate in silence as he again searched for the perfect words to form his question. He opened his mouth to speak but then reconsidered and simply leaned back against a boulder and watched her. She was finishing cleaning the dishes, putting them away, organizing the morning meal, when he suddenly realized that in every moment of the three years he had known her, she had always been doing for others. Isabella's giving was her receiving. There seemed to be no difference between the two.

She caught him watching her and tossed her towel at him. "What?"

He laughed as he caught the towel and patted the ground next to him. She did sit down, and together they watched the sun set across the canyon walls, changing its colors from bronze to a muted gray to soon a dark black silhouette reaching up into the night sky. He pulled her hand up, kissed her palm, and then cocked an eyebrow. "There's no one here."

She gave him a playful shove. "No mischief tonight. You need to rest."

He chuckled under his breath and reached for her, his hand traveling down her neck to the curve of her breast. She pushed him flat and put her knee on his chest. "I'm serious."

"So am I," he grinned, his hand creeping up her thigh, stopping at the belt of her dress.

Her knee pressed even harder into his sternum. "You can't handle me in your condition."

He laughed out loud, and the sudden movement did indeed bring pain.

She gave him the look of a medical professional unhappy with her patient. "Your heart is too fast, pumping blood at a quicker rate, which will inflame your wounds and could break your stitches."

His index finger continued to play with the belt of her dress as he winked. "My blood flow may already be beyond my control."

She giggled and pushed him over to his right side, away from the wounds on his neck, shoulder, and arm, and lay against his back, nestling up against him as if seeking warmth on a cold day. Every part of the front of her body touched his back: the tops of her feet against his ankles, her shins to his calves, kneecaps to knee pits, thighs to hamstrings, pubis to buttocks, ribs to lower back, her breasts pushing against his shoulder blades. She rested her head against the back of his neck, her breath a smooth current against his shoulder. He matched her breathing, trying to make their breaths one inhalation and one exhalation. Her hand slipped between his left arm and ribs; there was no trembling in what this woman did. Every movement was one of confidence yet tenderness as she reached up and unbuttoned the top button of his shirt, then the second and the third. He was hoping she would continue on, but she did not, instead resting her hand against his heart, gently massaging his chest to the beat of the fire inside. He tried to turn to face her, but she held firm, grinding the front of her body deep into his.

"You need to heal," she whispered, and he let go of his need to see her, his mind finally letting go of what his body wanted and journeying back across the last seven days. He thought about Trieste: if not for that bad experience, he wouldn't know the bliss he felt right now. This day, this woman, this life, so perfect. How was Isabella able to see this world so much differently than others could, he wondered—to see the good in what others perceived as bad? How was she able to see beyond disappointment, beyond fear, and find the good in everyone and everything? Her words seemed to be water for a parched mind, her actions a bridge from sickness to health, from fear to love. Her garden was the holy ground that set its roots in firm soil and—given light and warmth—never left its source, only shining her goodness back on everything she touched. As his thoughts continued on, he felt her hand go still against his heart, her breath heavy on his back; she was already off in some sweet dream. He knew she couldn't hear his words, but still, he gently whispered, "I love you—and I always will."

CHAPTER 23

LUCCA, AUGUST 1920

"The Pauper from Puglia lives!" Antonio cried out when he saw the car turn down the Martellino's drive. When it pulled up, he hurried over and opened the car door. Franco gave him a huge love-struck grin.

"Ooh la la! I see Nurse Bella did her job well!" Antonio laughed as he helped a now red-faced Franco up from the passenger's seat. "Your color is back; your lips are bruised—I can almost see your heart leaping out of your chest!"

Franco's face went from red to crimson as Antonio pulled him toward the field.

"Come, my friend, before she finds out you have no money!"

Isabella was giggling as she was helped from the car by Angelina, who impatiently waited for the men to get beyond the courtyard before she asked, "Well?"

Isabella gave her a crinkle-eyed grin. "Well, what?"

"Franco's in love with you, Bella. I can see it in his eyes."

Isabella looked momentarily startled but then forced a smile. "He's in love with the ideal, Angie, but he's still hurting. Physically his wounds are healing, but emotionally his past still haunts him. He opened up more to me on this trip than he ever has."

Angelina raised an eyebrow. "Are you in love with him?"

Isabella didn't answer.

"Bella?"

"Franco's recovering, Angie. Both his mind and his body are healing."

"And you've been part of his recovery," Angelina said firmly. "He came back from the war half a man until you showed up."

Isabella didn't speak for a time as she looked out at the field. Joy did seem to be shining from Franco as he talked with Antonio. The heavy gray and dark eyes she remembered from when he had first arrived had changed. His skin was now a clear olive and his eyes a chocolate brown that seemed to brighten whenever she was near. It was then that he turned her way and gave a look of such love and trust that her heart tightened. She swallowed hard and turned back to Angelina. "Two halves may make a whole in mathematics or baking, but two halves don't make a whole in a relationship. Each person must complete himself or herself."

"Not everyone's as strong as you," Angelina said, and then she looked directly at her friend. "Are you afraid of hurting him?"

Isabella said nothing.

"You're not responsible for Franco's happiness, Bella."

Isabella nodded but remained quiet.

Angelina drew in a deep breath. "I was afraid when I lost Mariano—and there are times when fear creeps in, when my children are late coming home from school or I can't see them at the market. But you've taught me to trust in something greater than myself." She touched Isabella's hand to make sure she heard her next words. "I've seen you in the field when you go somewhere deep, listening to that quiet voice the rest of us do not hear. I know you like to go there because you're comfortable being alone. God is indeed your refuge and security. But you were born to share your love."

Isabella wiped one tear from her cheek and stared out again at Franco. Strong and happy, feet set firm on the soil he loved.

"Do you love him, Bella?"

Isabella nodded.

Angelina smiled sweetly. "Perhaps it's time to trust what you've been teaching us."

ଓ ଅଡ

"Sorry to have to rip that love-struck look off your face," Antonio said as he crossed his arms over his chest, "but with you gone in Trieste for a week and then convalescing on Romance Ridge, it's been impossible for the farmers to talk with you. We just heard the news yesterday."

"What news?" Franco asked, suddenly alarmed. "And why do the farmers need me?"

"They've come to the villa three times, but Susanna failed to tell us—"

"Tell you what?"

"Angelo from the Mancini vineyard stopped by yesterday to tell us that Tuscany's farmers want you to be part of their solidarity. He said this could be the largest agricultural strike in Italian history."

Franco's shoulders dropped. "Dear God, no. We've made great strides the last two seasons, and I refuse to let this crop be ruined by outsiders."

"You can't be so closed-minded, Franco. It's not just the field workers, but also the factory men who are angry. The wealthy believe sharecropping works, but they don't struggle the way the workers do, with little to eat and homes with dirt floors."

Franco couldn't believe what he was hearing. He thought about getting back into the car and running away to the mountains with Isabella, just forgetting about the rest of the world and…He gave a frustrated exhalation and stared out at the vineyard, so bright and full of potential. He knew he should at least meet with his fellow workers.

"What does Giovanni say?"

"He's with other landowners right now, trying to decide how to handle it. But over five hundred thousand peasants are striking, and Signora Martellino thinks we are the enemy."

Franco shook his head sadly. "What a surprise."

"She believes we've already joined the union and are in the process of striking, even though we've been in the field every day. She even accused Isabella of taking you to the mountains as part of the strike."

Franco touched the wound on his neck. "I guess she thought my stitches were all part of our master plan."

"I don't know what to think," Antonio continued. "Part of me is with the workers, and part of me thinks that with our economy struggling, this is not the time to strike."

"There will be trouble."

"It's already here, Franco. The unions in Turin want a Sovietization of Italian industry, while in San Marino the Socialists made violent comments about the rich."

Franco exhaled loudly. "This 'all or nothing' mentality is only going to make people angry, and I'm worried it will set back everything the unions have worked for. I'm afraid I saw the beginning of it in Trieste."

"Enough about trouble. Let's join the ladies." Antonio put his arm around Franco and led him back to the courtyard. "Hey Angie!" he called out. "Should I tell him the good news?"

She nodded proudly, and Antonio clapped his hands together.

"So I'm in Lucca two nights ago with a few of bottles of our red for owners to sample, and who do I see but the restaurant owner from Viareggio who bought our wine in January."

"Signor Torelli?"

"The one and only. Anyway, he had a wine buyer from Pietrasanta with him who represents hotels and restaurants. Both were very worried about the strike and how it could affect the grape harvest and their prospects for acquiring a quality wine. I assured them we'd make our harvest and that we already have barrels ready from last year's wine that people from all over Tuscany have been raving about."

Franco gave Antonio a confused look. "We haven't even debuted last year's wine yet. Who's talking about it?"

Antonio squeezed Franco's shoulder. "Angelina, Bartolo, Rosa—even Little D. and I talked about the wine last week when we went fishing."

Franco's mouth fell open.

"It helped to have a few bottles of Martellino red with me," Antonio winked. "Nothing relaxes a wallet better than free booze."

Isabella let out a laugh that could be heard throughout the vineyard. "You're the best salesman ever, Sergeant Tony!"

As they celebrated in the courtyard, a fuming Susanna watched from the window. Their joy was her confirmation that her worst fears would be realized. The peasant union was coming to the Martellino vineyard. She felt a furious surge of disgust that they should think her such a fool. She would not let it happen. She must get her husband to understand the importance of defending what was theirs.

CR SO

Giovanni returned from the landowners' meeting in a dark mood, and Susanna was determined to keep him that way.

"Don't you think we're close to being successful?" she opened their dinner conversation that night.

He slowly nodded.

"Then why did you landowners roll over and sign a deal making the poor equal to us?"

He was indeed discouraged about the contract but was tired of talking about it. "We signed a deal to allow them to have their own management council for the estates where they work."

"And of course, they'll get all kinds of welfare demands—all at the expense of us, the landowners."

"I'll talk about it with Franco." He stood to leave, but she grabbed his hand and gave him an affectionate squeeze. "Thank you, darling. I'm sure you'll remind him that this vineyard is ours."

CR SO

They met outside the barn that afternoon. Franco carried two wooden chairs down to the vineyard while Giovanni brought two glasses and a bottle of wine. Giovanni poured each a small amount, they emptied their glasses, and the landowner told his winemaker about what had taken place at the landowners' meeting.

Franco took his time before answering. "Let me first say I was unaware of the union demands because I've not been in Lucca for almost two weeks. I'm very happy working for you, and I believe we are making great strides with both your grapes and your olives."

Giovanni nodded and offered another glass. Franco accepted.

"That said, signor, I'm from Puglia, where the peasant farmers barely make half of what the government says it takes for basic sustenance. There's no opportunity for the workers to save." He paused and nodded at the vines, already heavy with bright purple fruit. "It's better here in Tuscany, but with so many soldiers coming back from the war, competing to find jobs, it's easy to understand why the workers are angry."

Giovanni took a sip and leaned forward. "My wife believes we need a corporate system to save Italy. She says it's human nature—survival of the fittest. She thinks we need a strong government to control the masses. One Italy. One dynamic man to lead us."

"Did Susanna say that, or is she repeating the words of Mussolini?"

Giovanni's arched brow twitched up.

"Mussolini may have lost the election in 1919," Franco continued, "but his Fascists are gaining ground every day. They talk about returning Italy to our empire days, but what I saw in Trieste shows they'll crush anyone who gets in their way."

"Why won't Mussolini condemn the violence?" Giovanni asked.

"Because they're his base. Alienate them, and he'll lose their support."

Giovanni took a deep breath and glanced at Franco. "Do you think Italy's workers will revolt as they did in Russia?"

"I don't know. I'm just a simple winemaker." Franco paused and then raised his glass. "But I'm your winemaker—and I've been loyal to you."

Giovanni nodded. "We need each other for this to work."

"It's already working, signor. Antonio met with a wine buyer from Pietrasanta and made inroads with several hotels and restaurants."

"When did that happen?"

"While you were at the landowner meetings and I was convalescing, Antonio was out selling."

A small grin began to crease the landowner's face. "I doubted your decision to hire him, but he's a good man."

Franco sat silently for a long moment, as if deep in thought. "Remember when I first arrived at your vineyard?"

Giovanni nodded.

"You asked me about the war, but I was reluctant to tell you what I saw."

Giovanni remained silent.

"It was fear and death and cold and suffering," Franco said with a blank look, but then suddenly his eyes brightened. "But there were men like Antonio who were heroes; men who led without fear and inspired us, the young, to follow them. He's the same with you, Giovanni. You gave him a job when no one else would. He believes in the wine, and when his day work is done for you, he heads to Lucca with samples for the restaurant owners. That's where he met the wine buyer. I used to think Antonio was born to be a soldier, but I was wrong. He was born to sell."

Giovanni stared into his glass of wine, a reflection of what everyone who lived on his property helped create, from pruning to bud-break to flowering to *veraison* to harvest to wine. Each person he employed was part of what he held in his hand. He brought the glass to his lips, took a sip, and turned back to Franco. "I think we have an opportunity to show other landowners that there can be balance between owner and worker."

Franco only smiled and shook his landowner's hand.

As they picked up their chairs and headed back to the villa, Franco slowed his pace, searching for the right words to discuss another matter that had long been on his mind. He closed his eyes and took a deep breath.

"Is there something else you want to talk about?" Giovanni asked.

The question startled Franco, whose eyes flashed wide open. "Yes—uh—I want your advice about something personal."

Giovanni snorted with amusement and gave him a playful shove. "You're in love with Bella, aren't you?"

Franco flushed with embarrassment. "I'm crazy about her, signor! I—I can't sleep. I see her face in everything. The grapes. The olives. The night sky. I can't get her off my mind."

Giovanni laughed out loud and handed the bottle of wine to Franco. "Drink up, my friend, for you are indeed lost in love."

Franco did drink, with half of the wine finding his throat and the rest running down his chin and onto his shirt. "I'm both lost and found every time I see her, signor. But being without Bella scares me more than being rejected by her."

"Why do you think Bella would reject you?"

"Because she's everything I'm not—and everything I want. She has this—this absolute conviction about life. She has no fear. She's tough. She's safe. She's confident."

"Not the most romantic declaration of love I've ever heard," Giovanni chuckled.

"I want to marry her!" Franco gushed. "I want her to live with me! Here!"

Giovanni's face went from delight to near distress as he glanced toward the villa where his wife was waiting. "I—uh—have no problem with Bella living here, Franco. But for some reason, her confidence bothers Susanna. I don't know how she'll take this news."

It was as if Franco hadn't heard him as he took another big gulp of wine. "How does one propose to a girl who lives in a convent? I mean—Bella has no blood family. Who would I talk to—to seek permission to marry?"

Giovanni stood quite still, willing himself to let go of what his wife might think. Susanna had been the one who convinced him to send their winemaker to Trieste, where Franco had sustained his injuries, which had led to Franco and Isabella's time in the mountains. Thus, Susanna held some responsibility for their falling in love. His face softened into a slight smile. "What about Sister Anna?"

Franco's face lit up. "That's a great idea!" He gulped down the last of the wine, picked up his chair, and started for the barn. "I'll go to the convent right now and talk with Anna."

Giovanni hurried after him and grabbed him by the elbow. "I think Anna will be honored you came to her," he said. "But could you please wait until tomorrow? I want you at that union meeting in Lucca tonight. It's very important you be there."

CHAPTER 24

LUCCA, AUGUST 1920

"You can't be serious!" Susanna hissed as she stormed between her bedroom and Giovanni's, fists balled in anger, still unsure she had heard her husband correctly. "You met with Franco to discuss the challenges facing Italy and this vineyard—and you return with a marriage proposal?"

Giovanni gave a loud sigh and turned to face his wife. "I told you, Franco and I will work this out."

"As soon as they see the money we'll be making from this year's wine and oil, they'll want their cut."

"Franco made no demands, and it was my idea he attend tonight's union meeting."

Susanna hesitated before saying what was really on her mind. "I don't want that damn Isabella living here."

He threw his hands up in frustration. "Why? She's only been kind to us. She was here for you when DeAngelo was born and cares for our son as if he were—"

Susanna cut him off. "She's turning the workers against me!"

Giovanni gave a look of disbelief.

"It's true!" she hissed. "Have you seen the way they look at me? And now she'll be even closer to DeAngelo and turn him against me too!"

"The only one who's turning DeAngelo against you is you. If you changed your attitude about them—"

"I see what I see!"

"You see what you want to see, Susanna. Franco told me Isabella believes the two of you have something to learn something from each other."

"That's bullshit!"

"Maybe"—he paused, suddenly amused by her fury about something so frivolous—"there's something you can teach her."

"Don't patronize me."

"Then lets deal with the facts, darling. And the facts are that Franco's going to ask Isabella to be his wife and they'll need a place to live."

She stomped her foot. "I don't want her here all the time!"

"So you want her here only when you need her?" He was unable to contain his smile any longer. He walked over to her closet and pulled out a red dress. "Just in case Bella says yes to Franco, I think this is the dress you should wear to their wedding."

She grabbed the dress out of his hands and threw it back into her closet. "There isn't going to be any damn wedding!"

 CR   SO

As Franco walked the four kilometers to town to attend the union meeting, he had anything but labor strife on his mind. After spending every minute of the last seven days with the love of his life, he was consumed by thoughts of how he would propose to Isabella. There was simply no way he could honor Giovanni's request to wait until tomorrow to ask Sister Anna for permission to marry. Now, as he walked along the Via de Camaiore rehearsing his proposal, his feet seemed to take him farther away from the union meeting at Bosco's and directly to the Blessings Convent.

CR　SO

He arrived at a most serendipitous time. The very woman he wanted to talk with first, Sister Anna, was outside sweeping the front steps of the convent.

She smiled when she saw him and waved him over.

"I understand you've had quite the adventure," she said, the corner of her mouth twitching in amusement. "Tension in Trieste, a battle with villains, and recovery and romance in our northern hills."

Anna's knowledge of their affair sent him reeling, and he suddenly forgot what he was going to say. He shook his head to straighten out his thoughts and finally blurted out, "I wanted to talk with you about Bella."

"Let's go inside to discuss"—Anna looped her arm through Franco's and opened the convent door—"the subject of your romantic interest."

"Uh—yes. Bella has no family…" he said, and then he gritted his teeth, humiliated by his choice of words.

"Bella may have no blood family," Anna grinned, "but every home in Lucca welcomes her as family."

"Yes, of course," he stuttered, "but—it's—only proper to get permission from the head of the family when you're interested in the family's child."

"Interested?" She led him into the sanctuary. "If you're in love with Bella, there are a few questions I'd like to ask."

"Anything!" Franco gushed.

"Why do you love her?"

The question threw him off, and the speech he had rehearsed on his walk to town was suddenly lost to him. "I—I love being with her."

"Good answer." Anna bit her lip to keep from giggling. "And why do you love—being with her?"

These are tough questions, thought Franco, and he paused for a moment. "I—I like the way I feel when I'm with her."

"That's good. But what do you want from Bella?"

"Nothing—only her love!"

"That's a fine answer." Anna opened the door to the convent kitchen, and there stood Isabella with her back to them, preparing the night's meal. Anna leaned close to Franco and whispered, "You have my permission." And then she nudged him inside and closed the door.

Isabella turned and gave him a look of delighted surprise. "Franco!"

"I—I was on my way to the union meeting," he said quickly, and then he forced a smile.

"The meeting is at Boscos," she said with a raised brow. "That's on the other side of town."

He took a deep breath. "There's something I have to ask you first."

She looked up, her green eyes wide open, tender and gentle, a dreamy smile on her face.

"Bella—" He swallowed hard. "Will—uh—will—"

At that moment they heard a car door slam and looked outside to see Susanna walking purposefully to the convent.

"Dear God, no!" Franco groaned. "Susanna can't see me here! She knows I'm supposed to be at the union meeting. If she finds me here—"

Isabella grabbed him by the collar and shoved him underneath the table. A curtain attached to the front would keep anyone from seeing him.

Susanna burst through the door. "I know what's going on! And I'm here to prevent you from making a terrible mistake!"

"What's going on?" Isabella asked innocently.

"Franco's going to propose to you, and you have to say no!"

Underneath the table, Franco's head snapped up and hit a wooden support. Isabella kicked him and began chopping peppers to hide the noise.

"Why are you so concerned about my relationship with Franco?"

"He's a damn Socialist, Isabella! He and that foolish sergeant want our land, and I don't want you to be drawn into their vicious scheme. I'm—I'm here to protect you!"

Isabella nodded politely. "Thank you—for thinking of me."

Susanna crossed her arms over her chest. "I'm sure you've heard that soldiers returning from the war have been causing problems."

"But not one problem from Franco or Antonio?"

"Not yet," Susanna said. "But agriculture strikes are on the rise. We had only ten last year, and there already have been over one hundred this year. Why, in the south, peasants and returning soldiers have invaded farms and are demanding a redistribution of land."

"How does Giovanni feel about this crisis?"

"He's too soft. He still feels guilty about Franco getting hurt in Trieste. But how do we know that Franco didn't simply mishandle the sale? Why is my family the only one to suffer from this financial loss?"

"I'm a little confused," Isabella said as she sliced into an onion and stealthily dropped half of it under the table near Franco. "How does my saying no to Franco affect the redistribution of land in Italy?"

Susanna looked away, still stewing about the thought of this convent girl living on their property. And if Isabella and Franco were married, there would be no way to break up these Socialists who would take what was hers.

"I'm just trying to save you," Susanna said very slowly, "from making a terrible mistake."

"Thank you for your interest in my well-being," Isabella nodded, and then she glanced down to see an onion slide out from underneath the curtain. She bit the inside of her cheek to keep from smiling. "But if Franco were here right now and was to propose to me, how do you think I should reject him?"

Susanna shrugged slightly and gave an annoyed look.

"Why don't we try a little role play?" Isabella said.

Susanna's mouth opened as if she was confused. "What?"

"Come on, it will be fun. I'll be Franco, and you be me." Isabella kicked Franco underneath the table and lowered her voice. "Oh, Isabella, you're so beautiful and talented. Will you marry me?"

"No."

"You can't just say no, Susanna. That would be hurtful—let's try it again. Isabella, you're not only beautiful and talented but a fabulous chef, the best in Lucca. Will you marry me?"

"No. We're just friends."

"We're more than just friends after our rendezvous in the mountains, Susanna. Franco was quite the affectionate Romeo."

Franco slid his hand through the curtain and under Isabella's skirt, rubbing her ankle in a seductive manner. She kicked his hand away and tried to focus on Susanna. "Let's reverse roles—you be Franco, and I'll be myself."

Susanna exhaled her irritation. "This is stupid."

"Please."

"All right—um—Isabella—will you marry me?"

"That's boring."

"You're—uh—a kind person—and a good cook. Will you marry me?"

"I need more feeling!" Isabella implored as Franco's hand again came through the curtain and under her skirt, this time reaching up past her knee. She swatted it away as if it were a persistent mosquito and smiled at Susanna. "You need to say the three most important words of any marriage proposal."

"No." Susanna's blood was beginning to boil.

Isabella pushed out her lower lip in mock disappointment.

"All right, dammit—Isabella—I—I love you. Will you marry me?"

She looked Susanna squarely in the eyes. "I'll think about it."

"You'll do more than think about it!" Susanna demanded. "You'll say no."

"I said"—Isabella narrowed one eye—"I'll think about it."

Susanna opened her mouth to reply but instead just shook her head in anger, stormed out of the kitchen, got into her car, and drove off. As soon as she was out of sight, Isabella reached under the table and helped out an embarrassed Franco.

"I can explain," he said.

She crossed her arms over her chest. "I'm waiting."

"I—I can't do it now. I want it to be special."

"How do you know I'm going to say yes?"

"Give me a chance, Bella. How about we meet for dinner at Buca di Sant'Antonio as soon as the union meeting is over?"

She drew a deep breath and looked him straight in the eyes. "What time?"

"Eight."

She tried to hide her grin as she straightened his collar and gave him a kiss on the lips. "Don't you dare be late."

CB   SO

Franco arrived at Bosco's at seven. The union meeting had started an hour earlier, and the restaurant was filled with field and factory workers deep in conversation—some laughing, some arguing, but all drinking beer and wine that were flowing freely. When Franco walked through the door, it was as if Antonio had been waiting for him, for he immediately ran over. "Where the hell have you been?"

"I went to see Bella."

"Before the meeting? These lads can't make a decision without you."

Franco gave a confused look.

"You're the cock of the block, brother! You manage one of the biggest vineyards and olive orchards in the Province. My friends here say that ever since you arrived, the Martellino red and white have been the talk of the territory."

Franco's mouth fell open. "They have?"

"Damn right, with me as your public relations manager!" Antonio winked. "Unfortunately, not everybody likes you, Franco. Some are jealous of the Martellino success, but they all respect the work you've done. That's why they want your opinion tonight."

"But I don't have one."

Antonio put his arm around Franco and led him to the bar. "This is a time of change, my friend, with so many questions that need to be answered. Will kings still rule? Should the government or business run our economy? Should we peasants be allowed to own land?"

"I—I just want to produce a good wine and oil."

"As do I," Antonio continued. "And I'll follow your lead. But the division between rich and poor has never been greater. The Socialists want a revolution."

Franco shook his head. "That will bring suffering."

"Then tell them that. Because in this place, I'm the private and you're the sergeant." He lifted a glass of beer above his head and roared, "Here's to Franco!"

The crowd turned when they heard his name and raised their glasses with a cheer. "To Franco!"

And then the Martellino winemaker was engulfed by a sea of union men. He was besieged by questions about sharecropping and strikes and lockouts and Lenin, plus other questions about the earthy and oaky aromas in his Sangiovese and the improvement of his olive oil. He found himself defending his landowner, whose past work ethics were said to have been outrageous. Franco told them Giovanni had changed and that his boss had been one of the driving forces behind the July union contract that favored the workers. Some agreed, some wanted more, and some wanted revolution. By the time Franco finished and fought his way through the crowd to check the clock on the wall, he was horrified. It was nine o'clock.

CR   SO

Franco's lungs burned as he sprinted through the San Pietro gate and down Via Beccheria to Buca di Sant'Antonio. He arrived out of breath, gasping Isabella's name to the host.

"Bella left about ten minutes ago," the man said, and Franco bolted off into the night, darting down streets and alleys, past filled trattorias through the Porta Elisa to the Blessings Convent. He banged on the door until someone finally answered. It was Sister Emmilia, and she had not seen Isabella all night. He was frantic, trying to think of all the places she might go. He stopped by the Church of Saint Francesco, then the Piazza dell'Anfiteatro, and finally San Frediano. But no Isabella. Old doubts began to creep back into his brain as he started up the ramp that led to the top of Lucca's walls.

"You fool," he told himself. "Papa warned you about this, and you let her get away."

He headed west past Saint Agostino, his mind filled with regrets.

"I should have asked her at the convent. I should never have gone to the union meeting. Now I've lost her."

His walk took him past the lights of the city, along the northwest walls and into the shadows of the plane and chestnut trees that lined the path. It was an eerie gloom that drew him in, and it reminded him of something Isabella had said when they explored the caves of the Alpi Apuane mountains.

"This darkness is only the absence of light," she had said, "much as fear is only the absence of love. True vision is not physical but comes from deep within you, giving you the strength to see the light that guides you home."

Was he holding back, he thought? Had he been putting up some kind of resistance to love since the war? He knew love came with risks. He had seen cruel and horrible things in his life, and perhaps he was still staring at the darkness instead of seeking the light. As his eyes adjusted to the shadows, he saw someone at the edge of the walls.

"Bella?" he asked.

She turned but did not answer.

"I'm so sorry!" he called out as he ran to her. "I lost track of time!"

She stood quietly, a pleasant look on her face, but one that revealed nothing.

"I went to the restaurant, the convent, the market, and San Frediano, searching for you!"

She continued to look up at him, the full moon reflecting off green eyes that seemed to be smiling, yet he wasn't quite sure. Her face did not change with affection or question or give him that crinkle-eyed look he'd come to adore. She was stoic, patient, listening as he poured out his heart.

"I love you, Bella! I've loved you from the first moment I saw you! Please! Please be my wife!" He paused for a moment, a bit surprised by the ease with which his words flowed. "There! I said it. Now give me your answer!"

She inhaled deeply and stared out at the walls for a spell. Finally, she turned back to him. "Walking near these walls always helps me answer my questions. Sometimes I walk inside the city; sometimes I walk outside; sometimes I walk atop the walls." She paused to make sure his eyes met hers. "And sometimes I have to walk through the walls to find the answer I already know."

He took her hand. "What is the answer you already know?"

"When I was at the restaurant," she said, one eyebrow arched defiantly, "waiting, and waiting, and waiting. I did have questions flying through my head—'Is Franco the one? Can he let the past go? Should I share my life with him?'"

He swallowed hard. "And?"

"And I prayed on that while circumnavigating our city—twice. But when I stopped here, a voice came to me. It was clear and concise—and only one word."

He moved hesitantly toward her, uncertainty in his mind. "What was the word?"

"Trust."

Franco's voice was unsteady as he asked, "Do you trust—us?"

Isabella's eyes glowed as she smiled up at him. "Yes."

CHAPTER 25

AUGUST 1920

As the sun burned off the fog on an August morning, the sound of bells ringing in the steeple of a nearby church filled the Piazza del Mercado. Isabella was busy working her stand with Sisters Anna and Emmilia, and their table was surrounded by eager customers. Many of them had heard the news that the girl from the convent would be married, and wished her well.

Chef Vincenzo, who was buying vegetables for his restaurant, cried out, "Tell me it's not so, Bella, Bella! I dreamed last night that you said yes to me!"

She laughed and shouted back at him over the crowd, "You had your chance, Vincenzo! You could have kissed me that day in church when we were children, but you were too scared! Now, I must settle for a handsome hunk who worships the ground I walk on!"

"My heart breaks!" he yelled back. "How will I ever survive?"

"It's time to move on! Now, what can I get you? Tomatoes? Peppers? A Protestant woman?"

They all laughed, and then Sister Anna joined in. "Vincenzo, do you think the Princess of Patience even allowed Franco time to propose?"

"He asked me!" Isabella cried out. "My Franco, he loves me!"

Sister Emmilia interrupted the frivolity with a note from the Mother Superior. Bella read it and turned to Anna. "Our good Mother wants me to take some refreshments to a political rally at Piazza Napoleone. I shouldn't be long."

She prepared several trays of bread, fruit, and salad, put them on a cart, and headed to the Piazza.

CR ꙮ

Several townspeople and politicians were already in the square, setting up for the evening's festivities. A security man told Isabella where to set up, and she weaved her cart through the Lucchesi elite and entered a private dining tent.

It was warm inside, the afternoon sun baking the dark canvas, with only a dim light in the corner giving her enough light to see. As she leaned forward and placed a tray of vegetables on a table, she felt a hand slide up her right side and squeeze her breast. She tried to spin around, but her captor held her tight, grinding his pelvis into her buttocks.

"Mmmm," a man's voice moaned as he thrust his tongue into her ear. Isabella grabbed an eggplant off a platter and blindly jammed it backward, striking the man in the eye.

He shoved her to the ground and clutched his eye in pain. Isabella leaped to her feet and waved the eggplant in his face. "Get away from me!"

The man had already been drinking and slurred his words. "I was only havin' a li'l fun."

Isabella said nothing, just stood her ground, defiantly pointing the eggplant at the man as if it were the sword of the famed Roman gladiator Tetraites.

"Do ya know who I am?" the man growled.

"You're a coward who preys on women when they're alone."

Her words seemed to sober him up. "That's no way to talk to an important Fascist leader. I'm Alfredo Obizzi—the host of this party."

"Then why don't you act like a leader instead of a dog in heat?"

He reached for her, but she slapped his hand away with the eggplant. Her eyes narrowed as she studied him, believing she had seen this man before—but where?

"Why don't you just calm down." He began to remove his jacket. "Let's get to know each other a little better."

She suddenly remembered where she had seen him before: once at a restaurant in Lucca, and the other time in the arms of Susanna Martellino.

"Come on, sweetie—we have a little time before the party begins."

Isabella raised the eggplant to his face and stared him down. "I'm engaged to a gentleman who could teach you a thing or two about manners."

Obizzi unbuttoned the top button of his pants and smiled seductively. "But he's not here."

"No," Isabella said, "but this eggplant is."

She threw the vegetable at him, hitting him squarely in the nose. He yelped in pain as Isabella grabbed her cart and spun back to face him. "By the way—I'm to live and work at the Martellino vineyard. Does that mean anything to you?"

Obizzi's head jerked up, his hands frozen to his injured nose.

"I don't know what you think you've seen or heard," he said, trying to blink the tears from his eyes, "but I'm not a man to be fooled with."

Isabella shoved her cart at Obizzi, forcing him to stumble backward, out of the tent and in front of startled patrons. As she swept by him, she looked over her shoulder and said in a voice loud enough for all to hear, "You may not be a man to fool with, but you are certainly a man who acts like a fool!"

An incensed Obizzi wanted to chase her down, but with the Lucchesi elite watching, he held back, trying to calm his fury as Isabella pushed her cart back to the Mercato.

ന്ദ   ഇ

Susanna was livid when she found out Isabella had accepted Franco's proposal, but she remained quiet about it with Giovanni. She knew her husband favored the wedding, and she didn't want to start an argument she knew she would lose. Yes, the vineyard finances had improved, but she was convinced their field workers would use the gain as leverage to break up the Martellino property. Her payback would be simple. With her husband off on a sales trip, she would visit Alfredo at a Fascist rally in Pisa. Why not go? She had not seen her lover in over a month, and the thought of their last tryst left her wanting more.

ന്ദ   ഇ

She contacted him that night and left the next morning, an eager smile on her face as she drove to Pisa, thinking about what her sister would say when Mussolini finally governed Italy. Margherita's family may have enjoyed the spoils of success under the Socialists, but soon that would be part of the past. Fascism would be the rule, and her sister would finally be looking up to her. What would Margherita say if she saw a newspaper photograph of Susanna standing next to the great Mussolini? Would Alfredo include her in his rise to glory? Would he perhaps have her as his wife?

ॐ ॐ

"Hello, my darling!" Obizzi beamed as he opened his hotel room door and swept Susanna off her feet. "You should have heard me at today's rally!" He kissed her full on the lips, stopped, and then kissed her again. "I spoke to the spirit of the people! War veterans fed up with the government and patriots who would die for Italy. All are worried about a revolution."

"I'm sure you gave them good news," Susanna said as she traced her finger down his neck to the top button of his shirt.

"Indeed, I did," he boasted. "I told them of how our young patriots have stopped several Socialist rallies."

Susanna froze, thinking of the violence her winemaker had experienced in Trieste. "Did they stop the rallies—peacefully?"

"Let's just say they had—serious discussions with some of the rural workers' groups."

"What about Giacomo Matteotti?" Susanna asked as she reached for a bottle of wine on his desk.

"Fuck Matteotti!"

Susanna knew Obizzi hated the Socialist leader, but for some reason she had never told him that Matteotti was related to her brother-in-law. "But Matteotti has his allies," she said as she poured them each a glass of Chardonnay. "The liberals love him because he spoke out against the war, and the rural workers love him because he's helping them organize a union."

"He's a pacifist worm. He'll have to join us, or we'll remove him, because Fascism is Italy's future." Obizzi accepted a glass and then gave Susanna a cold look. "By the way, I had an interesting conversation with a young lady in Lucca the other day. She said she works at your vineyard. Thin, dark hair, fiery little bitch—said she is going to marry soon?"

Susanna's eyes narrowed in fury. "Isabella."

Obizzi slowly nodded as he studied her reaction. "She asked me an interesting question that led me to believe she knows about—us."

Susanna's mouth fell open in shock. "What? How? I've said nothing. We've been discreet in all our meetings—"

He grabbed her arm and squeezed until he brought pain. He wanted her attention. "No one is to know I'm seeing you, Susanna. If it's discovered I'm having an affair with a married woman, I could be thrown out of the party. Do you understand?"

She winced at the pain he was inflicting, "Yes. I—I understand."

He released his grip and unbuttoned the top button of his shirt. "Good. Now let's enjoy the rest of this lovely afternoon."

C3   80

With Giovanni and Antonio away on a sales trip, Franco asked Isabella for help. It was still August, and the grape berries that had been so hard two weeks earlier were changing color and softening. Harvest was about a month away. But Franco was interested in the vine by the creek that was just about ready.

"This is the Barbera plant you brought from the convent?" he asked.

Isabella nodded.

He pulled a berry off and tossed it into his mouth. "They're better than I thought they'd be."

She gave him a sly grin.

"It's sweeter—a little more complicated—fruity—less tannic."

"Isn't that what I said yesterday?"

"No." Franco bit his lip. "You just said they're very hardy plants and will grow practically anywhere."

She crossed her arms and gave him a crooked smile. "You do know I planted that vine?"

Ignoring her, Franco held a grape up to the sun as if he were some professor of viticulture from a university in Rome. "Impressive."

"Did you hear me?"

Franco tried to keep from laughing as he picked up his pruning shears. "Come with me, pagan woman. It's time to cut away any dense growth that's crowding the grape clusters and position them better to reach your sun god."

Isabella followed in mock respect. "If a grape falls off the vine, should I nail it back on?"

"Don't you dare let one of my precious grapes fall to the ground, peasant girl!"

She gave him a playful shove. "Is this how you expect me to behave after we marry?"

"I hope so," Franco laughed. "I gave instructions and you listened. That's a first."

"So, you want a brainless twit, do you?" Isabella jumped onto his back. "Is that how the girls are in Puglia? Oh, Franco, you're such a master vintner! Teach me all you know! Should I water my plants or use limoncello?"

He fell to the ground and she straddled him, tickling his ribs. "You're not the boss of me! Our marriage will be one of equality!"

"I surrender!" Franco pulled her on top of him and kissed her powerfully.

They heard a cough and looked up to find Josephine, hands on hips, staring down at them. "I'm sorry to interrupt your preparations for harvest," she frowned, "but I must warn you, the signora has been watching you from the villa, and the more you enjoy each other, the madder she gets. She's been on a tirade lately. She's angry with Giovanni, impatient with her son, wants everyone fired, but most of all"—Josephine paused and nodded at Isabella— "she doesn't want you living here."

"I don't understand," Franco said as he helped Isabella to her feet. "Sales are up. The grapes and olives are on schedule. Why is she looking for trouble?"

"It's my fault," Isabella sighed as she brushed the leaves from her blouse. "I've put this off for too long."

ଓ &ଠ

Susanna was in her study going over the vineyard ledger when Isabella knocked on the open door. Susanna looked up but said nothing.

"Signora Martellino." Isabella walked directly to her. "I think it's important we talk about my living here."

Susanna pushed herself away from the desk but remained quiet.

"Now that Franco and I will be married, I want to make sure there's peace between us. I'm sorry if I've done anything to upset you."

Susanna gave an exasperated sigh. "You went against my wishes when you agreed to marry. What did you expect?"

"I love him."

"Now the two of you think you can control my husband."

"I have no interest in controlling anyone."

Susanna cut her off with a flip of her hand. "You've never understood your place, Isabella. Until you do, you'll have many difficulties."

Isabella placed her hands on her hips, too irritated to be tactful. "Where's my place, signora?"

"When you marry, it will be working my field and cooking for my family." She cocked her head to the side and gave a look of complete arrogance. "Remember—I'm the landowner, and you'll now be my employee."

"Why do you put a wall between us?" Isabella asked. "Do you really believe we are that much different because you have money and I do not?"

"You Socialists are all alike!" Susanna snapped. "You want equality as if it's a right! But Socialism is a fraud, a comedy, a phantom, a blackmail. I believe we become strong when we have no friends upon whom to lean or to look to for moral guidance."

Isabella snorted in amusement. "That's a very accurate quote of Mussolini. But I don't belong to any party—and I believe we become stronger when we have friends to lean on, to help us through difficult times, to inspire our moral guidance." She paused to make sure she had Susanna's full attention. "Good friends should be there for us when we fall—or when we are led into temptation."

Susanna quickly turned her back to Isabella, incensed with how this peasant girl knew about her and Obizzi. "It's—it's time for you to leave," she said through clenched teeth.

Isabella headed for the door but then suddenly stopped. "I will cook and work for you—and be your friend. I'm sorry if I've angered you in any way. But if you ever need someone to talk to—about anything—I'm here for you."

CR BO

September's harvest went well. Despite Susanna's protests, Giovanni paid Isabella to prepare a feast to celebrate the end of the season, and invited the neighbors and the sisters of the Blessings Convent for dinner. As he helped carry the grapes in to be crushed, he stopped to tease the nuns as they tied their robes above their knees to stomp the berries into juice.

"Speed it up, Sister Anna!" Giovanni called out. "The shorter the time from vine to juice, the better the wine!"

"I believe this is an excellent harvest!" Anna grinned as she lifted a grape-stained foot to show Giovanni. "My feet are a much more robust purple this year, and the color under my nails seems to have a hint of cinnamon."

He laughed. "What should we call this divine vintage?"

She pointed at her foot. "Anna's Sole-full Sangiovese, of course."

Her fellow sisters groaned and pelted Anna with grapes. Giovanni tossed one himself and then picked up his son and walked over to join Franco.

It was a beautiful day for a harvest, with the green vines contrasting against the tan fields as the nuns and workers sang and laughed while picking the grapes and hauling them to the barn. Giovanni watched the scene with Franco and then lifted DeAngelo to his shoulders and smiled. "What a day, my friend. The joy on this farm is something much different from the way I was raised."

Franco nodded but said nothing, respecting his landowner's thoughts.

"All these years I've dreamed of making the perfect wine. A wine to be respected, a pride to be felt by everyone who worked this vineyard." He was quiet for a moment, listening to the laughter coming from the barn. "My father has been dead almost ten years, and still I tried to please him." He paused and looked back to the villa. "I've been doing the same with Susanna. Trying to get her to see what I have seen take place on this vineyard. I don't care anymore. I know what's happening."

The confession caught Franco by surprise, and he turned to face his landowner. Giovanni's eyes seemed to open and deepen, more like the eyes of a friend than those of an employer.

"It wasn't until DeAngelo was born, and then you and Antonio came aboard, that I discovered the joys in the simple things that take place in this vineyard every day. Watching my son pick a grape, or this—" He nodded to the nuns playfully pulling the Venero children into the vats to help with the crushing. "I just wanted to thank you, Franco—and let you know I'm looking forward to having you and Bella live here."

☙ ❧

Susanna pulled the curtains shut to keep the September sun from pouring through the dining room window. She wanted her husband's total attention for the speech she had planned. Since the war's end, more and more unemployed soldiers were growing frustrated with the government and claiming uncultivated and private lands for themselves. Labor strikes were up, some workers had seized factories, and Susanna feared a Communist revolution would be next.

"I think it's time you take a closer look at our Fascist effort, darling," she said as she poured Giovanni a glass of wine. "Our workers need to understand that Italy needs order. Why, one of the Socialist leaders sounds like an absolute terrorist. He had the gall to say that no ruling class ever surrendered its despotic power unless forced to do so by violence."

Giovanni placed his nose over the glass and inhaled deeply. "The only violence I've seen has come from the Fascist side. Your friends might be exaggerating information to recruit angry young men to the party."

"That's not true." She tried to stay calm. "The workers are demanding too much."

He took a sip. "What was it Lussu said last year? 'Imagination always plays a great part in times of political stress.'"

"Emilio Lussu?" she scoffed. "Don't tell me you're listening to that leftist revolutionary."

"He simply has been asking our leaders to seek common ground."

"The Socialists want all the ground!" she snapped, her calm suddenly broken. "If we don't do something right now, the workers will be storming our palace."

"Yes," he laughed. "I can just see Bella leading the mob. Straight from the chapel in her wedding dress with a pitchfork and panini raised over her head."

Susanna fired her wineglass across the room and stormed out of the house. Her eyes blazed with anger as she watched Angelina, off in the distance, tie a scarf around Isabella's eyes as Sister Anna showed the Venero children the wedding dress the nuns had made for her. It took all of Susanna's strength to keep from screaming.

Was she the only one in this vineyard who could see the cancer that was spreading inside Italy and in her vineyard?

She went to her car, revved the engine, and spun the tires up the drive and far away from the vineyard. She already knew where the car would take her, and why not? She deserved to see Alfredo. It had been weeks since their last tryst, and she had followed up with two messages that had gone unanswered. She wasn't surprised he had not responded; he was busy planning their country's future. While the Fascists may have lost the 1919 election, they had not lost their determination to rule Italy. Alfredo had echoed Mussolini's words in Pisa, saying, 'Only the intelligent and strong-willed have the right to decide Italy's fate.' Now Susanna would take those words to heart and decide her own fate. She would go to Massa, where Alfredo was speaking, and give herself to him. She would again be a part of something important. She would no longer be an insignificant farmer's wife.

The drive comforted her and gave her confidence. As she pulled into the hotel drive in Massa, her heart was filled with excitement until she glanced up to see a limousine parked in front. For an instant she froze, staring in panic. Obizzi was stepping out of the limo with a young woman holding on to his arm.

"Checking in, signora?" a valet asked as he opened her door.

She didn't say anything, but her face changed from shock to fury.

"Excuse me, signora—are you checking in?"

"Get out of my way!" she snapped, and she pushed past him.

Obizzi turned when he heard the outcry, and his eyes went wide when he saw who was headed his way.

"Susanna, what are you—"

She slapped him across the face. "You bastard!"

Every dignitary at the political rally turned to see what the commotion was about.

An embarrassed Obizzi threw his hands into the air.

She raised her hand to strike him again, but this time was caught by security.

"Signor Obizzi!" The security chief came running over to help his man hold back Susanna. "Are you all right?"

Obizzi saw that everyone was watching.

"Do you know this woman?" the security chief asked.

Obizzi inhaled a deep breath, glaring at Susanna and then back at the security chief.

"No," was all he said as he took the hand of his date and walked into the hotel.

CR   RO

The drive home was miserable. Susanna found it difficult to breathe and had to stop the car twice to be sick before arriving in Lucca at sunset. There were so many people to blame for her misfortune: her mother, her father, her sister, Giovanni, DeAngelo, Alfredo, and of course—Isabella. She turned her car down the road to the Blessings Convent and parked in front. At this time of night, she knew where she would find her.

CR   RO

A soft summer breeze swept through the trees as Isabella sat alone in the garden, legs crossed, hands in her lap, eyes closed. This was her precious time, when every morning and every evening she let go of all thoughts and reconnected with her higher self. She inhaled a deep breath of the cool night air and slowly exhaled, concentrating on the inflow and outflow of her breathing as she became more comfortable and more at peace.

"Isabella!"

She heard her name called out and immediately knew it was Susanna, stumbling through the darkness in search of help.

"Where are you? I need to talk with you!"

Isabella remained quiet and took in another long, deep breath and then let it go.

"Ow!" Susanna cried out as she walked headfirst into an olive branch, which only clipped her already diminishing patience. "I said—I need—to talk with you."

Finally, Isabella opened her eyes. "I'm over by the little tree."

Susanna pushed the branch out of her face and hurried over. "I need your help."

Isabella nodded but said nothing.

"I need to get away," she gushed, "Josephine is in Bologna taking care of her ailing mother, so I need you to take care of DeAngelo while I'm gone."

For a moment Isabella only stared up at her, too stunned to speak. Her wedding was only a week away, and she had many chores to finish at the convent before her special day—and then, of course, her move to the Martellinos'. She wanted to challenge Susanna's selfishness, but the look of desperation in Susanna's eyes made her pause.

"I will help you."

Susanna gave a deep sigh of relief. "Thank you."

"On one condition."

"Anything. I won't just donate to the convent this time. I'll pay you directly."

There it was, thought Isabella. The money. The wall Susanna always seemed to build to separate herself from the rest of the vineyard staff. The damn feeling that she was better than the rest of them because she had so much more.

"I'll help you if you tell me what has been troubling you."

Susanna looked away. "My troubles—are none of your business."

"Then I can't help you."

The ease in her statement infuriated Susanna, and she turned back to face Isabella, who was staring at her as if looking into her soul. "The people—the things that trouble me—you wouldn't understand."

"Try me."

Susanna balled her fists at her side. She couldn't believe the gall of this damn church cook. Yet she needed her help, so she softened her approach.

"I have"—she swallowed hard—"made some mistakes. I need time to be alone. To think things through."

"Do your troubles have anything to do with the man I met at the political rally?"

Susanna froze, mouth open, shocked at the question. She knew Isabella already knew of her affair, but hadn't thought she would go there. "I—I told you my troubles are none of your business."

"I thought he was very rude, Susanna. You're better than that."

"Alfredo Obizzi is a great man!" she snapped. "He's the future of Italy!"

"Great men have great character," Isabella said matter-of-factly. "That man is not interested in improving Italy. He's only interested in bettering himself."

"How dare you!"

"I'm sorry, but I think he's a con artist."

"You don't know what you're talking about! Alfredo will soon be at Mussolini's side, crushing any Communist uprising by you damn Socialists! We'll not allow what happened in Russia to happen in Italy."

"As I've told you before, I'm neither a Socialist nor a Fascist. But I certainly won't listen to men who spread fear to get themselves elected—or vote for men who prey on married women."

A furious Susanna kicked over Isabella's glass of water. "Damn you! I came here for your help, and all I get are insults from a—a—"

"A common orphan?" Isabella said as she calmly picked up the glass and placed it away from Susanna's wrath. "I'd like to think I'm your friend, Susanna, a friend who would let you know you're walking into dangerous territory with that letch. He'll use you and use Italy to get what he wants—and he won't care if he breaks up a family or breaks up a country to satisfy his ego."

Susanna was so angry she was shaking. "You disrespectful bitch! You're just like all the other Communists in this country! We give you jobs, let you live on our property, and you turn around and take advantage of our kindness!"

As Isabella stood up and started toward the convent kitchen, she shook her head. "And what time does your kindness want me to drop by tomorrow to take care of DeAngelo while you're away—getting your thoughts together?"

"Go to hell, Isabella!"

"No thank you, signora. I wouldn't want your son spending time with any of your friends."

CR   SO

Alfredo with another woman! Isabella had been right. He was selfish, greedy, and manipulative. But he had a power that both intimidated and excited her. Alfredo's being with another woman only made her want him more. And the agony of jealousy filled her days at the spa in Viareggio with despair and left her nights restless. The head cold started on the third day, and by the fourth she was on her way back to the villa, searching for comfort.

But the staff was busy, busy finishing up the primary fermentation of the newly crushed grapes and busy preparing for Isabella's wedding. Giovanni, whose wine sales had taken him to Livorno, arrived home on Friday, gave his wife a quick kiss on the forehead, and joined his workers outside. Once again, Susanna was left alone to suffer, and as Friday turned to Saturday, she was determined to use her illness as a way to avoid the wedding.

CR   SO

"I'm sorry I'm late," Giovanni said as he closed the back door to the villa and walked to his car. The vineyard staff were all sharply dressed and ready for the drive to the convent. "Susanna's not feeling well enough to attend, but said she will be with us in spirit."

Isabella's shoulders slumped forward. She had not talked with Susanna since their argument and knew the signora had been avoiding her. As the others climbed into Giovanni's car to head to town, Isabella headed to the villa.

"Bella, we need to go!" Franco cried out. "You have a rather important role in today's event!"

She turned and gave him a cockeyed smile. "Anna already has everything set up. You go on ahead. I've got my bike and I'll be along shortly."

He opened his mouth to disagree but felt Angelina's hand on his shoulder. "Don't try to stop her. I've seen mules give in before Bella."

She went to the kitchen, put a pot on to boil, clipped rosemary and thyme leaves, and tossed them into the water. When the water was ready, she took it upstairs along with apple cider vinegar and opened the door to Susanna's bedroom.

"What are you doing here?" Susanna coughed.

"Sit up," Isabella said as she poured a little of the apple cider vinegar into a shot glass. "Gargle this and then spit it into your washbasin."

Susanna did as she was told, grimacing at the taste, but the vinegar did seem to release some of the mucus that was caught in her throat.

"Now put your head over this pot and let the steam clear out your sinuses."

As Susanna leaned over the pot, Isabella draped a towel over her head to direct the steam to where it would do the most good. Susanna inhaled deeply, coughed, and finally mumbled, "I'm sorry I can't be there for you."

"And I'm sorry you're sick."

There was pause, as if the steam was releasing more than just the illness in Susanna's body. "Why are so many problems happening to me right now?"

"The mind is very powerful, Susanna. Perhaps your thoughts inspired your head cold."

"I rarely see you sick. Is that because you 'think' it away?"

"No, it's because I pray."

Susanna peeked from underneath the towel. "Prayer keeps you from getting sick?"

Isabella pushed Susanna's head back over the pot. "I pray in the morning to get my mind pointed in the right direction and pray at night to help it rest in God."

"Sounds as if you need a compass."

"Prayer is my compass."

Susanna paused for a long moment and then asked, "Does it work?"

"The body holds on to what the mind projects, Susanna. But if my needle is pointed in the right direction in the morning, the distractions of the day don't bother me as much. My prayers at night get that needle back to north and allow me to rest peacefully with God."

There was another pause in the conversation until Susanna lifted the towel off her head and looked up at Isabella. "You know I don't like you."

Isabella couldn't keep from grinning. "You'll hate me now. Your face is as red as a lobster. Let me get some lemon butter, and we can have lunch."

Susanna bit her lip to keep from laughing. "You take great joy in making me look bad, don't you?"

Isabella's grin widened to a broad smile. "It's my daily quest."

Susanna pulled the towel back over her head. "Get out of here, Bella. You'll be late to your own wedding."

CR ℀

Sister Anna stood at the edge of the convent path, hands on her hips, as Isabella came riding up on her bicycle.

"Where in Jesus, Mary, and Joseph have you been, Isabella Roselli?" Anna cried out. "I've had Sister Emmilia sing every verse of 'Santa Lucia' as slowly as possible to stall things. If this wasn't your wedding day, why I'd—"

"I love you too, Anna!" Isabella gasped as she tossed her bike aside and ran to the convent. "Now help me clean up and put my dress on!"

ⓒⱭ   ℰⱰ

Four Blessings nuns immediately went to work on the bride, wiping Isabella's sweat off with cool, wet towels while fanning her face to keep her cool. Sister Claudina slipped the wedding dress over Isabella's head as Sister Theresa went to work on her hair.

Anna hurried outside to join her co-maid of honor, Angelina, by the garden altar. Beside them were Franco and Antonio, smartly dressed in black tuxedos Antonio had bartered in exchange for four bottles of Martellino red. Antonio leaned forward and asked Angelina if he looked handsome. She nodded her approval.

The music started, and Giovanni and DeAngelo hurried to sit down next to Franco's parents. All heads turned to the kitchen door.

Isabella stepped out wearing a white silk gown made by the sisters, a crown of small daisies on her head. Her dark brown curls fell about her smiling face, still flushed from the four-kilometer bike ride.

Franco's mouth fell open, eyes locked on Isabella. He thought she was the most beautiful sight he'd ever seen and stood silently, hearing only the pounding of his own heart as she walked forward and took his hands.

Father Arturo cleared his throat to get everyone's attention. "The couple would like to share their thoughts on this blessed union with you."

But Franco was in another world, deaf to the priest's words, until he looked down at Isabella's bare feet.

"You forgot your shoes," he mumbled, and the crowd broke out in laughter.

Isabella giggled innocently. "Thank you for pointing that out."

An embarrassed Franco suddenly forgot what he was going to say.

"Family and friends," he finally blurted out, "uh—thank you for having us—I mean—thank you for being here."

His confusion was greeted with another round of laughter as Antonio stepped in front of his friend. "Would all of you just act like grapes? He was really amazing when he was practicing in the vineyard this morning."

Franco pushed Antonio out of the way. "I'm sorry—uh—I'm just a simple farmer from Puglia."

"You got that right!" his father roared from the front row. Maria elbowed her husband in the side.

By now, Franco's face was as red as the rose petals that lined the path.

He took a deep breath. "Do you remember the first time I met Bella?"

Most of them nodded, but some did not.

"It was the night I almost ruined the harvest by forgetting to block the creek that flows by the Martellino vineyard. Isabella came to the rescue with nuns from all over Lucca—many of you are here today—and the way she ordered us around was like—well—like Sergeant Tony leading an army up a hill. Don't ask questions, just charge!"

The congregation laughed, and he began to feel more comfortable.

"Bella was tough on me when I first met her, but she thought that I, like a good Tuscan wine, had potential. Thank goodness my friends and my parents encouraged me," he grinned at his father, "and embarrassed me into realizing I'd be a fool to let her get away." He smiled down at Isabella and touched her glowing face. "There was a time I didn't think I deserved this woman, but that is no more. I believe in love—and believe in us."

He turned back to the crowd and smiled broadly. "As you know, the final step in winemaking is bottling and sealing with a cork, so I want the first step of our marriage to be sealed with a kiss." With that, Franco took Isabella in his arms, bent her back, and kissed her soundly. The crowd cheered.

Now it was Isabella's turn. She looked at her sisters of the Blessings Convent and smiled. "I've been blessed to live the last thirteen years at this convent. I have made many dear friends who have been patient with me, taught me, raised me, and loved me." She wiped a tear from her cheek as she smiled at Anna. "My sisters helped me to realize that through forgiveness, beautiful things would happen, that through forgiveness and letting go, I would understand God's grace."

She looked up at Franco. "From the moment I saw you running around in the vineyard trying desperately to save the grapes, I was captured. Captured not by your effort, but by your desire to help others. Since that day, I've grown to love you more than words can describe. You are honest, kind, loyal, and open to learning and growing. Every year the harvest is a bit different from the last, and every year our lives will change. It's important to embrace those situations and understand that everything works together for our good, and ultimately for everyone. God is our source, and I am so grateful that He brought us together—not to complete each other, but to empower each other. We are here, Franco, only to be truly helpful, and by doing that I will joyously walk home to God with you."

When Isabella turned back to the congregation, she saw her Blessings sisters in tears, crying with joy for the young woman they had raised and now were giving to Franco. Isabella felt a tug on her dress and looked down. It was DeAngelo, holding their wedding rings on a kale leaf. Franco placed Isabella's ring on her finger, and Isabella did the same with the silver ring Sister Anna had had made for her at a local smithy. Father Arturo blessed the union, and the party erupted in cheers. When Isabella looked up again, she saw Susanna standing in the back, biting her lip to keep from crying.

CR SO

"What is that?" Isabella's eyes opened wide as Giovanni drove the newlyweds home that night to show off his surprise.

"We had it built during your wedding," Giovanni beamed, proud of how quickly the townspeople had come together to build the Carollos a tiny little cottage next to the barn. "It wasn't as difficult as you might think." He opened the car door and helped Isabella out. "Antonio and I had little difficulty finding volunteers to help."

"But who?"

He cupped his hands to his mouth and roared, "Who built this house?"

The barn doors suddenly opened, and out poured the citizens of Lucca.

"Oh my!" Isabella squealed as she reached for her husband's hand. "It's Cesare Bosco and Pascal Esposito! There are Henri and Stefano from the olive mill, and the Moscollonis all the way from Pistoia. Isn't this wonderful?"

Franco laughed, but he wasn't surprised. It was true. The little girl who had been adopted by the Blessings Convent had long been a light to all who were in need of help: from peasant families who were hungry to local chefs starting new restaurants, to the broken men returning from the war in need of healing. Isabella's thirteen years of giving were now coming back to her.

The newlyweds stood in the middle of the courtyard as over sixty people surrounded them: friends who had brought wood and stone and hammers and nails and built this tiny cottage. It was a simple yet comfortable structure with a wood-floor entryway, a small fireplace, and two small bedrooms at the rear. Three rooms were all this couple would need: a bedroom for the newlyweds, a bedroom for their future children, and a kitchen for Isabella to create her masterpieces in. The sisters had knitted a colorful bedspread, with Anna's gift hanging over the bed-—her artwork of hundreds of grape, olive, lettuce, and tomato seeds that spelled out Anna's favorite quote from Hebrews 11:1: "Now faith is the substance of things hoped for, the evidence of things not seen." A grapevine wreath with a "Welcome to the Carollos" sign hung on the front door, and a small wooden box was nailed next to the door.

Anna stepped forward and put her arm around Isabella. "You get what you give, my friend. You've given so much to so many ever since you arrived in Lucca. This is our humble way to say thank you."

CR   SO

They danced, they sang, and of course, they drank plenty of wine far into the night. As the reception drew to a close, the newlyweds searched out their hosts.

A dart of jealousy struck Susanna when she saw Isabella and Franco head their way, hands clasped, cheeks rosy from too much dancing and laughing. There was a ring of dirt around the bottom of Isabella's wedding dress, and her crown of daisies was now a lopsided mess, barely clinging to the side of her head. Isabella didn't seem to care as she hugged Giovanni with a joy that left him breathless and then turned to Susanna.

"I know you didn't feel well today, but it meant the world to me to have you at our wedding."

"Your steam concoction did seem to help—" Susanna started to say, and then she was overwhelmed as Isabella threw her arms around her and gave her a hug that almost cracked her ribs. They separated to an awkward pause, Isabella still smiling as Susanna looked away and busied herself with a loose thread on her husband's jacket.

"Our home is beautiful," Isabella said, "and we'll always remember it began with an extension of your love."

A frown drew Susanna's brows together as she glanced at the cottage. "Calling it an extension of my love is a bit presumptuous. I have not yet seen the bill for this project."

Giovanni's head jerked around. "I forgot to tell you, darling—we didn't pay for a thing. Every nail and piece of wood was a gift from friends of Bella!" He pointed at a man by the cottage who was visiting with Antonio. "You remember Filippo, who runs the lumberyard?"

She gave an uninterested nod.

"Isabella took care of his family when his wife fell ill. He donated all the lumber." He pointed to another man who was checking the seal on a windowsill. "That's Zanobi. He couldn't find a job when he returned from the war until Bella talked Filippo into hiring him. Now, Zanobi's his best carpenter." Giovanni nodded to other men who surrounded the little cottage—one with a hammer, pounding down a loose nail; another with sandpaper, going over a rough edge. "Those men built the floor, walls, and roof at the lumberyard and then brought them here and put the house together as if they were putting together the pieces to a puzzle. Rather industrious, if you ask me."

Susanna raised one eyebrow. "We didn't have to pay for anything?"

Giovanni shook his head.

"That was—very kind." She paused as she watched the scene for a moment, resigning herself to the fact that Isabella would now live here. On her property. Watching her every move. She massaged her forehead, feeling another headache coming on, and then turned and headed for the villa. A hand touched her shoulder. She immediately knew it was Isabella and turned to face that damn triumphant smile.

"Thank you again," Isabella said softly, "for a day I'll always remember."

CHAPTER 26

LUCCA, 1921

An all too familiar anxiety followed Susanna into Lucca's Fascist station on an April day of 1921. The seeds of want she had nurtured for the previous four years had blossomed into loneliness and disappointment. It had been so exciting to be part of the Fascist rise, next to Alfredo, a man she knew would soon be part of Mussolini's cabinet. Mussolini was Italy's future! He was the only man who could right the wrongs of the last decade and return Italy to greatness. He would indeed fight for the country she so loved. But now, as she glanced at her reflection in the office window, she saw only a common farmer's wife. Her days had become a dreary repetition of maternal chores, from taking care of her son to poring over the vineyard ledger, trying to make sense of the assets and debts, as if they held her own life in their balance. It also bothered her to see the vineyard blooming with joy. The sap that flowed through the trunks and canes of the vines was pushing the buds to swell...much like the newest addition to the Martellino staff. Isabella Carollo was now seven months pregnant, and Susanna was convinced that all of Lucca's attention was focused on the former convent girl, from the townspeople at the city market with their constant congratulations to the convent sisters who hovered about like mother hens.

Susanna straightened up with a small sigh of impatience and opened the door, oblivious to the conversation that buzzed about the Fascist office.

"He's Roberto Farinacci's most trusted ally!" a young volunteer gushed as she dusted the entryway, anxiously awaiting the arrival of an advisor to one of the thirty-five Fascists recently elected to parliament. "He's one of the men who protected Empoli from those awful Communists."

"Those people are animals!" a secretary said as she placed a bouquet of flowers in the entryway. "Did you hear that one of their women attacked a member of our party and bit off his ear?"

"I've heard that the Communists cut off the genitals from the men they kill."

"How horrible!" came the reply. "These people are certainly not Christians."

The office manager placed a vase of flowers on his desk and smiled proudly. "That's why it's such an honor to have one of the men who pushed the barbarians back into the countryside come all the way from Cremona to visit us."

The very mention of Cremona startled Susanna.

"Excuse me—who is this new advisor you're talking about?"

"He's very handsome!" The secretary picked up a newspaper that bore his picture. "It's Alfredo Obizzi."

Susanna's face went white just as the door opened, and there stood Obizzi.

"Susanna!" he said with a look of delight. "What a wonderful surprise!"

Her mouth fell open as she tried but could not even breathe.

The office manager ran to Obizzi and shook his hand vigorously. "Signor Obizzi! What an honor to have you visit our headquarters!"

"The honor is all mine," he said humbly. "I've heard great things of the work you've done here, enlisting young people to our cause."

"Thank you, signor, and—and congratulations on cleansing Empoli of those terrible Communists."

Obizzi put his hand on the man's shoulder. "My friend, a force greater than us guides me. During the war we had external enemies. Now, there are internal foes—enemies of Italy that must be eliminated."

The office manager's head bobbed up and down excitedly.

"Now, if you don't mind"—Obizzi squeezed the man's shoulder—"I'd like to have a word alone with Signora Martellino."

"Certainly, Signor Obizzi. My office is all yours." The manager quickly turned and motioned for his gawking young volunteers to leave the room. He then bowed and closed the door.

Alarm tingled up Susanna's spine as she heard the doorknob slowly click into place. She swallowed hard and looked up at Obizzi, whose black eyes danced as if amused by her discomfort.

"Why haven't you responded to the letters I sent to this office?" he asked. "I wanted to see you."

She kept her distance. "Remember Massa? The—other woman?"

"She means nothing to me!" he laughed, casting his hand in the air. "You have to understand, I'm now an important member of the Fascist Party, and sometimes it looks good to have an escort at your side."

"Why," she hesitated, "didn't you invite me?"

"You're a married woman, Susanna. Or did you forget that? Our leadership would frown on one of its advisors being involved in adultery."

Her face turned red, but Obizzi moved quickly to comfort her. "But I'm here now, darling. There are great things happening in Italy, and I want you to join me in being part of that future."

She took a step back. "I—I don't think that would be right."

Her lack of interest only made him more determined. "I'm only in Lucca one night. Why don't you join me for dinner?"

"I can't go to dinner with you, Alfredo. Lucca's a small town, and as you said—I'm a married woman."

He tossed his head back in laughter. "Which makes you all the more attractive to me." He looked her up and down with obvious approval. "And we don't have to dine at a restaurant. I'll have dinner prepared at my suite at the Hotel Universo."

She turned her back to him, but her heart was racing. "I—don't think that would be wise."

But Obizzi moved closer, and the touch of his hand on her shoulder excited her. He smiled slyly as he pulled a hotel key from his pocket and placed it on her desk. "Just in case you change your mind, my love. I'll plan our room service for eight o'clock."

ℭ ℭ

Nine months after the Carollo wedding, Isabella delivered a baby girl: seven pounds, eleven ounces. They named her after Isabella's mother, Liliana, whose name meant "love and joy." The day after she was born, Franco was back at work in the vineyard, and ten days later Isabella returned to her table at Lucca's market. All her produce came from the new garden she had constructed between the barn, vineyard, and olive grove. It was almost four times as large as the small convent garden she had known as a child, and the size allowed her to share her profits with the Martellinos and the Blessings Convent.

∞

July in Tuscany could be hot and humid. Even though Josephine opened every window in the villa, there was no breeze, and the walls seemed to hold in the heat of the day. Susanna tried to smooth back her tousled hair, but her face was damp, and her body was already wet with sweat; she was also frustrated by her son's constant chatter. DeAngelo had been pleading with his mother to let him go with Isabella to the market. An exasperated Susanna finally gave in, grabbing her four-and-a half-year-old son's hand and pulling him out to the truck that would take the produce to the Piazza del Mercato. Looking tired and haggard, Susanna sighed heavily as she gave her son to Isabella.

"Don't let him out of your sight. There's been trouble in some of our northern towns, and I'm sure the Communists are behind it."

"We have three very capable young ladies who will take good care of him," Isabella said. "I'll put Little D. in charge of selling the apricots; he's a fine little salesman."

Susanna gave her son a kiss on both cheeks and grabbed him by both collars. "If you did your studies with the same passion you use to bark at the markets, you might grow up to be a person of some influence." DeAngelo grinned, which did not sit well with his mother. "I'm serious, young man. Your aunt's little boy was reading at the age of four."

"The market's fun, Mama!" He took his mother's hand and walked to the truck. "Come with me! I help you sell—ap-ree-cots! Tasty ap-ree-cots!"

Susanna frowned as she struggled to lift him onto the back of the truck next to Rosa and Elisa. "Not today, dear. I'm too tired."

○ ○

As Obizzi passed the Piazza Napoleone in Lucca, he couldn't help but wonder how the great leaders always seemed to have the strength and courage to control the masses. Napoleon had done it in the previous century in Europe, and Obizzi was sure Italy would give the continent its next great ruler.

"Mussolini is growing in power," he said to his aide, Frederico Bartoni, as they walked along the Via Beccheria. "Benito understands there are times when violence is necessary, and now that we have a common enemy in the Bolsheviks, the money and support are beginning to pour in."

"We can't win without the support of the corporations," Frederico agreed.

"The heads of industry and the rich and powerful know the time is right to join the Fascist Party."

Frederico struggled to keep up with Obizzi's pace. "But Benito's genius is in his timing. He's been very patient in waiting for the perfect time to seduce the monarchy, the church, and the capitalists."

"With our help, he'll get them on board. The Communists have scared everyone into believing the peasants are ready to start a revolution. The rich know that Mussolini is the only man who can stop it."

As they turned right on Via Santa Croce, Frederico asked the question that had been more than an irritation to Obizzi. "What of the woman? What should we do about that situation?"

Obizzi stopped abruptly in the middle of the street and stared at his assistant. "There is no—situation. No one can know about Susanna and the baby. I don't even know if it's mine."

"But she said you're the only one she's slept with in months."

Obizzi articulated his next words with a cold and blunt cadence. "I had a courier hand-deliver her the name of a doctor in Cremona who could end this pregnancy."

"But she refused," Frederico fumbled, pulling the letter out of his pocket. "She wrote that she would leave her husband to be with you."

Obizzi slapped his aide's hand away and continued walking. "Do you think I'm a fool? I don't want that pregnant bitch getting in the way of my destiny—and Italy's destiny."

Frederico hurried after Obizzi as he weaved his way through the weekend shoppers. "Now where are we to have our 'coincidental' meeting with Signor Esposito?"

"The Piazza del Mercato," Frederico replied. "He's there every Saturday."

CR &

Isabella smiled sweetly as she watched DeAngelo adjust the blanket to protect Liliana from the sun. The Martellino boy had been a tremendous help since her daughter was born, caring for her as if he were her older brother. He made sure she was comfortable before organizing his apricots, apples, and pomegranates in small neat piles on the market table. He then cupped his hands to his mouth and called out, "Ap-ree-cots! Nothing better than Mar-tell-ee-no ap-ree-cots!"

A buyer from a local restaurant heard him and yelled back over the crowd, "I'll take a dozen, Little D.!" The man hurried over and handed Isabella money as the boy bagged the fruit.

"He's a fine young salesman," the buyer said with a wink.

"Indeed, he is," Isabella replied. As she handed the buyer his purchase, she caught a glimpse of Obizzi entering the market.

Obizzi saw her at the same time and waited for her buyer to leave before walking over.

"Well, well," he said in a condescending tone, his eyes traveling over Isabella as if she were something to be bought at the market. "If it isn't the saucy little girl from the Piazza Napoleone."

Isabella tried to ignore him, but he picked up an apricot from her table and took a bite. "Do you have anything succulent that might satisfy my appetite?"

She remained silent but held his gaze.

He seemed amused at her discomfort and lightly tossed the apricot at her. She snatched it out of the air with one hand and dropped it into a wastebasket.

"May I help you, signor?"

He cocked his head to one side and raised one brow. "You've always had something you could help me with, young lady." He then saw the wedding ring on her hand. "I see you're now married—but as you know, I find married women rather desirable."

Isabella tried to calm herself in front of DeAngelo and the Venero girls. "I have a wonderful husband and a fine daughter—"

He laughed. "Yes, I hear the Martellino fertilizer is quite good. A lot of little seeds sprouting up in that vineyard."

Isabella's mouth fell open; she was a bit puzzled. "I—beg your pardon?"

Obizzi realized his mistake. "Well—I—uh—heard the Martellinos were going to have a baby—please congratulate them for me."

Isabella was stunned. She took a step back and thought about seeing Susanna that very morning. That was the reason she had put on weight and looked so tired. A sudden fire began to burn in Isabella's belly, and her eyes blazed a green as dark as the caves in the Alpi Apuane mountains.

"I didn't know Susanna was with child," she said calmly, "and I'm rather surprised she would tell you before she would tell the person who helped deliver her first child." She nodded toward DeAngelo. "That beautiful little boy who looks so much like—Giovanni."

Obizzi froze, jaws clenched in fury, and then leaned in so only she could hear. "Don't fuck with me, bitch—I can make your life miserable."

He turned to leave but found himself face to face with Pascal Esposito, the influential landlord he desperately wanted to meet.

Esposito walked right past him and opened his arms to Isabella.

"I was hoping you would be here!" He swept Isabella off her feet and spun her around. "Please tell me you brought your baby!"

She took his arm, walked over to the bassinet, and pulled back the blanket.

"She's absolutely lovely!" Esposito gushed and then pulled from his coat pocket a silver baby spoon with several liras wrapped around it. "Just a little something for your darling girl."

"You are so thoughtful," smiled Isabella as she stood on her tiptoes and kissed Pascal on the cheek.

"A-hem," said a loud voice behind them, and Esposito turned to find a man bowing dramatically before him. "Signor Esposito, what a surprise to see you here this morning. What good fortune for both of us."

Pascal shook the man's hand, but the look on his face told Obizzi that the important Lucchesi landlord did not remember him.

"We met last year at the political rally in Piazza Napoleone."

Esposito looked puzzled for a moment and then slowly nodded. "Yes—yes—I believe I do remember. If I recall, it was a government rally—the new Fascist Party, yes?"

"Absolutely, signor. I was the featured speaker. I'm Alfredo Obizzi."

Pascal put his arm around Isabella. "And what brings you to the finest table of any market in all of Italy? Have you met the delightful Isabella Carollo?"

She offered her hand to Obizzi, and he reluctantly shook it.

Isabella turned to Pascal. "Signor Obizzi has offered to make a generous donation to the workers' relief fund. He wants to buy four crates of tomatoes, four crates of lettuce, and some apricots that he's taking to those in need of a good meal."

"Good for you, Alfredo!" Pascal responded happily. "That's one of my favorite causes. I didn't know you Fascists were interested in the workers. I took you for a corporate man."

Obizzi forced a smile. "I want to—help everyone, signor."

"And so do I! We've been so fortunate in our lives to be given much, and I believe God is telling us to be men of service."

"Of course," Obizzi said through clenched teeth.

Esposito put his arm around Obizzi. "May I help the two of you carry it over?"

Not wanting to make a bad impression on the rich landlord, an indignant Alfredo reached into his billfold, handed Isabella the money for the food, and then picked up a crate of tomatoes and dropped it onto the pushcart.

Pascal offered Isabella his arm.

"I would love to join you," she said, and then she pushed out her lower lip in profound disappointment. "But I must stay with my daughter and the Martellinos' little boy." She then reached up and gripped Obizzi's bicep. "But you have an ox of a man here to help you take this produce to those in need."

Obizzi gave her a cold stare. She smiled back and then silently helped him load the rest of the food onto the pushcart.

He gave her one final hateful glare before pushing the cart out of the market with Pascal Esposito chattering away next to him.

ೞ ಐ

Isabella sat quietly in her garden that night, praying for Susanna and the baby she carried. She tried to concentrate on her meditation, but a million thoughts flashed through her mind, all pulling in a direction she did not want to go right now. She wanted to crawl into bed with Franco, simply feel the warmth and comfort of her husband, and forget about everything. And yet the thoughts remained. She knew she had to talk to Susanna. The woman had been handling it all alone and would need her help. Both the emotional and physical stress of the pregnancy would negatively affect not only Susanna but the baby as well.

Isabella stood up and glanced at the villa. The lights were still on. She took a deep breath and started in, whispering to herself, "My only purpose is to be a light, to be truly helpful, to represent

Him who sends me. Give me the words, dear Lord, to help bring this woman peace."

She found Susanna in her study, dressed for bed, staring blankly at a book in her lap. Isabella knocked on the open door, and Susanna slowly turned to face her. Her skin was pale except for dark circles under her eyes, and she gave a look that was both defeated and defensive.

"I wanted to thank you for letting DeAngelo come with us to the market," Isabella started out, still searching for the right words to get Susanna to open up. "He had such a good time."

Susanna turned away with a restless gesture. "Thank you, for watching him."

"He's a good boy."

"Yes, he is." She paused for a long moment. "But that's not why you're here."

Isabella swallowed hard. "I'm here for you."

Susanna only shook her head.

Isabella moved closer. "For some time, I've felt that there's something troubling you—and I think I know what it is."

Susanna inhaled a deep breath and placed her hands over her belly as if to hide her secret.

"You're not alone," Isabella said softly. "I want you to know that God is with you, and I'm with you. Please let me in so that I can help."

As Susanna struggled to hold back her tears, Isabella knelt down and took her hand.

"I'm such a fool!" Susanna suddenly poured out. "I don't know what to do!"

Isabella said nothing as Susanna let go all she had been holding in. "I never should have gotten involved with that bastard! But I thought he—I thought we—oh God, what am I going to do?"

Isabella held her as she cried. "I should have known when I saw him at the hotel. I should have known better when he came to find me in Lucca. I'm such a damn fool."

"You're not alone," Isabella whispered.

"I have no one."

Isabella squeezed her hand. "You have me."

Susanna wiped the tears from her cheeks and looked up at Isabella, only to suddenly gasp.

Giovanni was standing by the doorway, and the look in his eyes was that of a man who had heard their conversation.

"What is it you should have known, Susanna?" he asked.

She burst into tears. "I'm so sorry, Giovanni! I'm so sorry!"

It was if he already knew the answer to his own question. "What are you sorry about?"

She dropped her head into her hands and sobbed. "I'm—I'm pregnant."

Giovanni felt as if he had been punched in the gut, knowing it had been months since he and his wife had shared the same bed. And even then he had felt it had been an act. Now, he knew it was to cover up something terrible she'd been hiding.

"How far along are you?"

She couldn't dare look at him. "Three months."

He was silent for a moment, his head bowed, his pain evident. "So that's why you've gone to Lucca or Pisa or wherever the hell it is you go so often? You wanted me to believe it was my child, didn't you?"

She said nothing, only stared into her hands. For a time, Giovanni hung suspended, hardly breathing. And then, finally, he exhaled loudly, as if trying to clear his mind, and he started for the door. Susanna reached for him. "Where—where are you going?"

He turned and gave her a look of absolute disgust. "I have no fucking idea. I just can't be here with you."

With that, he walked out of the room and out of the house. Susanna sat frozen, gripping the sides of her chair, listening to the sounds of tires on gravel as her husband drove away. Only then did she turn to face Isabella, and with tears streaming down her cheeks, she cried out, "Why? Why do you have to meddle in everything?!"

Isabella's mouth fell open. She had never expected Susanna to turn her guilt onto her.

"Get out, damn you!" she screamed. "Get out!"

ଓ   ଚ

Obizzi paced the floor of his office in Cremona. His aide, Frederico, showed him another letter from Susanna. "What should we do? This letter says her husband has left her and that she needs you."

"That blasted bitch will ruin everything I've worked for." Obizzi dragged his hands through his hair in frustration, "She doesn't want me. She wants my money and will blackmail me to get what she wants."

"She hasn't asked for anything, Alfredo."

He grabbed the letter, crumpled it into a ball, and flung it to the far side of the room. "But she will! And I know that damned peasant girl has something to do with it! She probably wants in on the scam!" He pounded his fist on his desk and then glared at Frederico. "Have you found anything on her husband and his coworker? They were both in the army and are most likely Socialists. Perhaps we can dig up something on the two of them and end this fucking distraction for good."

Frederico looked through his notes. "There's nothing on Antonio San Stefano. He was given the Silver Medal of Valor for his courage and leadership on the Isonzo and then lost a hand at Caporetto. The last thing Mussolini would want is to discredit a war hero." Then Frederico pulled out a letter he had received from a friend of his who was an army officer. "But we may have something on Isabella's husband. This letter shows a record of Franco Carollo entering the army, but there's no record of his being discharged. The only thing this letter says is that Private Carollo was reported missing in action, presumed dead, after Caporetto."

"A damned deserter," Obizzi hissed, and then his face slowly creased into a wicked smile. "Good work, my friend. You've given me the ammunition I've been looking for. It's time we load our guns."

CHAPTER 27

LUCCA, SEPTEMBER 1921

G iovanni had been gone for two months, and Susanna's belly was growing with another man's child. If she could have turned back the clock and erased that day with Alfredo, she would have. The affair had been a disaster. It had been exciting at first, but he had used her, and the mere thought of him made her nauseated. She knew she had sinned, and now she felt as if God was punishing her. His punishment was to take Giovanni from her. Yes, she had to admit, she missed her husband.

As she sat next to the window of her bedroom, she jealously watched Isabella and Franco walking in from the field, holding hands. He pulled her hand up to his mouth and kissed it gently, and she laid her head on his shoulder, a look of absolute bliss on her face.

Isabella glanced up, saw Susanna at the window, and waved for her to come down. She shook her head no. She was still angry with Isabella for the conversation that had prompted her husband to leave her, and she'd even thought about firing the lot of them, but what then? Who would run the vineyard, and who would pick the damn olives? But Isabella certainly had to share the responsibility for the misery Susanna was now going through, and the only retribution Susanna had been able to think of was to dock half the Carollos' pay until Giovanni returned. Now, as she watched the Carollo couple outside their tiny cottage, she recalled that last dialogue.

"Your husband had nothing to do with Giovanni leaving," Susanna had started out. "I will not penalize Franco. But YOU were involved in a decision that could hurt this vineyard financially, so it's only fair that you share in my hardship." She had then paused to allow Isabella to speak, but no words came as the young woman just stood quietly with that pretentiously unflappable look on her face— not even an apology, which only angered Susanna more. She had sent Isabella back to the field and had not talked with her since. At the time, the conversation had satisfied her, but as time passed, her guilt only seemed to multiply.

CR   SD

On the morning of their anniversary, Franco woke early and went to the kitchen to make a special breakfast for Isabella. Although it was simple, for Franco it would show a little of how much he adored his wife. He sliced up some apples and an olive loaf and made a pot of tea, which he delivered to Isabella in bed.

"Happy anniversary, sweetheart!" he whispered, not wanting to wake their daughter, who was asleep next to Isabella. "One year and I'm still filled with the joy of having you as my bride!"

Isabella popped an apple slice in her mouth. "*Still?* Did you use the word *still?* Fifty years from now, Franco Carollo, you'd *still* better be filled with the joy of having me as your bride."

He laughed softly as he picked up his daughter and laid her in the bassinette. "What more do I need in life than the two of you?" He gently stroked Liliana's hair for a long moment and then turned back to his wife. "Finish your breakfast, Bella. Let's get our work done, because I'm taking you into town to celebrate."

She pulled back the quilt to reveal her nakedness and winked. "What's the rush?"

He stared as if seeing her for the first time, admiring her thin figure, the swell of her breasts, the flat stomach that drew his eyes down to her very being.

"Good God, you're beautiful," he said as he unbuttoned his shirt, never taking his eyes off her, which only seemed to embarrass her.

"We've done this before," she giggled, and she reached for his hand and pulled him on top of her.

"I still have my pants on, Bella."

But she was already busy, unbuckling his belt and shoving his pants to his knees. He bent his head to bite her breast, and she let out a sharp gasp.

His head jerked up. "Did I hurt you?"

"No," she smiled, and she brought his face back to her breasts. "Please, continue."

CR   SO

As they lay together later, cuddling in the afterglow, they heard voices in the field.

"I would love to stay here all day," Franco groaned, and then he rolled up and sat on the edge of the bed. "But if I'm going to take you out tonight, I'd better help Angie and Antonio."

320

Isabella threw her arms around his waist to prevent him from leaving, but she knew there was work to be done. She simply kissed his back and released him.

Franco dressed and then gave a confused look as he walked around the entryway to their home. "Have you seen my shoes? I always put them by the door."

She looked over. "Mine are gone too."

He walked out to the porch, where a paper sign hung from one end of their cottage to the other and broke into a wide grin. "Bella! Come here! You have to see this."

"Happy First Anniversary to the Carollos," was written in big letters, and below that was a smaller message. "Every couple needs more than one pair of shoes. Love from Antonio and the Veneros."

When Franco looked around the yard, he noticed Antonio and Angelina coming from the vineyard, holding hands.

"Check out Tony and Angie," he muttered with a look of surprise. "Love must be in the air."

Isabella gave him a playful shove. "Husband, if you would pull your head out of those wine barrels for one second, you might see that they've been sweet on each other for months. Haven't you heard him singing to her at night?"

"I thought it was just Antonio being Antonio. Why am I the last to find out about anything?"

Antonio and Angelina arrived with grins on their faces.

"Where are your damn shoes?" Antonio called out. "You'll get dirt all over those beautiful toenails!"

"Someone stole them," Franco chuckled.

"What sick, demented fool would steal those stinky old dogs?"

Franco crossed his arms over his chest. "That's what we were wondering."

Antonio looked to the sky as if he were talking to the clouds. "If you'll just raise your vision a little, you might find that the good Lord has provided."

Isabella pointed to the roof of their house, where their old shoes had been tossed, and sitting next to them were two pairs of shiny new shoes.

"Everyone should have more than one pair of shoes," Angelina laughed. "You can use those old pairs in the field, and tonight you'll have new pairs to wear to your first anniversary dinner."

CR   ʀɔ

Susanna heard their laughter and looked out the window. She tried to suppress the feeling, but yes, she was jealous—jealous of the love these families had for each other. These workers, who had nothing, always seemed to be filled with joy, while she, who had everything money could buy, was drowning in misery. As she fought back tears, a black car turned down the drive. Could this be Giovanni, she hoped? The car stopped, and two men in military uniforms got out and began talking with Antonio and Franco. Antonio became animated with the men, while Franco stood stone-faced with his hands at his sides. Isabella threw her arms around her husband. What was happening? One of the men went to Franco and handcuffed his wrists. She must go outside to stop them; how dare they take her vintner! She threw a shawl around her shoulders and hurried down the stairs, but as she reached the back door, all she saw was the car heading up the drive with Franco in the back seat.

"What's going on?" she called out. Isabella was in tears, being comforted by Angelina.

Antonio's face was grave as he walked over. "Military police. They've accused Franco of being a deserter during the war."

Her hand went to her mouth. "Where are they taking him?"

"To prison."

"What will they do?"

Antonio moved closer so Isabella could not hear. "If he's convicted—they'll hang him."

 (a   so)

Antonio went to the barn and pulled out the locker from under his cot. He opened it up and dug through it to find his army papers. Included was a list of the men he had fought with and the officers he had served under. They would know of Franco's service to his country and understand the chaos of Caporetto.

(a   so)

In a grimy jail cell in Pisa, Franco sat alone. The cramped quarters reeked of urine, cigarettes, and unwashed bodies. His cellmates weren't common criminals; he was incarcerated with some of Italy's worst: murderers, pedophiles, and rapists, all on death row awaiting their sentences. But even though he had been arrested for a lesser crime, it seemed as though his case was being pushed forward sooner than the others. As he pulled the damp woolen blanket around his shoulders, he thought of his wife and child growing up without him, and his body began to shake with a grief-stricken shudder he couldn't stop.

(a   so)

Antonio waited impatiently inside Susanna's car, still surprised the signora had loaned it to them for their trip to the jail in Pisa.

"Would ya hurry up!" Antonio called out to Isabella, who had insisted on baking cookies for the prison guards before they left. Finally, he saw her step from her cottage with a bright smile and a plate full of cookies.

"Should I bring some milk to thank the guards for locking up your husband?" he grumbled as she sat down next to him.

"It's rude not to bring a gift when going to someone else's home."

"This isn't a day spa, Bella." He tried to lift a cookie off the plate, and she slapped his hand.

He gave her a sour look, started the car, and headed to Pisa. Both were thinking the same thing: Why was Franco being singled out when thousands had left the battlefields and returned home after Italy's failure at Caporetto? Why Franco? And why almost three years after the end of the war?

CR   BO

The officer in charge gave a look of guarded surprise when Isabella came through the door with her plate of cookies.

"This is for treating my husband, Franco Carollo, with kindness while he stays with you," she said with a bright smile. "You know he's completely innocent of these silly charges."

Antonio rolled his eyes as he lifted a cookie off the plate and took a bite. "Don't worry, my good man, she left out the rat poison."

The officer took a cookie and led them to the cell that held Franco.

Antonio waited for the guard to leave before he spoke. "I talked with the military police who arrested you, but since none of them were in the war, they don't understand what happened at Caporetto." He slid the list of the names of the army officers they had served under to Franco. "I did find out that General Cadorna is in the town of Bordighera, up near the French border. There's a colonel in the same area that we served with. I'll talk with them about this ridiculous mistake." He scratched the stubble on his chin. "Nothing about this makes any sense. I mean—why the hell you?"

Franco's face was filled with regret. "I deserved this."

Antonio gave a puzzled look.

"If I had not gotten on that train in 1915," Franco continued, "if I'd not followed my brother off to the war—I've been paying for that mistake ever since."

Isabella sat quietly off to the side, watching her husband struggle with past regrets. His face was gaunter than it had been the last time she'd visited. His voice was breathy and seemed defeated as he turned to her.

"I'm so sorry to have brought this on you, Bella. My past should not bring you pain. Please forgive me." He paused to calm his emotions, his voice quivering. "If I die, teach Liliana what you've taught me—unconditional love."

Isabella sat up straight and glared at her husband. "What's this, 'If I die, teach Liliana' bullshit? If you believe in unconditional love, Franco, then why are you putting conditions on it?"

His eyes went wide, as he'd never heard his wife use such language.

"Do you believe in miracles?" she demanded, and he nodded dumbly.

"There are NO conditions on miracles, Franco. They happen naturally when one surrenders totally to love." She tapped his forehead as if hammering home a point, enunciating every syllable. "Un-con-di-tion-al-ly! That means no doubts! No fears! It only works if you are certain it will work! Not because of the conditions YOU put on it!" She stood up and put her hands on her hips. "In every little thing that you call a mistake, there's been a blessing. Remember—that train brought you and Antonio together. That train led you to me and Liliana." She paused for a moment. "Do you trust Antonio to find a miracle?"

Franco only nodded.

"Then TRUST him!"

She then gave Franco a firm kiss on the lips and headed for the door.

Antonio bit his lip to keep from grinning and waited for Isabella to leave before turning back to his friend. "I'll find the miracle, brother. But now's a good time for you to have that faith Isabella's talking about."

CR   SD

When Antonio arrived in Bordighera, there was a telegram waiting for him at his hotel. "WE MAY HAVE THE NAME YOU ARE LOOKING FOR—(STOP)—ALFREDO OBIZZI—(STOP)—FASCIST LEADER." It was signed, "LOVE, ANGELINA."

He drove to the address given him by the officers in Pisa and knocked on the door. A maid greeted him suspiciously, but when he told her he had served under General Cadorna in the Second Army, she told him to wait in the foyer. Several minutes later, the general came down the stairs, dressed in tan slacks and slippers but wearing his old military jacket. Medals were dangling from the left breast pocket. The man had aged well, thought Antonio; however, there was a bitter look about him.

"May I help you?" Cadorna asked.

Antonio came to attention and saluted the general. "Sergeant Antonio San Stefano. I served for you on the Isonzo."

The old man sighed. "We fought well, but there are bastards who wish to blame me for their mistakes. They gave me inexperienced, arrogant, jealous officers who failed me, and our government still holds me to blame."

"I'm sorry, sir," Antonio said, "but I'm here on behalf of one of your soldiers, Private Franco Carollo. He fought bravely for you, sir. Helped lead the charge up a hill we captured near Gorizia and took out a machine gun nest. He was in shock after seeing his brother die at Caporetto. Everyone was retreating, sir. Franco was one of thousands who went home. Now, for some reason, after four years, he was arrested last week and accused of deserting. All I'm asking, sir, is that you write a letter on his behalf. It could save his life."

Cadorna shook his head sadly. "He left the field of battle, Sergeant. It's better that he die for his country—that's what loyal soldiers do."

Antonio hesitated to keep from raising his voice. "Sir, I beg of you. He's a good man who served his country well."

Cadorna went to the door and opened it, letting Antonio know it was time for him to leave. "And I also served my country well and look at the misery it brought me. Good day."

Antonio did not move, waiting for the old man to catch his gaze. "Does the name Alfredo Obizzi mean anything, sir?"

The general's eyes fluttered. The abrupt answer came. "No. I've never heard that name before."

CR &

Antonio had the same trouble with the colonel he visited in Bordighera. As soon as he brought up Obizzi's name, the colonel shifted uncomfortably and told him he couldn't help.

A frustrated Antonio headed back to Lucca, studying the list of officers who might still be living in the area. He came across the name Captain Arnaldo Cervelli in La Spezia. Antonio remembered him. Tough guy who trusted his gut and loved the foot soldiers more than the generals. Captain Cervelli never let his troops go up a hill without him. It took Antonio much of the afternoon to get to La Spezia, but he finally found the address on his list; however, nobody was home. He knocked on a neighbor's door and was greeted by an old woman who knew the captain.

"Yeah, I remember Arnaldo. Moved away. I think he lives over a restaurant where he works. It's in town. Some place called the Wine and Chicken. He's a drunk."

Antonio drove down to a seedy part of La Spezia and parked his car outside the *Wine* and *Chicken*. The place was a dump; dark and dreary. There was a reason they had put the word Wine before Chicken in the sign. He grabbed a bottle of red he had recently purchased for this occasion and headed inside.

"Where the hell is Captain Arnaldo!" he roared. "Sergeant Antonio San Stefano wants to drink with him!"

From behind the bar an unshaven man whipped around. "You, sir, go fuck yourself—and your wife and mother!"

Antonio yelled back, "Oh yeah, well, your mother gives it away!"

The captain slammed a glass down on the bar, grabbed his old friend by the neck, and pulled him in, kissing him on both cheeks.

"What the fuck are we drinking to, my friend?"

Antonio pulled the bottle out of his bag. "The best! Roagna Barbaresco!"

Arnaldo's eyes got as big as saucers. "You bust my balls!" He pulled him in and kissed him one more time.

Antonio poured him a glass of the good wine. "You remember Private Franco Carollo?"

"He's a damn good soldier!"

"He fought with honor. After watching his brother die at Caporetto, he went home. He was recently arrested for deserting."

The man's face drew down in a furious scowl. "You mean some fucking politician—who never fought a fucking day in his life—accused one of my fucking men of cowardice?"

Antonio whipped out a note he'd already typed up, and the good captain signed it and had another drink.

CR   ℘

Four days after he had left, Antonio arrived back at the jail. But when Antonio showed the officers the letter signed by Captain Cervelli, they all laughed.

"What good is this? You'll need to go higher than a simple captain to get this man off."

Antonio balled his fists at his sides in fury, but he knew there was nothing he could do. These guards were simply following orders.

The news devastated Franco. "They executed a man two days ago," he said with a look of gloom, "and someone seems to be pushing my case ahead."

His old friend wanted to say something, anything, that would pick him up, but the only words that came to him were old ones from Isabella.

"Be strong, Franco. Keep believing that we'll find a miracle. Somehow."

∝ ∾

When Antonio turned down the Martellino drive, Isabella raced out of her cottage but immediately saw the frustration on his face.

At dinner he explained what had taken place on his travels to Bordighera and La Spezia.

"I don't understand," Angelina said. "Bella's the one who had trouble with Obizzi. Why would he crucify Franco?"

"The greater the power, the greater the ego," Antonio growled. "And the ego must have its revenge."

"But how will arresting Franco benefit him?"

"Several Fascists have been promoted by having anti-Fascists arrested," Antonio continued. "Why not throw Franco in that cage and get two for the price of one?" He shook his head slowly. "It doesn't matter if the accusations are false. If you're poor and accused of being unpatriotic—you're screwed."

Angelina gave a loud exhalation. "We have to find a way to get Franco out."

"I know a way," a voice said.

They turned to find Susanna by the open door.

"Alfredo is trying to hurt me—any way he can." She walked inside. "He's a very vindictive man who has not answered any of my telegrams or letters."

Angelina was puzzled. "Why would he want to hurt you?"

Susanna took a deep breath and placed her hand on her belly. "Alfredo Obizzi—is the father of my child."

Angelina's hand went to her mouth in shock.

Susanna paused for a moment to compose herself. "Only Giovanni and Bella know my story. I had an affair. I was foolish. I'm the one who sinned, and I'm very sorry Franco got in the way of God's punishment."

The statement bothered Isabella. To her the thought of a loving God punishing anyone seemed preposterous. But she remained quiet and let Susanna continue.

"I sent a telegram to my sister. Her response came today, insisting we come to Rome. Margherita's husband is related to one of the members of the Italian Chamber of Deputies, Giacomo Matteotti."

Angelina's eyes went wide. "Your sister knows Matteotti?"

Susanna nodded grudgingly, still embarrassed about revealing her affair to Angelina.

"Franco's met him," Isabella added. "Before the war. He said he's a good man."

Antonio got up from the table and looked at Susanna. "With your permission, signora, I'd like to find this Matteotti guy by morning."

Susanna nodded and started to walk back to her empty house until she felt an arm come around her shoulder. It was Isabella.

CB   BD

Although he was exhausted, Antonio was back on the road heading to Rome that night. The old sergeant slapped his face to stay awake and reminded himself that he'd been through trouble before and could survive this midnight ride to Rome. When he arrived at the address Susanna had given him, security was there to meet him. After he explained that he was a friend of Susanna Martellino, they let him through the gate. A butler led Antonio to a sitting room that was decorated with beautiful photographs of different Italian cities. He stopped in front of a picture of a city he didn't recognize.

"That is Bologna." The voice came from a man by the door. "That's where Aldo and I went to law school. I loved those days, learning from professors who challenged a young man's mind. Simple times." He sighed. "Not anymore."

Antonio stood up to shake the hand of Giacomo Matteotti. He was a man with a serious look, deep-set eyes and a square jaw, but a man, thought Antonio, who cared—a man who truly cared about his country.

"I'm Antonio San Stefano. I served with a—"

"I know why you're here," Matteotti said. "Margherita told me about what your friend has been through."

"Did she tell you that you've met him?"

Matteotti looked up.

"You met Franco Carollo at a political rally in Rome before the war. Apparently he insulted Mussolini."

A broad smile creased Matteotti's face. "I do remember. I was very impressed."

"A man named Alfredo Obizzi had him arrested."

Matteotti shook his head sadly. "The Fascists will stop at nothing to rule our country, and people like Obizzi make life miserable for anyone who gets in their way."

"Is this Obizzi one of Mussolini's aides?"

"Not yet. But he wants desperately to be part of his inner circle. If Benito's elected, I'm afraid we'll see more of what happened to your friend come to anyone who speaks out against the government."

"But Franco's never criticized anyone."

"Then this must be personal."

Antonio thought back to the Great War and all the soldiers lost to some general's ego. "I remember you were against Italy going to war."

"Because of my unfavorable opinions, I was interned in Sicily. The hawks needed to muzzle me."

Antonio put his arm around the great politician. "You sound like a man I'd vote for."

Matteotti laughed. "Then I shall enlist you as my campaign manager, Antonio San Stefano. Now tell me what you have."

"I've been all over. I went to Bordighera to see General Cadorna, but he wouldn't help. I've a signed letter from a captain who fought with Franco and vouched for his service. Please, signor—if you don't help him, I believe Obizzi is determined to see him hanged."

Matteotti read the letter and shook his head. "It's difficult for me to understand how someone who did not serve can be critical of anyone who fought for his country."

Antonio only nodded.

"I'll do whatever I can," Matteotti said with a determined look. "I believe in Franco—and I believe in justice."

CR   BO

Although Antonio had been up for forty-eight hours, he was invigorated by Matteotti's words and drove straight through to Lucca that night. By nine o'clock that evening, he had arrived outside the city walls, but instead of heading home, he turned in through the Piazzale Boccherini and drove to Giovanni's hotel. As he walked through the lobby, he saw his landowner sitting alone in the bar. He quietly walked up behind him and said, "I don't mean to interrupt the fascinating conversation you're having with yourself, signor, but if you've got a moment, I'd love to buy you a glass of Martellino red."

"Antonio!" Giovanni jumped up to give his friend a hug. "It's good to see you! Please, join me."

Antonio did and told his landowner of his past week's travels. Giovanni listened intently and then paused in thought as he poured his friend a glass of wine.

"You're a true friend, Sergeant. You fought for your country, and now you fight for your friend."

"You're also a true friend, signor."

"No, I'm not. I've been very selfish."

"You gave me a job when no one else would."

"I wanted to fire you."

Antonio shrugged. "Franco may have had to twist your arm and tell a few lies so you'd give me a break." He raised his glass. "But you trusted him, and here we are, good friends having a glass of wine together."

Giovanni reluctantly took a sip. "These past few years I've spent so much time running around Tuscany trying to build the Martellino empire, trying to prove—I don't know—that my wine would be better than my father's, so that others would look at me with envy." He paused. "But in the process I neglected my duties as a husband and a father, and look at what it's brought me."

Instead of comforting him, Antonio gave him a playful shove. "Don't take yourself so seriously, Signor G. We all stumble in life. We fall down. We get up. Only to fall down again. The key is to keep getting up."

But Giovanni was lost in his thoughts. Antonio tried to distract him by raising his glass a second time. "How about a toast to me, signor. Did you know that Angelina and I are in love?"

Giovanni's head snapped up.

"It's true." He touched his glass to Giovanni's. "I mean, how could a fool like me be so lucky as to get a beautiful woman with three children already grown? I don't have to do any work!" He gave a look of pride. "But if they turn out good—I'll take all the credit for raising them."

Giovanni finally laughed and raised his glass. "To you and Angelina." Then his smile slowly faded. "I remember her husband. He was a good man. I regret to say I didn't get to know him as I've grown to know you. I wasn't very kind."

"Ah, the past, how it haunts us," Antonio said with more than a hint of sarcasm. "But it's a great teacher if we're willing to learn."

Giovanni forced a smile. "Angelina has been through so much. She deserves to laugh, and married to you she'll have plenty of laughter."

"And you deserve to laugh as well." Antonio paused to make sure Giovanni heard his next words. "Do you know who's been helping us with Franco?"

Giovanni shook his head.

"Your wife. Susanna is the one who sent a telegram to seek Giacomo Matteotti's help."

Giovanni's mouth fell open. "Susanna reached out to a Socialist leader she despises?"

Antonio raised a hand. "Not so fast. Your wife still thinks Mussolini walks on water—but—she believes Franco is the victim of another man's revenge."

"Alfredo," Giovanni grimaced.

Antonio slowly nodded. "She told us why you left, signor. She made a mistake—a big mistake. But I believe she misses you—and there's also DeAngelo. He needs you, and the new baby will need you as well."

Giovanni stared past his friend, out the window, past the walls, across the Serchio, and toward their villa, where he imagined Susanna lay sleeping. "I don't know, Antonio. I'm lost right now."

Antonio sat back in his chair and glanced at his left arm. "I was lost, too, and wanted retribution after losing my hand in the war. I found only one way out."

"What was that?"

"Forgiveness," Antonio said. "There is no greater retribution than forgiveness."

Giovanni thought about that for a moment and then downed the rest of his wine. "I'll think about it, my friend. I'll think about it."

Antonio shook his landowner's hand and headed out the door, home to Angelina and the Martellino vineyard.

ೞ ಐ

After Antonio's visit, Giovanni decided to get out more. That Sunday morning while walking the walls of Lucca, it was as if he were seeing his city for the first time. Families were together; children were laughing; men were playing cards; older gentlemen were arguing about a football match. As he passed by a restaurant, the doors opened and he inhaled the aromas of cured meats, freshly baked breads, and faro soup. A bright smile lit his face as he walked down to the Cathedral of San Martino, realizing he had not been inside since he was a boy. He opened the door and made his way to the sarcophagus of Ilaria de Carretto. He remembered her story: Ilaria was the wife of Paolo Giunigi, the famous Lucchesi merchant from the fifteenth century. Paolo had married the love of his life, Ilaria, in 1403. Only three years later, she died giving birth to their second child. Giovanni stared at the sarcophagus; Ilaria appeared to be sleeping with her hands on her swollen abdomen, and her position made him think of Susanna. She too, was pregnant with a second child, and even though it was not his, he felt a responsibility to the baby who was yet to be born. As he placed a hand on Ilaria's abdomen, he thought about what Antonio had said about forgiveness, and wondered if his own anger was keeping him from happiness. For all of Susanna's exasperating qualities, he still loved her.

"What the hell am I waiting for?" he said to himself and headed for the door. His feet seemed to have a mind of their own as they led him to his own church, San Frediano. He was late for Mass and hesitated before opening the huge wooden door to join the other late arrivals in the rear of the church. He knew where Antonio would be: back left, waiting to offer his seat to any woman who arrived late. He opened the door and immediately found Antonio grinning back at him. Giovanni motioned for Antonio to join him outside.

"Thanks for bailing me out, boss," Antonio wisecracked when they were out in the courtyard. "The ushers were just about ready to hand me the collection plate."

Giovanni laughed. "Would you care to join me on my drive to visit Franco?"

"Let's stop by Taddeucci's on the way." Antonio rubbed his stomach. "I'm sure Franco would appreciate some good cannoli."

CR ℘

The autumn morning was cool on the drive to Pisa, but Giovanni found it refreshing. He'd spent so much time holding everything in that now he just wanted to pour it out.

"Was there a time you hated me?"

"Of course not," Antonio answered as he opened the box of pastries and offered one to his boss. Giovanni shook his head no. Antonio took the biggest of the cannoli. "Even the generals I fought under were intimidated by my brilliance."

Giovanni laughed out loud.

"Hell, Signor G., I didn't even hate the enemy I fought in the war." He took a bite. "I just figured they were as stupid and as scared as I was."

"You were scared?"

"Every day. But I guess the fear of not doing my job was greater than my fear of being shot."

Giovanni glanced at Antonio with one raised brow. "You saw General Cadorna last week. What was he like?"

"It was very sad. He seemed to have no compassion for the soldiers who died serving him. All he could talk about was how HE had been unfairly treated."

"Maybe he needs to practice some of that forgiveness you keep telling me about."

"That's a damn good idea," Antonio said and took another bite. "It sure cuts through all the bullshit a person holds on to."

"You're a wise man, Sergeant Tony," Giovanni nodded. "One of the wisest I've ever met."

Antonio gave him a wink. "Not bad for a Sicilian with a seventh-grade education."

CR ЕО

They arrived in Pisa expecting a quiet Sunday morning. Instead they discovered a black limousine parked in front of the jail and a loud argument coming from inside the main office. Antonio took a final huge bite of pastry, the powdered sugar covering his lips, and stepped out of the car.

"Franco Carollo is not to be released!" he heard a man yell.

Antonio stopped dead in his tracks and turned back to Giovanni, who was reaching for the box of pastries.

"Lee de canli n decr," Antonio mumbled, still chewing on one of the cannoli.

Giovanni cocked his head to the side. "What?"

Antonio pointed to the box and swallowed. "I said leave the cannoli in the car. I think you-know-who is inside the jail."

Very quietly, they hurried up the steps, opened the front door, and peeked inside.

"He's a damn deserter!" screamed Obizzi. "A traitor to the king and to Italy!"

"Please, Signor Obizzi!" The officer held up a document. "This pardon comes from the Chamber of Deputies. It confirms the letter from a captain who fought with Private Carollo. I have to release him."

Obizzi shoved the desk against the captain.

Antonio saw the officer's plight, raced into the room, and grabbed Obizzi's arm.

"That's no way to treat an officer of the law," he said in a voice that made everyone pause.

Obizzi's assistant took one look at the stranger with the ferocious glare and psychotic white lips and shuddered back against the wall.

Obizzi looked to Frederico for help, but his assistant stood motionless, mouth open, eyes wide. Obizzi tried to twist out of the stranger's grasp, but Antonio held tight and lifted his stump to Obizzi's face.

"I hit a bastard like you so hard last week my hand literally flew off." He curled his lip into a sneer. "His head hangs over my fireplace. Would you care for yours to join him?" He then shoved Obizzi to the middle of the room.

For a second Obizzi stood frozen in panic. Then he took a deep breath, trying to calm his nerves, and very slowly reached into his breast pocket and pulled out a piece of paper. "I—also have a letter. It's from an officer in Bordighera—who swears he saw Carollo run from battle."

"You're a damn liar!" Giovanni stepped forward, snatched the letter from Obizzi's hand, and tore it into shreds. "Franco served our country with honor!"

Obizzi gave this next stranger a confused look, as if he'd seen him before. "Who the hell are you?"

Giovanni slammed his fist into Obizzi's jaw, knocking him to the floor, and stood over him. "I'm Giovanni Martellino!" he growled. "The man who will raise your son!"

CR   SO

"That Antonio is such a rascal," Angelina said as she slid a crate of pears onto the back of the truck that Isabella would drive to the Pisa jail. "He was next to me at church, then he gave his seat to some old woman, and then *poof*, he was gone."

"He won't go far," Isabella laughed as she offered a slice of pear into her daughter's waiting mouth. "I promised to save him some of the pignoli cookies I baked at church today for the prison guards."

Angelina frowned. "Those men will never let Franco out if you keep feeding them."

"Nonsense." Isabella smiled as she wiped Liliana's face with a handkerchief. "They'll treat my husband with kindness if their stomachs are happy."

Susanna was off to the side, listening to the banter, astonished at how Isabella could be so joyful with her husband behind bars. Her own mind had been filled with worry and dread ever since her separation from Giovanni and then Franco's arrest, yet Isabella had a look of perfect peace. Susanna stared long at her, searching for some kind of discomfort, but found none. A cloud moved across the sky, the sun's rays casting a soft glow on Isabella's face and shoulders, giving the illusion that a light was shining from her very being. It was as if Susanna were seeing her for the first time, warm and welcome, clear and plain, beyond deception in her simplicity. An odd feeling of understanding came over Susanna, as if something familiar were being revealed to her, and then, as quickly as the thought came, it vanished, and the fear returned.

"Aren't you angry with the men who have imprisoned Franco?" she blurted out, surprising both Isabella and Angelina.

"Of course not," Isabella answered. "They're only following orders, and what would my being angry accomplish anyway?"

"But what if they hang him?" Susanna said without thinking, and as soon as the words were out of her mouth, she regretted them.

There was a long silence as Isabella stared at Susanna. For a moment she did see her husband as cold and alone in the prison, being marched by guards to the gallows.

"I'm sorry—" Susanna started to say, but Isabella cut her off.

"If you want to see a world that's angry and afraid, that's your choice. But please don't give your fears to me." Isabella then closed her eyes and forced herself to see Franco's smiling face surrounded in light. She opened her eyes and smiled at Susanna. "Unless you're determined to see things differently, miracles can't happen."

Before Susanna could answer, they were interrupted by the sounds of the children running in from the vineyard.

"Where's Antonio?" Bartolo asked cheerfully as he grabbed a pear and took a bite. "He promised to play chess with me today."

"I don't know where that old windbag is," Angelina frowned.

"Maybe that's why he ran off. He's scared of losing to me again."

Bartolo gave his mother a cockeyed grin. "He told me he's never lost to you, Mama, except for that one time he let you win."

"Let me win? That sounds like him, always with a good story that ends with him smelling like a rose."

Bartolo saw the anxious look on Susanna's face, and tried to lift her spirits. "Perhaps he's out selling the best wine in all of Tuscany!"

Susanna forced a smile. "Giovanni did say that Antonio has a way of making our brand sound as if it's won the Florence wine festival."

It was the first time in over a month she had mentioned her estranged husband's name. She felt suddenly afraid, not for herself but for him. Giovanni was the one alone, without his son, without his land, and without his wife.

Bartolo's hand on her shoulder brought her back to the present. "I'll bet Giovanni and Antonio are somewhere selling wine and playing chess—" The boy suddenly paused and squinted toward the valley at a black auto headed their way. "Hey, that looks like Giovanni's car."

Susanna's head jerked up.

Bartolo covered his eyes to block the sun. "It's Giovanni with Antonio and somebody else." His eyes went wide. "It's Franco!"

Isabella's heart skipped a beat when she heard her husband's name, and she grabbed her daughter and raced to meet the car. But Franco was out the door even before the car came to a stop, lifting his wife and daughter off the ground to shrieks of delight from their friends who surrounded them.

Giovanni hesitated before stepping out of the car, and with a cautious glance he nodded to Susanna. Antonio felt their discomfort and tried to lighten the mood the only way he knew how.

"You should have seen your papa rescue Franco!" he said to DeAngelo. "He shook that jailhouse so hard all the nails came out of the boards and fell to the ground! The prison guards were shaking in their boots when your papa bit the lock off Franco's cell and spit it against the wall, shattering a picture of Mussolini himself!"

As DeAngelo stood wide-eyed, Antonio dramatically crossed himself. "God forbid anything bad ever happen to our great leader."

He winked at Giovanni, who was trying to hide his embarrassment.

"That, my little friend, was the only mistake your papa made! He yanked those bars apart with his bare hands and pulled Franco to freedom! I tell you, DeAngelo, it was the greatest rescue I've ever seen!"

It took every bit of courage Susanna had to walk over to her husband.

"That's quite an adventure," she said softly.

Giovanni stayed silent, only watching with a contented smile as Franco held Isabella and Liliana. Their joy was his reward. He was aware of Susanna's presence but unsure of what to say or how to act. Finally, he simply nodded and said, "We were only successful because of the telegram you sent to contact Matteotti. Without his help, we had no chance."

Susanna felt a pride she'd thought she'd forgotten. She had indeed been part of Franco's release, and now she was part of this happiness. It felt good. She touched her husband's hand, waiting, hoping he would respond, and finally he did, curling his fingers around hers.

"Are you coming home?" she asked.

He stared out at his winemaker, who had brushed back Isabella's hair from her face and was kissing the tears from her cheeks. Giovanni stood frozen, both watching and wanting that same love. The past haunted him, his wife's infidelity still fresh in his mind, but he knew he had to have the strength to forgive or he would drown in his own misery. He squeezed Susanna's hand and slowly nodded.

CHAPTER 28

LUCCA, OCTOBER 1922

A nother year passed, another fine grape harvest, and as the calendar turned to autumn of 1922, the Martellino farm was busy preparing for olive season. The Carollos were in the grove, studying the purple-green olives, trying to decide when would be the best time to pick.

Franco dug his thumbnail into the fruit, the juice oozed out, and he licked his thumb.

"It's time, Bella. Taste the flavor." He handed his wife the Frantoio olive, and she took a bite and nodded. "It's good. Just a little bit of a nutty flavor, perfect for a good oil."

Franco looked across the grove with pride. "Giovanni said these olives come from the original trees planted by Pietro Martellino back in the mid–fifteen hundreds."

"The older the tree, the better the olive," she said. She slipped her arm through Franco's, and they started back to the barn. "We'd better get the troops together, because we couldn't ask for better weather to pick."

345

CR BO

Susanna was in her bedroom, folding diapers for a baby she did not want. She had wept with despair the day she gave birth to a baby boy her husband named after the man who had started the vineyard in 1541. Pietro means "stone" or "rock," and Susanna thought the child proved to be as stubborn as one. He was colicky at birth, and even now at nine months old he refused to take a nap or go to bed at a decent hour.

"What is it you want?" Susanna grumbled as Pietro stood screaming from his crib, wanting to be outside with his brother. She turned to Josephine. "I don't understand him. DeAngelo never was like this as a baby."

"We're all different," Josephine said. "He came into the world mad as hell, and until he learns how to speak, I think he'll tell us what he wants by screaming."

Susanna put a pacifier in his mouth, but the child spit it out.

"I'll never have another one of these," she fumed as she snatched the pacifier off the floor. "When will I stop paying for my mistake?"

"Don't say that! Pietro is not a mistake. With love and discipline, he'll be a fine boy."

Susanna gave her a sour look and stuffed the pacifier back into Pietro's mouth.

CR BO

"We're a little behind schedule," Franco said as he rolled a round green olive between his index finger and thumb. "These olives need to be processed as soon as possible, so we're going to drop them off at the mill tonight and then grab a beer."

Angelina and Isabella lifted a basket of olives onto the back of the flatbed and said in unison, "Who's *we*?"

"I—uh—thought we'd have a boys' night out," he said with a sheepish grin. "Even Big G. is bringing Little D. to show him how they process olives."

"We picked as many olives as you did." Angelina slipped by Franco and sat down in the front seat of the truck. "Which makes us just as thirsty as you are. Rosa and Elisa said they'll watch Lily for us."

Franco grinned at them and shook his head. "You already had us figured out."

"The more the merrier," Giovanni said as he lifted DeAngelo onto the back of the truck. "I just wish Susanna could join us, but she's exhausted after taking care of Pietro all day."

"We'll make it an early evening." Isabella pulled DeAngelo onto her lap. "A quick trip to the mill and a quiet dinner in Lucca."

The barn door opened, and out limped Antonio, grimacing as he stepped into the cab and sat down next to Angelina.

"Your back is bothering you again, isn't it?" she asked.

"I'm fine," he muttered. "I pulled a muscle picking olives."

"No, you didn't."

"Yes. It was a huge olive—at least fifty pounds."

She gave him a sour look. "We both know it's because you sleep on that awful cot in the barn. As soon as we marry, you can sleep with me, and your back problems will disappear."

Franco stifled a smile and kept his lips sealed. He'd heard this conversation before, and history had taught him that if he opened his mouth, he'd be in big trouble.

Antonio wasn't so lucky when he whined, "Woman, why do you ruin my moment?"

"I don't need a moment. I need you in my bed."

"But I want to romance you first," he sighed. "I'm writing a poem of passion that will bring a tear to your eye as I beg for your hand."

"You can have both of my hands! My parents are gone, and no one is going to give away a woman with three children."

He turned away from her and said under his breath, "Those children would love to give you away."

"What did you say?" she snapped. "Why, I'd smack you right now if your back weren't hurting."

"It's not my back," he groaned. "It's your mouth that's causing these spasms."

"Don't change the subject. Do you love me?"

"Of course."

"And I love you. Let's get married."

Franco bit his lip and started up the drive.

"Why don't you just reach down my throat and rip my heart out?" Antonio continued. "Just when I'm about to ask you—you ask me. From what everyone tells me, that's not how it works."

"So how's it supposed to work, Tony? You're the one with the bad back who's all over me in the field but must spend the night alone in the barn with the bugs and the barrels."

He closed his eyes and gave a look of absolute bliss. "Ahh, how I long for the peace and quiet they give me."

Everyone laughed except Angie, who elbowed him in the side.

"Ow! All right, I'll ask you!" He tried to get down on one knee in the cab of the truck, but the pain in his back made the move impossible. Instead he took Angelina's hand and stared into her eyes. "My bee-uh-yoo-tee-full angel, will you fulfill an old man's dreams and marry me?"

A bright smile lit Angelina's face, and she grabbed his head and pushed her mouth hard onto his. It was not so much a kiss as an act of desperate relief. "Of course I'll marry you, you silly goose."

A roar came from the entire truck as Franco turned down the hill toward Lucca.

ℰ ℋ

"I think tonight deserves more than a beer," Franco winked as he parked the truck in front of the olive mill. "Why don't you two lovebirds walk ahead to town and secure a table at Buca di Sant'Antonio?"

Antonio stepped out of the truck and offered his arm to his now fiancée. "Come, my darling, I shall sing you the love songs of Puccini."

She took his arm and rolled her eyes. "Please don't."

"I am happy and at peeeeace!" he belted out, "and my pastime is to make lilies and roses!"

As they walked to town, Giovanni stood alone, listening to Antonio's voice fading away in the distance. He then turned and saw Franco put his arm around Isabella and kiss the top of her head. For a moment, he wanted to go home and take Susanna in his arms, but something held him back. Instead, he felt a tug on his sleeve and looked down to see his son smiling up at him. He picked DeAngelo up and headed to the mill.

"Let's go see how they press olives into oil."

ℰ ℋ

DeAngelo was mesmerized. His bright eyes followed every step of the mill foreman from worktable to fireplace. As the foreman pulled

349

off a large piece of bread, placed it between tongs, and toasted it lightly on both sides, DeAngelo stood wide-eyed. The foreman rubbed a garlic-rosemary branch over the top of the bread and then dipped it into the Martellino olive oil paste, pulled off a piece, and placed it in DeAngelo's open mouth. The little boy took his time chewing, as if testing its worth, and then smiled.

CR   BO

They finished the tour and headed inside Lucca's walls to celebrate the engagement of Antonio and Angelina.

There seemed to be a nervous energy about the city as Franco parked the truck along Via Calderia. Several Fascist Blackshirts were patrolling the streets, waving black flags as if daring someone to challenge them.

He held Isabella's hand tighter and nodded to Giovanni to hold on to his son.

"I don't know what's going on," Franco said. "Let's just get to the restaurant as quickly as possible."

They made it to Buca di Sant'Antonio without incident, but Antonio was waiting for them outside the door.

"Has something happened?" Franco asked.

Antonio nodded. "Groups of Fascists from all over Italy are marching on Rome."

"Can't the prime minister stop them?"

"Facta was forced to resign," Antonio said as he guided them to their table. "Apparently King Emmanuel refused the liberal government's request for martial law."

Franco grimaced as he pulled a chair out for his wife. "The king is afraid of Mussolini."

Giovanni sat down and pulled his son onto his lap. "He knows that Benito's tight with the military and probably fears a civil war if he doesn't give him power."

All of a sudden, a door at the back of the restaurant opened and cigar smoke spewed out, along with the sounds of men who had had too much to drink.

Antonio leaned back in his chair to see who it was, then turned back to the table. "Well, if it isn't our old friend from Pisa."

Franco sat up straight as Alfredo Obizzi and his friends stepped out with cigars between their teeth and smug looks on their faces. When Obizzi saw who was seated at a nearby table, his smile turned to stone.

"This is a private party," he growled.

"That's why we're out here in the officers' club," Antonio joked. "Why don't you privates head back to your cave?"

Obizzi took a step forward, but when Antonio and Franco rose up out of their chairs, the Fascist official thought better of provoking men who knew how to fight. Instead he ignored them and flicked his ashes onto the table in front of Giovanni.

"I thought you had two sons, Martellino?"

Giovanni balled his fists and began to rise, but Antonio put a hand on his shoulder to settle him and flashed a grin at Obizzi. "Speaking of twos, Alfredo, are you still seeing double after Giovanni knocked you out last year?"

The rage that was building inside Obizzi almost boiled over until a colleague shouted from the back room. "Alfredo! They're talking about Benito's march on Rome!"

"Turn up the radio!" Obizzi roared. "I want these Socialists to hear it!"

The radio crackled as the volume was turned up to the sounds of a reporter.

"It's estimated about thirty thousand of Mussolini's Blackshirts participated in today's march, while the rest of his squadrists have spread out around the country. It also has also been reported that Il Duce's supporters have taken control of the Po Valley."

There was a glint of amused disrespect in Antonio's eyes as he said, "Was Mussolini in Rome today? One of the waiters told me he was directing the whole show from his telephone in Milan."

Obizzi glared at Antonio but again was reluctant to take on a decorated Italian war veteran.

"Sounds like the Isonzo to me," Antonio winked at Franco. "The generals enjoying a nice glass of port while sending the foot soldiers to do their work."

At this point, Obizzi seemed to notice that everyone in the room was looking at him to see how he'd respond. He inhaled deeply and crossed his arms over his chest.

"Italy finally has a leader we all can respect, yet worthless cripples like you still hold us back."

Antonio's right hand twitched at his side, but his face remained neutral.

"Yeah, I heard his bullshit," he said in a low voice, his eyes fixed on Obizzi. "'The state is absolute, and the only worth an individual has should be in serving the state.' Sounds like a dictatorship to me."

Obizzi could take no more and started toward Antonio, but Isabella quickly stepped between them with a glass of wine. "What do you say we toast the memories of this historic day?"

Her statement seemed to calm the room as Obizzi grabbed the glass from her. "At least some of us understand the importance of today." He gulped the entire glass down, wiping the remaining drops from his chin before shouting, "To Mussolini!" Then he turned and went back into the private room with his compatriots.

When the door closed behind him, Angelina turned to Isabella with a look of absolute shock.

"I can't believe you agreed with that horrible man!"

"Who said I agreed with him?" Isabella said as she poured herself a glass. "I don't care what memories HE was toasting." She lifted her glass above her head. "I'm drinking to the real history that was made today!"

The table gave her a puzzled look.

"To the engagement of Tony and Angie! That's the history that was made on this night!"

CR   SO

"I should have been there!" Obizzi grumbled as he paced the office of the new mayor of Cremona, Roberto Farinacci.

Farinacci was dressed in a dark suit that was perfectly tailored to his slight frame. The starch in his shirt, the polish on his shoes, and his deep-set eyes presented a look of absolute power.

"The new Italy began with the march on Rome," he said. "Our country will be going through many changes. Don't worry—you'll be a part of our future."

"Will democracy be thrown out?" Obizzi asked.

"Of course. It's been ineffective and corrupt. As Mussolini said the other day, 'National strength was conceived qualitatively, not quantitatively.' If Italy is to be a world power again, it should be ruled by a strong, disciplined leader."

"A man who can inspire," Obizzi gushed. "God, how I wish I had been there."

Farinacci turned to Obizzi with a raised eyebrow. "You know very well why Benito didn't invite you. After your disaster at the military jail, the last thing a leader wants is to surround himself with failure."

Obizzi's eyes went wide. He hadn't known Roberto knew of the incident in Pisa. His mouth was dry as he searched for the words to explain. "I—I was ambushed! I wasn't expecting the man to hit me."

"You didn't expect to be hit by the husband of the wife you were screwing?"

"But—"

Farinacci cut him off. "You're so arrogant, Alfredo. When you bring your personal problems to the new administration, you're only asking to be rejected."

"I contacted all the right people."

"You called Old Man Cadorna while your enemies were able to contact Giacomo Matteotti."

Obizzi swallowed hard. "I didn't know they knew Matteotti."

"You must always know your enemy," Farinacci said as he looked over his papers. There will come a time when you'll be able to take your revenge. But for now, I think you should stay in the background. Let Benito come to you."

CHAPTER 29

LUCCA/ROME, 1923

Three more letters arrived from Susanna's sister in Rome: one to congratulate the couple on the birth of their second child and the second practically begging Susanna to come see her in Rome. Not yet, thought Susanna. Not until her personal life was put back together. Despite a good season for the Martellino business, she and Giovanni were struggling to put their marriage back together. The memory of her infidelity seemed to carry too much pain, and the guilt they sentenced themselves to only separated them further.

Pietro cried out from his room, and an exhausted Susanna lay back on her bed in frustration.

"Pietro, that's enough!" Susanna groaned in exhaustion as she lay listening to her second child's incessant crying. But the boy screamed louder until suddenly he stopped. She raised up on one elbow to see her older son pull Pietro out of his crib and carry him downstairs. She went to the window and watched as DeAngelo handed his baby brother to Isabella, who began singing to him, and he quickly fell asleep in her arms.

Susanna didn't have the patience or the desire to pamper and train Pietro, but she resented watching Isabella do it. And it bothered her more to see DeAngelo spending so much time with the Carollos. The boy seemed to wait for his mother to leave before sprinting out to the vineyard to join the winemakers in the field. The jealousy simmered as the day went along, and then Susanna would lash out at her son when he came in late for dinner. She knew she was wrong in her actions but couldn't stop herself. She felt lost; she needed to get away, to feel again, to engage in life. Perhaps, she thought, now was the time to take that first step in letting go of her past. She would start in Rome and go see her sister.

CR BO

"Margherita is very rich," Susanna said with a slight edge to her voice. "My sister married a man who owns a twenty-room mansion in the hills north of Rome—family money—none of it they had to work for."

Isabella only smiled as Susanna drove to Lucca, chattering on about the marble statues, ornate ceilings, expansive balconies, and bustling servants that adorned her sister's massive estate.

Susanna dropped them off at the Porta San Pietro and waited for Rosa to take the children out onto the lawn before she grabbed Isabella's wrist.

"I don't want you spoiling the children today," she instructed.

"I won't," Isabella replied.

"No gelato after three."

"Of course not."

"Make sure Pietro takes his nap."

"I will."

"And he must go to bed by eight, or he'll be a devil for me tomorrow."

Isabella put her hand on top of Susanna's. "Just enjoy this time with your sister."

Susanna looked down at their hands. There was more she wanted to say, or perhaps she was just reluctant to leave. Either way, she wanted to talk.

"We fought the last time we were together."

"But today you come in peace," Isabella smiled.

"We're so different. She was given so much, while I—"

Isabella squeezed her hand. "Forget about the past and the future. Just be present with her today."

Susanna sighed. "I don't know how."

Isabella nodded toward the children who were playing on the grass lawn that surrounded the walls of Lucca. "Be like them. Let go of all plans and expectations, and just enjoy." The shadows of the chestnut and plane trees atop the walls seemed to form a perfect path for Isabella's words. "God wants you to be happy, Susanna."

Susanna sat for a moment longer, her eyes searching Isabella's face. "I don't deserve to be happy—I have sinned terribly."

Isabella gave her a crinkled-eyed grin and said, "What if there was no sin? What if the sun came up every morning, shining on what you consider the good and the bad? What if it was up to us to stay in the dark or come out into the light?"

Susanna shook her head and let out an exasperated exhalation. "You—are—impossible."

Isabella laughed out loud.

"It's true! You make everything sound so easy!"

"That's because I think we make our lives difficult."

Susanna scowled. "You come from this mystical, pagan, sacrilegious faith, yet you still go to church. Why?"

Isabella laughed again, as she had never had anyone describe her daily practice in such a way. "I go to church because that's where people are."

"So?"

"Church is filled with all kinds of people, Susanna. Rich people, poor people, the sick and the healthy, shopkeepers, tax collectors, butchers and bakers, landowners and winemakers. These people disappoint and hurt each other sometimes."

"And the church's responsibility?"

"To help anyone who comes through its doors to discover God's unconditional love."

Susanna accepted the answer even though she had a hard time believing it. "You don't think God is punishing me for my sins?"

"Do you think God punishes the grapes by bringing too much rain?"

"That's silly."

"Perhaps as silly as believing that God would punish you."

Susanna paused for a long moment. It was as if Isabella was turning her entire thought process upside down. Isabella squeezed Susanna's hand again to make sure she had her attention. "We can't find heaven alone, Susanna. We're here on earth to simply learn how to forgive and help each other."

Susanna sighed again. "Like my sister?"

Isabella nodded. "Think only love today, and everyone will benefit." She then reached into her pocket and pulled out an olive leaf she had picked up from the orchard that morning. "If you have an anxious moment today, touch this olive leaf. It represents peace."

Susanna took it and forced a smile. "Thank you."

CR SO

The morning sun warmed their shoulders as Isabella took the children to the top of the walls, first passing the Piazza Vittorio Emanuele and walking on to the Baluardo di Santa Maria. She waved to a friend who was unloading fresh fish for that night's menu at Caffe delle Mura and then continued on through a canopy of plane trees that swayed gently in the breeze. A loud yell came from behind a wall at the Baluardo di San Colombano, and suddenly several teenage boys shot out in front of them, chasing a boy dressed in his Fascist Blackshirt gear. Isabella knew one of the teens and called out, "Paolo Castiglia, you leave that boy alone! I know your mother, and she wouldn't be happy to hear about you bullying another!"

The boys scattered, and the young Blackshirt nodded his thanks to Isabella.

"You're Silvio Conti, aren't you?" she asked.

"Yes, signora."

"I've seen you at church."

The boy nodded but turned his attention to Rosa. "I—was in the same catechism class with Rosa."

Isabella could tell Silvio was smitten with Rosa.

"Why don't you join us on our walk?"

The invitation seemed to draw new courage from Silvio, and his brown eyes glowed eagerly at Rosa. "I'm running errands for my mama, but I think we're headed in the same direction."

They continued on toward the Porta Elisa, where the two towers of San Gervasio and San Portasio marked the impressive medieval gate. Rosa had yet to notice Silvio's interest as she asked, "Why were those boys chasing you?"

Silvio perked up, happy Rosa wanted to talk. "They don't like the squad I joined."

"The Blackshirts?"

"Yes. We have pledged our allegiance to Benito Mussolini."

"Why?"

He turned red, startled by a question about patriotism from a girl he had a crush on. He had never had to answer such a question before. The squad he had joined only talked of the brilliance of Il Duce. No one had ever asked why or why not.

"Because—" he stammered, "because only Mussolini can return Italy to being great again. Only he can right the wrongs that were done by the Socialists during the Great War."

Rosa's face was calm, yet serious. "My papa was killed in the war."

Silvio's face went crimson with embarrassment as he remembered Rosa's father's death, remembered the look on her face when their teacher gave her the news and her absence from school as the family grieved. He stood frozen, staring down at the ground.

Rosa seemed unaffected by his discomfort as she turned to Isabella. "Who are you for, Bella?"

Isabella glanced at Silvio. The poor boy seemed distraught with shame for the insensitivity of his words.

"I'm for Italy," she finally said, "and for Austria, and for France and Germany, and for Europe, and the rest of the world." She waited for Silvio's eyes to come back to hers. "There are no limits to the blessings we'll receive when we seek to help others."

Isabella could tell Silvio did not understand, so she let it go. The boy shuffled his feet and gave a desperate look to Rosa, as if he might never get another such opportunity to be near her.

"Rosa," he said with a hopeful tone, "will you be at the market on Saturday?"

She nodded innocently.

"May I—walk you home?"

Rosa again nodded, but this time with a smile.

As he left to finish the errands for his mother, Isabella called out to him. "Say hello to your mama! And be kind to everyone you meet! Blackshirts, blue shirts, and like Rosa here, green dresses!"

Silvio gave an embarrassed wave as the children giggled and Rosa watched him leave. "I still don't understand why the other boys were mad at Silvio."

Isabella put her arm around Rosa, and they continued their walk down into the botanical gardens.

"Italy has been in pain ever since the war ended, and our politicians know citizens are vulnerable," Isabella explained. "Several politicians want change and believe the best way to bring that change is through young people. They've formed groups called Blackshirts to promote their cause and make others afraid."

"Silvio did look scary when I first saw him," Rosa said, "but then I saw it was just Silvio."

"Fear is a great instigator of change, Rosa. When you make people afraid, they tell their leaders they want to be protected. The leaders promise protection in exchange for money and power."

They slowed their pace as Isabella eyed Lucca's walls. "It's a little like our city. There was a time when Lucca was a major banking and silk-trading town, and its citizens needed free access to the sea to ship their goods and wares. But Pisa controlled much of the western coastline."

"My teacher said Pisa wanted money from Lucca to ship their goods."

Isabella nodded. "For hundreds of years there was tension between the two towns, and by the early Middle Ages, city leaders felt Lucca had outgrown her pre-Christian walls and needed greater protection. Those walls were built in the thirteenth century."

"Did that bring peace?"

"No. Three hundred years later the Medici family of Florence wanted to expand. Our fear of an attack led to the building of the walls we walk on today."

They walked on through the Porta Santa Maria, down into the Palazzo Pfanner gardens, where they were surrounded by ornamental flowers, forest plants, and earthenware pots of lemons. Isabella paused in front of the octagonal fountain and asked, "Do you know how many times our walls have been militarily tested?"

Rosa shook her head as Isabella answered her own question.

"None. Lucca has never been attacked."

CR   ℬ

Susanna arrived at Margherita's villa late that afternoon. She stood in the parlor, nervously waiting to surprise the sister she had not seen since their mother's funeral. All she remembered about that day was being angry—angry at her mother for giving so much to Margherita and so little to her. Their mother had demanded that her daughters work for a seamstress outside Lucca and give their paychecks back to her to save. When Margherita became old enough, her mother used the money to send her oldest daughter to the finest private school in Rome. It was there she met Aldo, and they soon fell in love. When Susanna came to collect her savings, her mother could only apologize. It was all so unfair.

The doors of the parlor suddenly opened, and a tall, thin gentleman came in to greet her. "I'm sorry. Aldo and Margherita are upstairs changing for dinner. May I tell them who's calling?"

She nodded politely. "Yes—I'm Margherita's sister."

"Susanna!" the gentleman said with a look of surprise. "I should have known! You look so much like Margherita." He extended his hand, and she accepted. "I'm Giacomo Matteotti, a distant relative and college classmate of Aldo's. I'm certain your sister would love to have you stay for dinner."

Her hand tensed in his, but she forced a smile. Susanna was face to face with the enemy of Obizzi and the Fascists, the man who railed for Socialism and workers' rights, the very things she despised. But he was also the man who had helped Franco.

"It's a pleasure to meet you," she nodded. "Thank you for helping our winemaker get out of jail."

"Did you know I met Franco several years ago in Rome? He called Mussolini a fraud to his face. Benito was none too pleased."

Susanna's eyes went wide at the revelation, but she kept her voice under control. "I—was not aware of that incident."

Matteotti seemed to sense her discomfort and changed the subject. "Tell me of the gentleman who came to seek my help. Antonio, I believe, was his name. He seemed to be a man of good character, a fine friend to have."

Because Susanna wasn't sure how much Matteotti knew, she stayed away from any conversation about Obizzi. "Thank you, yes. Antonio is a good employee."

Giacomo offered her a chair. "These are difficult times, in which good people get hurt by the egos of politicians."

Susanna couldn't help herself. "Are the Fascists really so evil, signor? Italy certainly needs a new direction."

Matteotti raised an eyebrow. "The Fascists talk as though they're going to help the peasant farmers when their real plans will be a form of agricultural slavery."

Susanna's blood began to boil, and she stuffed her hands inside the pockets of her jacket to hide the fact that she was shaking with rage. Her hand touched the olive leaf Isabella had given her earlier in the day, and for some reason it immediately cooled her anger. "I think slavery is a rather harsh word to describe what the Fascists have in mind," she said calmly.

"Perhaps, but I'm always concerned when corporations do so well while workers struggle."

"Will you—try to stop Mussolini?"

"I've been trying, but the Fascists despise me even more since I interrupted his speech last year."

Susanna remembered reading about it, and at the time she had been furious. For too long all she had thought about was the Fascists versus the Socialists. For years those words had consumed her, driven her passion to be part of Italy's future, even justified her belief that Fascist violence was needed to control those who opposed Mussolini. Yet she wanted to show respect for the important politician who stood before her.

"I do remember your criticizing Fascism in front of Mussolini— I'm sure that took courage." Susanna paused to inhale a deep breath. "But Benito has also shown courage by exposing the failures of the Socialist government."

He raised one eyebrow. "Are you a Fascist, signora?"

Susanna squared her shoulders to draw strength. "I am very proud to say—yes."

Matteotti's gaze rested on her, his disappointment evident, but as he opened his mouth to speak, he suddenly paused, hearing someone coming down the stairs. They turned to find Margherita staring.

"Sister?"

Susanna's heart skipped a beat. "I'm sorry I didn't give you notice, but I've thought much about the kindness you, Aldo, and Signor Matteotti gave our workers. I thought it important that I come and thank you myself."

"What a great surprise!" Margherita hurried down to greet her. "Where's Aldo? He'll be so happy!"

They heard Aldo call out from their cellar stairs. "I'm on my way, darling. Just looking for the perfect wine for this evening. I thought maybe Chianti or a Barolo, or—oh my—Susanna!"

He put the wine bottles down and gave his sister-in-law a great hug. "What a wonderful surprise! I do hope you'll stay."

Susanna cast a curious glance at Matteotti, who nodded politely. "I think this should be a night for the three of you."

"You don't have to go," Aldo argued.

"Please," Matteotti raised his hand. "There is nothing more important than family." He then hesitated as if studying Susanna, and once again extended his hand. "It was a pleasure to finally meet you, Signora Martellino."

One corner of Susanna's mouth twitched as she shook his hand.

"My best wishes in your efforts to work with our new government."

CR &O

They talked of family and business, of wine and olive oil, and finally of their plans to stay connected.

"Why don't you come with me and see our children's school?" Margherita suggested. "You might find Saint Gregorio perfect for DeAngelo and Pietro."

All of Susanna's breath went out in a long sigh as she thought about her boys going to a boarding school so far from home. "I— would miss them."

"Which will only give you another reason to visit more often," Margherita beamed. "Saint Gregorio is one of the most respected schools in Rome!"

They walked arm in arm to the end of the hall, Susanna barely hearing Margherita as she chattered on about the attributes of Saint Gregorio and the distinguished professors who had produced some of Italy's finest politicians, financial officers, and elites. Susanna thought of her own life, one that had certainly fallen short, but she still had dreams. She had dreams for her own sons, and the thought of standing on equal ground with her sister excited her.

"Yes," she finally said. "DeAngelo is a very bright child—he's first in his class." She then paused, thinking of her second child's temperament, his outbursts of uncontrollable anger and defiance. "Pietro can be quite a handful, so perhaps the discipline of a private school would also help him."

They talked more about the school before Margherita spoke the words that had been hanging over both of them.

"I'm so sorry for the difficulty we had several years ago," Margherita began. "I was a stupid girl filled with ideas of how Italy should be led. I wanted so much to have you believe as I did, and that was foolish. A democracy should welcome many ideas."

Susanna was moved by her sister's admission, and myriad emotions welled up inside her, but she remained stoic. "We—you and I—will start anew. We shall let go of the past and make today a new beginning for our families. It would be wonderful if our children could go to the same school."

Margherita wiped a tear from her eye as she hugged her sister. "I would like that very much. A new beginning."

CR   ꙅ

"May I help you make dinner?"

It was DeAngelo, coming in from the field with a basket of tomatoes in one arm and Liliana in the other.

"I would love it." Isabella smiled as she picked up her daughter and placed her in a high chair. She nodded for DeAngelo to follow her over to the chopping block and picked a juicy red tomato from his basket. "Do you know why they call these heirloom tomatoes?"

The boy only shook his head.

"It's because their seeds have been saved from one season to the next and have been handed down through several generations. They're family heirlooms. Father Daniel from San Martino brought me seeds from America several years ago, and I've had a tasty crop every year." She cocked her head to the side. "What shall we do with your heirlooms, Little D.?"

He studied the tomatoes for a long moment. "Let's put them in pasta!"

"Then we'll need about six more tomatoes." Isabella took several from his basket. "I'll cut these up and boil the water. You get me some chives, basil, flat-leaf parsley, and tarragon."

She poured water into a pot, placed it on the stove, picked up a lemon, and tossed it over her shoulder to DeAngelo. "I think a couple of lemons, olive oil, and pine nuts will also go perfectly with this dish."

"Not so fast, Bella," DeAngelo frowned. "I'm not like you."

But she was already busy, slicing up the tomatoes and heating the oven. While the pasta was boiling and the pine nuts were roasting, she tossed everything else in a bowl. "Bring me two loaves of bread, DeAngelo. We'll warm them in the oven while we finish dinner."

She drained the pasta, tossed it with ricotta and Parmesan, and added a little of the pasta water to mix it into a creamy sauce. She grabbed a handful of the tomato mixture, placed it on top, added pine nuts, and voila! Her masterpiece was ready.

"Go tell your mama and papa we're ready to serve."

◌ ❦ ◌

"I'm the one who met Matteotti," Susanna repeated for the second time as she sat down at the dinner table, "and while I found him to be a gentleman, I still believe Italy needs a stronger man to lead our country out of our postwar troubles."

"And you think that egomaniac Mussolini is that man?" Giovanni argued.

"You didn't see what I saw on the streets of Rome! There were unemployed soldiers wandering around, looking for jobs but more than likely looking for trouble. Why, even the Vatican is afraid of criticizing the damn workers' movement."

"We do need a strong leader, Susanna, but a ruler without boundaries would be dangerous."

"Nonsense! Mussolini has the best interests of every Italian in mind."

Isabella sensed the tension when she walked into the dining room and tried to break it by placing the steaming dish before Giovanni.

"Well, aren't you the lucky ones, getting the first plates!" she smiled. "When I mixed the tomato sauce with this pasta, the bouquet of flavors almost made me go crazy."

The comment drew a grin from Giovanni but not from Susanna. He nodded to a chair next to him. "Isabella, why don't you sit down and give us your thoughts on our new leader?"

She paused as if in thought and then said, "I have a better idea." She picked up the basket of bread from the middle of the table and nodded for them to follow. "It's a beautiful evening. Grab your plates and silverware and children and join us outside." Before they could say anything, she was gone, with DeAngelo on her heels. Giovanni smiled at his wife. "It appears we'll be dining out."

CR SO

They stood quietly by the table as Franco and Antonio brought four extra chairs from the barn while Isabella served the pasta-and-tomato mix topped with ricotta and Parmesan.

"Angelina, would you do us the honors tonight?" Franco asked.

They held hands and bowed their heads, and Angelina said softly, "Bless us, O Lord, and these Thy gifts, which we are about to receive from Thy bounty through Christ our Lord. Amen."

As soon as Angelina said amen, Antonio clapped his hand to his leg and roared, "All right, let's start with Rosa! What's the best thing that happened to you today?"

Franco whispered to Giovanni and Susanna, "He does this every night. Same silly question, different funny answers."

Rosa spoke first. "Do you know that cute waiter at Vipore?"

"You mean Silvio?" her sister, Elisa, asked with a grin.

Rosa nodded. "I saw him at church and he winked at me."

"He did not," Elisa teased. "He winked at me."

"Elisa," Antonio interrupted, "it's not your turn yet. How about DeAngelo? The best thing that happened to you today?"

"Cooking with Bella!" the little boy yelled, holding up a fork dangling with pasta.

Susanna shook her head at her son. "We need to work on your goals."

Isabella was next. "The best thing that happened to me today was having my daughter tell me that her papa needs to take her mother out for an evening in Lucca."

Franco laughed as he put his arm around his little girl. "Is Mama putting words into your mouth again, bambino?"

They went around the table and finished with the Martellinos. "My good lord"—Antonio grinned at Giovanni—"what's the best thing that's happened to you today?"

Giovanni hesitated as he thought of his answer. He was impressed by his workers and the joy they found in the simplest of things: a good story, faith, friendship, and the conversation and laughter that came from simply being together at a family meal.

"I would have to say joining you for dinner tonight. *Grazie*."

Surprised at Giovanni's statement, the table was quiet for a spell until Antonio blasted out, "Then you're invited to dine with us whenever you and the signora want to share your joys of the day!"

Giovanni turned the tables on Antonio. "All right, Sergeant, your turn—what's the best thing that happened to you today?"

Antonio took a bite of pasta, wiped his mouth on his sleeve, and put an arm around Angelina. "Every morning I wake up next to this bee-yoo-tee-full woman, and I say to myself, 'Myself, how did you get so lucky that this woman—'" He turned to face her. "What's your name again, sweet cheeks?"

She rolled her eyes. "Angelina."

"Yes—my Angelina, she loves me. And I get to love her back. And front, too, if you know what I mean?"

The table broke up in laughter until DeAngelo cried out, "It's Mama's turn! What's the best thing that happened to you today, Mama?"

Susanna was suddenly aware that all eyes were on her, and she didn't know what to say. After an awkward silence she stumbled ahead with her thoughts. "Well—I—uh—was reading in the newspaper today that Italy is getting closer to economic stability. We all know that there has been bitterness between parties. I—I know the Fascists have been a bit rough on some who have objected—but now that Mussolini is in power—I believe we'll have peace."

Once again there was dead silence at the table. Antonio again played the part of icebreaker. "Well, I sure hope we get peace, signora, but we usually stay away from politics at dinner. Except for little Lily and Pietro. They argue all the time about the diaper union."

Giovanni chuckled, but the look on his face was anything but amusement. "You read the paper that's owned by Fascists, Susanna. The newspaper I read—the one that has a little more—journalistic integrity—predicted the troubles we're now having." He paused for a moment and shook his head. "When Mussolini railroaded his 'Acerbo Law' into parliament, we should have known something was up."

"There's nothing wrong with that law."

"You mean the law that says if a candidate gets twenty-five percent of the votes in the general election, he gets two-thirds of the seats in the Chamber of Deputies?" He snorted in disdain. "Mussolini found yet another way to get his friends into high positions while his Blackshirts intimidate voters into making sure he gets the majority. That's not democracy."

"Two years ago you believed in the Fascists—"

He cut her off. "Two years ago they told us what we wanted to hear so they could gain power. Now that they have power, they've gone back on all of their promises."

"Italy needs discipline!" Susanna slammed her hand down on the table." And only Mussolini is willing to give us that discipline!"

An angry Giovanni stood up. He wanted to speak but did not; instead he threw his napkin on top of the table and stormed back to the house.

After an awkward silence, Antonio picked up his fork. "Would anyone like pie? I helped Angie make it. At least, I helped put the cinnamon on top."

Angelina frowned at her husband as DeAngelo and Pietro ran after their father, leaving Susanna alone at a very quiet table.

CHAPTER 30

CREMONA/ROME, 1924

"This book will bring trouble!" Obizzi grumbled as he sat in the Cremona office of Roberto Farinacci. He was reading an excerpt of Giacomo Matteotti's recently published book, *The Fascisti Exposed: A Year of Fascist Domination*. He looked out the window to watch a group of protesters brandishing signs criticizing Mussolini's new government. "That damn Socialist has accused Benito of all kinds of corruption."

"Yes, I've read it," Farinacci nodded in a condescending manner, "but now that WE control parliament, it will be impossible for him to stop us."

Obizzi was so angry, his hand shook as he lit his second cigarette. These damn Socialists were traitors to the new Italy, and Matteotti had become the anchor that was keeping the Fascist ship from sailing.

"Matteotti must be dealt with, Roberto."

Never a man who liked being told what to do, Farinacci glared at Obizzi before handing him a letter that was postmarked from the

United States. "More troubling is this correspondence I received, saying Matteotti has uncovered information that Mussolini and his brother sold the exclusive rights to all of Italy's oil reserves to the American oil company Sinclair." He glanced at the protesters outside his office. "This information must never get out."

CR   SD

A happy look came over Susanna when she read the invitation from her sister, asking them to come to Rome to visit her son's boarding school. For days she had been searching for some way to get back into her husband's good graces after their argument at dinner in front of their field workers. Now, a perfect solution had fallen into her lap.

She presented her best smile and handed the invitation to Giovanni. "I think this would be a wonderful holiday for you and me."

He read the note and first thought about the vineyard. Franco had become a very capable farm manager, and Antonio could handle sales and deliveries. Perhaps this would be a good time to reconnect as a couple. He had not talked to anyone about Susanna's affair—he had not even discussed it with her since he returned home. But the memories of her infidelity haunted him every time they were alone. Susanna's stiff attempts at affection bothered him, but his clumsy rejections angered him even more; they needed to get away. Yes, Rome would be good.

CR   SD

They arrived in the nation's capital on May 30 with the city on edge. Hundreds of angry Blackshirts were pacing the streets, searching for anyone who would challenge their new power. There was a faint sound of shouts and screams from a block away, but Giovanni didn't dare to turn and look, afraid that a Blackshirt might think he was questioning the gang's authority. They drove past a protester who had been badly beaten. Susanna covered her eyes, but the image was still there—a man sitting on the ground, blood dripping from his nose as he held a now-damaged sign that read, "Mussolini Lies!"

Weaving the car through the trouble, Giovanni headed north and finally into the exclusive neighborhood where Margherita and Aldo lived. The homes were all magnificent—large, handsome estates with long curving drives lined by cypress trees, all with spectacular grounds filled with statues and flower gardens and fountains.

A security guard met them out front by a locked gate and let them pass. Margherita was in her garden, picking flowers for her guests.

"Giovanni!" she exclaimed when she saw who was driving. "What a grand surprise! I didn't know you'd be joining us!"

He waved as he parked the car and then got out to give his sister-in-law a hug.

"Aldo will be so happy to see you!" Margherita kissed him on each cheek. "Unfortunately, he'll be delayed with business in the city."

"I think we saw what's delaying him," Giovanni said. "There were Blackshirts everywhere in town."

Margherita suddenly became serious. "Even though the Fascists won the April elections, there are many who want parliament to challenge the outcome. Mussolini's loyalists are furious."

"I'm sure both sides have been causing problems," Susanna said as she gave her sister a brief hug.

Margherita's mouth fell open; she was stunned by her sister's statement. "The Socialist protests have been peaceful," she said, searching for words that wouldn't antagonize Susanna. "The Blackshirts are the ones who have been breaking into homes and newspaper offices and terrorizing our protesters."

"All very dramatic stories written by a liberal press—" Susanna stopped suddenly when she caught the angry glare from her husband. "But—let's just pray for peace and turn our attention to why we're here—Saint Gregorio!"

◯ ◯

Giovanni was quiet when they dined at a restaurant and even more so when they drove to the elite Roman academy. The school was indeed impressive—an immaculately cut stone building nestled in the hills north of Rome, surrounded by vineyards and olive orchards. The students wore uniforms, and the discipline and manners they displayed immediately impressed Susanna. She slipped her arm through her husband's. "When DeAngelo and Pietro are of age, I want them to be part of this."

He said nothing.

"Saint Gregorio was founded in 1690," Margherita said as she took them on a tour of the grounds, "not as a seminary but for the education of Italy's future intellectuals and leading social class. This school has everything your boys could ever want. Fencing, horseback riding, all kinds of athletic and academic programs that would bring out the best in your sons."

Giovanni again remained silent, not wanting to crush his wife's enthusiasm. He was already missing the sons he'd grown close to. He wanted them to have a good education, but couldn't understand why they had to go so far away. DeAngelo loved being in the field, and the Lucchesi schools were excellent. Pietro, more than his older brother, needed the love and attention he received from his vineyard staff. This would be a difficult battle he would have with Susanna, and one he would likely lose.

CR   ꙮ

It was nearly five in the evening when they returned to the villa. Aldo was in the living room, pouring himself a drink. He had a look of absolute defeat. "I'm sorry I couldn't join you today—I would have much preferred showing you our school."

Margherita hurried over. "Did you attend the parliament hearing?"

He nodded solemnly.

"Did Giacomo speak?"

"Yes." He relaxed just a little and swallowed. "He was brilliant. He challenged last month's election results and accused the government of committing fraud. He said the balloting, especially in northern Italy, had been marred by violence and intimidation and that with Fascist bullies overseeing the voting, the results were predetermined and therefore corrupt." He poured each of them a glass of wine. "When he called for the election to be declared invalid, Mussolini and his deputies were outraged. As Giacomo passed by, he said, 'Now you can prepare my funeral oration.'"

Susanna gave a dramatic sigh, for she could bear no more of this exaggerated drama. "The Socialists are blowing this way out of proportion. If they would simply agree to work with the new government, everything would be all right."

There was a very long silence as Aldo stared at Susanna. "You don't understand—when I left parliament today, there were Fascists threatening to kill Giacomo."

"Angry young boys making foolish threats," she said with a flip of her hand, "only to recant them tomorrow."

"These weren't boys, Susanna. These were Fascist leaders. Leaders who are responsible not only for what they say but also for what their supporters hear."

"Please," she said with a patronizing tone, "let's not spoil a truly wonderful day with any more talk of politics." She grabbed Giovanni's hand and kissed it. "I came to show this handsome man your marvelous school in hopes that our families will be part of Italy's dynamic future."

☙ ❧

They shared a great meal, went to bed late, and arrived back in Lucca the next afternoon. Susanna had done her part to sell her husband on the Saint Gregorio boarding school by seducing him twice the night before, and he'd slept peacefully until after sunup. Now, as she turned her prettiest smile on him, he seemed to beam with a renewed energy as he pulled down the drive and parked the car. The first thing she saw was their children in the vineyard with Isabella and Franco. Their faces, browned by the sun and dirt, flashed white smiles of joy as they played among the vines. A pang of jealousy gripped Susanna as she waved for them to come in. The image of her sons working with their winemakers made her even more determined that when

378

DeAngelo and Pietro were of age, she would get them into Saint Gregorio.

"Both of our boys deserve the best life has to offer," Susanna said as her husband waved to DeAngelo and Pietro. "I don't want them to become common farmers."

"Farming has been a noble profession in my family for centuries." Giovanni lifted her suitcases out of the back of the car. "And it's allowed you to keep up with all the latest fashions."

She wrinkled her nose. "There are more people losing money trying to grow grapes than getting rich. Why don't we sell and move closer to Aldo and Margherita?"

He exhaled a loud breath. "And do what, Susanna? This is what I know"—he then nodded to their sons running in from the field—"and this is what they love."

"But there's so much more to life than simply being a farmer and childbearer."

He shook his head sadly. "We just returned from a wonderful trip, darling. Please, let's just enjoy today."

"Bella's snap peas came up!" DeAngelo said excitedly as the boys hugged their parents and then pulled at their father's hand. "Come, Papa, help us pick them!"

As Giovanni swept Pietro off the ground and followed DeAngelo out to the garden, Susanna stood alone, a scowl on her face.

‹಼ ಌ›

Susanna woke up late the next morning to the sound of silence. None of the usual morning chatter from Giovanni and the children filled the halls. She dressed quickly and went outside, only to see her husband and the boys in the field with their workers. Her insides clenched tight at the sight, a reminder of what her future would be like. She wanted to turn around and go back inside. Instead, she exhaled a loud sigh and walked out to join them.

It was a lovely morning, with the sun shining and the grapevines bearing their early green clusters, still so small one could hardly see them. Franco only gave a silent nod as Susanna approached, but Isabella never raised her head, only stared down at the vine with a distant look on her face. Susanna was in no mood to get involved with whatever troubled them, so she continued on to Angelina.

"What's the matter with Bella?" she asked in a condescending tone. "I didn't think Mother Nature ever had a bad day."

Angelina hesitated for a long moment, and a small flush rose to her cheeks. "She miscarried this morning."

"I didn't know she was pregnant," Susanna said with a bit of surprise. Then she glanced at her own sons digging in the dirt. "Perhaps she should consider herself fortunate; one child is more than enough."

Angelina's eyes went wide.

"I'm simply being honest," Susanna continued. "I love my children dearly and want the very best for them, but the entire process, the nine months of being tired, the incessant crying—why, it's surprising to me that any woman would want more than one."

Angelina couldn't stop herself. "My children aren't a burden—"

Susanna cut her off. "How many years have we known each other, Angelina? Ten? It appears to me that your life has always been a struggle."

All of a sudden Susanna was distracted as she saw Isabella tying a rope to her younger son's waist.

"What in the world are you doing with Pietro?" she called out.

Isabella walked over. "He keeps wandering off." She pulled a snap pea out of her pocket and popped it into the little boy's mouth. "I'm afraid he'll fall into the creek if I don't tie him to myself."

Susanna's eyes traveled beyond to watch her oldest boy follow Liliana and Franco. DeAngelo had become very protective of the Carollos' little girl. He copied Isabella's idea with the snap peas and dug one out of his pocket. He cut open the pod, placed the pea in Liliana's waiting mouth, and kissed the top of her head. Susanna watched her oldest child copy their winemaker's every move, from the way he studied the plants to the way he nurtured the Carollos' only child.

Dear God, no, thought Susanna, her eyes riveted on DeAngelo with his arm around Liliana. This was a friendship that certainly needed some boundaries. The longer she allowed her son to mingle with their workers, the more difficult it would be to separate them in the future. She inhaled a deep breath and turned back to Isabella.

"Angelina told me you miscarried. I'm sorry for your loss."

"Thank you," Isabella whispered.

"I pray your longing for another child isn't the reason why you mother my children as if they're yours."

Isabella didn't say anything, but her face changed, like a shadow across the vineyard when a cloud moves in front of the sun. Susanna could see it plainly, and the look of vulnerability gave her a feeling of power, of finally cracking the indomitable spirit of Isabella.

"I'm sorry to bring this up at a time when you're suffering," Susanna continued, "but I would appreciate it if you would encourage my DeAngelo to give as much time to his studies as he does to spending time in the dirt and vines with your family." She nodded to the children playing in the field. "I mean, look at him—

imitating your husband's every move. I don't want this farm to stifle his future. He's so much more than a common farmer."

The deep hurt that burned inside Isabella suddenly cooled with a calm understanding. This wasn't about her; it was about Susanna— Susanna's guilt and dim-witted illusions of what she deemed success. It was about Susanna's obsession with both her past and her future, and until she forgave herself, it would continue to be her enemy. As Isabella watched DeAngelo show Liliana how to dig around the vines, she suddenly called out to him. "Little D., how deep are you digging?"

"Just two inches, Bella," the boy yelled back. "Franco said if I went any deeper I could hurt the vine roots. He told me the roots are the source of the plant and if I take care of the source, we'll have a good grape."

Isabella untied the rope that held Pietro and handed it to Susanna. "This farm isn't stifling your sons' future. It's inspiring it."

CHAPTER 31

LUCCA, JUNE 1924

I sabella was at the market when she heard the news. Lucca was
alive this Saturday morning, with Sister Anna's booming voice
carrying across the market.

"Did I ever tell you about the time Bella set out a plate of apples
in the market with a sign that read, 'Take only one apple—God is
watching'?" Anna called out to DeAngelo and Pietro.

DeAngelo shook his head as Anna tried to cover up her widening
grin. "Well, a little boy put a plate of chocolate cookies at the other
end of the table with a sign that read, "Take as many cookies as you
want—God is watching the apples!" Anna laughed at her own joke
as Isabella shook her head.

"Little D., your favorite nun has a great imagination and never
lets accuracy get in the way of a good story." She tried to keep a
straight face but could not and joined Anna's laughter as she took
each boy's hand. "Gentlemen, it's time for us to get to work and
make a little money for the convent and your farm."

They sold to their usual customers, men and women they had
known for years who now teased them from across the market with

shouts of, "Isabella, did you save me some of your best truffles?" or "Bella, where's the good kale? Are you holding it in the back for someone special?"

The chatter continued much of the day until Isabella saw her husband's truck turn into the market. It wasn't like Franco to be this early to pick them up.

He stepped out with a grim look on his face and walked over. There was something in his expression that scared her, and she took a deep breath.

"Giacomo Matteotti has been kidnapped," was all he said.

Isabella stood frozen, as if his words did not register.

"He was taken outside his home—in broad daylight."

Isabella felt faint and steadied herself against her husband's chest. Matteotti was the great man who had helped rescue Franco, the man who had tried to keep Italy out of the war, the man who helped workers unite for better working conditions. She knew the Fascists were angry after Matteotti's speech to Parliament, but she had never thought they would...

She looked up at Franco, who was staring blankly ahead, shoulders slumped in despair.

"Was it the Blackshirts?" she finally asked.

"No one knows," Franco said in a barely audible voice. "But Mussolini said he had nothing to do with it and will begin an investigation."

ᙣ   ᙧ

When Susanna heard the news, she cried. Her tears surprised her because she remembered the time when she had believed Matteotti to be the man who was holding Italy back—a liberal elitist who refused to see the potential greatness of Mussolini. But kidnapping

Matteotti was evil. And Susanna knew this was not something that had begun a week or a month ago. It had not begun with the Treaty of Versailles or with the march on Rome, or with Matteotti's speech to parliament. It had begun with people who were afraid. This was the politics of hatred and division. What Italy needed, now more than ever, was an even stronger man to control its citizens. A man who would stand up to terrorism and govern their country with an iron fist. A man who would do what he promised: find those who had kidnapped a rival politician and bring them to justice. This was a tragedy that, if handled properly, would give Mussolini even greater power.

Susanna lifted her head and found Giovanni standing over her, the newspaper telling of Matteotti's disappearance in his hand. He knelt down, wrapped his arms around his wife, and let her cry.

CB   BD

"Let them leave parliament!" Alfredo Obizzi screamed at his aide. "Those bastards don't know what's best for Italy! I hope they're gone for good!"

Frederico scrambled to pick up the newspaper Obizzi had thrown across the room. He couldn't understand his boss's arrogance after the members of parliament had abandoned their chamber to protest the kidnapping of Matteotti.

"You can't be so cavalier," Frederico said. "This action could mean the end of the Fascist party. These are our nation's deputies who walked out on parliament. They're furious about what happened to Matteotti."

Obizzi waved his hand in the air to dismiss any concerns. "They don't have any fucking proof of who did it!"

"But they've blamed Mussolini. Even if Benito is innocent, he'll take the fall. They've already forced him to step down as minister of the interior, and now the Socialists are asking for the king to return our government to legitimacy."

"The king has no power—he's afraid of Il Duce. This will all blow over."

"What if they find the body?"

"They won't." Obizzi picked up his glass of wine and took a long drink. "And even if they do, Benito will take care of it."

CHAPTER 32

EMPOLI, 1926

A ntonio slowed his truck as he drove into Empoli to deliver wine to the shop where his stepson worked. There were several Blackshirts standing in the middle of the street as if daring him to honk his horn. Instead, he drove up onto the sidewalk and parked the truck in front of Bartolo's wine store.

"Greetings, comrades!" Antonio grinned as he stepped out of the truck. "What brings our government to a humble wine shop?" The squadrists gave Antonio a cold stare as he lifted a barrel off the truck. "Please forgive me—I'm just a poor farmer trying to sell a few barrels of my lord's best to the good citizens of Empoli."

One of the Fascists spit on Antonio's boots as he walked past them into the shop and winked at Bartolo. "How about a little help in bringing this to the cellar?"

They unloaded the ten barrels and moved down to the cool quiet of the cellar. Antonio asked, "Why all the Blackshirts outside your store?"

Bartolo frowned. "They've been hanging around to enforce the new law against all opposition to Mussolini."

Antonio remained quiet as he rolled one of the barrels up against the wall.

"The Fascists have formed a secret police that will arrest anyone causing problems for the new regime," Bartolo continued. "The men outside are waiting for us to do something they don't like."

"Have you been causing any problems?"

"No, but one of my coworkers used to work as a printer for a newspaper that was critical of the way Mussolini handled the Matteotti assassination."

"There are a lot of people pissed with Benito," Antonio said. "Why would he pick on a lowly printer?"

"Ever since the workers' unions were dissolved and newspapers critical of Fascism outlawed, Benito's secret police have been picking fights with anyone who disagrees with them."

"Where do you stand on these new laws?"

"It's 1926, Antonio! In the last two years, more than ten thousand anti-Fascists or those simply accused of being anti-Fascists have been arrested, sentenced to death, or exiled. Who's next? You? Me? Mama?"

"Did you help the boy who printed the paper?"

"No—but I know him."

"Have the Blackshirts seen the two of you together?"

"Of course. I work with him. But when you can get thrown into prison for simply talking with the wrong person—well—that's no government I want to be a part of."

"I don't like what's going on in our country either, Bartolo, but responding with violence will only empower the squadrists and encourage the police to support them."

"The squadrists—are the police."

"I still want you to be strong enough to walk away from the trouble they'll try and draw you into." Antonio paused to make sure he had his stepson's full attention. "Do you understand?"

Bartolo looked past his stepfather and up the cellar stairs at the Blackshirts still lingering outside the shop. "I understand."

◌ ◌

Obizzi was frustrated. Ever since Mussolini had named Farinacci his secretary of the Fascist party, making him the second most powerful man in Italy, Roberto had distanced himself from Obizzi.

The setback only seemed to fuel Obizzi's desire for a greater role in the new government. He had his allies. Frederico had stayed by his side, and if he was patient, he was sure Farinacci would reach out to him again. Obizzi had met Mussolini only one time, in his chambers with Farinacci, and he was sure Il Duce had been impressed. If he could do one thing that could catch the leader's attention, he was convinced, he could be the party's future secretary.

"Frederico, tell me about this new decree on public safety," he said.

His assistant barely looked up from his papers. "Mussolini's people are calling for a tighter surveillance of anti-Fascists."

"He's finally doing what Roberto had always suggested," Obizzi said. "It is indeed time to satisfy the radicals in our party. This decree may be just what we need to receive an invitation into Mussolini's inner circle. WE shall be the ones to root out Benito's enemies."

A slight shock ran through Frederico as he realized what his boss was implying.

Obizzi's smile grew even wider. "And I know just the family we can put on top of that list."

෬ ෨

Two weeks later, Obizzi and his aide sat down at down at a table in a dark corner of Vicentini's restaurant in Viareggio. This was a place known for its criminal element and ties to the Sicilian Mafia.

"I don't know if this is a good idea," Frederico said as he looked over his shoulder at a grizzled man who eyed his briefcase.

"Grow some balls," Obizzi laughed as he pounded his assistant on the back. "The world is looking at Il Duce as if he's saving Italy from Leninism. Believe me, when he took out the Sicilian Mafia recently, the world stood up and cheered."

Two rough men walked into Vicentini's, talked with the bartender for a bit, and then headed to the table where Obizzi and Frederico were seated.

"You looking for us?" the smaller man asked.

Obizzi nodded as he looked down at the envelope he had in front of him. "Just call me Signor A."

The two Mafia men looked at each other and grinned. "So— Signor A.—what is it you want from us?"

Obizzi straightened up in his chair. "As you know, Mussolini has had great success controlling your Sicilian Mafia." He inhaled a dramatic pause. "I'm here to help you get back into his good graces."

The man frowned. "I worry when the government says it's here to help me."

Obizzi laughed. "I completely understand! But I'm only here to root out anti-Fascists who do business and bring trouble to your

390

city. These men are enemies of the regime. If you can prove or—how should I say—come up with information that shows they're anti-Fascists, it could benefit you greatly."

"So, what's in it for you?"

"I'm just a simple businessman," Obizzi said matter-of-factly as he pushed the envelope across the table. "Their names are Martellino and Carollo. Here's a list of the places they do business. Find out the information I need and let me know when you are going to—meet them."

As they walked out of Vicentini's, Frederico shook his head. "I still don't know if working with the Sicilians is a good idea. We don't have any evidence that Giovanni or Franco has done anything against our government."

Obizzi held up his hand to silence his aide. "That's why I want the Sicilians to find that evidence or rough them up in the process." He turned and gave Frederico a cold look. "I want revenge for what they did to me in Pisa."

CR   SO

The year 1926 ended well for the Martellino vineyard. Franco crossed his Trebbiano with another grape to produce a dry, crisp white wine, better than Giovanni had ever tasted from his vineyard. Franco also matched his Sangiovese grape with a Caniola and another grape whose identity he had not revealed even to his landowner. He blended them together into a full-bodied red that had drawn praise from wine critics throughout Tuscany. The accolades opened the eyes of the prestigious wine club Buonamici, an organization that invited only the top vineyards to join. While the membership was voluntary, to be invited by a top producer meant your brand was highly respected. It was an honor Giovanni did not take lightly. It was also an opportunity for the vineyard fortune to prosper.

As he looked out beyond the blue-gray olive trees toward his hometown, a rush of exhilaration hit Giovanni. It was time to celebrate, he thought, to share this feeling with everyone. Another Christmas party would be planned.

Giovanni did make one mistake. He wanted to surprise his wife with a special Christmas gift. The day before the surprise was to arrive, Susanna knew something was up when she walked into the study and caught her husband whispering to their son.

"What are you boys up to?"

Her words surprised them, and DeAngelo started giggling as Giovanni quickly put his index finger up to his lips.

"Nothing, Mama," DeAngelo grinned. "It's a secret!"

"You know I don't like secrets!"

"That's why you're DeAngelo's target," Giovanni said.

Susanna gave a look of genuine interest. "I'll bet I can guess your surprise with only one clue."

DeAngelo's eyebrows came together as if he was in deep thought. Then suddenly a bright smile began to crease his face, as he thought he had the perfect clue.

"What's the capital of Italy, Mama?"

The question, of course, was elementary, but as soon as she heard the words, Susanna's eyes went wide with shock, and she turned to her husband. "You did not invite Margherita and Aldo!"

"She guessed it, Papa!" DeAngelo squealed.

Giovanni seemed to be scrutinizing his wife's face, waiting for a look of delight, but he found none. "They've had us to their home several times, darling, yet we've never invited them to ours."

"Their home is a mansion! Ours is a—a farm!"

"I don't think they're coming to compare houses."

"You don't understand, Giovanni! This villa needs to be painted! The front drive is nothing but gravel, and our dishes and wineglasses are as old as—as DeAngelo!"

"Margherita and Aldo are family!" Giovanni laughed. "They don't care how old our plates are."

"But I do!" Susanna cried out as she hurried to the closet to grab her coat and purse and headed out the door to Lucca's most exclusive shop for glassware.

⊂ঽ &ɔ

She had Franco and Antonio up until midnight, cutting the hedges that lined the drive, trimming the trees that faced the street, and raking the gravel into neat little lines. She knew there was no time for painting, but she had Rosa and Elisa up late polishing and dusting until the villa met Susanna's most stringent satisfaction.

⊂ঽ &ɔ

"DeAngelo, move the peppers," Isabella said, as she needed room to place the antipasti before plates of cheeses, olives, grilled peppers, sun-dried tomatoes, and bruschetta. The courtyard was a noisy, lively place this Christmas Eve as preparations continued for the Martellino party. Angelina and Antonio grilled the sea bass while Rosa and Elisa made the *ravioli di magro* with spinach. Everyone was welcome.

The Martellinos' closest neighbors, the Bianchis and Marinos, were the first to arrive. It was the first time they had been on the Martellino property in two years, and even then it had only been to get help from Franco about a mildew problem they were having with their vines.

393

"Thank you for coming!" Giovanni greeted them at the front door. "We have a wonderful holiday feast planned for you!"

Susanna smiled politely and then looked beyond their neighbors to where a pearl-white 1925 Alfa Romeo RL Super Sport Castagna turned down the drive. It was her sister's family, and the auto was yet another example of what Susanna did not have.

She did the best she could to greet the Bianchis and then waited uneasily for her sister. When Susanna saw the dress Margherita was wearing, it made her feel even more inadequate. Her sister looked radiant in a jeweled chiffon dress new to the 1920s, and Susanna was certain Margherita had traveled all the way to Paris or Milan to make such a purchase. She tried to hide her disappointment as her sister hurried up the path with a look of absolute joy. "Susanna, darling, what a beautiful home you have!"

But Susanna was sure the compliment was insincere, and she forced a smile, hoping her sister could not read her mind.

"Thank you," was all she could think of saying as she gave Margherita a modest embrace. When they separated, Margherita's gaze was one of such confidence, Susanna had to look away. "Please, come in," she finally said. "We have a wonderful day planned. Dinner and of course Midnight Mass at San Frediano."

Aldo gave an appreciative smile but remained quiet.

Susanna wasn't sure what next to say or do, and stood awkwardly next to Margherita for a moment until Isabella came out of the kitchen with a platter of glasses filled with Martellino red.

"You must be Susanna's sister!" Isabella exclaimed as she handed Margherita a glass. "I'm Isabella. My husband, Franco, is the Martellino's winemaker—the one you were so kind to help."

"I was hoping to meet you," Margherita said sweetly. "Thank you for the letter of condolence after we lost our dear Giacomo. Your prayer gave me such comfort."

The conversation surprised Susanna, who hadn't known Isabella had corresponded with her sister after the murder of Italy's Socialist politician.

"It was a tragedy for all of Italy," Isabella said. Then she introduced herself to Aldo and their children before taking the last glass of wine and handing it to Susanna. She didn't let go until Susanna made eye contact with her.

"Enjoy today, my friend. This is a special occasion."

Then she turned back to their guests. "The red we're serving is Susanna and Giovanni's finest! It's the wine that prompted the invitation into the Buonamici!"

The mere mention of the organization turned the head of their neighbor, Dante Bianchi, who was across the room, and he raised his glass. "Congratulations to one of the finest vineyards in all of Tuscany!"

Susanna beamed with pride and raised her own glass before taking a quick sip and turning back to her sister. Margherita was already gently swirling her glass, bringing it up to her nose to inhale the aroma, and then letting the wine run over her tongue and across her palate. A broad smile followed. "Absolutely marvelous!"

Isabella gave a quick wink to Susanna, excused herself, and went back to the kitchen. For a moment Susanna watched her leave, until Dante Bianchi grabbed her elbow and pulled her toward Giovanni. "You must seize the day, my friends. This is your golden opportunity. Now show me where you make these heavenly red and white wines the Lucchesi newspapers have been raving about."

CR SO

Antonio inhaled the fragrance of grilled fish drifting across the courtyard, and stirred the embers of his fire into a red heat. The juice from the bass trickled down into the coals as he scooped a slice of it onto a platter and carried it over to Angelina. She took the platter but stared past him to the young man who was walking down the drive. Her daughter Rosa was running to greet a boy who was wearing the uniform of a Blackshirt.

"Who's that, Antonio?"

"That's Silvio."

"And WHO is Silvio?"

"He's one of the waiters who work at Vipore's. Rosa's had a crush on him for years."

"Why am I the last to know about him?"

He put his arm around her. "Because you spend all your time loving me."

She elbowed him in the side. "How long have they been— dating?"

"I don't know, but the way she's been dressing lately, she sure has his attention."

"He has MY attention by what HE is wearing to a Christmas celebration."

Antonio moved behind his wife and wrapped his arms around her. "I know Silvio. He's a good boy. I remember being his age once, passionate about defending my country when I didn't know why the hell we were fighting. Let's make this night one of peace and fellowship."

CR SO

Rosa kissed her boyfriend and then held him at arm's length. "This is a Christmas party, Silvio. Why did you have to dress as if you're going to a Fascist rally?"

Silvio stood tall and proud. "I love you, Rosa. It's important that your parents know everything about me for what I am about to ask them." He took her hand and walked down to the courtyard where Angelina and Antonio were waiting.

Inhaling a deep breath, Silvio extended his hand to Rosa's mother. "Signora Venero, I am Silvio Conti. I am a friend of your daughter, I am a hard worker at the restaurant Vipore, and I am a follower of Benito Mussolini."

Angelina nodded coolly as she shook the boy's hand. As soon as she released her grip, Antonio grabbed the boy's hand and shook it enthusiastically. "Good to meet you, Silvio Conti. I'm Antonio San Stefano from Sicily. I too am a hard worker, and I'm a follower of Signora Angelina."

Antonio started laughing at his own joke but quieted when he realized his wife did not share in his humor. He did, though, continue to grip the young man's hand. "Interesting outfit you chose to wear to a Christmas party."

Angelina elbowed her husband in the side, reminding him he was the one who wanted peace and fellowship.

Silvio stood in front of them with a renewed determination. "I only wanted to be completely honest with Rosa's parents. It's important you know everything about me. I am a good worker, and I will soon be one of Mussolini's warriors who will make the country I love strong again."

Antonio chuckled dryly. "Young man, being a Fascist isn't who you are. That's simply what you support. The 'who you are' that Rosa's madre and I are interested in is, are you a good and kind person? And do you treat Rosa like the saint that we all know her to be?"

This time Rosa was the one elbowing Antonio in the side.

"I have great respect for Rosa." Silvio straightened up as if getting ready to salute an army general. "I truly do."

Rosa's brother, Bartolo, walked up to join them as Silvio continued, "I have a good job, I'm a good Catholic, and I love your daughter." He paused to collect himself. "And tonight—I would—I would like to ask permission for Rosa to be my wife."

Rosa squealed and threw her arms around Silvio as her brother groaned, "Oh Jesus."

Angelina gave her son a stern look before turning back to her daughter's boyfriend. "Silvio, it's been very nice meeting you, but this is a discussion Antonio, Rosa, and I will have in private. Now please—both of you—enjoy the party." With that she grabbed her husband's arm and pulled him along into their house.

ር8 ፪ე

The rest of the evening went much more smoothly. As the families celebrated Midnight Mass at San Frediano. Isabella sat in the back pew next to Franco. It pleased her to see Susanna and Giovanni enjoying the time with family and neighbors. There was something wonderful in seeing Susanna finally relax and be part of the moment—no pretensions, no expectations, just savoring the right now. As they began to head home, Margherita climbed into the back of the truck with the children and Isabella.

Aldo called out from his Alfa Romeo, "Sweetheart, you'll ruin your new dress!"

"I don't care!" Margherita laughed out loud. "I've never ridden on the bed of a produce truck before! This day has been absolutely delightful!"

Aldo laughed as he opened his door for Giovanni and Susanna to join him. The first half of the drive home was filled with song and merriment until the children went off to dangle their legs off the end of the flatbed, leaving the two women alone. Margherita was the first to speak.

"Isabella, I must tell you—when we left Rome earlier today, I was a bit uneasy about coming to see my sister."

Isabella only smiled.

"For the longest time I thought she didn't like me. I've always wanted a relationship with her—my goodness, she's my only sister—but—something always seemed to push us apart. Political differences, sibling jealousy perhaps—I don't know—but every time I've tried to reach out to her, she seems to push me away."

"Have you told her?"

"No."

Margherita leaned closer so only Isabella could hear. "You know I'm a Socialist. Aldo and I have friends who have fled Italy to escape Fascist persecution."

Isabella nodded.

"I've heard that Susanna was at several important Fascist rallies."

Isabella did not smile. She was waiting.

"They said she was always in the background, as if she were expecting someone."

"She still is," was all Isabella said.

Margherita's brows came together as if forming a question. "Who?"

Isabella looked ahead to the car that was carrying Susanna. "Herself."

CHAPTER 33

VIAREGGIO/LUCCA, 1927

O bizzi and his aide waited in the shadows at the back of Peppino's bar in Viareggio. He wanted to see for himself when the men who had embarrassed him at the jail in Pisa were taken down. The Fascist police would completely understand why he approved of an assault on alleged anti-Fascists. It was a time in Italy during which an accusation held almost as much power as the truth.

Three men walked into Peppino's and took their places at the bar. Obizzi remembered two of them from their meeting weeks before; however, this time they had another bigger, tougher fellow who looked as if he had seen his share of violence. The proprietor had told the men that the Martellino wine would be delivered that day at three o'clock. As the hit man sat down at a table opposite the bar, Obizzi noticed he had a wooden club hanging from his belt. Obizzi smiled. Yes, this payback would be worth the wait.

℞ ℁

"So, in love does my lady enjoy me, that death by drowning shall not destroy meee!" Antonio sang as he and Franco pulled up to the side of Peppino's.

Giovanni was usually with Franco, but today he was busy in Lucca, so had sent Antonio in his place.

"Life on the tide will run before meee! The long wave—the gray waaaave—shall be my stor-eeee!" Antonio belted out as he pulled the tarp back from the barrels of wine. "Anteo Peppino, get your ass out here and try the best red in all of Tuscany!" he yelled out as Franco hoisted a barrel of Martellino red onto his shoulder and walked into Peppino's.

Franco was barely through the door when he felt something sharp slam against the backs of his knees, sending him tumbling to the floor. He dropped the barrel, wine bursting out from the broken slats. A man jumped on top of him, slashing a wooden club at his head, but Franco rolled to his right, the club barely missing. The hit man raised his club again, but Antonio came flying through the front door, blasting the man to the ground. Two Mafia men bolted from behind the bar and grabbed Antonio, shoving him up against the wall. The hit man scrambled to his feet and raised his club to strike, but his eyes suddenly narrowed as he stared at his target.

"Antonio San Stefano from Messina?"

"The one and only!" Antonio snarled, and then he too saw who was speaking, and he broke out into a huge grin.

"Ferruccio Vencini? What the hell are you doing in Viareggio?"

The pair grabbed each other in a bear hug.

"Times were getting rough in Sicily," Ferruccio said. "Mussolini's been dropping the ax on some of our old compadres, so we thought we'd lie low for a bit. Came over here a few months back looking for work. Thought we found some until today. Then you walk in with a barrel of wine."

"You're telling me I was part of your job?"

"Not you." Ferruccio nodded toward Franco, who was being helped to his feet. "There was a guy wanting damaging information on your partner and landowner. We couldn't find anything bad, so he wanted us to rough them up."

Antonio's jaws clenched as he tried stay calm. "So, where's this guy now?"

"He's sitting over—" Ferruccio looked to the dark corner of the room at a booth that was now empty. "Damn—he's gone."

"I think I know the bastard you're talking about."

"He called himself Signor A."

"As in *asshole*!" Antonio growled.

◯ℛ ℰ◯

When Obizzi saw that his setup had failed, he and Frederico slipped out the back door and hurried to their car.

"How did our hit man know that fucking Antonio?" Obizzi hissed.

"He has many friends." Frederico pulled a letter from his jacket. "I've found nothing that ties them to any anti-Fascist plot except this."

Obizzi snatched the note as Frederico continued. "I did some research and discovered that Bartolo Venero is no longer working for the Martellinos. He's taken a job at a wine store in Empoli. Apparently one of his coworkers was once a printer for a Socialist newspaper in Florence."

Obizzi remained quiet as he read the note.

"All you have to do is talk to a certain police officer in Empoli, and I believe we can have both of them arrested as anarchists."

Obizzi handed him back the note. "Let's make sure the prefect in Empoli knows WE are the ones who turned them in. That information will eventually get back to Mussolini's people. He needs to know he has a great ally in Alfredo Obizzi."

"One more thing," Frederico said. "Did you notice the Buonamici seal on the barrels they were delivering to Peppino's?"

"No."

Frederico gave the look of a man who had discovered a golden nugget. "The Martellino vineyard has been invited into a rather prestigious wine club in Tuscany."

A wicked smile spread across Obizzi's face. "Perhaps we can kill two birds with one stone."

ଔ   ಖ

Isabella took a deep breath of the morning air as she sat on a blanket in her garden. Her clothes were wet from the mist as she watched the sun lift the fog from the cold ground, sending a soft glow across the olive grove. She had started her prayers a bit early this morning, after hearing Franco's story of what happened in Viareggio the night before. There would be more trouble from Obizzi, she thought. He was not a man who would take defeat lightly, and she wondered what strategy he would try next.

The sound of footsteps interrupted her thoughts, and she turned to see her daughter with DeAngelo. The Martellino boy had a sad look on his face.

"What's wrong, Little D.?"

He only shrugged his shoulders.

Isabella picked up an olive from the ground, squeezed it in her hand, forcing the juice to flow into her palm, and dabbed a bit on his forehead, "My father used to tell me the Spanish said of the olive, 'Aceita de oliva, todo mal quita,' which means, 'Olive oil makes all pain go away.'"

But the boy only stared out at the olive grove with his hands stuffed into his pockets.

"You seem to be studying the trees," she said, trying to lift his spirits. "Do you remember the five ingredients needed to create the perfect home for an olive tree?"

DeAngelo remained quiet.

Liliana answered for him. "The sun."

Isabella nodded, and her daughter continued. "Stones—drought—uh—"

Again, nothing from DeAngelo.

"It appears that Little D. is acting out the last two," Isabella said.

"Silence and solitude," said Liliana with a quick smile.

Isabella brushed her hand through DeAngelo's hair. "Is there something you want to tell me?"

He sighed and finally said, "Mama and Papa fight all the time. They fight about money. They fight about who runs the country. They fight about my school."

His words surprised Isabella, and she paused before answering. "Your parents sometimes disagree on what they believe is best for our country—but this conversation is not about our government, is it?"

He shook his head.

"What is it you want to say?"

"Do you think children should do whatever their parents want?"

"That depends on the situation. But all parents want what's best for their child."

DeAngelo's shoulders slumped. "Then I guess I'll do what Mama wants."

She waited for DeAngelo to continue but was suddenly distracted by a car racing down the drive. It was Bartolo with a boy she didn't know.

"Something's happened, children!" Isabella lifted up Liliana and hurried to the courtyard.

CB   BO

Angelina's cry brought Antonio and Franco from the barn. Bartolo was trying to comfort his mother, who was sobbing against his chest.

"What's happened?" Isabella called out as she arrived, out of breath.

Bartolo looked up. His face was grim. "The Fascist police came to our wine shop to arrest us. We were lucky to be making deliveries when they arrived. Our boss came to warn us."

Antonio looked at the boy who was with Bartolo. "Is this the young man who worked for the Socialist newspaper you were telling me about?"

Bartolo nodded. "Tullio and I work at the wine shop, but someone accused both of us of working for a paper that was critical of Mussolini."

Tullio's face was filled with guilt. "I did once work for a man in Florence who printed everything from newspapers to school books—I didn't always read what was in his papers, but one of his writers accused Mussolini of cheating on his wife."

"So, it was truth in journalism," Antonio chuckled.

Angelina gave her husband a dirty look before she turned back to her son. "Did you work for this printer?"

"No," Bartolo said. "But the Fascist police don't care. I'm guilty by association."

Tullio raised his hand. "I'm very sorry, Signora Venero, but I must get home. I have to get my things before we escape."

"Escape?" Angelina gasped. "Escape to where?"

"I don't know—" was all Tullio said, and then he was gone, back in his car and speeding for home, leaving a stunned Bartolo unsure of what to do.

Isabella looked down at her daughter and DeAngelo, who were staring up at her with frightened eyes. She then glanced at Bartolo and Angelina, who seemed numb with horror.

"Everything's going to be fine," she said, and then she winked at DeAngelo. "But I need you take Lily inside your villa."

DeAngelo nodded and took Liliana's hand, and off they went.

Isabella turned to Angelina. "Why don't you help Bartolo pack?"

She waited for them to reach the cottage before she turned back to her husband and Antonio. "It appears Alfredo Obizzi won't rest until he's hurt one of us."

Franco's jaws clenched as he attempted to stay calm. "He still wants revenge after I was released from jail, and he failed at Peppino's."

Isabella nodded and stared out at the horizon. She recalled meeting Obizzi for the first time at the Piazza Napoleone. She remembered eyes that burned with arrogance, blood red from both wine and ego.

Antonio stood quietly watching her, but his patience finally wore out. "I know the wheels in your mind are turning, Bella."

She heaved a deep sigh. "I'm trying to think of a peaceful solution."

"And I'm trying to think of one of that doesn't involve my throwing a hand grenade into his office."

She shook her head. "Violence will only bring more trouble to this vineyard."

"Unfortunately, we don't have a man like Matteotti to help us out this time," Franco grumbled.

"No, we don't—and if Bartolo is arrested, his trial will be a sham." Isabella paused for a moment and then smiled up at Antonio. "But we do know people who could be of assistance, don't we, Sergeant?"

Antonio raised an eyebrow.

"Susanna's sister has friends in the anti-fascist movement who have fled to Paris to avoid persecution." She put a hand on Antonio's shoulder. "And didn't you recently reconnect with a friend from Sicily who might be willing to help?"

"Yes, I did." Antonio's face broke into a wide grin. "And Asshole Obizzi himself set up our reunion."

CR BD

Angelina and Bartolo came out of the house with a bag of clothes and food. The boy's eyes were moist as he scanned the property, wondering how long it might be before he would return. Where would he go? What would he do? The farm was all he knew.

Isabella seemed to know what he was thinking and took his hand. "We'll hide you at the convent until we come up with a plan."

All of a sudden, Antonio's head jerked up at the sound of an automobile coming up the road. He grabbed Bartolo and Franco and ran to the barn. As soon as the door closed, a police truck turned down the drive, and out stepped the police chief of Lucca with three Blackshirts. Angelina knew one of the men as the office manager from the city's Fascist headquarters, but the other two she was unfamiliar with.

The police chief gave an embarrassed look. "I'm sorry to be here under these circumstances, Angelina, but these men are here to arrest your son."

"On what grounds?" she demanded.

One of the Blackshirts she didn't recognize stepped forward. "Bartolo Venero has been conspiring against the Italian government."

"My son has no interest in politics. He's a simple apprentice at a wine shop."

"Is he here?"

"No. He lives and works in Empoli."

"We've already been to the wine shop and his apartment." The Blackshirt crossed his arms defiantly across his chest. "Your son must have been tipped off that we were coming to arrest him. We were told he was on his way here."

Just then a car turned down the drive. It was Susanna returning from an afternoon of shopping in Lucca, and her pleasant demeanor turned cold when she saw the Blackshirts in her courtyard. She stepped out of the car and nodded at her coworker from Lucca's Fascist headquarters.

"What brings the law to my property, Marco?"

Her embarrassed coworker said nothing, only stared down at his feet.

The Blackshirt next to him spoke up. "One of your former workers has been accused of being a traitor to Italy."

"Preposterous!" Susanna snapped. "I know everything that happens on—"

"Then you won't mind our searching your farm?"

Susanna's eyes went wide with fury—partly because this rude stranger had interrupted her and partly because of his insult of calling her vineyard a damn farm.

"Who the hell do you think you're talking to?" she hissed. "You damn well need my permission to search my estate. The last time your buffoons were here, they falsely arrested my winemaker and cost me a lot of money. Why—I'll have you know I've been a supporter of Benito Mussolini since before you could spell his name. If there's an anti-Fascist on my property, I won't turn him in to your band of misfits—I'll shoot him myself!"

The barn door then opened, and out stepped Franco and Antonio with two barrels of wine. Antonio spoke first. "When do you want us to take the sacramental wine to the Blessings Convent, signora?"

The question caught Susanna by surprise, and her eyebrows narrowed as if forming a question. Antonio had never asked her opinion before about when or where the wine was going; she cared only whether it sold or not. The management of the grapes and olives was left up to her husband and winemaker.

"I'm sorry," Franco added. "Sister Anna asked to have these barrels yesterday, but I've been busy in the cellar all day."

Susanna made no movement, still puzzled by being included in a discussion about sacramental wine. Finally, it was the young Blackshirt officer who spoke. "May I get on with the search, signora?"

For an answer, Susanna looked to Isabella, who nodded her approval.

"Uh—yes," Susanna stammered, and her loss of control suddenly infuriated her. She straightened up and shook a finger in the Blackshirt officer's face. "But if I find one scratch on any piece of my furniture or one grape stolen from my barrels, I shall write a letter to Benito myself, complaining of the rude and careless treatment given to one of his most loyal supporters!"

The search found nothing, and Marco and the police chief apologized profusely as Susanna stood in the middle of the courtyard with her hands on her hips, giving them a dark stare.

Finally, Lucca's embarrassed police chief said, "I'm very sorry, Susanna—is there anything we can do that would put your mind at ease after this unnecessary intrusion?"

She looked around the courtyard until Antonio raised his hand.

"They could give us a lift to the convent, signora."

Susanna pointed at the Blackshirt officer who had irritated her the most.

"Put those barrels on the back of your truck immediately."

A grimace of displeasure drew down the mouth of the young Blackshirt as he grabbed one barrel while Franco and Antonio lifted the other and jumped into the back. Antonio gave a mock salute to Susanna as the truck started up the drive and headed for the convent.

As Susanna watched the truck leave, she slapped her hands together as if she had just finished a hard day in the field and turned to Isabella. "I'm not going let anyone push me around on my own property."

"No, signora." Isabella bit her lip to keep from smiling.

Susanna then gave Angelina a patronizing look. "I want you to know that if Bartolo had been here, it would have been my patriotic duty to turn him in to the authorities."

"Yes, signora."

"If you see him, tell him he must straighten out his difficulties with the law before he's welcome back here. The Martellinos do not hide enemies of Benito Mussolini."

CR   SO

Twenty minutes later, the wine barrels were delivered to the Blessings Convent. One barrel was indeed filled with sacramental wine, but the other held an enemy of the Fascist state. After the Blackshirts left, Franco broke the top of the barrel open and helped Bartolo Venero climb out.

CR   SO

Obizzi read the letter from the OVRA and smiled proudly. The Organization for Vigilance and Repression of Anti-Fascism praised him for his efforts in arresting anti-Fascists throughout Tuscany. While the Venero boy was still on the loose, this letter was proof that Mussolini himself was likely aware of Obizzi's determined support.

As he walked into his Cremona office, he waved the letter for his assistant to see. "Good work, Frederico. I received a document from the head of the Secret Service praising my 'passion for the party.' Now we can tighten the noose around the necks of the Martellinos and their fucking winemakers."

Frederico gave a look of doubt. "I don't think that would be a good idea, Alfredo. The authorities still haven't found the boy."

"They'll find him. Every police officer in Tuscany has the picture I handed out."

"But if you continue to torment this one family, the party may think you have a personal vendetta against the Martellinos."

411

"Bullshit."

"They still have the letter from Matteotti," Frederico argued, "and they know of your trouble at the jail. Mussolini doesn't like his war heroes put in a bad light, and Sergeant San Stefano certainly is one of those—"

"He doesn't scare me!"

"Pissing off Benito should scare you." Frederico pointed at the letter from the OVRA. "You have a future with the party, and it begins with this letter. Let's not mess it up."

⊗ ⊗

Giovanni shaded his eyes as he looked across an olive orchard that was missing one important worker. He was now doubting his decision to let Antonio help Bartolo escape the law, but these workers had become his family, and he was responsible for their safety. It had been his idea to keep the plan to a select few: Angelina, Franco, Isabella, and Susanna's sister, Margherita, were the only ones who knew about Antonio's efforts to get Bartolo out of the country. Giovanni knew Susanna would throw a fit if she had even an inkling that they were going against Fascist law. Now, as he opened the car door and sat down next to Franco, a feeling of guilt gripped him. "Shouldn't we tell Angelina where we're going?"

Franco shook his head. "She already has enough to worry about. It's best she still believe that Bartolo's safe and that her husband is out selling wine."

Giovanni started the car and looked back at Angelina in the orchard, all alone. With a deep sigh he headed up the drive and turned west, toward the docks of Viareggio.

⊗ ⊗

Angelina wiped the sweat from her brow and closed her eyes, trying again the deep-breathing techniques Isabella had taught her to help let go of her fears. She had not heard from her husband or son in more than a week, and when she confronted Giovanni and Franco about their whereabouts, they would mumble, "Still working the border," but they never looked her in the eye. She had her doubts.

"Signora San Stefano!" a voice said. "I have an important question before I leave for work!"

She turned to see Silvio and Rosa headed her way. Rosa's boyfriend was beginning to grow on her. He was a good young man who treated her daughter well, but she thought that his fanaticism for everything Mussolini was dangerous. She tried to understand Silvio's passion, but the Fascist government's pursuit of her son, as well as, now, her worry for her husband, was trying her patience.

"When your daughter and I marry," Silvio said happily, "I would like a big family, but Rosa wants a small one. What do you say?"

Angelina sighed. "I think a big family would be difficult in these times."

"But Benito wants more Italians. He's honoring the families who produce the most children."

"He's only interested in those children becoming Fascists. But he has no interest in helping to raise them."

"Il Duce loves children, Signora San Stefano! His babies will be the warriors who will return Italy to an empire. They'll defend our great country and push out the Communists and subversives who threaten us."

"So, we are not to question any of Mussolini's decisions?"

"Why would we?"

She looked up to face her future son-in-law. "You did hear that one of the deputies of Italy's Chamber, Antonio Gramsci, was sentenced to over twenty years for simply criticizing Benito's government."

"Criticizing?" Silvio scoffed. "How about conspiracy to incite civil war and class hatred?"

"Accusations!" she snapped. "Just like the false accusations the Fascists brought against my son!"

Silvio's eyes went wide with shame. "I'm sorry. I—I shouldn't have—"

"It's not your fault." Angelina touched his hand as she tried to calm her own anxiety. "I'm just worried. I don't know where Bartolo is, and I didn't think my husband would be gone this long."

Silvio stood silently, embarrassed, with a look that suggested he wanted to be far away.

Angelina forced a smile and squeezed his hand. "You're going to be late. Go on to work."

He nodded respectfully, gave Rosa a quick kiss on the cheek, and hurried up the drive to start his walk to Lucca.

When he was far enough away, Rosa turned back to her mother. "Bartolo and Antonio are fine, aren't they, Mama?"

Angelina stared at her hands, spotted and dry from years working the fields under the Tuscan sun. She had held it in for so long, but the memories of her past were too much. As she thought back to the death of her first husband, the loss of her daughter to the influenza, and now her son being hunted by the Blackshirts, she broke down and cried. Just when she had found happiness again with Antonio, she was worried now that he too might be gone.

CR   SO

A haggard old drifter stumbled down the boardwalk in Viareggio; he appeared drunk as he picked through trash on the side of the street. Underneath the rags and filth was a man of tough, thick muscle. Antonio was playing the part of a derelict to throw off the fascist police, who were searching the shipyard for anti-fascists they had heard were trying to escape Italy.

Franco and Giovanni were huddled underneath a dock with Bartolo and Tullio, awaiting an all clear from Antonio, who continued to scan doorways and alleys for any sign of the Blackshirt police. Finally, he saw what he was looking for. Two men were hiding behind barrels of trash. Antonio shuffled along the boardwalk, trying to make as much noise as he could, and then stopped to sift through one of the barrels.

"Get the hell out of here," one of the Blackshirts ordered as quietly as possible.

Antonio jerked up in false surprise.

The Blackshirt officer peeked out of the shadows. "Keep moving, old man."

"Yer like the bastards I jes' ran off," Antonio belched. "Tryin' to steal wus mine."

The officer showed a sudden interest. "Who did you run off?"

"Mmph." Antonio grunted and went back to digging through the trash.

The officer came out of the shadows and grabbed Antonio's arm. "Where did they go?"

"Said they was lookin' for a ship captain—but they's lyin'." Antonio pointed south toward Viale Europa. "Trespassin's what they's doin'! I run em off!"

Antonio then farted, which only sped up the police pursuit down Viale Europa. He dug through the trash until they were out of sight and then ran north to the end of the block to Giovanni's truck and flickered the lights to alert his Sicilian friend, who was waiting in a small boat about one hundred meters offshore. Antonio continued down the dock, lay on his stomach, and flashed an upside-down grin to Franco.

"Who's ready for a cruise?" he wisecracked, and then he pulled Franco up. The other three followed, and they hurried to the end of the dock, where Ferruccio Vencini was waiting. Bartolo let Tullio board first, as he wanted time to say goodbye to the two men who had been like fathers to him over the years.

"I—I can't thank you enough—" Bartolo struggled with his words.

Antonio kissed his stepson's cheeks and then pushed him aboard. "No time for nostalgia." He gave him a hearty pat on the back. "The law will be back soon."

As the boat pulled away from the dock and out into the dark night sea, Bartolo saluted him. "Tell Mama that I love her and that she's lucky to have you, Sergeant Tony!"

❧　☙

On the drive back to Lucca, Franco and Giovanni dominated the conversation, while Antonio was uncommonly quiet.

"This is the second time this trio has pulled off a great escape!" Giovanni grinned as he pounded on his steering wheel.

"You're right," Franco laughed. "You busted my ass out of jail in Pisa, and now there's tonight's fantastic flight to France!"

They turned to Antonio, who had a miserable look on his face as he stared out the front window.

"What's wrong?" Franco asked.

"I forgot something."

"Did you forget to give Bartolo money?"

"Worse."

"Do you think the police came back?"

"Way worse."

There was a long silence as Antonio dragged his hand through his hair. Finally, he gave a loud exhalation of complete surrender. "I just realized I told Angie I'd only be gone a few days—and it's been two weeks. I'm in deep shit."

Giovanni and Franco roared with laughter.

"We'll come up with a plan!" Giovanni yelled out. "There's still time for one more great escape!"

ଓଃ   ଞ

The crickets' chirping helped mask the triumvirate's stealth as Giovanni cut his engine and silently coasted his car down the Martellino drive. Giovanni and Franco covered their mouths to keep from laughing as they watched Antonio remove his shoes and tiptoe into his house. Everyone was asleep. He opened the door to his bedroom and saw Angelina sleeping. Sitting down beside her, he softly started to sing. "How you are beautiful—more beee-yoo-tee-full tonight. A star smile shines in your bluuuue eyes. Even if tomorrow the destinnneeeee will be adverse—tonight I am near yoooou, sigh! Do not think—"

Angelina opened her eyes. "Antonio!"

She threw her arms around him as he continued to croon, "Tell me of love, Angelinaaaa—you are all my life! Your beee-yooo-tee-full eyes shiiiiine!"

Angelina was in tears as she pulled him on top of her, and Antonio responded. "Ooh la la—I must leave more often, my beautiful princess."

She kissed him fully on the lips and then shoved him off her. "Where's Bartolo?"

Antonio started to sing again. "Dream flames twinkle—tell me it is not illusion—tell me that you are all for meeeee—"

Angelina put her hand over his mouth. "I'm serious. I'll make you sleep outside!"

He pushed her hand away. "I must be losing it. My songs usually work. I thought I had you at 'your bee-yoo-tee-full eyes shine!'"

She tapped her index finger against his chest as if nailing him to a tree. "If you ever want to share my bed again, tell me what you did with my son."

He rubbed the two-week growth of whiskers on his face. "Bartolo's off on a grand adventure to France."

"What!"

"Shhh—you're going to wake the whole house."

Angelina's face became serious. "Go on."

"The Blackshirts were a bit of a headache, but it was nothing this old sergeant couldn't handle." He slipped a strap off Angelina's shoulder. "It was easy. Kind of like taking your nightgown off."

She pushed him away. "Continue."

"We got him on a boat with political refugees. They even have a job for him at a restaurant in Paris. Don't worry—they serve good wine."

She giggled and snuggled up to him. "When can I see him?"

"He has to lie low for now." Antonio shrugged. "And you and I have to act as if we don't know anything, or we'll all wind up in jail. That's why you can't tell Rosa or Silvio."

He pulled out an envelope from his pocket. "Bartolo wrote you a letter. That boy loves his mama."

Angelina wrapped her arms around him. "And Bartolo's mama loves you."

She slipped a strap from her nightshirt over her shoulder and gave Antonio a sexy look. "Now, my Sicilian liberator, take off your clothes."

Antonio unbuttoned his shirt as he softly sang, "Here on your heart I do not suffer anymore! Tell me of love, Angel-ee-nuhh!!"

CHAPTER 34

LUCCA, AUGUST 1927

Susanna paced back and forth in her living room. She wasn't sure about any of her decisions anymore. Now that Pietro was five years old, both boys were eligible to attend Saint Gregorio, but her last argument with Giovanni had not gone well. He had insisted that the Lucchesi schools were just fine; they would give their sons a strong education and allow them to live at home and help on the farm. But Susanna wanted more, particularly for her eldest son. DeAngelo was at the top of his class and had a natural gift with people—perhaps politics or a professorship, she thought, could be in his future. Pietro was completely different. Their youngest child was a fearful boy with little interest in learning how to read and write. He was distant around the neighbor children. He constantly teased his brother and followed Isabella around like a lost puppy. His only joys seemed to be his toy soldiers and the stories Isabella read to the children every night. He was also the daily reminder of the mistake Susanna had made six years earlier. Pietro was Obizzi's son. His features were sharper and more forceful than Obizzi's, but his dark eyes were nearly identical; there were times she felt as if those eyes were looking directly into her soul.

She delayed telling Isabella about her plan to send the children off to boarding school, because she knew how disappointed she would be. But a part of her wanted to get DeAngelo and Pietro away from Isabella. When her boys came home from school, they would immediately run to their winemaker's house to share the day's adventures or troubles. It also bothered Susanna when Giovanni praised Isabella's talents as a mother: he marveled at her patience, her capacity to see life through a child's eyes, and her ability to forgive. Susanna remembered walking to the garden with her husband only to find Isabella talking to her boys and Liliana about something as simple as how to eat an apricot. Isabella laughed as Pietro devoured the fruit and had the juice dripping down his chin and onto his shirt.

"Yes, that's one way to eat an apricot," Isabella had told Pietro, "but this time, I want you to close your eyes and think of how the apricot was created. The sun, the water, the soil, and the tree itself are all in the fruit. Now bring the apricot up to your nose and breathe in its aroma; feel the texture of its skin. When you take a bite, really try to taste the flavors that burst forth. I want you to understand that when you bite into the apricot, you taste the sun, the water, the soil, the tree, and the entire universe in that simple bite. The children were mesmerized, and so was Susanna. She was also jealous.

It was Josephine who told Isabella about the imminent departure of the Martellino boys, and Isabella recalled DeAngelo's sadness in the orchard a month before. "I don't understand why the boys have to go so far away to school."

Josephine frowned. "Susanna wants someone else to raise them."

"But she loves her sons."

"Love has nothing to do with it, Bella. She doesn't trust herself as a mother."

The statement made Isabella stiffen.

"She thinks she's better than we are." Josephine's lower lip began to tremble. "That woman judges everybody and everything."

"She holds on to the past," Isabella said in a voice barely above a whisper, "and holding on to the past only strengthens her fears and doubts about the decisions she's making right now."

"Her sons need her love right now." Josephine wiped a tear from her cheek. "I'm already missing them. I pray this new school doesn't change them."

Isabella turned to watch DeAngelo climbing an olive tree with Liliana. He was playfully trying to grab her as she dropped an olive onto his head. Their laughter could be heard throughout the grove.

ଓଃ ଶୠ

When her mother told her that DeAngelo would be leaving for a boarding school, Liliana was heartbroken; she ran to her bed and broke into tears. "It's not fair! He's the best friend I've ever had!"

Isabella sat beside her. "He'll be back."

"No, he won't. I'll never see him again."

"Of course you will." Isabella rubbed her daughter's back. "He has breaks at school, and we can visit him in Rome for a holiday."

Liliana looked up. "We can do that?"

"Of course. Why, I've never been to our nation's capital. Papa may have to stay and work—but you and I could have a holiday."

Liliana started to smile. "And Pietro too?"

Isabella nodded. "DeAngelo and Pietro can both tour Rome with us."

CR   ℘

After reading the acceptance letter from Saint Gregorio for perhaps the tenth time, Susanna pinched the bridge of her nose to stifle the headache she knew was coming on. Giovanni walked into the living room. "I hope your headache is about your decision."

"Don't say that!" Susanna shot back. "This is just as difficult for me."

"In what way?"

"We're doing what's best for the boys. Saint Gregorio will be an excellent school for them, and—with our wine and olive oil sales doing well—we can afford it now."

"Our sales have improved, but this is a big expense."

"Giovanni." She rubbed her forehead, barely able to speak the next words, but they needed to be said. "Think about our son's potential. DeAngelo is a very smart boy, and this school will give him opportunities he would never have in Lucca."

"What about Pietro?"

"Pietro," Susanna sighed. "I think Pietro needs the discipline Saint Gregorio will provide. This is a school that will bring out the very best in our sons."

"What if I don't want to go?" It was DeAngelo, who had been listening from the kitchen.

Susanna's head jerked around as if she'd been slapped. "DeAngelo!" She held her arms out, but he stayed by the doorway. "Please, my love, there are times when a mother has to do what she thinks is best for her children."

423

"But I want to be like Papa. I want to grow grapes and olives."

Giovanni gave his wife a look of disappointment.

She walked over and knelt down in front of her son. He backed away.

"DeAngelo, this school will give you so much more. It will teach you leadership and discipline. Why, you could be a banker like your uncle Aldo, or even the next leader of our country."

"If I go there and don't want those things, can I come home?"

"Of course you can, my precious child," she said gently, and for a moment DeAngelo thought his mother was going to cry. Instead she took his hands in hers and looked him in the eyes. "But I want you to give this school a chance."

He nodded sadly and then headed outside to find Liliana.

As soon as his son was out of sight, Giovanni asked, "What is it about Saint Gregorio that makes it so much better than our schools in Lucca?"

"That's not it. Giovanni, you know that—"

"Did you see the look on DeAngelo's face? Everything he loves is right here in Lucca—his family, his friends, this vineyard. Why can't you just let our boys enjoy being children? They'll have the rest of their lives to work."

"Margherita and Aldo insist it's an incredible school. One that will help young people discover their talents and work toward their goals."

"Their goals, Susanna? Or YOUR goals?"

"Don't say that! I just want them to realize their potential."

"Would you rather they be rich and famous, or happy?"

"Why can't they be all three?"

He looked up slowly. "Does it bother you that the Carollos have very little yet are very happy?"

"No!"

"Have you ever thought, Susanna, that their simple life allows them to enjoy life's simple pleasures? Planting, growing, harvesting, crushing, turning those grapes into a fine wine. I watch them. I watch them live simply—and love fully."

"There's so much more to life, Giovanni."

"Then let our sons discover it on their own." He then paused before offering a soft smile. "Spending time with our workers has changed the way I look at the world. Isabella even makes a boring task such as slicing tomatoes a fascinating experience."

She glared at him. "You think she walks on water."

"No, I think she enjoys every moment of walking on the green grass of the right here and right now."

"You don't understand, Giovanni. Our boys have never received the proper Catholic education while we've lived on this vineyard."

"Just about every school in our country has been indoctrinated in Catholic teaching for centuries," Giovanni laughed. "But what I saw at Saint Gregorio was Fascist educators teaching children elitism—that there's a pecking order and a chain of command in how we citizens do things."

"This school has only the best teachers."

"But what if the government is telling our schools how they should educate our children, Susanna? Reading and writing have become secondary to—Mussolini. He wants to train our children to obey and follow without question. That's not education; that's the military. You and I both know DeAngelo will be lost in that environment."

Susanna closed her eyes and again rubbed her forehead. Her headache had arrived and with it the realization that she would be alone in this decision. The fact that their field workers had influenced her husband only heightened the pain. Finally, she opened her eyes and sighed. "Let's just try this school, Giovanni. Let's see how it works. I have a feeling this could be very good for both our boys."

☙ ❧

The following week, Liliana rarely left DeAngelo's side. When DeAngelo pulled weeds from the garden, Liliana pulled weeds from the garden. When DeAngelo went fishing on the banks of the Serchio, Liliana baited his hook. Together they helped Franco and Isabella in the field and ate all three meals sitting side by side. The very scene at dinner convinced Susanna that she was doing the right thing. If her son was to become the man she knew he could be, those two must be separated.

While DeAngelo complained about leaving home, Pietro said nothing. Only Josephine heard the younger son's soft footsteps shuffling outside to find Isabella when his parents began to argue. If the Carollo's lights were out, he would curl up on their wooden porch and pull his blanket around himself. Franco spent the final few nights carrying the boy back to his bed.

On the night before they left, Isabella held Liliana as she cried, and then she said prayers for DeAngelo and Pietro with her. Isabella went outside and took her wooden rocking chair to the middle of the yard to begin her evening meditation. She inhaled deeply as the full moon lit up the vineyard and olive orchard. As she sat down and closed her eyes to begin her prayers, she felt a tug on her arm. It was Liliana. "Mama, I can't sleep. I'm still sad they're leaving tomorrow."

Isabella lifted her daughter to her lap. "I'm sad too. I'll miss DeAngelo and Pietro very much, and tonight I'm asking God to watch over them on their new adventure."

"Can we say another prayer for them?"

"Of course, my sweet girl."

"What should we pray?"

Isabella pulled Liliana in tightly and kissed the top of her head. "When I was a child, one of the prayers Anna said that helped me fall asleep came from Proverbs: 'If you sit down, you will not be afraid; when you lie down, your sleep will be sweet.'"

"Is that why you always pray sitting down? To help you sleep better?"

Isabella laughed. "I sit down to be still. Being in nature helps quiet my mind."

"What do you pray?"

"I give God any thoughts of sadness or anger and just relax in His peaceful world."

"What does He tell you, Mama?"

"That I'm never alone. That His love is with me every step of the way. I close my eyes and bless everyone;starting with your father, then you, then the Veneros, and Martellinos, and Antonio. And if I know of anyone else who is suffering, I bless that person too. People need love as plants need water."

"I'm still going to miss them, Mama."

"DeAngelo and Pietro may be leaving tomorrow, but they'll still be in our hearts, and no distance can take that away." Isabella hugged her daughter. "Now say a prayer."

Liliana closed her eyes and took a deep breath. "Please, God, take care of DeAngelo and Pietro. When they're sad, help them be happy. Don't let anybody take Pietro's toy soldiers. He really likes them. And let DeAngelo make friends," she paused, "just don't let them be girls."

Isabella laughed again, then lifted her daughter and carried her inside to bed, touching the wooden box next to the door as she entered the house.

CR   BO

Isabella was up at her usual time the next morning: it was five forty-five prayers and six-thirty breakfast for the three families that lived at the vineyard. After her meditation, she went to the Martellino kitchen to begin breakfast, only to hear screaming coming from upstairs.

"Put your shoes on right now, young man!" It was Susanna's voice.

"I don't want to go! I'll run away!" Pietro yelled.

"Really? Where will you go?"

"Anywhere that's away from you!"

"Don't threaten me!"

"I hate you!"

"You ungrateful little brat!"

"You hate me too! That's why you're sending me away!"

"We're paying a lot of money for this excellent school!"

"I don't want it! Leave me alone!"

"You get back here right now and put your shoes on!"

But Pietro walked downstairs in only his socks, his eyes puffy from crying.

Franco and Liliana came through the door and saw the tension, and then DeAngelo came bounding down the stairs. "What's for breakfast?"

Franco pulled down a pan that was hanging over the stove and bowed deeply. "Young lords of Lucca, this is your day. We'll cook whatever your hearts desire!"

"Eggs!" shouted DeAngelo. "With cheese and onions and peppers and spinach and tomatoes!"

Isabella looked at Pietro, who did not answer as he stewed in his seat.

DeAngelo stood up. "Can I help with the toast?"

Isabella shook her finger at him. "You take a seat, my royal of Tuscany. Franco and I will serve you like kings. Now sit down and wait for your feast."

DeAngelo and Pietro were indeed treated like royalty. When the meal was ready, Liliana did a curtsy as she delivered the morning meal to DeAngelo. "Breakfast is served, Your Highness."

DeAngelo winked as he took a bite and then pointed to the open chair for Liliana to join him.

Franco grinned as he watched the scene and then took breakfast out to the Veneros, leaving Isabella alone in the kitchen.

"You certainly know how to make this difficult, don't you?" It was Susanna, who closed the door to the dining room to give them privacy.

Isabella wiped her hands on her apron. "I'm not trying to make anything difficult."

"Then please let me be their mother."

"I—I love your sons. I've never tried to—"

Susanna cut her off. "I know you and Giovanni are very disappointed with my decision to send them to Saint Gregorio, but you don't understand the influence this school will have on my sons' future. We've had this discussion in the past about my place in this household and your place in working for us. I've watched you dote on my boys the last two days, making it very difficult for them to separate from this vineyard, and now with this 'special meal', you're determined to make them homesick for you." Susanna walked around the stove to face Isabella. "You and I have come a long way in our relationship since you arrived, and I would appreciate it if you would mind your own family."

Isabella looked Susanna squarely in the eyes. "I can assure you, Signora Martellino, it's never been my intention to intrude in your decisions as a parent. I love your sons and only wanted to make them a breakfast to remember."

Susanna exhaled slowly and put her hand on Isabella's shoulder. "I'm sure you mean well, but remember—this is difficult for me also. I am their mother. Remember that. Please don't make this mistake again."

Isabella nodded as she picked up a plate and opened the door to the dining room. "Would you like to join your sons for breakfast?"

For a moment, Susanna watched the children chattering away as they devoured their meal. Her gaze finally rested on Pietro, who was staring back at her through angry eyes. Susanna stood up a little straighter, attempting to be unfazed by her youngest boy, and took the plate from Isabella. But instead of joining the children, she headed for her study to be alone.

CHAPTER 35

FLORENCE/LUCCA, 1928

"**W**e've been robbed!" Giovanni screamed at the railroad security assistant at the Florence station. "My winemaker and I loaded twenty barrels of our best red and white onto boxcar six in Lucca! Now where the hell are they?"

His anger had the young man backpedaling up against the platform gate.

"I checked twice in every car, signor! There's no wine with your Martellino seal on it in any car."

Giovanni shook with fury as he shoved the receipt into the face of the inexperienced security man. "This shows our wine was loaded in Lucca and was to be unloaded at your station! It's already been purchased by one of the finest hotels in Florence!"

"And as I told you, signor, what you're holding is not our standard rail receipt."

"Well then, who the hell were the two men who gave me this receipt in Lucca and said they were with railroad security?"

The young man scanned the receipt and looked up in anguish. "Signor, these names are none I'm familiar with."

At that moment Franco ran to them, out of breath. "I watched the men lock boxcar six when we left Lucca, but someone must have broken the lock off between Lucca and here. I can't even find evidence of a padlock near the car."

Giovanni collapsed on the ground and dropped his head into his hands. The men they had met in Lucca had claimed to be part of the mayor's new team in the transition from Mayor Guidi to Mayor Grossi. It had been a lie, yet Giovanni had been the fool who trusted them. In his excitement to get to Florence, he had not even asked for their badges or identification. He had simply signed off on the shipment and boarded the passenger car. His thoughts had still been on the flattering write-up in the Lucchesi newspaper about his Martellino brand. Now, it was over. Their wine could have been stolen in Lucca, or at the stop in Pistoia, or even at the Florence station.

"God, what are we going to do?" he gasped, his face distraught as he looked up at Franco. "I can't pay this month's bills. This shipment was going to a brand-new buyer who will never trust me again. The word will get out that the Martellinos don't deliver."

Franco knew Giovanni had borrowed against the vineyard to send his sons to that expensive school in Rome, and thought of the only chance they had to hold on to the new customer.

"All we can do is tell him the truth." He reached for Giovanni's hand and helped him to his feet. "Tell him what happened. We have several barrels left of last year's vintage, and we can deliver the rest when this year's is ready."

"We can't afford that."

"We can," Franco said, "if you withhold my salary until you can afford it."

Giovanni stared at his winemaker. "I can't do that."

"We're in this together, Giovanni. That wine was just as much a part of me as it was a part of you."

☙ ❧

Isabella sat on the top of Lucca's walls with Cesare Bosco. She had never seen the restaurant owner so troubled; he explained to her what had happened after he was accused of being a Communist.

"I have to be honest with you," Cesare said, dragging his hands through his thick gray hair. "I did have union meetings at my restaurant, but we all did after the war. Those meetings helped the government strike a deal with the agricultural workers. I'm sure there were a few landlords and politicians angry about the results, but I thought time would take care of any future trouble. Nobody accused me of anything until the lease on my restaurant came up and another man bid on it and lost."

"As he should have," Isabella said. "That restaurant has been in your family for years."

"But with the outcome came accusations that I was a Communist. Two weeks after the new mayor took over, they reversed the decision."

Her eyes went wide in shock.

"Yes. I've lost my trattoria, and I may be sent to prison."

Isabella had known Cesare since she was a little girl. He frequented her table at the market, and gave to the Blessings Convent. She sat up straight and looked at him intently. "Do you know who made these accusations?"

"Of course—the same man who bid for the lease to my restaurant."

"Is he another restaurant owner in town who wants your business?"

"No, he's a man who's never spent a day in the business, but he saw the money our trattoria was making."

"May I ask the man's name?"

"Obizzi."

Isabella's jaw dropped. "Alfredo Obizzi?"

"That's the name. Do you know him?"

Isabella stood up from the stone wall and clenched her fists. "I know him! He's ingratiated himself with every single Fascist leader in Tuscany!"

Cesare sighed. "Apparently he has the produce and wine to take over immediately."

"If he has no experience, where did he get the food and wine?"

"I don't know, but I believe he has ties to Lucca's new podesta."

Isabella was furious. "Then I shall talk with this new podesta! Because—because this is wrong!"

"What can you do?"

For once Isabella was at a loss for words. "Why—why—I will—I will make him my crostini! He'll listen to what I have to say after a bite of my crostini! Yes, he will!"

CR SO

The mayor's secretary was a friend of Isabella's and set up an appointment the following day. After morning prayers, Isabella made her acclaimed crostini and then experimented with a new vegetable dish. She sliced several eggplants, grilled them, brushed on olive oil, added a little red pepper and sea salt, and topped it off with two mint leaves. She smiled broadly, knowing Lucca's new podesta, Lorenzo Grossi, would be impressed.

"This is fantastic!" Grossi exclaimed as he bit into Isabella's eggplant appetizer. "What do you call it?"

Isabella shrugged her shoulders as she offered him another piece. "I haven't given it a name. I usually just experiment in the kitchen, but if the vegetable is of good quality, the experiment usually works."

Grossi took another bite of the appetizer. "My secretary told me of your excellence in the garden and the produce you sell in our city market."

"Regina attends my church, so she's enjoyed my cooking for years."

The mayor took another bite and then paused. "But Isabella, you didn't come here to dine with me. You have something else on your mind, don't you?"

She lifted the cloth from the crostini and placed them on a plate before the podesta. "I came to talk with you about Cesare Bosco's restaurant." She pushed the plate closer to the new mayor. "It's been in his family for three generations and is very popular because his patrons are the common workingmen from Lucca." She pushed the plate even closer. "They're the textile- and olive-mill workers and vineyard farmers—good, hardworking people."

The mayor eyed the delicacy as if it were his last meal. Suddenly he realized what this woman was asking. He shook his head vigorously. "I'm sorry, signora. Cesare Bosco has been accused of being a Communist and speaking out against Mussolini."

"Nonsense," Isabella laughed. "The people who come to his restaurant are only there to let off steam and brag after a hard day's work."

The mayor frowned. "And criticize our leader?"

Isabella's expression remained neutral. "I would imagine they might complain about what's going on at work with wage cuts of 10 to 20 percent by the Fascists this year. But I've known Cesare for years. He's an honest man who gives to his church and his community—he's certainly not a Communist. The accusation is false."

Grossi took a bite of one of the crostini, closed his eyes, and smiled. Isabella nudged him out of his trance.

"Signora Carollo," he stammered, it—it's not my investigation that's brought this difficulty to light—" He took another bite. "I'm merely the new podesta of Lucca, and this goes much higher than me. I'm simply following the government's rules."

Isabella's blood was beginning to boil. "And allowing people like Alfredo Obizzi to spread lies in order to steal the restaurant from Cesare Bosco?"

Obizzi was listening on the other side of the podesta's office door, and when he heard his name mentioned, he shoved the door open. "How dare you accuse me of stealing his restaurant? I'll not have you slander my good name!"

When she saw him, Isabella immediately cried out, "Good name! YOU have a good name?" She shook her finger in his face. "Alfredo Obizzi, I try very hard to be a woman of peace, but when so many of my family and friends have been hurt by your attacks, I have—I have—well—I have a hard time biting my tongue."

The podesta stepped between them. "Please! Let's settle down!"

"I will not be insulted by this bitch!" Obizzi hissed.

"And I demand you look into the accusations he's made about Cesare Bosco!" Isabella fired back.

"I promise you, we shall get to the bottom of this," Lucca's new podesta said to Isabella. "But signora, you cannot make such statements about a Fascist leader of Signor Obizzi's importance."

Isabella stood boldly with her hands on her hips. "Who then protects the innocent, the poor, and the simple workers from people like him?"

Obizzi looked tempted to lash out, but instead placed his hand over his heart and bowed respectfully to the new mayor. "Please, Your Honor, may I have a word in private with Signora Carollo?"

The podesta nodded and left the room, closing the door behind him.

Obizzi was formally dressed in a black suit with a white silk shirt, whose cuffs he now pulled sharply out from his jacket sleeves as if to exhibit an air of superiority. He pointed to a chair. "Please sit."

She did not. She only crossed her arms defiantly across her chest.

He slowly exhaled, eyes fixed on her face. "You should be afraid of me—"

"I'm not."

He smiled slyly. "I know—and I don't like women accusing me of—"

"Did you steal our wine?"

Obizzi's eyes flew open with momentary shock. "I don't know what you're talking about."

"Did you steal our wine?" she asked again, and she saw a small twitch at the side of his face as he tried to compose himself. He drew a deep breath and seemed to resist the urge to strike her. "Accusing an important leader of the Fascist Party of such a heinous crime as the theft of stale Sangiovese could get you arrested."

"I never accused you of anything," she smiled. "I only asked a question." She then paused and looked him directly in the eyes. "And I never said the wine was Sangiovese…"

Obizzi said nothing. He didn't even draw a breath. He simply stared and waited as if he were a wolf in the weeds, waiting for its prey to move closer. "You may not be afraid of me," he said at last, his fists clenching and unclenching at his sides. "But you should be afraid for your family—how old is your little girl now?"

A knock on the door ended the tension. The podesta entered and nodded to Isabella. "I'm very sorry, Signora Carollo, but I have a very busy schedule today. I'll take your request under advisement."

Obizzi grinned defiantly and picked up one of Isabella's crostini. But as he raised the toast, thick with cheese, garlic, cilantro, and tomatoes, to his mouth, Isabella's hand suddenly shot out and snatched it from him.

"That's not for you!" She glared at him and took one step toward the door. Then she spun back to face Obizzi. "But since you've touched it, no one else will want it." She threw the crostino at him, splattering the tomato and cheese all over the front of his new white shirt, and stormed out of the podesta's office.

 CZ ƎO

"You took it out of his hand and threw it at him?" Antonio could not contain his laughter at dinner that night.

Isabella tried to hide her embarrassment as she prepared the evening meal. "I can't remember a time when I've been so angry."

"I wish I could have seen the look on his ugly face when that tomato plastered his shirt."

The conversation about Obizzi was already bothering Giovanni, and he cleared his throat to change the subject. "Did you have time to discuss the theft of our wine with the new podesta?"

She didn't know how much she should tell them. Supporting a friend like Cesare was one thing but accusing a high-ranking Fascist of stealing without proof would surely bring trouble. In Milan, workers were beaten, and hundreds arrested, all on suspicion of being Communists.

"No," she finally said. "Alfredo came charging out from behind the door as soon as I said his name."

Franco reached for his wife's hand. "I'm proud of you. You stood up for a good man."

"Then why was it that on my walk home today all I could think of was how I let my ego get the best of me?" Isabella grabbed a knife and sliced a pepper with the force of a blacksmith hammering on an anvil. "I yelled at him, and he defended himself. He yelled at me, and I defended myself. It's a vicious cycle that makes attack seem justifiable."

"Don't be so hard on yourself," Franco said. "You were right to go to the mayor."

"But I let my anger get in the way of doing what was right. It may have momentarily satisfied my ego to throw the crostino at him, but if that action comes back to hurt Cesare or our families, then I've given in to the same insanity that enslaves Obizzi."

Giovanni winced every time he heard Obizzi's name, and thought about all of his friends who had been hurt by the new government. But Cesare was one of many who had been beaten down by the Fascists. He raised his glass to Isabella. "I think you raised a good question when you asked, 'Who protects the innocent, the poor, and the common workers?' In this dictatorship, I don't know anymore."

Susanna wanted to say something to defend Mussolini. This was not Benito's affair. This was simply one of his rogue lieutenants abusing his power. There was much to be thankful for under Mussolini's leadership. He was indeed making Italy great again— empowering the corporations, controlling the unions, and building a relationship between his new government and the Catholic Church. Of course, Susanna was disappointed that a few of Benito's overenthusiastic supporters were making life difficult for some outside the Fascist Party. But Mussolini couldn't be expected to control all of his followers.

Finally, it was little Liliana who asked, "Who is going to help the poor people, Mama?"

"We are," Isabella answered. "Our leaders and politicians aren't going to change the world for us, Lily. We're going to have to do it ourselves."

"But how?"

Isabella inhaled a deep breath and smiled down at her daughter. "Who made you, Lily?"

"You and Papa."

"But even bigger than that, who made you?"

"God made me."

"And what do you think God is?"

"You always say God is love."

"So, if God is only love, how can He make something that He is not?"

"He can't."

Isabella gently brushed a lock of hair away from her daughter's face. "Every day it's my job to show the world who created me by being truly helpful."

"But how do we stop the bad men?"

"By being vigilant with our kindness. Each one of us has the power to help heal this world, but it will take great determination and faith to make it happen."

Susanna wanted to scream. Not only were Isabella's words naive, but they also made her afraid. And Susanna understood fear. She had used fear to push people away her entire life, and that same emotion rose up now. It was time to defend themselves, to demand justice. Finally, she spoke up. "And how are we supposed to change the world 'peacefully,' Isabella?"

"By being determined to see things differently."

"That's difficult when a rat like Obizzi has the ear of our leaders."

"I still won't give him the power to affect my happiness. No person or situation can take that from me."

"Then you're a fool who will be taken advantage of by the Obizzis of the world!"

Isabella shrugged her shoulders as she placed two slices of grilled peppers on top of the crostini. Her silence only angered Susanna more.

"We need action, dammit!"

"I didn't say I wouldn't do anything." Isabella handed her a plate. "I shall continue to serve, continue to be active in our community, and"—she winked at the crostini—"sometimes take matters into my own hands when I think what they're doing is wrong."

Giovanni raised his wineglass. "Here's to throwing crostini on those who are wrong!"

Susanna swung around to face her husband. "We've been robbed, Giovanni! Our wine was stolen! Franco was thrown in prison, and Cesare may soon be sent there as well! All caused by the same evil man!"

He looked down.

"Yet we do nothing!" Susanna hissed. "And nothing will happen to Obizzi because of who he's connected to!" She turned back to Isabella. "What does your faith say about that?"

Isabella gave a lopsided grin as she placed a plate before Giovanni. "It tells me to help those who are suffering and make crostini for those who are hungry."

Susanna was now completely distraught. Her entire thought system was being questioned. All she could see was Obizzi taking what was hers, and the only thing she knew how to do was to fight back. Isabella's idea of defense was absurd, and it would keep her in the same desperate state as the rest of the peasants of Italy. As she stared out the window, past their farm into the black of the night, she saw only trouble. "These are dark times," she grumbled. "Dark times for our families, and dark times for Italy."

Isabella looked out the same window and instead saw the soft moonlight dancing on the dew-covered grapevines. Those grapes needed both the darkness and the light to reach their potential— they were grapes that, even when picked, never left their source. The roots were still there, ready to replenish for the next season, and the next. She turned back to Susanna and only smiled.

CHAPTER 36

LUCCA, 1929

As 1929 came to a close, those who worked the Martellino vineyard watched the leaves change from green to yellow to a golden red before falling off the vine, giving the field the look of winter. The cold also bit the world economy, with the Great Depression two months in, not yet blasting Italy with its full storm but enough to drop crop prices, forcing the Martellinos to halt pay to their staff. The farm survived because of Isabella's thriving garden and Italy's unquenchable thirst for a good Sangiovese.

Franco tossed his spade aside and knelt down to work on the first vine. "With the boys coming home, I'd like to get everything finished before the cold snap."

"You just want time off to take DeAngelo and Pietro fishing," Isabella said.

"That's a great idea," he grinned as he mounded the soil around the plants to protect the roots. "So, get to work, fair maiden of the hills, instead of accusing your husband of something you'd like to do."

She laughed out loud and threw a handful of dirt at him. He tried to dodge out of the way, but the majority of the soil found its way down the front of his shirt.

As he stood to untuck his shirt and let the dirt fall free, he saw Giovanni's car turn down the drive. "It looks as if my fishing partners have arrived."

They watched their daughter race from their cottage to greet the Martellino boys. As soon as the car came to a stop, DeAngelo was out the door, running to Liliana, lifting her up and spinning her around in delight. Their laughter could be heard throughout the vineyard, but it brought no joy to Pietro, who sat alone inside the car. Only when Liliana opened the door did the Martellinos' youngest son join them.

"*Ciao il mio ragazzini!*" Franco shouted as the children ran to the field. "Now that you're home, we can officially celebrate Christmas!"

DeAngelo stopped suddenly and looked out over the vines with a bit of sadness. "I missed the harvest. I missed the fermentation and racking. Now you've mounded the plants without me."

Franco put his arm around him and pointed to the last row of the field. "I left one for you, DeAngelo. But we must finish tonight because I feel a frost coming."

As Isabella hugged Pietro, in the distance she saw Susanna waiting for her sons. She looked completely alone as she held on to the cold iron fence that separated her villa from the workers' living quarters.

"Boys, I'm so happy you're home," Isabella said, and then she turned the Martellino sons toward their villa. "Now run along to your mama. She needs a good hug."

As he ran off, DeAngelo yelled back at Franco, "Don't you work those vines without me! I've been waiting forever to be in the field!"

That night Isabella fixed them their favorite meals. Pietro's mouth and fingers were covered with tomato and olive oil from the bruschetta he was devouring. He smiled a toothy grin as he peeled off little slices of garlic and basil leaves from his chin and dropped them into his mouth. The aroma of vegetable kabobs on the grill filled the air: a medley of corn, onions, bell peppers, squash, mushrooms, and cherry tomatoes sizzling on skewers over a hot fire. Isabella removed one of the skewers, poured cilantro sauce on it, crushed garlic and black and cayenne pepper over the top, and handed it to DeAngelo.

"Now this is home!" he grinned as he slipped a bell pepper off the skewer and into his mouth.

"We don't get this at Saint Gregorio," Pietro added, but then he saw his mother frown. "I like school, Mama. I'm the fastest!"

"It's true." Giovanni gave a proud nod. "His teacher said that Pietro is a fine athlete and that the school devotes time every day to physical education and sports." He then became serious. "But I attended Pietro's fitness class and was a little concerned about how much time his teacher spent preaching to them about Fascism."

"I'm sure he wasn't preaching." Susanna crossed her arms over her chest. "Every Italian child should be so fortunate as to have an instructor who can inspire both the physical and moral health of students."

Giovanni rolled his eyes but said nothing. He had heard stories of children repeating their parents' criticism of the Fascist state at school and ending up in prison.

"I can sing our state song," Pietro said proudly.

"Let's hear it," Susanna beamed.

Pietro waved his knife and fork in the air as if he were conducting an orchestra. "Long live the king! Long live Italy! Long live the army! Long live our chief, Benito Mussolini! Down with Russia! Long live our chief and the founder of Fascism! Long live Italian Rome!"

Susanna clapped her hands, but Giovanni was not amused. "What about education?" he asked DeAngelo. "What are you boys learning in school?"

"We learn math and science and Mussolini."

"And how to be soldiers!" Pietro shouted.

DeAngelo nodded. "They teach us how to march and tell us one day we'll be the soldiers of the new Italy."

Giovanni raised an eyebrow. "What do you mean—soldiers of the new Italy?"

"Our teacher told us we'll play an important part in returning Italy to the Roman Empire, Papa. He said this is year seven of the new calendar, which signifies the beginning of Fascist history. That's the day Il Duce marched on Rome in 1922."

Giovanni turned to his wife. "Did you hear that, Susanna? I didn't pay all this money to send our boys off to a military school."

"It's not a military school. Aldo and Margherita would never let their children attend such a school."

"I talked to Aldo," Giovanni countered, "and he is indeed concerned about the Fascist indoctrination at Saint Gregorio. But every other school he's looked at has been forced to teach the same principles. The only reason his children continue at Gregorio is because it's close to their home and many of their friends' children go there."

"I get a marching uniform!" Pietro shouted. "I want to be a Fascist soldier!"

Giovanni walked over to Liliana. "What do you learn in school?"

"We learn numbers and letters and science, and at home Mama teaches me reading and plants and animals and God. Last week our school went to San Cristoforo and saw Matteo Civ—Civ—Civitali's house."

"Who's he?" asked Pietro.

"He was a painter and sculptor."

"I thought that was Vincenzo?" DeAngelo chimed in.

Liliana shook her head. "No, Vincenzo was one of the men who helped build Lucca's walls."

A disgusted Giovanni turned to his wife. "And you think the education at this school in Rome is better than the education our sons would get in Lucca?"

ଓଃ ଛେ

The week before Christmas brought one of those crisp, blue, cold December days when the frost inhales the dust from the air, providing a crystal-clear view all the way to the end of the horizon. It was like old times for the children, Liliana teasing DeAngelo about how he followed her father around the vineyard, copying his every move. When Franco knelt down to study the branches of the vines, DeAngelo went to one knee with him; when he overheard Franco telling Antonio how to handle the orchard if the temperature dropped below ten degrees Celsius, the boy parroted the information later to his father.

Liliana climbed an olive tree with a pocket full of olive pits and waited. DeAngelo counted to twenty and began his search.

Something deflected off his shoulder; then a stone or pit bounced off his forehead; then, like rain, seeds from the sky pelted him, followed by the giggles of a girl. He looked up, found his assailant, and playfully shook the branch she was on. Liliana swung around, dropped smoothly to the ground, and ran off, DeAngelo in pursuit. He finally tackled her into a pile of leaves he had raked earlier. Their shrieks of laughter carried through the orchard.

"They have a wonderful friendship," Isabella smiled as she watched with her husband.

Franco had a far-off look. "I hope what's happening in Italy doesn't change that."

She rested her head on his shoulder. "What do you see?"

"A country—afraid."

"Is that the truth or what you choose to see?"

He stopped to listen to the quiet of the farm, the few blue jays calling out from trees bared by winter, and DeAngelo and Liliana giggling in the distance. He then turned to see Pietro alone by his bedroom window, staring out at them. "What about the fear that's inside that child?"

"He'll be fine."

"How do you know, Bella? There's a dark side to Pietro. You heard how the neighbors found him down by the creek after he killed their cat."

She only nodded.

"You don't think his behavior has anything to do with his past—with who his biological father is?"

"I think that's an excuse. We should try to understand what torments him."

"What do you think torments him?"

"He wants to be loved." She pointed to the field. "Look at your olive trees and vineyard, Franco. They thrive because you care for them. Every plant, animal, and person, struggles when not nurtured and loved."

Franco reached down and picked up two olive pits. They looked old and dead, but he knew of their potential inside. "Maybe if Susanna would stop comparing him to DeAngelo…"

"That's why he cries out for attention. He wants to be punished."

Franco looked doubtful. "She punishes us by sending him to his room. That boy should be out working the fields. That's the lesson he needs."

"He's just confused. He joined me this morning for prayers—and there were many tears." She paused to watch the little boy line up his toy soldiers on the windowsill as if preparing for an imaginary battle. "I know Giovanni said he's popular with his classmates, but Pietro told me he has no friends."

"What did you tell him?"

"That I love him—and that his mind is part of God's, and that he's very holy."

Franco stared at the two seeds in his hand. "Did you ask him why he killed the cat?"

"He told me he didn't know why he did it."

Franco tossed the seeds to the ground. "Now his mother will send him back to that elitist school to learn how to be one of Italy's perfect soldiers."

She reached for his now-empty hand. "We all have our lessons we must learn." Franco looked out at his daughter, who squealed with laughter as DeAngelo tickled her. Isabella squeezed her husband's hand. "This is our earth school, Franco. You had your lessons—and they'll have theirs."

CHAPTER 37

LUCCA, NOVEMBER 1930

"I don't understand," Obizzi grumbled as he looked over the restaurant's books, which told of a third straight miserable month. "This was one of the most successful restaurants in Lucca. What the hell happened?"

Frederico fidgeted nervously, trying to find the right words to explain the demise. "The depression has hurt everyone."

"Other restaurants in Lucca are doing well."

Frederico chose his words carefully. "I believe Cesare Bosco had a loyal clientele that was like him, common people who came to his restaurant to be together."

"I don't give a shit if our patrons are rich or poor!" Obizzi snapped. "I just want them spending money at a great restaurant! We hired a better chef, changed the menu, and upgraded the food—what's not to like?"

"I don't know if these are the kind of people who are interested in *scottiglia di cinghiale* or *torta di limone*."

"Shut up!" Obizzi pounded his fist on top of the ledger. "Someone did this to me! Someone spread lies about my restaurant!" He stared at the list Frederico had made of the three most successful restaurants in town. They all had one thing in common. They all bought their produce from Isabella's stand at the market. The rage in his gut was boiling, and his eyes burned with a hatred that scared his assistant. "It was—that fucking bitch—from the market. She knows—we stole the Martellino wine. She's trying to ruin me." He crumpled the list in his hand and fired it across the room.

Frederico swallowed hard. "Let it go, Alfredo."

"I'm tired of the Martellinos and their fucking workers getting in my way!"

Frederico knew his boss was wrong, but also knew when to keep his mouth shut.

"Believe me," Obizzi hissed. "They'll get what's coming to them."

CR   BO

Most grapes do well in a tough environment. It doesn't matter if the soil is rocky, broken with gravel or slate—grapes will survive. One of the toughest grape seeds is the Barbera plant, and while its flavor may not be as smooth as others, its ability to adapt and grow when others struggle is indeed impressive. Isabella was with her daughter on a steep hill some forty meters from the vineyard. She had planted the Barbera plant three years before, and believed this year would be its season. "Do you know what I find interesting, Lily?"

Lost in a daydream, Liliana ignored her mother and picked at the dirt around the plant.

"Liliana, are you listening to me?"

No response.

Isabella decided to have a silly conversation with herself to see if she could get her daughter's attention. "I thought you might be interested to know I took this lovely plant fishing the other day—we caught an alligator in the Serchio River. Yes, that's very interesting because I've never seen an alligator in the Serchio before. We invited him for dinner and he's bringing his friend—oh, he is? Who's his friend? It's a giant owl. Well, where will they sleep? That's a good question—I think I'll put them in your bed for the night. Then where will you sleep, Lily? I'll just put you on the roof of our house with a blanket. I'm sure you'll be fine." There was still no response, so Isabella changed strategy. "Did you hear DeAngelo grew a second nose on his forehead?"

Liliana's head snapped up. "Is DeAngelo coming home?"

Isabella gave her daughter a playful shove. "I've been talking to you for the last five minutes, and you were lost in your own little world. Do you have something on your mind?"

Liliana pulled a dry leaf off the plant. "I haven't had any letters from DeAngelo in over a month. He usually writes me every week."

"He'll be coming home in a few weeks," Isabella said as she dug into the soil to loosen it around the roots. "But I want you to know that DeAngelo is now thirteen. Boys that age go through many changes, so try not to take anything personally."

Liliana cocked her head to the side. "What do you mean, Mama?"

"DeAngelo may want a little space."

"Why?"

"Because he's growing up."

"So am I."

"Yes, you are. But there's a difference."

"How?"

Isabella took a vine in her hand. "It's like this plant, Lily. When it was young, it needed to stay close to its source to survive. But as it grew, even though it was still connected to its source, it needed space so the air, water, and sun could help it mature."

"That plant isn't very big, Mama."

"It may look small above ground, but its roots go down over six feet. Those roots are its foundation. Those roots help it survive life's challenges and allow just enough water and oxygen to help the plant reach its potential. Even in the worst of times, this plant will never leave its source. If your friendship with DeAngelo is strong, it too will survive."

Isabella took her daughter's hand and walked back to the Martellino villa to prepare dinner. Liliana tried to hide her smile as she asked, "Are the alligator and owl coming for supper?"

Isabella laughed. "You were listening, weren't you?"

Liliana giggled as she took off running toward their house. "Whoever loses has to sleep on the roof!"

Isabella watched her daughter run off and then placed her hand on her belly. Three months, she thought, but barely showing. She had yet to tell Franco. After Liliana almost nine years ago, she had had difficulty conceiving again. She was sure she had had several early miscarriages over the years and had been tormented by the look on Franco's face when he would find her crying in the garden during her prayer time. Her husband was a worrier who couldn't bear to see someone he loved in pain. But it was time, thought Isabella. It was time to tell him. She waved for him to join her, and he arrived a bit agitated. "This better be important, because I have a lot to do before olive harvest. The wet weather's come early this year, and I want to make sure it doesn't lead to disease or fungus or—"

Isabella pointed to their daughter. "Look at Lily. Isn't she a cutie?"

Franco cocked his head to the side. "You called me in to tell me I have a cute daughter?"

"Don't you think she needs someone to play with?"

"I hope you're talking about someone who can help in the field."

"Perhaps in a few years," she grinned.

"Years?" Franco whined. "If we don't take care of the olive trees right now, we've got problems. I saw a few brown and silver spots on the undersides of the leaves, which means infection. With Antonio gone selling, I need someone to make sure the roots don't get too much water."

Isabella took his hand and placed it on her belly. "You're going to have to be patient for that help, Franco."

His eyes went wide. "Are you—?" He couldn't even say the word, he was so struck with joy.

She opened her arms and welcomed his embrace. In his excitement he lifted her up to the sky, but he suddenly thought of his wife with child and gently lowered her to the ground. "I'm sorry, Bella. Are you all right?"

"You big old ox." She gave him a playful shove. "I'm not going to break. I worked until the end with Lily, and I'll be fine with little Benny."

"You think it's a boy? And you're going to name him after my brother?" His smiling eyes brightened. "Oh, sweet Jesus, bless my wife and bless this baby!"

She pulled him in close. "Angie's the only other person I've told about the baby. Let's keep it between ourselves until I'm further along."

CHAPTER 38

LUCCA, DECEMBER 1930

I sabella felt wonderful; her mothering instincts had taken over as she felt the baby growing inside her, and the daily joys with Franco and Liliana were never-ending. Her face was a constant smile with the inspiring sensation of this new life, the first heartbeat and playful kick reminding her she was never alone. Even the worldwide depression couldn't dampen her spirits; neither could the added work at the market, the cut in pay at the Martellino farm, or the troubling news from the south.

Franco walked into the kitchen reading a letter. "The landowner my parents have worked for for the last thirty years didn't renew their agreement."

"I'm sorry," Isabella said as she took the bread out of the oven and placed it on the table. "What will they do?"

He sighed and handed her the letter. "Mama's sister invited them to help at their restaurant in Naples."

"That could be just the change they need, Franco. Our economy is doing much better in the bigger towns."

Angelina joined the conversation. "But I wonder if that's because Mussolini has encouraged the poor to leave Italy."

The thought reminded Franco of the time before the Great War in 1914, and all the broken promises made by politicians. Mussolini had always told Italians he was a man of the common people—one of them, a man of hope and determination. But now he had done what all the other leaders had done in the past. He had done nothing for the poor or middle class. He followed the money and made agreements with the most powerful corporations in Italy. Mussolini's parliament had created the National Council of Corporations: twenty-two of Italy's most influential companies representing agriculture, industry, and God knows what else. Franco knew the Fascist laws were probably designed to make sure those corporations would prosper.

Isabella sensed what her husband was thinking and hugged him from behind, resting her head on his back. "You can tell Benito what's on your mind next week, because he'll be in Lucca when we dedicate our triumphal arch to him."

Angelina rolled her eyes. "I'm sure Il Duce can't wait to hear Franco's ideas about improving the economy. Be sure to ask him where Lucca found the money to pay for this arch. From what I've seen, it will be expensive."

The discussion came to an abrupt halt with the sound of wheels tearing down the drive. It was Giovanni, with a broad smile on his face. "Open up our best red, Bella!" he cried out as he parked the car. "It's time for a celebration!"

As Franco opened the kitchen door to welcome him inside, Isabella went to the pantry where she kept the 1925 Martellino Sangiovese.

Giovanni held a contract over his head. "The Buonamici has chosen the Martellino vineyard to represent our city in next week's celebration!"

"Hooray!" they cried out as Isabella pulled the cork from the wine bottle and handed it to Giovanni. But instead of pouring a glass, he took a long drink and handed the bottle to Franco. "Drink up, my friend. Drink the wine that Mussolini himself will enjoy!"

Susanna heard the commotion and came downstairs to join them. Giovanni quickly poured his wife a glass. "We did it, my dear! We did it!"

Her face was filled with questions, but the delight in the room told her the news was good.

"Our Martellino red has been selected," he said with a dramatic bow, "to represent Lucca in next week's dedication of the triumphal arch!"

Her eyes went wide, and a laugh spilled out that surprised even her. "How? Why?" was all she could think of saying.

Giovanni raised his glass to Franco. "Because our brilliant winemaker has put together the perfect blend of grapes to create Tuscany's finest!" He turned back to his wife. "This is just the beginning, darling! When Mussolini's entourage samples our wine on such a lovely day—word will get around that Il Duce chose the Martellino brand to satisfy his royal palate!"

CR ꙩ

Liliana was waiting outside the door of her parents' cottage for the Martellino boys to come home from Saint Gregorio boarding school. She missed DeAngelo terribly. Although she had made friends at her Lucchesi school, DeAngelo was the best friend she'd ever had. She could hardly wait to show him the new buds on the vines and take him to her favorite new fishing spot on the Serchio. As she looked down at the lures she had made for him earlier that week, she positioned each hook to make her gift appear as if it were a smiling face, perfectly set all the way down to the feathers that represented eyebrows.

She heard the car before she saw it, bounced out of her chair, took a glance at her reflection in their front window, and smoothed her hair. As Giovanni's car made the turn into the Martellinos' property, she ran to the driveway and waved enthusiastically as the car came to a stop. DeAngelo and Pietro stepped out wearing their boarding school military uniforms: black shirts, black hats, shorts, and gray socks. Liliana ran over, threw her arms around DeAngelo, and kissed him on the cheek. The thirteen-year-old boy arched his back, a bit overwhelmed by Liliana's affections. He hugged her stiffly as she exclaimed, "I'm so glad you're home! I missed you so much! We fixed your favorite meal! I made some lures for you! We can go fishing! We can go see Mussolini! You and me! Do you want to—do you—"

DeAngelo held up his hands in surrender and gave her a reserved smile. "Slow down, Lily. I just got home. Some friends from school are going to come over, so I don't know what my plans are yet. Let me take my things upstairs, and I'll see you a little later."

Pietro gave Liliana a quick hug and then followed his brother into the villa.

Liliana was crushed. This was not what she had been expecting. With a look of complete disappointment, she slowly walked back to their cottage and glanced at the lures she had set in the design of a smiling face. She slapped the smile with her hand, sending lures flying off the table—except one that stuck in her thumb. She pulled it out quickly, stuck the wounded thumb in her mouth, plopped down in a chair near her parents, and gave a dramatic exhalation. "DeAngelo is odd."

Both parents bit their lips to keep from laughing.

"Odd?" Isabella asked. "Really? In what way?"

"He thinks he's so important wearing that stupid uniform."

Her father came over and put his hand on her shoulder. "Give him time, sweetie. He just got home. I would imagine after being cooped up in that boarding school he just needs time to get outside and breathe again. But you might try giving him a little space this week until he adjusts to being back home."

"I'll give him space, Papa," Liliana said with a look of defiance. "I don't need that little soldier boy telling me what to do."

A half hour later DeAngelo knocked on their door, and Isabella walked over to give him a hug. Franco followed his wife to greet the Martellinos' son, but Liliana stayed silent in her chair with her back to him.

"How's school?" Isabella asked.

"I've made some friends," DeAngelo said. "We even had a dance with a girls' school that's near us. I danced with a girl named Sandra whose twin brother is a classmate of mine. They don't live very far from here and may come over to play this week."

Franco looked at his daughter, who was staring out the window. He knew she was hurting inside and was acting as though she had no interest in the conversation.

DeAngelo glanced at her. "Lily, would you like to check the buds?"

"No, thank you," she answered curtly. "I—have to help mama."

DeAngelo turned to Franco, who nodded yes. "I haven't been out there today. I should probably take a look." His eyes stayed with his daughter as he put his arm around DeAngelo and led him out of the house.

After they left, Liliana continued to stare out the window and then gave a dramatic exhalation. "I think I'm going to be a nun."

Isabella turned away from her daughter and covered her mouth.

"Maybe I'll join the Blessings Convent. Sister Anna seems happy."

Isabella's shoulders shook as she tried to stifle her laughter. Liliana thought her mother was crying and walked over to comfort her. "Don't cry, Mama. We'll get through this together. My roots are deep."

Isabella could control herself no longer and broke up laughing. "I'm sorry, Lily! It's not right for me to laugh!" Liliana looked at her mother in surprise as Isabella put her hand to her mouth to keep from giggling. "I said the other day that, like the roots of the grapevine, the roots of your friendship with DeAngelo are deep, and because of that strength, a little disappointment won't hurt you. She hugged her daughter. "This too shall pass. Your friendship is strong"—she bit her lip again—"and your roots are deep."

ൟ   ൟ

"It's good to be home," DeAngelo said as he felt the little bumps on the canes of the vine. "It won't be long before the shoots break open and reach up to the sun."

Franco smiled at him. "It's all part of creation. From the bud-break to the flowering to the *veraison* and then the harvest. We worry far too much about how to do life, rather than trusting it to happen perfectly."

The boy scanned the vineyard with a far-off look. "I didn't want to go to Saint Gregorio at first, but I'm enjoying it more now."

Franco only nodded, allowing DeAngelo to continue.

"I like learning about science, history, and language, and I have made some good friends." He paused. "But there are some things I don't like."

Franco handed him a pair of pliers but remained quiet.

"I really don't mind wearing the uniform, but why are they training all of us to be soldiers?" He tightened the trellis wire and looked up at Franco. "Do you know what my teacher told us?"

Franco shook his head.

"'War is to the male what childbearing is to the female.' They said being soldiers is what we were born to do."

One corner of Franco's mouth twitched. "What do you want to be, DeAngelo?"

"I want to finish school and then come home and work the vineyard." His gaze stayed with Franco, but it was distant, as if looking through him. "Pietro wants to be a soldier, but I don't. I want this—I want to be in the field, planting seeds, growing grapes, and turning them into wine." He picked up a rock and threw it toward the creek. "But our teachers at Saint Gregorio told us that Il Duce needs soldiers. They've divided us into training groups. Pietro belongs to the Sons of the She-Wolf. My group is called Balilla. We march and use toy guns and act out battles." DeAngelo paused before asking, "Papa said you were in the Great War. What was it like?"

461

This time it was Franco who picked up a rock and heaved it toward the creek. "It was cold—" were the only words he could summon.

"Were you afraid?"

Franco slowly nodded. "We were told, much as you've been told, that war is about honor and patriotism. But the Great War was about power and greed and—" He paused as an old misery came rushing back to him, jagged and painful. He swallowed hard, trying to force down the dark thoughts. "No," he finally said, "I don't think man was born to wage war."

"What do you think we were born to do?"

"Perhaps it's something that I'm still working on."

DeAngelo looked up but remained quiet.

"Forgiveness," Franco said in a voice barely above a whisper. "Bella says our sole purpose on earth is to know forgiveness."

The boy stared up at Franco, admiring the rock of a man who had been his mentor for most of his life. But for the first time in his thirteen years, DeAngelo also saw grief, suffering, and loss. He reached down, picked up a stone, and put it in Franco's hand. The big man smiled and threw it as far as he could.

03   80

Isabella finished the last of her prayers, opened her eyes, and looked out at the horizon. The sun had just broken over the southeastern hills, but hadn't yet reached the row of olive trees on the western slope. With last week's rains, the creek was now rushing happily down to the Serchio, nourishing the plants that framed its banks. She sat quietly for a moment, listening to the faint heartbeat of the child growing inside and feeling the cool December breeze lift her hair from her face. Finally, she stood up, looked to the sky, said a grateful thanks, and headed to the villa to start breakfast.

DeAngelo met her at the door. "I lit the fire for you and got out the eggs."

She gave him a quick hug, grabbed an egg in each hand, and deftly cracked them open into a wooden bowl.

Liliana wandered in half-awake, her dark curls plastered like seaweed to the side of her face, and collapsed into a chair. DeAngelo dipped his fingers into a water bucket and sneaked up behind her, flicking the spray onto the back her neck. She leaped up in surprise and chased him around the stove, giggling in delight. Before long it was like old times, Liliana telling DeAngelo what was happening in Lucca and DeAngelo telling Liliana of his school adventures in Rome. The Martellino boy pulled Liliana onto his lap, and she leaned back and rested her head on his shoulder, a bright smile lighting her face. The rest of the families soon joined them for breakfast, with the sounds from the kitchen only laughter and teasing and exaggerated stories of holidays past.

Then suddenly there was a knock on the front door, and DeAngelo looked up to see whom his mother was greeting.

"Marco! Sandra!" he cried out when he saw it was his friends from school. In his excitement, he jumped up, and Liliana slid off his lap onto the floor.

"Sorry, Lily." He helped her up and then ran over to welcome his friends.

Liliana sat alone in the chair and pulled her knees to her chest, her face a jealous blank stare as she watched DeAngelo give particular attention to the girl named Sandra.

"Mama, can Marco and Sandra go fishing with me today?" DeAngelo asked. "I promise we'll only be gone a few hours."

Susanna happily nodded, and the three children raced out of the house to gather their fishing gear and head to the river. When Liliana realized she wouldn't be invited, a jealousy burned inside her, but she said nothing until DeAngelo and his friends were out of sight.

"I've been DeAngelo's friend way longer than they have. I don't know why he's so much nicer to them."

"He's still your friend," Isabella said.

"That Sandra girl isn't prettier than me, is she, Mama?"

"I think you're both very beautiful."

Knowing her mother would never understand the pain that only she was feeling, Liliana left in a huff to find her father in the field, leaving Isabella and Pietro alone.

Pietro handed Isabella his empty plate and gave her a proud look. "I'm a Son of the She-Wolf!"

Isabella smiled as she took his plate and dipped it in soapy water. "Please tell me what a Son of a She-Wolf is."

"Only the top students are selected," he answered seriously. "I'm one of our school's best soldiers."

"Congratulations."

"I'm going to be a warrior for Il Duce."

"And I'm sure you'll be a very good one. One who brings peace and kindness to everyone he meets."

"Not the anti-Fascists."

"Did they do something wrong?"

"My teacher says they're evil and Mussolini must punish them."

"What did they do?"

"I don't know, but they're bad."

"That's a shame."

He looked up. "What is?"

"That they would be punished simply for having a different opinion."

"Benito doesn't like them, so we must do what he says."

"Will your Mussolini ever forgive them?"

He shook his head. "Only God can forgive them."

Isabella placed a slice of apple pie in front of him. "But if God is love, then He has never condemned. And if He has never condemned, then He has nothing to forgive. That's why WE must forgive."

Pietro hadn't thought of that before and sat down at the round table and stared at his pie. Finally, he looked up. "My teacher told us Mussolini is like Jesus. That God blessed him over all others."

She handed him a fork. "Aren't we all blessed sons and daughters of God?"

He grabbed the fork and stabbed it into the pie. "But Mussolini is like Jesus."

"And so are you, Pietro."

The little boy dug into the dessert and took a bite. Isabella's words always confused him. She constantly told him what a good person he was, but in his mind he saw himself only dark and unloved. He straightened up in his chair and shook his head. "No. I will never be as good as Benito. My teacher told us we were all born into sin."

"That doesn't seem fair," Isabella said as she took a bite of pie. "Why, I think you're a very good boy."

"No, I'm not." Pietro struggled with his words, his lower lip trembling. "I'm bad."

Isabella came around and knelt beside him. "I assure you, Pietro, that deep within you is everything that is perfect love, ready to shine through you and out into the world. If God made you in His image, you are perfect. You are not a sinner."

"Yes, I am." He refused to look at her. "There are times I know God hates me. I have done bad things."

"Then don't do them anymore."

He bit his lip to keep from crying. "I think—that if I do what Benito tells me to do—I'll be a better person."

"I think if you listen to your heart, you'll be just fine."

"I don't want to talk about it anymore." Pietro turned away and looked out the window so she wouldn't see his tears. "I just want—to be a good Son of the She-Wolf."

Isabella placed her hand on his shoulder. "You're a good boy, Pietro. I love you."

☙ ❧

When DeAngelo and his friends returned from fishing, Isabella waited for Marco and Sandra to leave with their parents before asking the children, "Who would like to go with me to see the new stadium and the archway our city has made for Signor Mussolini?"

DeAngelo raised his hand. "I'll go!"

Pietro was still stewing about their conversation and shook his head. "If Il Duce were there I'd go, but he won't be there until tomorrow."

Isabella frowned. "But the crowds will be huge tomorrow, and it will be difficult to move around."

"I don't care. I don't want to see a stupid archway. I want to see Mussolini."

Liliana, still hurting from not being invited to go fishing, looked at DeAngelo and then at his brother. "I'll stay here with Pietro. We'll play games or—go fishing."

"They can help me in the field," Franco said, sensitive to his daughter's pain. "You go on ahead. But write down everything you see, because I'll be wanting a good story at dinnertime."

Susanna came into the kitchen. "I have to drop off some things in town, so I can give you a ride."

ʘ ʅ

Obizzi stood atop the stage that would welcome Italy's great leader. He took two steps out onto the apron and thrust his chest out. "Mussolini will stand exactly where I am tomorrow." He then nodded to his left. "Lucca's podesta will be here, and I will proudly stand on the other side of Il Duce."

He had a glass of wine in his hand, took a drink, and then bowed dramatically. "Frederico, tomorrow will be a grand day. I'm sure Benito has heard that I'm responsible for uncovering many anti-Fascist plots throughout Tuscany."

Frederico had heard this monologue before and remained quiet as Obizzi began to slur his words. "He knows it was I—who shupported him in the Matteotti trial—and I backed him—when he drained the Pontine marshes." Obizzi poured another glass of wine and toasted himself. Frederico failed in trying to grab the wine from his boss's hand; it was Obizzi's fifth glass, and it was not even four in the afternoon.

"You still have to win approval from Mussolini's security," Frederico warned him. "Benito's surrounded himself with the rich and powerful. Remember, we took a financial hit on your restaurant idea—"

Obizzi glared at his assistant. "Why the fuck did you have to bring that up?" He took another healthy gulp. "You'll thank me when I'm part of Mussolini's team."

⊂⊃ ⊂⊃

Isabella and DeAngelo walked along the eastern walls of Lucca, by the cedar of Lebanon that marked the entrance into the botanical gardens. It was a lovely day, and they wanted to enjoy the seasonal change of Lucca's gardens on their way to the triumphal arch. They passed rhododendrons, so bright and beautiful in spring, now seeming to cower with their leaves curled in to protect themselves from winter dehydration. The pond was next, where hundreds of water lilies seemed to emerge from the murky depths, filling the water's surface with color and vibrancy, all the while keeping the pond and creatures underneath safe and healthy. Isabella had come here many times as a child; it always gave her peace.

"Do you remember the first time I brought you here?" she asked.

DeAngelo shook his head no.

"You were only three years old. We came out of the arboretum, you saw a fish in the pond, and you ran right into the water, all the way up to your waist. Oh, was I in trouble."

DeAngelo had been home only two days and was already tired of his mother's criticism. "Why does Mama always blame you for my mistakes?"

"She was just upset because you were wearing brand new shoes."

"I'm tired of her telling me what to do all the time," DeAngelo grumbled as they walked past the botanical school. "As soon as I got home, she told me what to wear, how to act, and who I should choose for my friends."

"She just wants what's best for you."

"She wants to control me. She thinks I spend too much time with your family."

Isabella remained quiet as DeAngelo kicked a rock from the path. "She treats me like a little boy, but I'm thirteen. I'm almost a man!"

"Be patient," Isabella laughed. "You have plenty of time to grow up. Enjoy right now, being young, without responsibilities. You're home in Lucca. Laugh! Smile! *Divertirsi!*

愈 愉

Obizzi was annoyed with his aide and sent him home for the day. He was tired of Frederico's pessimism every time he came so close to glory. Pouring himself another glass of wine, he took a long drink and walked toward the triumphal arch outside the Porta Elisa, where Mussolini would be the next day. It was lined with huge sunflowers, bright magnolias, and carnations. As he looked to the south, he thought he saw someone who looked familiar.

"Damn, is that the bitch from the market?" He gulped down his wine, threw the glass against the stone wall, and stumbled toward them. "Ishabella!" he screamed out. "You fucking whore!"

She looked up, and seeing it was Obizzi, she grabbed DeAngelo's hand and started in the other direction.

Obizzi ran after them. "I knows why yer here! Yer spyin' on me!"

She sped up their pace as DeAngelo stared back at the man who was yelling at them.

"You ruined my restaurant!" Obizzi caught them and shoved Isabella off the path. "You told lies about me and no one came!"

She stepped in front of DeAngelo to protect him. "You did that on your own, Signor Obizzi. I didn't say a thing. You failed on your own."

He slapped her across the face. DeAngelo tried to defend her, but Isabella pulled him back. Obizzi grabbed her by the throat and pinned her against a chestnut tree, his breath hot against her face. "I warned you not to fuck with me!"

She tried to push him away, but he was beyond angry and threw her to the ground. DeAngelo lunged, but Obizzi grabbed the boy's hair and held him down as he kicked the heel of his boot into Isabella's belly. She cried out in pain, which only seemed to feed Obizzi's rage as he shoved the boy aside and yanked Isabella to her feet. He spit in her face and then threw her down the ramp at Baluardo San Regolo. She skidded on her hands and knees before crashing against the side wall. DeAngelo ran to her as she clutched her abdomen.

A victorious smile creased Obizzi's lips as he clapped his hands in perverse satisfaction of justice finally brought.

But a sudden fury lit in DeAngelo. He found a rock that had broken loose from the wall and slowly stood up. With a newfound resolve, he hurled the stone, and it found its mark, slicing the side of Obizzi's forehead.

The Fascist leader fell to one knee, blood gushing down his face, blinding his vision for a moment. He clutched at the wound as he struggled to stand up and ran off.

Isabella lay grimacing in pain. Her hands and knees were bloodied. She tried to get up, but a deep burn shot through her lower belly.

"DeAngelo—" she gasped.

But the boy only stared in shock at the blood that now appeared on Isabella's dress.

She grabbed his hand and pulled him close. "Get your mother—but—you can't tell her—what happened!"

"I have to!"

"No!"

"Then I'll tell Franco!"

She gripped his hand tighter. "I'm losing my baby, DeAngelo—I'm very sorry about that—but you can tell no one—particularly Franco—what happened."

"I want to kill that man!" DeAngelo was in tears as he tried to pull away. "I have to tell Franco or Antonio!"

She pulled him in again. "If you tell them what happened—they'll want vengeance—and that will only bring trouble—to our families."

"No!"

"Listen to me! I don't want to lose my husband or Antonio because I was hurt."

"They need to know!"

"You can't tell them! Swear to me, DeAngelo—that you'll never tell anyone—what happened today!"

"I can't!"

As she held him with one hand, she took hold of his chin with the other, forcing him to look her in the eyes. "You must do as I say. I love my family. I don't want to lose them. I'm going to give my anger to God. All I'm asking is that you do the same. Please."

As the tears rolled down his cheeks, he finally nodded, and she released him.

"Find your mother."

As soon as DeAngelo was out of sight, Isabella turned her face to the wall and let out a scream of all she'd been holding in.

Ɒ ଞ

Susanna gripped the wheel tighter as she sped to Lucca's hospital. Isabella's head was in her lap, sweat pouring down her face.

"Franco—" Isabella coughed. "I want him—with me."

"I'll get him! I promise!" a terrified Susanna gushed as she placed her hand on Isabella's head and tried to maintain her own calm. Isabella cried out in pain and Susanna pushed the car faster. "Stay with me, Bella! Please! You're the strong one! I can't do this without you!"

Ɒ ଞ

As they walked in from the field after a good day of work, Antonio put his arms around Giovanni and Pietro, and with the humblest sincerity he could muster, he said, "I think it's time you congratulated me for having my wine selected for Lucca's big celebration."

Giovanni raised an eyebrow. "YOUR wine?"

"That's what I had to tell Benito the last time he was in town," Antonio continued to joke. "He always sends that big black limo to pick me up so we can play a little dice with Sister Anna."

"You're a big liar," Pietro frowned. "You don't know Mussolini."

"Sure I do, little man," Antonio grinned. "I beat him in a big game in the basement of Saint Freddy. Benito rolled a five, Sister Anna dropped six, and yours truly fired snake eyes to win. I told Il Duce I didn't need that yacht he offered me that's anchored off the Amalfi Coast—told him to taste the wine I've been making at my vineyard."

Angelina dumped her entire canteen of water on her husband's head as everybody exploded in laughter.

"Hey, hey, hey!" He danced off, shaking the water from his hair. "Our leader owes me! I could have you all arrested!"

Their laughter stopped when they saw Susanna's car tear down the drive. "Isabella's hurt!" she cried.

CR   SO

Franco raced up the hospital stairs and burst through the front door. Sister Anna was in the corner, rosary beads in her hands and a look of desperation on her face.

"The doctors are with her, Franco. I'm so sorry."

His face went white. "Where is she?"

Anna nodded to Isabella's room but held his hand. "They're trying to save her, Franco—but she's lost a lot of blood."

He collapsed into a chair and stared at the floor. Once again, he thought—the damn randomness of life. Images of the day flashed across his mind: from the joy he had felt in imagining this child to the laughter of his friends, and now this overwhelming fear of losing his wife and child. He buried his face in his hands. "Dear God, please help me believe." All he could see in his mind was Isabella: her smile, that adoring look she gave only to him. The images then changed to her suffering alone in the room; he wanted to be with her, holding her, kissing her face, taking the pain from her. Suddenly words came to him he knew were not his own. "Father, I know my real home is with You. I give You my fears and ask only that You change my vision." He then imagined his wife surrounded by light. She was smiling.

Franco opened his eyes and found his family and friends surrounding him: Sister Anna, Liliana, Giovanni, Susanna, Antonio,

Angelina, Rosa, and Elisa were all there, yet Franco wondered why DeAngelo was alone in the far corner of the room. The poor boy had a tortured look on his face.

Liliana went to him.

"I'm sorry!" DeAngelo sobbed. "I tried—I tried to—"

Franco sat frozen, staring at the Martellino boy sobbing into his daughter's arms. Finally, he stood up and went to them. "Come with me."

Since the war, Franco had separated himself from God. He believed in God; he even prayed to God; he prayed daily for Isabella and Liliana and his friends, but still he was unsure of his own personal connection to any higher power. He did, however, believe in Isabella. He was often awed by her quiet familiarity with the Holy Spirit. She had once said to him, "You doubt God because you don't see him, Franco. Why do you trust your physical eyes so much? It's that lack of faith that tells you how weak you are, how helpless and afraid, born into sin and wretched in your guilt. Don't listen to that voice, for there is a voice deep inside you telling you that you are God's perfect creation."

Franco led them all down the hall to the hospital chapel. As he opened the door for his family and friends to enter, his daughter took his hand. Liliana had a tiny hint of her mother's crinkle-eyed smile lighting her face, innocent yet confident. Her look seemed to lift him from the cloud of worry and fear that had gripped him only moments before. He swallowed hard and together they walked to the front of the altar.

"You know I'm not a religious man," he started out, forcing down his emotions. "I've had my battles with God. But Bella told me that to join with others is a holy connection. To pray and truly join together is love in its purest state." He squeezed his daughter's hand and closed his eyes. "I want all of you to see my wife healing— to visualize her smile and surround her in light. See the hands of God blessing her this very moment."

ଔ ଛ

They prayed that night in the chapel. Though no one said it, there was a belief that they had joined with the Holy Spirit, that together they were a part of God's will. It was a will that still left Franco asking questions. One person lives while another dies, and in our confusion we humans decide that it was God's will that brought about such tragedy. In pain, we either connect or separate from our source. But on this night, Franco was determined to see things differently. He did believe that God was with him, simply waiting for him to change his mind and reconnect to the love that had always been available.

ଔ ଛ

The hospital nurse closed the door to Isabella's room and told the families her patient needed to rest. Franco sent his daughter home with Angelina, but he stayed, pacing the waiting area until the nurses tired of the click-clack of his shoes on the floor and gave him permission to be with his sleeping wife. As he pulled open the curtain that surrounded her bed, his eyes filled with tears, seeing the scratches on her face and the gauze dressing that covered her arms and legs. Quietly pulling up a chair next to her bed, he took her bandaged hand in his and rested his head on the inside of her elbow, feeling her heartbeat against his cheek. It seemed as if each heartbeat brought him peace; each breath infused him with her love, and he soon joined his wife in a peaceful sleep.

CR SO

Susanna arrived at the hospital the following morning and was told that her friends were still sleeping. She waited by the nurse's desk, drumming her fingers on the edge of the table. The nurse frowned; Susanna countered with a condescending glare and tapped even louder until the nurse got up and left. Glancing down at the hospital's ledger of patients, Susanna recognized a name and had to blink twice. Her mouth fell open in shock—Alfredo Obizzi. He had been admitted thirty minutes before Isabella and had left forty-five minutes later. Susanna buried her face in her hands and wanted to scream, but the sound of footsteps brought her back to the now. It was a doctor coming down the hall and opening the door to Isabella's room. Susanna moved closer to listen.

Franco woke at the sound and shook the sleep from his eyes. He'd been by his wife's side through the night and now leaned over to kiss her forehead. Bella's eyes flickered open, but Franco didn't move, just stayed there with his lips pressed to her skin.

"Good morning," she whispered.

Her words startled him, and he rose up. "I never should have let you go."

She gave him that crinkled-eyed grin. "When was the last time you kept me from going somewhere? I was only four months along. I'll be just fine."

The doctor tapped the end of the bed frame with his pen to get their attention.

"I'm glad you're here, Franco," he said with a serious look. "I told your wife last night—her hands and knees are fine, no broken bones; she bruised a rib. That will be fine also." He hesitated for a moment. "I'm sorry to tell you, though—she did lose the baby, and after an examination I believe that it will be impossible for you to have children again. Your wife must have landed very hard when she fell, because her uterus was damaged."

A deep sadness swept over Isabella. Having this baby was all she had wanted. She had dreamed of giving her husband a son and her daughter a brother. Now that dream was gone. Her lower lip began to tremble as she looked up at her husband and forced a smile. "I'm sorry, Franco—I wanted to give you a son."

"I have all I ever wanted," he said softly. "I have you. I have Lily."

She took his head in her hands and kissed the tears from his face.

He raised up a bit and stared into her eyes as if searching for answers. "But I have to know—what happened?"

"I fell."

"Why won't DeAngelo talk? The boy hasn't said anything."

"It was an accident, Franco." She then turned to the doctor. "Are we finished? I want to go home."

The doctor tried to stop her, but she already had her feet off the bed and into the stirrups of a wheelchair, motioning for Franco to push her to the exit. "My bed and food are way better than anything here. And I want to hold my Lily."

Susanna slipped into an adjacent room and hid behind the door as the Carollos passed by. She wasn't ready to greet Isabella yet—not with all this new information she had discovered. It was all too much. She waited for Franco and Isabella to leave, then headed to town.

CR   SO

The podesta's office in Lucca was filled. Dignitaries from all over Tuscany were there, hoping to catch a glimpse and perhaps shake the hand of the great Mussolini. Obizzi glanced in the mirror, straightened his tie, and then pulled his hat down over the bandage that covered the stitches on his forehead. That damned kid wasn't going to keep him from getting what was rightfully his. He imagined where he'd stand, how he'd turn and salute, and then how he would bow when Benito shook his hand.

A politician from Pistoia recognized him and hurried over to say hello. "Alfredo, so good of you to be here! We've all heard of your great efforts in shutting down Socialist papers and silencing anti-Fascists who would bring harm to the party. Will you be on the stage today?"

Obizzi nodded proudly. "It's in the hands of the press secretary, but I've been told that I'll be next to—" He stopped mid-sentence as he heard the applause start to build from outside the office. At that moment the doors opened, and Mussolini with his security came through. There were shouts and cheers for Italy's leader. Obizzi tried to push his way to the front, but Benito's security chief grabbed his arm and pulled him to the side.

"And you are, signor?"

Obizzi came to attention. "I'm Alfredo Obizzi, from Cremona. I've been a vigilant advocate for our great leader for many years."

The security chief told him to wait a moment and walked over to Mussolini's press secretary. Obizzi watched the two in a quiet discussion before the chief nodded and returned to Obizzi with a map of the stage. "We'd like you to stand here, in the VIP gallery."

Obizzi was shocked. "There's been some mistake! I was told I'd be on the stage next to Mussolini."

The security chief shook his head. "Il Duce is very concerned about image—health and fitness." He then pointed to a man across the room. "Look who Benito has in charge of the youth groups."

Obizzi looked over to see the handsome and athletic Renato Ricci talking with Mussolini.

"He can't have someone with a bandage on his head next to him," the chief continued. "There will be photographers here, and one of these pictures could wind up in the New York or London press."

"I can remove it." Obizzi took his hat off and started to undo the bandage. "No one will be able to see the cut—"

The security chief waved him off. "We've made our decision. But if you continue to help the Fascist cause and uphold Mussolini's laws, there will be other opportunities for you to have your picture taken with our leader."

"I'm not here to have my picture taken!" Obizzi snapped. "I'm here to talk with Benito about a position on his staff!"

"Calm down," the security chief said in a hushed tone as he grabbed Obizzi's upper arm firmly and led him from the room. "I'll let him know all about your efforts, signor. Now please, take your place in the gallery."

As Obizzi stormed out of the podesta's office, he turned to see his broken image in the window. He shoved his hat down over the bandage on his head, winced in pain, and turned to find Susanna Martellino next to him.

"What happened, Alfredo?" she asked in a calm voice.

He tried to hide his disappointment. "What the hell are you doing here?"

"I want to know what happened to you."

"It's none of your business."

"I stopped by our Fascist city office, Alfredo. My friends told me you'd be at the right hand of Mussolini. Obviously, they were mistaken."

His eyes narrowed with fury, and he took a step toward her.

"Did you hurt Isabella?"

He froze.

"I was told she fell while walking with my son on their way to see Mussolini's triumphal arch." She paused to make sure her next words found their mark. "Did you know she miscarried her baby?"

But instead of showing any compassion, Obizzi curled his mouth into an evil grin. "I have no idea what you're talking about. I was with my assistant, preparing for our leader's visit."

"Then how did you get that awful cut on your forehead? Is that why you've been relegated to sit in a box at Benito's feet?"

His hands twitched slightly, resisting the urge to clench into fists. "I thought you despised your winemaker's wife. Perhaps old age has softened you."

His tone, his smugness, and the sneer on his lips did indeed shake her. She wanted to claw his wound until blood ran—she wanted to say something, anything, to wipe the conceit off his face.

"What a shame that Mussolini's lackeys tossed you aside," she finally said, and then she paused to make sure she had his full attention. "But at least you'll be able to drown your sorrows in our Martellino red—our leader's own choice for today's festivities."

Obizzi's face went ashen.

"That's right, Alfredo. OUR vineyard will represent Lucca in our city's historic moment. So while YOU are with the commoners looking up at Il Duce, our great leader will be sipping the finest wine in all of Tuscany."

She watched as he tried to swallow his anger. His eyes turned black with envy, and then he withdrew into the crowd. Susanna watched him disappear into the sea of adoring Mussolini humanity with the buzz of gossip and chatter swelling over him like foamy waves. She turned, feeling victorious, and left.

Obizzi watched her from the crowd and then headed not for his box but below, to where the food and wine were being stored for Lucca's important day.

ʘ ⁊

The drive home was a quiet one for the Carollos. Franco knew his wife needed time to grieve, so he said nothing. He pulled the car up next to their cottage and helped her inside, where she lay in bed with Liliana and told her that she had fallen and lost her baby. Sleep came quickly, and she slept for several hours, woke up in the afternoon, and went outside to pray. As she sat in her garden, trying to concentrate on her breathing, inhaling the warm air to begin her meditation, she felt a presence next to her and opened her eyes. It was DeAngelo.

She patted a spot on the blanket next to her. "Pray with me."

He sat down, closed his eyes, and waited for Isabella to begin. She started by blessing each member of their families and then paused for a long moment before blessing the child that she had lost. DeAngelo opened his eyes and watched Isabella, knowing each slow inhalation and exhalation meant something—likely recognizing any suffering or anger she was experiencing and letting it go. Her breathing was light and calm, her face serene, as if cherishing only the present moment, her pain healed, her misery replaced with joy, yesterday's tragedy gone. Finally, she brought her hands together in one final exhalation and turned to DeAngelo.

"I'm not as strong as you," he said.

She smiled. "Peace and happiness are always here for you. What you see is your choice."

"I didn't choose yesterday."

"I said what you SEE is YOUR choice. This world is our classroom."

He winced as if in pain. "Why would God give us that lesson?"

"He didn't give us that lesson. But everything that happens to us can be a lesson that helps us return to His love. That's our choice. If I let what happened make me vengeful, then I'm allowing Alfredo to take my peace—and I won't give him that power."

He touched her bandaged hand and gently turned it over, staring at the dried blood that had seeped through, revealing her vulnerability. He had always looked at her hands as perfect. They were hands made for deft movements when preparing a meal or for healing. She seemed to know what he was thinking.

"The world you see right now is a vengeful world—and when you see a vengeful world, the only answer that comes to you is revenge." She waited for his eyes to meet hers. "That's why it's so important to forgive."

"But he must be stopped."

"That's not always so easy—and I don't want my being hurt to infect the ones I love. Don't let what Alfredo did yesterday stand in the way of your discovering who you are."

He looked up at her, the sun silhouetting her face in light. "Who am I?"

"You are a holy child of God, DeAngelo. Fear and grief are visiting you right now, but they are strangers to who you truly are. I want you to remember that the man who attacked us is also a child of God, and that you will meet people like him throughout your life.

Use them as reminders to turn to the light that is always with you." She put her hand on his heart. "There's a little spark in here that is part of a light so great that it can sweep you out of all darkness forever."

DeAngelo took a deep breath and stood up. "I'll try."

Isabella extended her hand and smiled. "Now help me up. Franco's making the meals for everyone the next few days, and I need a good laugh."

As they started their walk in from the vineyard, the Martellino car turned down the drive and came to an abrupt stop. Giovanni was obviously upset about something as he slammed the car door and stormed to the villa. Susanna started after him and then suddenly stopped and stared out at Isabella with her son. An intense look was on her face: one of frustration and anger, but also one struggling with guilt. She headed their way, rage growing with every step.

"We're ruined!" she yelled out. "Our wine was destroyed!"

Isabella stopped, too stunned to speak.

"Giovanni and I went to present our wine to Mussolini, but the spigots had been broken, and our wine had been drained into the gutter!"

The only thing Isabella could think of saying was, "Couldn't we get another barrel from our cellar?"

"It's too late! The organizers have already obtained barrels from another vineyard! We've been disgraced!"

Isabella understood the disappointment of the moment and knew of the importance this day would have had for her husband.

"Why would someone do such a thing?"

"We both know who it was," Susanna hissed. "It was Alfredo!"

Isabella's heart went to her throat, and she squeezed DeAngelo's hand as a reminder to stay silent. "But how would Alfredo know that the mayor's office chose our wine for today's celebration?"

"I don't know," Susanna lied, and then she looked away. There was tenseness about her, an anger boiling inside, but she couldn't tell them it was she who had told him. "I—I just know he was involved."

"We can't make accusations without proof, Susanna."

"Oh God, that's just like you! That man's driven to hurt our families, and he won't rest until we're ruined!"

"And attacking him without proof would benefit us in what way?"

Susanna's eyes slowly rose up to meet hers. "You have proof, don't you, Isabella?"

"I have no idea who destroyed our wine."

"That's not what I'm talking about. I'm talking about yesterday. When you were walking the walls with my son. I know Alfredo was there." She paused for a moment to try to read doubt in Isabella's eyes, but she saw none. "Did he hurt you?"

Isabella said nothing.

"Did he cause your miscarriage?"

Again Isabella gave no answer.

Susanna kicked at the ground. "Why are you protecting him? That bastard has to be stopped!"

DeAngelo's eyes flashed up to Isabella as if pleading for her to tell, but she only smiled back at him, which only infuriated Susanna more. She turned to her son. "What happened, DeAngelo?"

But he refused to look at her, so she grabbed his chin to make sure he looked directly into her eyes. "Tell me, DeAngelo—did Alfredo hurt Isabella?"

His lower lip trembled, but he did not speak.

Isabella could take no more and pulled DeAngelo back. "Let it go, Susanna. Please."

"No!" Susanna hissed, fists clenched to her side. "That man must pay for his sins!"

"He's already paying for them."

Susanna glared at her, furious with Isabella for refusing to defend herself. Obizzi had thrown Isabella's innocent husband in jail, and now he had likely caused the miscarriage of her child, and yet she still talked of forgiveness.

They heard a door slam in the distance and turned to see Giovanni in an animated conversation with Franco by the barn. It appeared Giovanni was explaining what had happened to their wine, and when Isabella saw her husband's shoulders slump forward in disappointment, it broke her heart. She, too, was angry with Obizzi, and it took every fiber of her being not to lash back at him. But in her heart, she knew that now more than ever she had to be vigilant in choosing forgiveness. Any other path would bring trouble to their families. She turned back to Susanna.

"I've never asked you for anything." Her voice was calm, yet serious. "But I'm asking you now—I'm begging you. Let this go—please."

But Susanna's fury boiled over to tears as she thought of all she had lost, and greater than her sense of loss was her sense of how she would now be perceived by the people she desperately wanted in her life: the politicians, the power brokers, and the Lucchesi society. That, of course, would never happen now. Not after their vineyard had been humiliated—humiliated in front of Lucca's elite and in front of Mussolini himself. As the tears streamed down her cheeks, she felt as if she were outside the walls of Lucca, screaming to be let in. There had been so many walls that had blocked her path throughout her life. This was yet another one. She raised her eyes to Isabella with a look of bitterness.

"For years I've watched people walk over you, steal from you, and hurt your family. As long as you refuse to defend yourself, your life will continue to be one of suffering."

Isabella closed her eyes and searched for the words to help her friend understand. She knew in her heart that there was only one way, that all the troubles in the world would dissolve into nothingness if only she could surrender. Then, and only then, would Susanna find the gifts that were already waiting for her. Finally, she opened her eyes, but instead of speaking, she only reached for Susanna's hand.

For a tense moment, there was silence. The vineyard was so still, Susanna could almost hear her own heart pounding. The shame and guilt she felt were too much to bear. She had to do something or she would go mad. Then, suddenly, she shoved Isabella's hand away.

"No! I will have justice!" She stormed off to the villa, with Isabella following as swiftly as her pain would allow. The courtyard was already filled with all the members of the vineyard who wanted to know what had happened to their wine.

◌ ◌

"This doesn't make any damn sense!" a furious Giovanni grumbled. "Why would someone want to sabotage our wine?"

"Isabella knows why!" Susanna yelled out.

All eyes turned to see Isabella being helped to the courtyard by DeAngelo. Franco raised his head. His eyes were filled with hurt, but he had a look of distant curiosity. He walked slowly toward his wife.

"Tell them!" Susanna screamed.

Isabella said nothing, but her entire body softened as she opened her arms to Franco.

He could not accept her embrace, instead stopping several feet away, his old defenses rising up to protect against the agony he knew would come next.

"Tell them!" Susanna screamed again, but again only silence followed, and the quiet tension seemed to light an anger in her that could not be stopped. "Tell them Alfredo attacked you! Tell them he's the reason you can't have any more children! Tell them he's the one who destroyed our wine!"

Franco's face went white. The shock of Susanna's words was like a blade cutting deep into his chest. His heart ached as he stared at his wife, knowing the suffering she had endured. His family was all he cared about, yet he had done nothing to protect them.

"Tell me—" he pleaded, his voice heavy. "Tell me the truth."

But Isabella only stood there, her bandaged arms still open, waiting, hoping he would come to her. He did not.

"Forgive him," she finally whispered. "Please—I can't lose you again."

But there was no way he could forgive, and as she reached for him, he recoiled as if Isabella were a threat. The look her husband gave her was devastating. It was a look of both guilt and pain, and he turned away as if lost, searching desperately for an answer, any answer that could end this nightmare. His mind was back in Puglia, seeing the disappointment on his father's face; it was back in Caporetto, watching his brother die. And now he was tortured by his inability to protect his wife and child. His imagination conjured vicious scenes of Obizzi's hands on Isabella, of his attacking her and killing their child. The images played over and over, and with them his anger grew.

ʘ βɔ

The sun had set across the Tuscan hills by now, and the soft light of lamps shone out from the kitchen windows. Susanna had gone inside and now returned to the doorway, holding something wrapped in a dirty rag. She peeled the corners back to reveal a small revolver.

"No!" Isabella cried out, but Franco was already there, accepting the weapon Susanna willingly offered. His hands shook as he opened the chamber to check the load.

"This is something I should have done a long time ago!" he said, his face flushed with fury.

"Forgive him!" Isabella begged as she stood in front of her husband, tears streaming down her face. But Franco was beyond listening and pushed past her to the car, his mind filled with hate, his body with rage. He ripped the door open and started to get in, only to feel two arms come around his back and clasp at his waist. It was DeAngelo.

"Let go of me, boy!" Franco growled as the contained misery of his entire day reached a boiling point. But DeAngelo would not release him. Franco tried to peel the boy's arms from his side, but DeAngelo held tighter. Franco grabbed his wrist and twisted; DeAngelo cried out but still held firm. Franco felt two arms take hold of his right leg and two more grab his left. He looked down to find that Liliana and Pietro had locked themselves to him; all three children were in tears. Suddenly Giovanni, Antonio, and Angelina were at his side and placed their hands on his shoulders; Rosa and Elisa joined them. Isabella was sobbing as she wrapped her arms around her husband's neck. They stood before, beside and behind him, as if begging him to surrender. And finally, he did, collapsing onto the ground in a heap. For an instant, perhaps a holy instant, he truly felt love's presence. It was in all things he looked upon and in every hand that touched him, and in that moment, it seemed as if time disappeared, for what surrounded him and kept him safe was love itself. He felt it. He knew it. There was no source but this.

But not everyone understood. The scene drew only anger from Susanna as she ran to the car.

When Franco heard the engine start, he shook his head to clear the dream he still was in. It took him a moment to grasp his mistake.

"Dear God!" he gasped. "I left the gun in the car!"

But Susanna was gone, chasing her own insane nightmare. Her mind was prisoner to a law no god had made—vengeance.

CR   ßO

Giovanni was horrified when he realized where his wife was headed. Still, he drove, pushing the truck faster to keep Susanna's car in sight. Franco and Isabella were with him. He'd tried to stop his winemaker's wife, but she had given him a look so bold he immediately caved in. Now, as he pushed the accelerator to the floorboard, he searched the road to try to stop a mistake that seemed inevitable.

CR   ßO

There was one word that Isabella spoke that gnawed at Susanna. It was a word she'd heard countless times in their years together, but it always seemed an admission of defeat. Forgiveness to a woman like Susanna was frail and foolish, and there was no way she would give Obizzi the satisfaction of victory. Not on this day.

She turned in to the Hotel Lucca, host to this Fascist celebration. Mussolini and his security detail were long gone by now, the detail protecting his every move on his trip back to Rome. But she was sure Obizzi would still be there, spouting his lies to any lingering Il Duce supporters to promote his own political career. She grabbed the revolver, stuffed it into her purse, and headed to the front door. Another Isabella message pried its way into her mind—"If you want to be loved, you must love."

Susanna shoved the thought aside, but another crept in—"If you want just treatment, you must be just."

She shook her head savagely, trying to focus on the task ahead, but there was another—"If you want to be forgiven, you must forgive."

"Damn you, Bella!" she snapped. "Get out of my head!"

A startled front desk employee turned her way. "May I help—"

"Where's the Fascist rally?"

"Ballroom A, signora. May I—"

But she was already gone, down the hall, unclasping her purse and reaching for the gun.

ೞ   ಐ

"There she is!" Isabella cried out as she saw Susanna moving past the hotel windows. Giovanni slammed on the brakes and shut off the car, and they raced inside.

CR · SO

Obizzi spotted Susanna a split second before she saw him. He slid out a back door and headed for his room. He wasn't going to let that bitch embarrass him in front of all his new political contacts. These were the most connected and influential men in all of Tuscany, and he was sure they'd been impressed with his commentary that afternoon.

CR · SO

Susanna hurried after him, her anger building with every step. She saw a flash of his jacket as he turned down a hallway and entered a room. She followed and then stood for a moment to gather her strength. She knocked, and the door opened as if he'd been waiting for her.

"Hello, Susanna," was all he said, with a look of arrogance that only stoked her fire more. She pulled the revolver from her purse and pointed it at his head.

CR · SO

"Where's Alfredo Obizzi?" Isabella pleaded to a waiter as they rushed into the ballroom. The band was playing as the young man looked around the room and then shook his head. "He was here just a moment ago—perhaps he went out the back door."

They ran through the crowded ballroom and out into the hall, where they heard the sharp crack of the revolver.

"Dear God, no!" Giovanni gasped, and they raced to where they'd heard the shot.

CR · SO

"Justice," Susanna said, her hand still calm as she held the revolver.

Giovanni shoved the door open only to find Obizzi cowering on the floor. He had wet himself after Susanna had fired a shot by his ear that shattered a mirror behind him. He stared wide-eyed in horror.

"I know everything." Susanna pointed the revolver at his head. "I'm ready to walk into that ballroom and tell them what you've done—destroyed our wine and hurt my friend."

"You—you have no proof," Obizzi stammered as he tried to calm his nerves and somehow turn his defenses on Susanna.

"I have proof your government friends won't like hearing," she continued, and the anguish of what she was about to say made her hand start to tremble. "I'll tell them—I'll tell them you're the father to my second child." She hesitated, watching him. "While it may hurt my reputation—it will ruin yours."

Obizzi cursed Susanna, cursed the very day he had met her. "They won't believe your words over mine. You're a common whore and an adulterer while I'm an important Fascist leader."

Her dark eyes blazed at Obizzi, sending a shiver down his spine, and suddenly she saw none of the confidence she'd always admired. Instead he wore the same fear-stunned look of the child they had both created in little Pietro. Her voice was calm but dangerously low as she said, "The Fascists don't care about truth, Alfredo—only perception. Your great Mussolini has been screaming to the masses about the importance of ethics and family while he gallivants around the country with other women." She drew the hammer back on the pistol. "Unfortunately, you're no Benito."

He winced in fright and threw up his hands to protect himself. Tears of frustration and shame streamed down Susanna's face, the revolver shaking uncontrollably in her hand. "Swear to me you'll leave our families alone."

He hesitated for a moment, his jaw clenched with anger, but finally, he nodded.

And then Isabella was by Susanna's side, gently removing the revolver from her hand. Giovanni's arm came around her as he guided her out, back through the ballroom, where the band was still playing, and out into the cool night air.

The lights of Lucca had illuminated the walls with a soft glow that seemed to Susanna to define both the city's strength and its vulnerability. She watched as Franco and Isabella walked down the steps of the hotel, their arms around each other in a loving embrace. Isabella took her husband's face in her hands and whispered something that made him smile. It made Susanna smile too. Perhaps she had finally given in to Isabella's relentless insistence that she try forgiveness. There had indeed been release in what she had done. Now, as Isabella walked over to join her, Susanna let out a tired exhalation. "Your earth school exhausts me."

Isabella laughed out loud. "God placed no walls between Himself and you, Susanna. He needs you as much as you need Him. You can reach over anytime you want, take His hand, and be pulled up to the heaven that's right here and now."

It was just like Isabella, thought Susanna: always saying something that made her think, as if trying to awaken some ancient truth in her that had long been asleep. Isabella's words always seemed to require more from her—like a grapevine's roots, digging deep through rocky slate and soil so they could finally discover their divine potential. The thought stayed with her a moment longer, until the enormous weight of the entire day pushed it aside. Susanna was tired, so tired; she just wanted to go home and sleep. She took her friend's hand and sighed, "Take me home, Bella. Take me home to our family."

The End

This is the end of Book One, and the sequel to *The Walls of Lucca* will debut in the fall of 2018. It picks up the story in 1938—where Fascists and partisans, loyalty and love, and World War II become the walls which need to be lifted before the Martellino wine can finally realize its potential.

GLOSSARY OF REAL HISTORICAL CHARACTERS

Benito Mussolini: Italian journalist and politician who created the Italian Fascist Party. Mussolini and his followers combined their power through a series of laws that changed the nation into a one-party dictatorship. He ruled Italy from 1922 to 1943.

Giacomo Matteotti: Italian Socialist politician who opposed Italy's entry into World War I. In 1924 Matteotti spoke openly in the Italian parliament alleging the Fascists committed fraud in the recently held elections, outraging Mussolini and his loyalists.

General Luigi Cadorna: Chief of Staff of the Italian Army during World War I. His autocratic leadership led to failures in the battles of the Isonzo and Caporetto.

Roberto Farinacci: A leading Fascist politician who came to represent the most radical faction of the party. Farinacci played a strong role in establishing Fascist dominance over Italy in 1922.

Lorenzo Grossi: Lucca's first true Fascist Podesta (Mayor) who came to power in 1927 and followed the strict requirements and guidelines of Mussolini's new government.

Father Antonio Costa: Christian monk from the hermitage of the Camaldoli in the Province of Arezzo. In 1938, Father Antonio would become Procurator of the Carthusian monastery near Lucca.

ACKNOWLEDGEMENTS

I am so grateful for all the people who inspired me to write *The Walls of Lucca*. The journey started on a simple vacation to Italy in 2005, where upon arriving in the charming town of Lucca I was immediately enchanted. But sometimes one must be pushed to write a novel, and that first push came from my mother, Bette Physioc, who gave me my love of reading at a young age and encouraged me to start this project.

Then, there was my friend and sage from Southern California, Mark Mendizza, who pressed me through revision after revision with the battle cry, "Keep going, it's actually getting better!" And, when I did finally improve he said, "OK, it's now good enough to hire a developmental editor." That's when Nicole Ayers, of Ayersedits came into my life. Nicole is a great developmental editor. She is a professional who not only cares about the writer but has the unique ability to understand the soul of a story and how best to improve that message. Did she tear it apart? Absolutely, but every change she suggested strengthened my characters, improved their dialogue and built the storyline. Ayersedits is magnifico!

There is no greater gift for a new writer than to have friends and fellow writers who patiently answer my never-ending questions. Kansas City author Bob Sommer challenged my thinking, Sister Rosie Kolich inspired it, and romance novelist, Jennifer Robinson was an awesome mentor/critic/guide who worked with me on creative style and helped me build a social media platform. Grazie to

Beth Kallman Werner of Author Connections, for her brilliance in marketing and promotion, and to my sister, Cathe, whose cover art and interior maps brought readers closer to my favorite Italian town.

I am also indebted to KC's terrific mystery writer, Joel Goldman, who has been my coach every step of the way. Joel helped me find Ayersedits, tutored me in self-publishing, copyediting, format and cover-art. I am so thankful for his friendship.

But, the very heart and soul of The Walls of Lucca is my wife of 32 years, Stacey St James-Physioc. She is the inspiration for my lead character, Isabella. Both Stace and Bella are women of conviction and spiritual devotion who bless everyone they touch. They see light where others see darkness and find lessons in what others consider misfortune. As an example, when I was let go as broadcaster of the Los Angeles Angels of Anaheim after fourteen years, Stace met me at our front door with her typical enthusiasm, "What cool new adventure is ahead for us?!" For life is indeed an adventure, a journey of ups and downs, of happiness and disappointments… perhaps the best way to acknowledge my wife is to steal a line from Book 2 of *The Walls of Lucca*. (Spoiler alert!)

The scene is of Franco and now 22-year old DeAngelo Martellino after a Christmas celebration. DeAngelo asks Franco about the love he has for Isabella. Franco tells him, "My wife taught me the importance of forgiveness. That everyone will get their share of joy and sadness, of love and heartache—that all will happen—but if you have a friend to share it with and help you through the tough times—a true friend—well, that's heaven. The easiest thing I've ever done in my life is love Bella."

That's the way I feel about the inspiration for this book—for the easiest thing I've ever done in my life is love Stace.

ABOUT THE AUTHOR

Steve Physioc has been telling stories for the past forty years. He has been a play-by-play announcer for football, baseball, and basketball. Physioc is currently the radio-tv broadcaster for the Kansas City Royals and gives play-by-plays for Fox. He won an Emmy in 2013 for excellent announcing. Physioc's new historical romance was inspired by *A Course in Miracles,* which perfectly reflects his protagonist Isabella's view on inner peace and the power of forgiveness.

CPSIA information can be obtained
at www.ICGtesting.com
Printed in the USA
LVHW08s0352110918
589776LV00016B/201/P